Written in Blood

TWENTIETH-CENTURY BATTLES

Spencer C. Tucker, editor

Written
✠ IN ✠
Blood

The Battles for Fortress Przemyśl in WWI

GRAYDON A. TUNSTALL

INDIANA UNIVERSITY PRESS   *Bloomington & Indianapolis*

This book is a publication of

INDIANA UNIVERSITY PRESS
Office of Scholarly Publishing
Herman B Wells Library 350
1320 East 10th Street
Bloomington, Indiana 47405 USA

iupress.indiana.edu

Manufactured in the
United States of America

Library of Congress Cataloging-in-
Publication Data

Names: Tunstall, Graydon A.
  (Graydon Allen), author.
Title: Written in blood : the battles for
  Fortress Przemyśl in WWI /
  Graydon A. Tunstall.
Description: Bloomington : Indiana
  University Press, 2016. | Series:
  Twentieth-century battles | Includes
  bibliographical references and index.
Identifiers: LCCN 2016024511 (print) |
  LCCN 2016025866 (ebook) |
  ISBN 9780253021977 (cl : alk. paper) |
  ISBN 9780253022073 (e-book)
Subjects: LCSH: Twierdza Przemyśl
  (Przemyśl, Poland) | World War,
  1914–1918—Campaigns—Poland—
  Przemyśl. | Przemyśl (Poland)—
  History, Military—20th century.
Classification: LCC DK4800.P7 T86 2016
  (print) | LCC DK4800.P7 (ebook) |
  DDC 940.4/22—dc23
LC record available at https://lccn.loc
  .gov/2016024511

1 2 3 4 5 21 20 19 18 17 16

To

ALLEN, ALISON, ISABELLA,
GRAYDON, AND CHLOE

Contents

Maps

Acknowledgments

I would like to express my sincere thanks to Vannina Wurm for her enormous assistance on my behalf. A special debt of gratitude is owed to Benjamin Sperduto, David Beeler, and Philip Davis for their editorial finesse and unflinching willingness to assist in the typing of this manuscript; to my good friend, Casimir Robak, and to Natalie Misteravich for their valuable assistance with Polish sources; and to Robert Sloan for his patience and faith in this work. Kudos to Laurie Andrews for the excellent maps.

Last, but not least, to Wendy for her continual support and to Willy and Nicky.

Written in Blood

1

✠ ✠ ✠

Introduction: Fortress Przemyśl

IN THE EVENT OF WAR, AUSTRIA-HUNGARY—WITH ITS PRE-carious location in Central Europe—had to defend its interests on multiple fronts and against multiple opponents. Constructing fortresses was a necessity to hold or delay enemy invasions, particularly because of the Dual Monarchy's extended frontiers; however, sufficient funds rarely became available for such construction. In a two- or three-front war against numerically superior enemies, fortresses enabled Habsburg war planners to spare troops to deploy on all fronts. As field armies used interior lines to defeat one enemy at a time, fortresses assumed an important role in Austro-Hungarian as well as German military planning—strategic and operational.

The numerically inferior Habsburg army could not compete against potential enemy troop numbers; therefore, fortresses had to be erected to compensate for its lack of mobile forces.[1] The defense of the Galician frontier depended largely on the neighboring Carpathian Mountains because fortifications could not secure the bow-shaped, extended terrain. This led to the necessity of fortifying the open frontiers against Russia, which had become a European great power and eventually a potential enemy of the Dual Monarchy over their Balkan Peninsula competition. Repeatedly, however, financial problems intervened, because Vienna had fallen into enormous debt and bankruptcy after the Napoleonic Wars. Fortress Przemyśl would soon serve as the first line of defense against a tsarist invasion of Galicia. Because the Russian army had many light infantry and cavalry units, this made it increasingly important to protect Habsburg rear echelon connections in that province. The

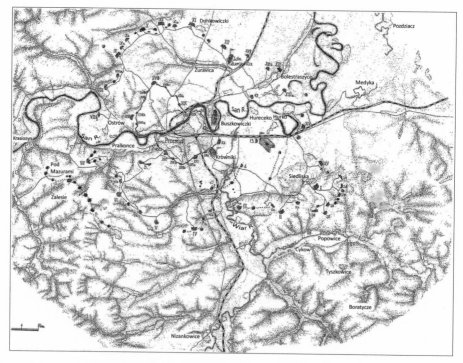

Map 1.1. Overview of Fortress Przemyśl.

inferior and insufficient Galician roads and railroads and lack of significant geographical barriers to halt a tsarist advance into the province also
had a major effect on military planners.

Fortress Przemyśl, an isolated and basically unknown garrison town
on the San River that was surrounded by a series of hills only twenty-
eight kilometers from the Galician frontier, slowly assumed a pivotal role
in Habsburg eastern front military strategy and the battles against Russia during the disastrous 1914 deployment, the chaotic September retreat, the fall 1914 Habsburg offensives, and the ill-fated Carpathian
Winter War campaign during the first half of 1915. As the strongest
Habsburg bulwark in the region, Fortress Kraków, 140 kilometers to the
north, became significant because it represented a flank threat to any
enemy force attempting to cross the San River and proceed into the
Carpathian Mountains. During the Habsburg military campaigns of late
1914 and early 1915, one specific objective stood out—the liberation of

Fortress Przemyśl, the strongest northern Dual Monarchy bulwark, initially under siege in September because of the disastrous mid-September 1914 Austro-Hungarian retreat, liberated on October 10, and besieged again during early November 1914. By the following spring, the fortress had become the eastern front's Verdun.[2]

For eight months during 1914–1915, the fortress became the focus of Habsburg offensive operations against Russia. From its initial besiegement in September 1914, after the Habsburg retreat that followed the two devastating Lemberg field battle defeats, until its capitulation on March 22, 1915, the fortress remained the bellwether for General Franz Conrad von Hötzendorf's strategic planning. Following the ill-fated battles of Lemberg, Habsburg troops mounted offensives in October, November, and December 1914 in conjunction with allied German operations in an attempt to reconquer the beleaguered fortress. Then, during winter 1915, Conrad, under extreme time pressure, launched three separate, strikingly similar frontal offensives to liberate the San River bastion before it had to capitulate, reputedly because the inhabitants were starving. Conrad's strategy compelled his armies to initiate the ensuing frontal assaults over rugged, snow-covered mountainous terrain in harsh fall and winter weather conditions because of the pressure relative to Fortress Przemyśl. Before the last rifle fell silent in mid-April, the 1915 Carpathian Mountain Winter War offensives had claimed hundreds of thousands of Austro-Hungarian, Russian, and German soldiers' lives. The Russians maimed, incapacitated, or captured countless other Habsburg troops—mostly resulting from the futile and desperate Habsburg efforts to liberate the 130,000-man Fortress Przemyśl garrison. In hindsight, Conrad's obsession with liberating Fortress Przemyśl, though in some ways commendable, produced a tragic and woefully misguided military strategy that almost annihilated the kaiserlich und königlich (k.u.k.; Royal and Imperial) Armee once again by mid-April 1915.[3]

The desperate 1914 and 1915 battles to liberate besieged Fortress Przemyśl also constituted the first example of total warfare in mountain campaigning, and the horrendous weather and terrain conditions and casualty numbers have led some European scholars to describe them as the Stalingrad of World War I. The three-month 1915 battle losses during

the Carpathian Winter War proved greater than the western front bloodbath battles at either Verdun or the Somme. Although this significant
campaign remains largely unknown in English-speaking countries, and
despite the Russian General Staff's assessment that fortresses were of no
particular military value due to their obsolescent artillery and numerous
deficiencies, the fortress played a critical role on the Austro-Hungarian
portion of the eastern front during the first nine months of the war.[4]

The origins of Fortress Przemyśl can be traced back to the seventh
century, when Prince Przemyslaw constructed its first bulwark. A mo-
nastic settlement was established there sometime during the ninth
century. When Hungarian tribes invaded the heartland of the Moravian
Empire in 899, the region around Przemyśl declared its allegiance to
Kiev, making it a site of contention among Poland, Hungary, and Kiev.
This rivalry provided the oldest and most widely accepted historical
mention of the fortress. In the year 981, a date that is widely accepted as
the oldest historical mention of Przemyśl, it became a wooden stronghold. Between the eleventh and twelfth centuries, it became the capital
of a Ruthenian principality. During the fourteenth century, it was incor-
porated into the Polish-Lithuanian Empire, which lasted for almost four
hundred years. During the Renaissance period, the Przemyśl area was
home to multiple nationalities and served as an important trade and
population center.

The first partition of Poland, in 1772, brought the province of Galicia
into the Austrian Empire (Holy Roman Empire until 1806). By 1778, the
Habsburg military displayed serious interest in its new Galician territory
and conducted reconnaissance missions in these areas the following
year. In 1793, the French Revolution caused the second partition of Poland, and the province of Galicia swiftly became a part of the Habsburg
state system. During the third Polish partition, in 1795, West Galicia also
entered the Austrian Empire, bringing with it 46,000 square kilometers
of flat terrain as well as approximately one million inhabitants. The
years between 1772 and 1846 witnessed the development of plans to
construct a major fortress that could defend the Vistula and San Rivers
against a Russian invasion.

As early as the Napoleonic War period (1799–1814), Viennese military planners had contemplated erecting defensive fortifications along

the extensive Carpathian Mountain range. In 1804, construction commenced at the present Fortress Przemyśl location; however, builders did not erect a surrounding wall. Encircled by little more than a trench, the fortress remained far from completion. Construction was interrupted again in 1809 when Napoleon conquered significant Austrian territory, including Galicia. The Austrian Empire regained the territory following the Congress of Vienna in 1815, which again revived the question of how best to defend the province from invasion. Some Habsburg military leaders believed that the province could not be protected by a fortress, but only by launching an offensive at the outbreak of any hostilities. Fortress Przemyśl could provide a central location to assemble and deploy such an offensive operation.

A lingering question concerned whether or not the fortress could protect the approaches to the critical Dukla Pass—a key area for an invasion of Hungary. Plans to construct a depot fortress near the Dukla Pass had been discussed between 1810 and 1814, but nothing resulted because the Austrian army was preoccupied with fighting the French. Following Napoleon's defeat, these and other plans could be reconsidered. In 1818, Habsburg archduke Johann released a report that proposed the construction of a fortress to protect the road junctions at Przemyśl extending from Warsaw through Moravia to Vienna. The inspector general claimed that a large fortress could protect the area against an enemy invasion through Galicia by blocking all roads leading east-west at the San River, while simultaneously preventing any crossings of the Carpathian passes, or at least making them more difficult to achieve. Most Habsburg military planners agreed that the first natural obstruction capable of checking an enemy advance into Galicia would be the San-Dniester River line. Przemyśl, situated at the major transportation intersection between the San and Dniester Rivers and the Dukla Pass, and controlling the most accessible Carpathian Mountain passes and roads leading into central Hungary, was thus an ideal strategic location. It was designated a second-class fortress and transportation center in 1819.

In 1821, plans were put in place to construct the Przemyśl fortress along the hilly terrain extending north to south on the banks of the San River. Habsburg military plans authorized the construction of new entrenchments five kilometers from the center, or *noyau* (core), of the fortress town of Przemyśl in 1830. Between 1833 and 1836, a fifteen-kilometer embankment was constructed around the inner city and reinforced with thirty bastions and gates. Although a series of high-ranking officers had become convinced of the necessity of constructing fortresses, the Przemyśl project had its critics, and construction was consistently plagued by a lack of funding.

Fortress Przemyśl controlled the roads leading south and southwest with two main defiles in the Carpathian Mountains (Dukla and Turka). Military leaders generally accepted the necessity of constructing a major fortress, but no agreement could be reached about the bulwark's size, the number of garrison troops, or other important details. This led to the creation of a Fortress Commission, which noted that Przemyśl's location in the middle of the province provided a major road junction that blocked enemy egress from Lemberg and Brody, as well as flanking northern and southern secondary routes. It would also block egress to all main Carpathian Mountain crossing areas between the Dukla Pass and Eperies.

During the 1840s, fortress planning was overshadowed by the fear of a war with Russia. Fighting such a war required fortified areas that could also serve the army's logistical needs, and until the end of 1846 the Austrian Empire lacked satisfactory fortifications to secure against the important Russian invasion routes. Even then, the protection of rearward communication lines became increasingly important because of the threat of massive Russian cavalry units attacking Fortress Przemyśl and cutting it off. Between 1845 and 1847, delicate relations with Russia delayed construction. Although Austrian strategy against Russia depended on this system of fortresses, it was feared that additional fortress construction might cause unnecessary political tensions.

During this decade, development of Fortress Przemyśl also slackened because of the continued lack of funds. As a result, the military command leaned toward less costly projects. In 1846, when Kraków, along with Russian portions of Poland, exploded in civil unrest, pressure increased to construct a fortress at Kraków to control internal disturbances. By 1848, the European-wide revolutions renewed the possibility of foreign invasion, and attention was again drawn to Przemyśl. In 1849, a new Central Fortress Commission serving with the Fortress Commission (Reichsbefestigungkommission) investigated the matter of fortress construction.

The growing conflict in the Balkan Peninsula between Austria-Hungary and Russia drew attention to the significance of the strategic location of Przemyśl as a railroad and road crossing point as well as a fortress that would partially protect the provinces of Galicia and the Bukovina. It also blocked three main tsarist military operational lines. Still, the fortress faced competition for funds. Plans for the expansion of Fortress Kraków, 140 kilometers north of Fortress Przemyśl and crucial to defending against a Russian crossing of the Vistula River from the Warsaw region, evolved after 1846. By the 1850s, Fortress Kraków had already become vital to Habsburg eastern front military planning.

Between 1854 and 1857, a workforce of some twelve thousand city laborers constructed a ring of fifteen forts containing thirty modern fortification works which began to surround Fortress Przemyśl with a fifteen-kilometer circumference, while work also commenced on Forts I, II, III, VI, and XII on the left side of the San River. Forts I and II encompassed the fortress inner city. The project enjoyed a high profile during this period of activity, with Emperor Franz Joseph himself visiting the fortress in 1855. Once again, however, political circumstances intervened. Although only nineteen of thirty-five planned Fortress Przemyśl positions were completed by 1857, the Habsburgs canceled further construction after the Crimean War.

Despite the renewed attention to Przemyśl, the fortress was not without competition for funds. As noted, plans for the expansion of Fortress Kraków, evolved after 1846. Construction commenced at Fortress Przemyśl in 1854 on the high terrain around the village of Siedliska at the southwestern frontier of the evolving fortification. By 1914, there would be six major fortress works in the critical Siedliska Defensive District VI. These works became vitally important during the two sieges of the bulwark in 1914 and 1915.

During 1861, the construction of a railroad line into eastern Galicia added to Przemyśl's importance by connecting it to Fortress Kraków and the provincial capital of Lemberg. It also greatly improved the transportation situation in eastern Galician, encouraging and resulting in accelerated economic development. Ten years later, a line was extended over the Carpathian Mountains into Hungary. Then, during 1863, the importance of building railroads for a potential war with Russia became evident with the 1863–1864 Polish uprising in Russian Polish territories.

On June 14, 1871, Emperor Franz Joseph determined that Fortress Przemyśl would be the primary Habsburg bulwark in Galicia. By 1878, several entrenchments built during the Crimean War received improvements, and the first fortress girdle works were constructed. During 1882, the perceived role of Fortress Przemyśl was modified following the 1879 Austro-Hungarian–German Dual Alliance treaty. Henceforth, officials placed emphasis on launching an allied offensive against the tsarist empire before its military could deploy its main invasion forces. Fortress Przemyśl's new mission became to block tsarist operational lines during a Russian invasion. Fortresses Kraków and Przemyśl, therefore, became major military bases for the strategic mobilization and deployment of Habsburg troops, while also protecting against a surprise enemy attack. The chiefs of the General Staffs of Austria-Hungary and its ally Germany agreed to launch offensives into the Polish Sack, the territory that jutted between the Prussian and Austro-Hungarian frontiers.

In 1906, when General Conrad von Hötzendorf became chief of the Austro-Hungarian General Staff, that mission would continue, although without significant improvement to the fortress's defensive power. To General Conrad, Fortresses Kraków and Przemyśl would serve mainly as depot centers intended to protect the initial Habsburg deployment. A major problem that affected the citadel's evolution involved the lack of local practical experience in constructing fortress positions and the inadequate training of the workforces, all of which resulted in defective workmanship. The immense cost of building fortress positions drew constant criticism from military and political leaders, particularly Hungarians.

The years between 1884 and 1890 proved most important in the development of the fortress. During this six-year period, smokeless gunpowder and heavy mortars made their appearance as the evolution of weaponry sped up during the Second Industrial Revolution. Fortress defense construction plans struggled to keep pace with the rapid improvements in artillery range and destructiveness. The period witnessed the massive utilization of concrete and iron in fortress construction as a reaction to the development of new weapons. Thus, between 1881 and 1886, building of permanent concrete artillery forts commenced. Expansion of Fortress Przemyśl's core works and half-hearted modernization efforts continued on a limited scale, and progress was made on perimeter works. Defensive District VI (Siedliska) was extended to higher terrain further to the east.

Przemyśl became the third-largest city in Galicia after Lemberg, the provincial capital, and Kraków. By the 1880s, it received the full designation as a fortress. Additional improvements included filling some of the twenty-five-mile gap that existed between the two major Galician river defense lines at the San River and the marshy Dniester River, then further strengthening the existing defensive positions of the fortress. Though Fortress Przemyśl's potential defensive value had become increasingly obvious, essential financial support for additional construction and improvements did not materialize. Increased tensions between Austria-Hungary and Russia during the Bulgarian Crisis (1885–1887) finally provided the incentive to further improve both Fortresses Kraków and Przemyśl.

Some modernization improvements included the construction of new positions and strongholds at the northern and southeastern areas of Fortress Przemyśl. The Fort Siedliska Defensive District VI bulwarks became the main offensive objectives of the Russian storm attacks of October 1914 during the initial siege of the fortress, as well as during the fatal November encirclement. The fortress defensive system became divided into eight groups, while new types of fortifications, such as the main armored citadel and smaller infantry positions, made their appearance.

Stationary artillery batteries and ammunition magazines were added between the various forts. Fort I/1, the strongest core and northernmost position of the Siedliska Defensive District VI, and critical during the 1914 and 1915 sieges, was erected between 1897 and 1903. A moat surrounded it, while barracks with steel and concrete ceilings, cookhouses, emergency rooms, and storage areas for food, fuel, and tools were added. During the 1890s, additional important fortress renovations commenced. Concrete now covered the old stoneworks to strengthen them, and other upgrades were undertaken throughout the decade. Small infantry positions were also constructed between the main defensive locations.

Artillery advancements made in the second half of the nineteenth century during the Second Industrial Revolution appeared to make fortresses obsolete. The added range of more-powerful rifled artillery pieces required much larger and better-constructed fortresses. They now also had to be capable of absorbing the greater firepower of the improved artillery pieces. Turn-of-the-century technological advancements utilizing steel and concrete construction, however, ensured that fortresses became less vulnerable to even the heaviest enemy artillery fire. By replacing bronze artillery barrels with steel models, both range and effectiveness were increased. In addition, new loading and recoil mechanisms improved accuracy and speed of firing, and the concrete roofs reinforced with steel beams over ring fortress positions protected heavy artillery pieces with armored plating. New artillery armor turrets and casements made their appearance as well.

Fortress Przemyśl's geographic location provided its strategic significance. Located on and overlooking the meandering San River, it stood at the juncture of several important north-to-south transportation routes. Moreover, it formed a bastion against large enemy army masses attempting to cross the river and then traverse the Carpathian Mountain ridges from the defenseless flat eastern Galician frontier. Fortress Przemyśl thus presented a serious flank threat to any potential enemy advance along the most likely mountain invasion route, the Dukla Pass, onto the Hungarian plains. The bow shape of the Galician frontier would allow Russian troops to invade from either flank of the province and crush any defensive forces in an envelopment movement. In the event of war, Habsburg forces would have to launch an offensive to preclude such an outcome.

The fortress protected against a tsarist invasion through the Carpathian Mountains, toward Vienna and Budapest, and even north toward Fortress Kraków. Galicia could not be surrendered to the enemy without a fight on political grounds, nor could the main rearward defensive positions project into the Carpathian Mountains. Thus, a Habsburg offensive had to be launched if war commenced to gain the initiative against a numerically superior enemy, which required the fortress to secure the deployment of the designated offensive field army troops. As the nineteenth century ended, the development and expansion of railroads significantly increased the importance of Fortress Przemyśl, the heretofore isolated province of Galicia, and the Carpathian Mountain range.

No one in 1914 foresaw that the deployment of million-man armies, which could now march over vast swaths of territory due to the two Industrial Revolutions and corresponding technological advancements in weaponry and railroads, would diminish the perceived role of fortresses. Vastly improved and expanded railroad and roadway networks made it increasingly difficult to interrupt enemy supply and communication lines, particularly before the unanticipated utilization of aerial reconnaissance, which proved very effective even early in World War I and transformed the art of intelligence gathering. It appeared to some military planners that fortresses could no longer perform a decisive role in major military operations. However, until its capitulation in late March 1915, Fortress Przemyśl influenced every tsarist attempt to traverse the Carpathian Mountains to invade Hungary and end the war, exerted a powerful but negative, influence on General Conrad's strategic planning, and played an important role in the early June 1915 phase of the enormously successful Central Powers' Gorlice-Tarnov offensive. The reconquest of the fortress on June 3, 1915, eliminated the Russian foundation for its San River defensive positions, forcing tsarist troops to initiate a retreat after their rapid defeat. It also removed the bulwark from the military limelight.

Fortress Przemyśl came to represent for the Dual Monarchy's eastern front what Verdun did for France on the western front. In addition to the defensive role of Port Arthur during the 1904–1905 Russo-Japanese War, the 1916 battle of Verdun marked the last successful defense of a major fortress in world history. Just as Fortress Sevastopol played a pivotal role for the Russians during the 1854–1856 Crimean War and as the Strassburg, Metz, Paris, and Belfort fortifications did in the 1870–1871 Franco-Prussian War, Fortress Przemyśl fulfilled its missions during 1914 and the first half of 1915. It bound significant tsarist forces—nine infantry divisions and two cavalry divisions (some 280,000 troops)—during its first siege after the disastrous Habsburg September defeats following the two battles of Lemberg. Thus, it became known as the Verdun of the east, although it was much larger, had far more garrison troops than the French citadel, and possessed a third more artillery pieces (1,000 to Verdun's 670).

Austria-Hungary and Russia had effectively placed the Balkan Peninsula on ice after 1897, allowing Russia to continue the imperialistic advances into Asia that had commenced midcentury after the Crimean War. The disastrous 1904–1905 Russo-Japanese War defeat not only halted that expansion but also demonstrated artillery's new combat effectiveness, particularly the huge new siege guns utilized against Fort Sevastopol and Port Arthur. It also previewed the nature of what one could expect in the next major war, World War I—for example, trench warfare and battles lasting weeks or months rather than days.

Once General Conrad von Hötzendorf assumed his position in 1906 as Habsburg chief of the General Staff, he opposed the continuation of construction and other improvements to Galician fortresses, maintaining that they required excessive garrison troops and that their maintenance proved much too costly. The Austro-Hungarian frontier extended more than 3,500 kilometers, which made fortifying the entire Galician Carpathian Mountain front impossible and far too expensive. However, the particular concern remained that eastern Galicia and the Bukovina possessed no geographical barriers that could delay or halt a determined enemy offensive effort. Attention also had to be directed to the Balkan and Italian frontiers, which left Habsburg planners facing a nearly unmanageable three-front threat.

Though the Russo-Japanese War demonstrated significant military advancements, it unfortunately had no effect on Habsburg military leadership. In particular, the sieges at Sevastopol and Port Arthur demonstrated that well-trained fortress troops could withstand a long siege. Despite this evidence, General Conrad willfully chose to ignore several important developments from what he termed a "colonial war."

Immediately before the outbreak of World War I, Conrad focused his attention on the Italian frontier and the Adriatic Sea coast for any major fortress improvement projects. Then, shortly before the 1908–1909 Bosnian Annexation Crisis exploded, he surprisingly proposed upgrading the Galician fortresses. He insisted that Fortresses Kraków and Przemyśl would provide security for a wartime troop deployment and initial offensive operations during a conflict against Russia. The possibility of conflict with the Russian colossus became a major concern in Habsburg military planning after 1904–1905, when tsarist attention refocused on the Balkan Peninsula. Conrad considered Fortress Kraków strategically more significant than Fortress Przemyśl since it protected against Russian encroachment at the Vistula River from the direction of Warsaw toward the capital, Vienna. Fortress Kraków also helped protect the railroad lines through Silesia, an important German industrial province. It would also serve as a vital military base and depot during a war while significantly providing access to cross or defend the critical Vistula River line. Thus, in prewar Dual Monarchy Operations Bureau planning, Fortress Kraków's mission included securing the initial troop deployment and operations, but it also had the disadvantage of close proximity to the northern Habsburg frontier, which placed it within Russian artillery range. General Conrad's main concern relative to both fortresses stemmed from the San, Dniester, and Vistula Rivers providing little protection against a Russian offensive.

In fall 1908, the Habsburg army's inspector general reported that both citadels required extensive renovation to fulfill their wartime missions. Renewed discussions concerning the role of fortresses in strategic planning ensued, although General Conrad would have preferred not having to upgrade either Fortress Kraków or Fortress Przemyśl because, in his opinion, they should serve mainly as depot centers for any offensive action.

Judged adequate for close battle, neither fortress possessed the capability to sustain long-range heavy artillery bombardment; but both fortresses' outer defenses had to be capable of absorbing the new heavy caliber artillery shells, such as 21- or even 24-centimeter rounds. Consequently, some construction commenced after 1910 to improve smaller defensive bastions and field fortifications. The expansive Habsburg northern frontier, however, could enable the tsarist enemy to circumvent either fortress, albeit with some difficulty. Nevertheless, doing so would leave a fortress with a garrison over a hundred thousand men threatening their rear echelon connections. Because of the lack of funding,

Habsburg Supreme Command determined to make the fortresses battle-ready only at the outbreak of a war.

General Conrad, however, supported the construction of fortified bridgeheads along the San-Dniester River line, particularly at Jaroslau and Sieniava, to protect the direct approaches to Fortress Przemyśl. Nevertheless, he continued to oppose building permanent fortifications along the Carpathian Mountain ridges because enemy forces could easily neutralize or bypass such isolated locations. In the interim, the critical financial constraints limited any improvements to either eastern Galician bastion. It should be mentioned that until 1911, much of the very limited Habsburg military expenditures financed Archduke Franz Ferdinand's naval construction, which paralleled the general naval race throughout Europe. That year also witnessed General Conrad's famous Denkschrift, where he demanded the improvement of the Dual Monarchy's fortresses, but mainly those on the Italian frontier. No money was appropriated for fortresses in Galicia.

Notable among Conrad's salient arguments against fully arming fortresses during peacetime was the possibility of them falling into enemy hands or the necessity to destroy the fortifications before preparations for battle could be completed. As a result of such concerns and the perpetual lack of funding, Conrad limited peacetime fortress supplies to a precautionary one-month period, and the majority of Galician fortress artillery pieces remained obsolete models dating from as far back as 1861.

The 1912–1913 Balkan Wars proved particularly devastating for Austria-Hungary as its perceived archenemy, Serbia, evolved into a much more dangerous potential military foe following its battlefield successes against Turkey and Bulgaria. This prompted the Habsburg General Staff to reevaluate the role of fortifications at the Russian frontier and consider the necessity of improvements. The years 1911–1912 also witnessed the introduction of advanced, heavy long-range mortars and artillery pieces such as the 30.5-centimeter cannon and 42-centimeter guns. These represented a major threat to contemporary fortresses. When the war erupted, no effective countermeasures had been developed to protect fortresses against such enormous firepower, as witnessed by the destruction and surrender without battle of Belgian fortifications in the early phases of the German 1914 Schlieffen Plan offensive against France.

The Balkan Wars also raised serious concern relative to the status of Romania as a reliable Dual Monarchy ally in a war against Russia. Though allied in a secret treaty to Austria-Hungary since 1883, Romania had fought as an ally to hated Serbia against Bulgaria during the 1913 Second Balkan War. Until then, Habsburg military strategists had expected that the Romanian army would fulfill the critical mission of cementing the Habsburg extensive extreme right flank positions during a war against Russia. After the 1913 conflict, suddenly facing the possibility of a Romanian invasion of Transylvania (part of Hungary), an irredentist goal of the "Great Romania" movement, General Conrad began contemplating constructing fortified positions along the long common frontier to delay a possible invasion until sufficient Habsburg defensive forces could be deployed to that potential war theater. The Habsburg Operations Bureau also prepared plans for a potential War Case "Ro" (Romania) for the first time. This naturally helped remove serious funding for improvements to Fortress Przemyśl and resulted in the initial planning for the drawing back (Rückverlegung) of the projected wartime deployment against Russia because tsarist action now seriously threatened Habsburg extreme right flank positions.

Habsburg war plans against Russia and Serbia, when war became a distinct possibility after the 1908–1909 Bosnian Crisis, adhered to the European-wide "cult of the offensive." General Conrad's sudden demand to fortify the Tyrolean frontier against a possible invasion by despised Italy also precluded allocation of significant financial support for the defense of the Carpathian Mountain invasion routes.[5] In hindsight, he should have concentrated on Carpathian Mountain fortress construction, because Russia posed a far greater military threat to the Dual Monarchy than Italy. During 1914, Habsburg Operation Bureau military planners contemplated using Fortress Przemyśl as a secure depot position behind the deployment line in an eastern front war; however, General Conrad continued to harbor concerns that the San River bastion could become a serious source of embarrassment.[6] On July 1, 1914, after the June 28 assassination of Archduke Franz Ferdinand, he revised

Habsburg Operation Bureau war planning for a War Case "R" (Russia) by considering ordering the mentioned rearward deployment (Rückverlegung) on July 1 from the originally planned Galician frontier to the San-Dniester River line, already discussed in 1913 during the Balkan Wars because of the threat of Romania not protecting the Habsburg right flank in a war against Russia. This immediately brought the little-known eastern Galician frontier Fortress Przemyśl to the forefront in war planning against the tsarist empire. Its significance commenced with the Habsburg mobilization.

In 1914, the Galician fortress was inadequately prepared for a major war. Serious preparation of Fortress Przemyśl for wartime activity occurred only during the six-week period between the initial Habsburg mobilization and deployment and the subsequent Galician military campaign. The expansive nine-hundred-kilometer eastern front, too vast for available German, Austro-Hungarian, or even Russian troops to defend, gave added significance to an obsolete citadel such as Fortress Przemyśl in blocking major enemy invasion efforts.

For decades, financial shortages dictated that only the most selective and necessary improvements would be made to the fortress. Even provisions of vital food stocks exceeding a one-month supply had to await a wartime deployment period, because the most pressing improvements would cost more than the annual allocation for all fortification expenditures.[7] Equipping the fortress for war involved stocking ammunition and artillery shells, food rations, uniforms, and fuel. It also meant building costly ammunition magazines and infantry and artillery positions, as well as making major improvements to the perimeter walls. Rations for an anticipated hundred-thousand-man garrison (equaling a quarter of the size of the peacetime professional Habsburg army) totaled 36 million food portions. One-half of the required meat rations alone represented 4.5 million tons of canned food. Not counting the expense of transporting them, such food supplies would cost an estimated 3.6 million kronen, or more than half the annual outlay for all Dual Monarchy fortification expenses![8]

In 1914, the plan for Fortress Przemyśl designated a garrison of 85,000 troops, almost 1,000 artillery pieces, and 7,500 horses. The actual 131,000 soldiers and 21,500 horses deployed there signified that the allotted fortress food supplies could not last either as long as planned or as long as necessary. The fortress's basic armament included almost 1,000 artillery pieces, over one-half consisting of short-range weapons. Another third consisted of obsolete, immobile light artillery guns lacking means of transport and many 1861-vintage 12- and 15-centimeter cannons that participated in the decisive 1866 battle at Königgrätz during the Austro-Prussian War. These obsolete artillery pieces utilized black powder instead of white and had a limited firing range, and thus proved of questionable value. Their shells also proved defective because of their age. The bastion also possessed 450 longer-range guns, but many consisted of the older 9-centimeter model M 75/96 and multiple 1905 field cannons capable of firing shells seven and one-half kilometers. It also possessed 12-, 15-, and 18-centimeter cannons as well as vintage 10- and 15-centimeter howitzers dating from the 1880s and 1890s. The new heavy 30.5-centimeter mortars represented the only modern long-range artillery weapons, but only three hundred shells would be provided for the four guns. Other artillery pieces possessed an average of five hundred shells per weapon. Interval positions between the various major fortress works and battle emplacements remained vulnerable to enemy assault; still constructed of wood and soil, they did not provide any protection from heavy artillery fire.

The fortress also possessed 114 machine guns; 42 were positioned at the perimeter walls to provide flanking fire against attacking enemy troops, and 72 served mobile field purposes, but initially possessed neither crews nor horses to utilize them.[9] The citadel's offensive force, the 23rd Honvéd Infantry Division, was composed of four infantry regiments and included four artillery batteries, or sixteen guns; two more belonged to each of the two March replacement regiments, which together possessed two batteries. The multiple Landsturm units initially possessed no machine guns; thus, improvised crews had to be trained in their use when and if made available. The number of machine guns, however, proved inadequate for the size of the fortress.

Fortress Przemyśl consisted of a series of three major defensive lines for protection, which included concentric rings formed by nineteen permanent and twenty-three smaller forts with a perimeter of forty-five to forty-eight kilometers, making it one of the largest fortresses in Europe.

The citadel's main positions remained unprepared for major battle, while the second and core elements had been only partially constructed for effective combat service.

The important high terrain around the citadel's defensive district fortress positions, a frequent and favored Russian target, was situated ten kilometers from the San River crossing and inner city. The overall fortress construction had produced an irregular elliptical configuration, which gave the Russians an advantage in their multiple attempts to encircle the Siedliska Defensive District VI lines during their October 1914 mass attacks. They would also utilize the fortress terrain close to the entire perimeter to advantage.

The tragedy for the Austro-Hungarian army was that only a small portion of the neglect of the armed forces during the past decades could be corrected before combat commenced in late August 1914. The feverish labor activity during the short preparation period between the first mobilization day and the siege of the fortress in mid-September 1914 could not compensate for the previous lack of support and services.

Some serious problems became glaringly evident when preparing the fortress for wartime action. Only twelve of the perimeter rings, for example, could be considered bombproof against the newest heavy caliber guns. Furthermore, the artillery complements consisted partially of old 15- and 24-centimeter cannons, while the infantry and artillery interval positions constructed between the various major fort positions did not possess sufficient protection even from shrapnel artillery shells. Many of the newly constructed interval infantry positions consisted of only wood and earth with no overhead cover. In addition, protective barbed wire entanglements were only three rows deep. Fortress commander General Kusmanek von Burgneustädten encountered multiple problems during the bastion's mobilization period, seriously compounded by General Conrad's decision to deploy the Habsburg Supreme Command headquarters within the citadel. This seriously interrupted fortress preparations for combat and negatively affected frantic daily fortress activity as well.

Once battle ensued, multihour enemy artillery battery fire often destroyed telegraph and telephone lines, initially overhead, disrupting fortress communications and forcing the utilization of mounted riders and other signaling techniques. The main artillery telephone connections were constructed in mid-September during the fortress's first siege.[10]

The 1914 Austro-Hungarian army consisted of forty-eight active infantry and eleven cavalry divisions as well as multiple other units including Ersatz (troop replacement) Brigades and National Guard (Landsturm) formations divided into three separate combat groups. An A Group, composed of twenty-eight infantry divisions and assorted other formations, would be deployed against Russia as a strategic defensive force in case of war, while a Minimal Group Balkan consisting of eight infantry divisions would serve as defensive forces at the Serbian frontier. The third, the swing B Group, consisting of twelve infantry divisions and ancillary units, could be deployed against either foe, Russia or Serbia, to launch an offensive (Serbia possessed twelve infantry divisions, Russia one hundred). This reputedly provided flexible Habsburg war planning for any contingency.

Meanwhile, General Conrad, instead of launching the promised forty infantry division offensive against Russia, initially deployed twenty infantry divisions (A and B Groups) against Serbia in an attempt to achieve a rapid victory on the Balkan front and perhaps gain Bulgaria as an ally before facing the Russian colossus. Conrad anticipated a two-week "window of opportunity" because of the reputedly slow tsarist mobilization. However, Russia's quick 1914 mobilization forced Conrad to extricate his B Group strategic reserve Second Army from the Balkan front operation immediately to counter the unanticipated tsarist threat. This exposed the invading forces' northern flank with the B Group's redeployment, which proved significant in the subsequent Serbian defeat of the invading Habsburg Fifth and Sixth Armies. Second Army units, encountering numerous railroad delays during their transfer to the eastern front, were hurled into combat against a massive and numerically superior tsarist force launching an offensive and suffered costly defeat there as well.

Earlier, between August 14 and 18, 1914, twenty-seven thousand workers arrived at Fortress Przemyśl to prepare it for wartime service as much as time permitted. By September 15, when tsarist troops approached the bastion, the workers, laboring fourteen hours a day, had constructed seven new fortress belts, twenty-four defensive posts, fifty kilometers of covered approach routes, twenty-three infantry defensive lines, and two hundred new artillery positions. Roughly one million meters of barbed wire and multiple minefields had also been prepared, but heavy caliber artillery did not protect most defensive zones.[11]

The northern and eastern fortresses, located on almost level ground, provided the most advantageous Russian attack approach direction. During 1914, construction commenced for a new series of defensive works beyond the present fortress's outer perimeter to extend seven to eight kilometers from the core and inner city.[12] This forced the Russians to deploy additional siege troops around the fortress perimeter and finally removed the inner-city area from enemy artillery range.

A fifteen-kilometer wall extended around the inner city, whereas from the center city it was one to three kilometers to the San River Bridge. These core positions protected the immediate San River area from an enemy crossing. The fortress's main resistance strength, however, was concentrated at the outer citadel rings or zones, situated up to ten kilometers from its center, seven kilometers from the inner defensive lines. Fortress Przemyśl's flanking position along the San River also prevented the Russians from launching an early envelopment offensive operation across the southern Vistula River area against Fortress Kraków, two hundred kilometers to the north, while threatening the flanks of any enemy offensive launched in that direction. It also protected the potential invasion routes through the northernmost Carpathian Mountain range. The bulwark's initial mission, again, entailed the protection of an undisturbed Habsburg Galician deployment and the defense of the most dangerous enemy approach routes, particularly along the San-Dniester River line. Habsburg Supreme Command, determined to block all major regional Carpathian Mountain approaches, constructed major bridgehead positions along the two river barriers, at Jaroslau and Sienieva on the San River and at Halicz-Mikolajov on the Dniester River. These positions became integrated into the fortress's defensive system.

Following the Habsburg army's devastating military defeats in August–September 1914 at the two battles of Lemberg, the resulting chaotic 150-kilometer retreat and the ensuing siege of Fortress Przemyśl created a quasi-mystical aura about the fortress, increasingly riveting General Conrad's attention to the citadel between September 1914 and late spring 1915. Many contemporaries believed that whoever controlled the fortress also mastered the province of Galicia, enormously increasing its moral and political significance.

The fortress's military importance became evident when it became besieged in mid-September 1914; in addition to giving the defeated and exhausted field armies adequate time to rehabilitate from their disastrous defeat, Fortress Przemyśl also blocked major tsarist supply routes between middle and western Galicia. Most significantly, the citadel served as a major bulwark against a Russian invasion onto the Hungarian plains. If tsarist forces had seized the main Carpathian Mountain ridges and invaded Hungary, it would have signified the end of the war. The bulwark initially halted, then delayed, a 280,000-man enemy army advancing toward the Carpathian Mountain passes and Fortress Kraków in September 1914, which probably saved the Habsburg field army from annihilation.

General Conrad bears much of the responsibility for the disastrous Habsburg military record as winter 1914–1915 approached. His obsession with launching offensives had blinded him to the importance of fortified positions should his field armies be defeated and forced to retreat. Fatefully, Conrad made no preparations for a retrograde movement if it became necessary. The hasty and ill-prepared withdrawal of September 11, 1914, resulted in Fortress Przemyśl becoming an indispensable asset to the Habsburg military, as noted earlier.[13] Successfully retarding the tsarist advance provided time for the rehabilitation and reorganization of the defeated Habsburg army, enabling it to launch an offensive with its German counterpart in early October 1914.

Once tsarist forces besieged the fortress in September, however, a significant disadvantage became glaringly obvious. No railroad line connected the fortress to the hinterland from its rear echelon area. In addition, enemy forces blocked the crucial main Habsburg Carpathian Mountain railroad route (the Karl Ludwig), which also proved susceptible to enemy artillery fire from the surrounding hills. Nevertheless, as long as the fortress remained unconquered, the enemy had to utilize a wide and laborious detour over extremely poor mountain roads to maintain its supply and communication connection to its field army front. This disadvantageous situation ended for the Russians when they constructed a field railroad around the fortress perimeter shortly after its second encirclement in early November 1914; but the situation never-theless continued to limit tsarist maneuverability because it interrupted rail traffic on the main railroad supply line extending between Lemberg and Fortress Kraków as well as lesser connections.

Maintaining the Dual Monarchy's military prestige remained a ma-jor priority for General Conrad, feeding his obsession with liberating the fortification during both sieges. The fortress successfully fulfilled its primary mission by binding a significant number of tsarist troops during the first siege period between September 23 and October 9—forces that could have been deployed against the already outnumbered Habsburg field armies. By fall 1914, eleven to fourteen enemy divisions participated in the initial siege.

With tragic consequences, however, General Conrad allowed politi-cal and morale concerns to overshadow critical strategic Carpathian Mountain front military events. The mounting public concern and dete-riorating frontline troop morale increased General Conrad's preoccupa-tion with the fate of the fortress. To him, Fortress Przemyśl's capitulation would be tantamount to the defeat of the Habsburg army and the Dual Monarchy; therefore, he felt that he could not surrender the fortress without a major military action to preserve its honor. He also feared that its capitulation could create a public panic. This resulted in an unneces-sarily bloody battle on March 19, 1915.

Neutral states played a pivotal role in Habsburg, German, and Rus-sian military strategy during World War I, as Italy, Romania, and Bul-garia had an enormous influence on 1914 and 1915 Habsburg military decision making. These countries (especially Italy and Romania, which had irredenta claims against the Dual Monarchy) considered the con-tinued Habsburg battlefield defeats by Russia and, importantly, the three devastating encounters with Serbia in 1914 as signs of military weakness. It was assumed that their declaration of war against the Cen-tral Powers would prove fatal. Therefore, Fortress Przemyśl could not capitulate as Rome, Bucharest, and Sofia closely monitored the Carpathian Mountain battlefield situation and waited for an opportune moment to enter the fray.

Fortress Przemyśl remained besieged for 137 days during its second encirclement, which lasted from early November 1914 to March 23, 1915. Until then, its fate influenced the entire Austro-Hungarian strategic situation. Comparing the bulwark's time under siege with that of other fortifications, Russia's Fortress Ivangorod surrendered in just one day (August 4, 1915), the major Novogeorgiyevsk citadel in seven days (August 13–19, 1915), and Brest-Litovsk in nine days (August 26–September 3, 1915).

Another interesting facet of the fortress's history was the role played by aircraft, which became increasingly important during the conflagration. During one of the largest and bloodiest fortress battles of the war, Fortress Przemyśl's only contact with the outside world, besides radio and telegraph, was by aircraft. Flights in and out of the fortress represented the first example of airmail service to a completely besieged fortress. During the first siege, no aircraft companies were deployed in the citadel area. Following its liberation on October 10, airplanes became a major factor in the history of Fortress Przemyśl as well as for Habsburg field armies.

However, the fortress's location at the foothills of the Carpathian Mountains presented severe obstacles for the utilization of aircraft. The extremely volatile weather, in particular, presented a major impediment. Pilots repeatedly braved unfavorable conditions even when their crude aircraft should have been grounded. Despite their best efforts, however, terrain, snow, fog, turbulent winds, and biting cold sometimes made flying impossible. Compasses proved useless in the fog, and thick clouds regularly loomed over the fortress at a height of a hundred meters for days on end. The turbulent winds often shifted direction without warning, making even the most routine flights dangerous.

A final consideration concerning the strength and military worthiness of any fortress involves the extent and effectiveness of garrison troop training, moral character, and the competence of its commander and staff. These factors proved critical in Fortress Przemyśl's saga, because the garrison was composed mainly of inferior Landsturm troops that were less-trained and experienced. A second key factor was the bulwark's obsolescence—it could not withstand artillery barrages from newer, heavy artillery guns. The Russians did not deploy such heavy artillery pieces; otherwise, the citadel would have had to capitulate much sooner.

This book also describes the fortress's March 22, 1915, surrender and the railroad transport of Habsburg prisoners of war into Russia and provides a description of the victorious four-day Gorlice-Tarnov campaign to recapture Fortress Przemyśl from the Russians, which succeeded on June 3, 1915. The fortress remained within Austro-Hungarian administration until the end of the war in November 1918. Finally, there is a brief description of the Polish and Ruthenian struggles for control of the fortress during the early postwar period, ending with its involvement in World War II in the final chapter.

2

✠ ✠ ✠

The Opening Battles

AUGUST–SEPTEMBER 1914

WHEN WORLD WAR I ERUPTED, THE GREATEST CHALLENGE relative to Fortress Przemyśl was the need to remedy the decades of neglect the citadel had endured before the 1914 alarm and mobilization periods. On July 31, the three Galician army corps (I, X, and XI) received notification of the alarm period prior to war. Habsburg Supreme Command had earlier deployed X Corps to the Fortress Przemyśl area partially because of the fortress's proximity to the battlefront and because its mission was to assist in protecting the July 1 rearward deployment (Rückverlegung) of the Habsburg army to the San-Dniester River lines. This change in deployment was significant for the fortress, as it protected against enemy assaults on the San River. Although Habsburg prewar planners had anticipated that tsarist cavalry masses would attempt to disrupt a Habsburg mobilization, such actions did not occur in 1914. At the time of the deployment, the skeleton Fortress Przemyśl garrison remained seriously under strength and inadequately equipped for any military action, consisting of a mere five infantry battalions, a field artillery section, three regiments of fortress artillery, and a number of sapper (engineer) companies.

On the battlefield, a combination of factors sealed the fate of the initial 1914 Austro-Hungarian Galician military campaign, not the least of which was General Conrad's faulty mobilization and deployment planning. On July 3, Conrad had ordered his troops to redeploy back to the San-Dniester River when they mobilized, though the prewar Operations Bureau had scheduled them to be railroad-transported far forward to the Galician frontier. This Rückverlegung resulted in long troop marches in the August heat back to the originally designated frontier lines following mobilization. In the process, any possibility of obtaining a victory over the rapidly assembling Russian units vanished. Moreover, the Habsburgs suffered 40 percent casualties during the initial Lemberg campaigns, and concomitant lack of reserve formations meant that those lost could not immediately be replaced. Consequently, Habsburg Supreme Command had to reorganize its shattered army in October 1914, but the new formations no longer possessed the capabilities of the original army. Too many professional officers, noncommissioned officers, and professional soldiers had been sacrificed, and the newly mobilized recruits and reserve officers could not match them on the battlefield.

The defeat of Habsburg infantry units on the battlefield was further ensured by a lack of adequate artillery support. In addition, the dense Habsburg troop formations became easy targets for the more accurate and more numerous tsarist artillery pieces. Compounding the increasingly dangerous military situation was the earlier decision to detain three Second Army divisions in the Balkan theater as the remaining forces were redeployed to Galicia. The three divisions quickly became embroiled in battle against Serbia, making it difficult to transfer them to the Russian front, where the enemy continued to hold a significant numerical superiority over the beleaguered Habsburg forces.[1]

Fortress vulnerability resulted from the terrain exposure to the enemy between individual bastion perimeter works and from the garrison's significant lack of manpower. No serious resistance could be anticipated to halt an early enemy foray against it, particularly with the order for the rearward deployment to the immediate fortress area. In addition, cement and earthen works only half-enclosed some citadel artillery positions, while infantry defensive lines had no protection except for the earth itself. If the Russian army had supplied its later siege troops with modern heavy artillery pieces, it could have quickly forced the garrison to capitulate.

Enormous quantities of building and other materials were needed to prepare the citadel for military action. The massive influx of troops, labor units, civilian workers, and tons of material produced enormous

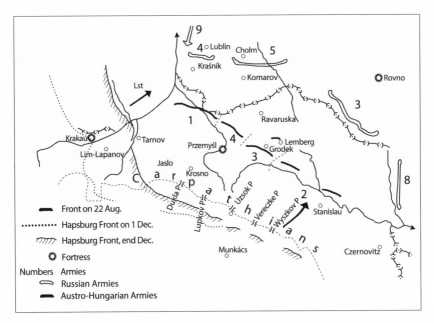

Map 2.1. Mobilization and deployment, 1914.

traffic jams and chaos in the fortress environs during early August 1914. While frantic construction commenced, numerous reconnaissance missions radiated out from the fortress. The construction workers had no military training, while inexperienced reservists comprised the majority of military labor crews. Most of the latter had been issued obsolete single-shot Wendl rifles and lacked adequate weapons training. Furthermore, obsolete fortress wagons, many fifty years old and utilized at the battle of Königgrätz during the 1866 Austro-Prussian War, proved much too cumbersome for fall and winter mountain supply column service. Use of local smaller wagons and Galician *panja* horses became standard.

Earthen embankments and dry moats blanketed the terrain around each fortress defensive structure. During the 1914 deployment period, the construction of multiple new field positions improved the citadel's defensive value. A series of new continuous infantry trench lines supplemented each of the external fortress rings, while workers also modified and improved existing structures. In addition, they dug new positions for field artillery batteries as well as improving and extending forward

positions beyond the important fortress perimeter at Helicha, Pod Mazurami, Batycze, and Na Gorach. These extended positions proved significant on numerous occasions during the September–October and
early November 1914 through March 1915 sieges, partly because they
compelled tsarist siege forces rearward, removing the inner citadel city
and military structures from enemy artillery range.

Workers had only partially completed the second infantry defensive
lines when construction had to be halted because of the disastrous field
army defeat at the second battle of Lemberg on September 11, 1914. The
outer fortress circumference measured about forty-five kilometers and
consisted of forty-two main positions. Fifteen of these, as mentioned
earlier, had been designated main fortress structures; the remaining
twenty-seven served supportive roles to them. Two of the eight major
military defensive districts that occupied the fortress's inner ring also
contained major support facilities. Defensive District I, situated on the
right bank of the San River, contained the fortress garrison hospital,
two railroad depots, ammunition magazines, fortress headquarters, five
barracks complexes, and multiple food magazines. Defensive District II
was located on the river's left bank. Defensive Districts III through V,
positioned outside the inner two, reposed along the left bank of the San
River, while VI through VIII occupied the right riverbank.

On August 2, 1914, preliminary measures were taken to prepare the
fortress against an anticipated Russian attack. Initial efforts protected
the garrison from the expected enemy mass cavalry strikes, which never
occurred. The X Corps deployment in the fortress area also provided
some protection for the citadel. The entire Fourth Army deployed before
the bastion. Prewar planning estimated that weeks and possibly even
months of preparation would be required to ready the fortress for effective military service; however, in 1914 only six weeks were available
because of the field army's disasters on the battlefield, which forced an
extended retreat behind the San River and Fortress Przemyśl to the
Biala-Dunajec River lines.

After Austria-Hungary's belated declaration of war on Russia on
August 6 to assure the success of the Minimal "B" rail transport to the
Balkan theater,[2] General Conrad was determined to establish his head-
quarters in Fortress Przemyśl. This greatly exacerbated the problems for

the fortress commander, General Kusmanek von Burgneustädten, who had received his command assignment just a few months before the outbreak of war. This also interfered with the efforts to place the fortress on war footing. In particular, it intensified security and communications problems. Adding to the chaos, the X Corps mobilization to prevent a Russian strike against the citadel also occurred within the fortress environs.

Garrison sorties, or offensive operations launched from the fortress perimeters, commenced after the Russian army initially encircled the fortress in late September 1914. They continued until early 1915, following the second tsarist siege in early November 1914. Their missions entailed binding opposing enemy forces to prevent their transfer against the Habsburg field armies, interrupting enemy transportation moves, and ascertaining enemy positions and troop concentrations. Unfortunately for the men under his command, General Kusmanek would repeatedly launch the sorties in the same direction and with 23rd Honvéd Infantry Division troop units, the fortress offensive unit. The failure to implement thorough preparations for the various missions and to utilize sufficient manpower for each endeavor was a classic example of Habsburg military ambition exceeding available resources.

The garrison's multinational composition further complicated its unenviable predicament. Many of its second-line Landsturm units contained a majority of Ruthenian (Ukrainian) troops, with the homes of their loved ones often located behind enemy lines. Of the sixty-five fortress garrison battalions, forty and one-half consisted of Landsturm troops, and of these, nineteen and one-half consisted of Ruthenian soldiers. Astute Russian propaganda influenced these troops, many of whom were considered unreliable in combat and a security threat. Exacerbating the situation, Ruthenian soldiers had not received adequate training, proper weapons, or the communications and signal equipment necessary for battlefield effectiveness, which left them wholly unsuitable for the rigors of fortress warfare. Officers encountered great difficulties in attempting to train the illiterate Ruthenian troops. Such troops proved incapable of performing even the most rudimentary military functions, such as challenging personnel at guard posts with single passwords.[3]

When offered it, Fortress Commander Kusmanek requested that he not receive Ruthenian Landsturm Infantry Regiment 19 for fortress duty, because it had left its neighboring units in the lurch, even abandoning its equipment on the battlefield during the fateful September Habsburg retreat. The reinforcing 111th Landwehr Infantry Brigade also reputedly possessed unreliable Landsturm officers. Very few active or reserve officers served in such units except at the highest command levels. Landsturm troops required training in the most basic military skills. Such officers, with the exception of regimental and battalion commanders and regimental adjutants, served with inactive Landsturm units. Thus, they lacked familiarity with many of the recent military advancements and, as older soldiers, often proved physically unfit for active duty. In general, all Landsturm troops lacked the physical fortitude for the severe rigors of offensive operations, particularly during winter weather conditions. Such units also lacked machine guns, proper artillery support, and other vital equipment, and had to implement multiple improvisational measures to form fortress supply trains properly and even to establish a functional supply transportation structure.[4]

The September 1914 battles at Lemberg decimated the 23rd Honvéd Infantry Division, which became the main Fortress Przemyśl offensive force for all major breakout (sortie) missions. The division soldiers, originally deployed on the Third Army's left flank, panicked during the Lemberg battle and fled from the front.[5] During the bloody October campaigning, the division again suffered 50 percent casualties while attempting to disrupt the tsarist siege! After the fort had been liberated from its first siege during early October 1914, the unit participated in the gruesome Magiera Mountain battle with the Habsburg Third Army, where it was bled white again. General Conrad ordered the division involved in battle east of the bulwark to return to fortress garrison duty before the second Russian siege commenced in early November 1914.

Returning to the chronological events, on August 3, Conrad ordered Fortresses Kraków and Przemyśl, as well as the improvised San-Dniester River bridgehead units, to be placed on war standing. By mid-August, the 97th and 111th Landsturm Infantry Brigades, both composed mainly of Ruthenian peasants, had arrived for fortress duty.

Transportation problems occurred immediately in the bulwark, largely because too few commissioned and noncommissioned officers had been assigned to organize the many wagon units. Initially only three commissioned officers and one noncommissioned officer commanded three thousand enlisted men while having responsibility for approximately fifteen hundred wagons and thirty-five hundred horses in the main fortress wagon park.[6] With the constant commotion and chaos during the early mobilization period, the number of available wagons and horses fluctuated daily, at times even hourly. Already during early August 1914, the unregulated utilization of horses and wagons had created incredible confusion that officials had to bring under immediate control. Hundreds of commandeered wagons simply disappeared. Until authorities instituted an effective control system, multiple teams of wagons and horses vanished for days at a time. Fortress provisioning and transportation duties had to be adjusted to accommodate these unacceptable circumstances. Finally, on August 12, a system for available wagons was established, along with critical measures such as provisioning for basic necessities such as feed for the horses. Between August 18 and 30, the wagon park commanding officer, on his own initiative, scavenged hay along the fortress perimeter to feed the starving animals.[7]

On August 16, Habsburg Supreme Command transferred its headquarters into the fortress. Armament and construction activities began in earnest with the arrival of twenty-seven thousand civilian workers, as well as many local farmers, four hundred officers, and three thousand horses mobilized specifically for this purpose. The civilian labor force's primary responsibility was to construct infantry defensive lines and artillery battery and blocking positions along the fortress rings, but they also helped build other vital structures such as depots, barracks, and ammunition dumps. The civilian workers also filled multiple gaps in interval positions between the major fortress works to protect against an enemy assault. When the first Russian units approached the fortress environs on September 15, workers had constructed seven new fortress rings, twenty-four protected heavy artillery posts, fifty kilometers of covered approaches and infantry line trenches, and two hundred new battery positions. Laboring up to fourteen hours a day, the workers also emplaced a thousand kilometers of barbed wire in three lines outside the fortress perimeter and laid multiple minefields. They also created artillery and infantry fields of fire through wooded areas by cutting down 1,000 hectares (247 acres) of forest, but prolonged periods of rain prevented

burning the wood. Seventy military labor sections, eight engineer companies, and the several thousand civilian workers made noteworthy
contributions during the fortress's six-week preparation period.[8]

In addition, the workers constructed ammunition dumps, a military
hospital, fortress headquarters, and other military structures. Four
airfields—the main one in Fortress Przemyśl-Zuravica with Flieger-
kompagnie (Flight) Company 8, an alternative location in Hureczko
village, a reserve site in Bakionczyce-Blonie, and a field airport between
Buszkourczki-Zuravica—were built. During the first siege, the citadel
did not have an airplane unit because the flight company had been redeployed. Workers also constructed two new bridges over the San River.
Fortress Przemyśl's overall resistance capabilities nevertheless remained
inadequate. If the enemy had possessed heavy artillery, many fortress
walls could have been destroyed, as most were twenty to thirty years old
and could not absorb the latest heavy artillery and mortars.

Meanwhile, garrison troops were shifted from one location to another, often disrupting unit cohesiveness. General Kusmanek decided to
extend some of the fortress perimeter positions forward from the citadel
walls, particularly in the areas where he believed the Russians would
attack, such as Siedliska (Defensive District VI). During the October
siege, Siedliska became the target for mass Russian assaults. Kusmanek
also launched sorties when he determined it to be necessary to protect
the new construction projects, and regular reconnaissance missions
launched from the bastion also served security purposes.

On August 21, an air reconnaissance mission flew over a wide stretch
of Podolio, where the Second Army's XII Corps located no enemy. One
day later (August 22), Conrad ordered the First and Fourth Armies to
launch an offensive toward Lublin and Cholm. Meanwhile, a tsarist
army was partially assembled to march in a southwesterly direction between the Bug and Vistula Rivers. There was a general uncertainty
regarding enemy intentions in the vital area between the Dniester and
Bug Rivers. On the Habsburg eastern flank, the Russian Eighth Army
had crossed the Zbrucz River at the upper Bug River frontier.

The next day (August 23), the Russian Third and Eighth Army left
flank forces entered eastern Galicia, while the tsarist Fourth Army advanced on a broad front toward Lublin. The Habsburg First and Fourth

Army offensive momentarily gave Conrad the initiative, but he ignored the growing threat from the east. He then ordered the Third Army to march to the north as rapidly as possible to defend the Fourth Army's exposed flank area. The First Army's success at Krasnik led to orders for the Russian Ninth Army to be redeployed to the endangered tsarist positions between the Bug and Vistula Rivers.

The Third Army received orders on August 24 for its troops to deploy to the high ground west of Przemyslany, while the Fourth Army launched its own offensive against reputedly weak enemy forces between the Dniester River and Tarnopol-Proskurov. As the military movements continued, gaps formed between the First and Fourth Armies and between the Fourth and Third Armies, and a rapidly increasing enemy threat to the eastern flank counterbalanced the favorable battle reports from the northern theater.

On August 25, the Third Army continued its movement without knowing that superior enemy troops had already invaded East Galicia on the eastern flank. The Third Army planned to defeat the Russians before they could unite all their forces; if it did not do so by August 26, it would have to calculate on much stronger enemy troop numbers. The Second Army's XII Corps mission was to halt any enemy incursions across the Zbrucz River. The Third Army received orders to launch an offensive in the general line to Zloczov to halt the enemy incursions against the Zlota Lipa to the north toward Ravaruska. The Third Army had to hold the enemy fast if it attacked from the direction of Brody and Tarnopol to the east. The battle at Zloczov began to introduce the factors that led to military disaster on the northern front.

It soon became apparent that the enemy intended to deploy troop concentrations on the high terrain before the southern fortress walls; simultaneously, long enemy troop columns approached the areas of Nizankovice-Rybotycze, deploying particularly strong forces in the vicinity of Nizankovice, a key railroad and railroad bridge site. Surprisingly, the enemy did not appear to threaten Defensive District VIII, as fortress command had originally anticipated; rather, they continued marching troop units to the west.[9] Significant enemy activity also commenced on the southwest fortress front, but no systematic effort to approach the fortress walls ensued.

General Kusmanek, determined to actively defend the fortress, implemented several active countermeasures on his own initiative. He launched sorties to disturb Russian troop movements around the fortress environs and to bind as many enemy troops as possible at the citadel. On September 2, General Kusmanek ordered the evacuation of the Ruthenian inhabitants living close to the fortress perimeter areas, which involved burning twenty-one local villages and twenty-three hamlets situated in the fortress line of observation or artillery fire. However, the uprooting of the poor, illiterate peasants proved to be a terrible undertaking. Participating troops witnessed the destruction and burning of homes, barns, crops, and even churches.[10] The villagers, often misunderstanding their dire predicament, were forcibly evicted from their homes by gendarme and military units, witnessing the destruction of their villages and losing many of their worldly goods. Soldiers helped peasants glean salvageable personal belongings, and even collected money to help ease the suffering of the villagers.[11] Many of the very old and very young struggled to keep up with the departing ragged wagons and horse-cart caravans and were ultimately abandoned. Livestock was often left in the fields. A good number of the mostly Ruthenian peasants, however, soon returned to their burned-out homes. The fortunate ones had some livable area remaining and moved back in. Those whose homes had been completely destroyed by fire moved into the cellars, mere holes in the ground, or lived in their small *panja* wagons to survive on their own.

Garrison units even razed larger structures such as grain warehouses. They demolished hundreds of wagons and extensive food supplies, which would have proved valuable in the latter months of the fortress's last siege. By September 2, garrison troops had deforested a thousand hectares of fortress terrain outside its perimeter area and leveled all large structures.[12]

During early September 1914, innumerable Second and Third Army stragglers passed through the fortress environs. To better maintain the flow of wagon traffic, Third and Second Army Commands ordered their supply trains to circumvent the fortress perimeter rather than travel through the bulwark. On September 4, General Kusmanek ordered the evacuation of all civilians who did not possess a three-month food supply or who were considered of questionable loyalty. Nonetheless, between

Map 2.2. Military situation, September 2–September 11, 1914.

twenty and thirty thousand inhabitants remained in the bastion city section. The poorest inhabitants suffered uprooting most frequently, since they could not fend for themselves. As September progressed, the sound of gunfire became increasingly pronounced in the fortress environs. Garrison troop units received assignments to their fortress works (Werke) and barracks and began preparation for twenty-hour duty as Landsturm troops continued retraining for fortress duty.

Fortunately for Fortress Przemyśl, a newly assigned artillery battalion had gained valuable combat experience in the Serbian campaign before being transferred to fortress duty. Newly designated fortress troop units during mid-September included the badly defeated Third Army, three Landsturm infantry brigades, the k.u.k. 93rd, 108th, and Hungarian 97th Infantry Brigades. The earlier mauled 23rd Honvéd Infantry Division and the 97th Landsturm Infantry Brigade had fled from the Lemberg battle to Fortress Przemyśl.[13] Fortress troops, meanwhile, had to defend the higher terrain areas where laborers raced to complete the construction of new positions outside the citadel's perimeter walls. Eventually, a sufficient number of laborers had become available for the projects, but it remains unclear why the elevated terrain outside the fortress perimeter had not been established as priority defensive positions in the original fortress plans. Meanwhile, Defensive District VII proved difficult to defend because the entrenched enemy occupied the opposing high ground. The outer perimeter fortress walls' close proximity to the citadel city enabled the Russians to fire artillery shells into it, which made it necessary to extend certain defensive positions forward to place the city out of tsarist firing range.

Habsburg Supreme Command calculated that the food supplies and ammunition hastily delivered to Fortress Przemyśl would prove sufficient for a three-month period. Original prewar plans provided 137 days of provisions, far greater than the specified 90-day supply for an anticipated 85,000 garrison soldiers and 3,700 horses. During the first bulwark siege from September 23 to October 9, however, the fortress garrison was over capacity, housing 131,000 troops, including the reinforcing troops and 21,000 horses. Thus, a ninety-day supply of items, particularly ammunition, did not exist.[14] The overly frugal prewar estimates ensured that the fortress would have insufficient provisions for a long siege, and the excessive troop and horse numbers dangerously strained the garrison food supplies throughout late 1914 and into 1915.

Meanwhile, farther east, the Habsburg Second, Third, and Fourth Armies launched an early September offensive to recapture Lemberg after its September 2 surrender. The ambitious strategy created a dangerous gap between the Fourth and the First Army that the Russians quickly exploited. Tsarist troops poured into the gap and threatened to encircle the Fourth Army's southern flank positions before that army successfully reversed its main forces' advance direction 180 degrees following the successful battle at Komarov. The Fourth Army's mission then became to attack the tsarist infantry divisions crushing the hopelessly outnumbered eastern flank Habsburg Third Army's seven divisions, but this maneuver, in turn, dangerously enlarged the gap between the First and Fourth Armies. When two enemy corps attacked the First Army's rear echelon positions, it produced a catastrophic situation, particularly because no replacement or reserve troops were available. The First Army received orders to delay the seemingly irresistible tsarist advance, while its supply trains continued a rapid retrograde movement before the army's infantry troops could retreat behind the San River.

The Habsburg offensive to reconquer Lemberg produced no positive results, as it could not overcome the deadly accurate Russian artillery fire and superior troop numbers. Reinforcements from the newly created Russian Ninth Army, originally intended to be deployed against Germany, reversed direction to the southwest Austro-Hungarian front. The Russians attempted to turn the tide of battle south of Lublin and Cholm, where Habsburg forces had originally achieved battlefield success. As Russian troop numbers steadily increased, so did their advantage. General Conrad ultimately had to withdraw his First and Fourth Armies. He did so to shorten his front lines, while simultaneously attempting to intercept the Russian Third Army forces bearing down on his right flank.

The First Army suddenly felt Russian pressure on its right flank. Simultaneously, superior Russian forces advanced into eastern Galicia toward defensive lines at Zlota Lipa. On September 10, the First Army was forced to retreat. Troops were exhausted and low on ammunition. The question was, could the First Army hold the enemy behind the San River? After fighting for seventeen straight days, the First Army was ordered to delay the Russian advance until Habsburg troops had been able to retreat behind the San River at Lemberg. The Fourth Army left flank forces had been threatened by encirclement.[15] Two enemy corps had broken through the First and Fourth Armies.

As it withdrew, however, the First Army received orders to prevent the enemy from severing Habsburg connections westward to the homeland so that the retreat could continue. Eyewitness reports from a small Galician village described the ensuing Habsburg retreat, noting the enormous amount of supplies discarded by the troops. Many horses died and hundreds of supply wagons were wrecked as a result of the terrible road conditions. The Russians captured vast amounts of valuable Habsburg war material such as supply wagons, artillery pieces, horses, rifles, and ammunition. The retreating troops also destroyed supplies and food items during the retrograde operation. Starving, exhausted, and dispirited troops begged for food as they passed through villages, but more often than not the villagers had none to spare. Increasingly

desperate, the soldiers scavenged for cabbages, carrots, and raw potatoes in the fields, and they often broke into homes, seizing whatever they
could find.

The second devastating Lemberg battlefield defeat finally convinced
General Conrad on September 11, 1914, that he had to initiate an immediate retreat to save his reeling armies from further disaster. The Habsburg
armies could not move to the southwest because they would lose contact
with the allied German forces at their northern flank. Simultaneously,
Conrad requested that his ally transfer at least three army corps to the
vicinity of Fortress Kraków to cooperate in the next allied campaign. The
mid-September retreat resulted in enormous losses. The demoralized
Habsburg troops initially retreated to the San River, but they desperately
required rest and rehabilitation, and could not defend the river line in
their present condition. Therefore, the retreat had to be continued
farther westward into the Carpathian Mountains. During the heavy
autumn rains that ensued, many weary soldiers fell ill. Four hundred
thousand Habsburg soldiers became casualties in the first campaign,
which constituted 40 percent of the original deployment numbers.
Only the enemy's failure to press its advantage, an often-repeated phe-
nomenon during the war, spared Conrad's armies from annihilation.

In addition to German reinforcements, General Conrad also requested to be in command of the resulting multinational military
endeavor. This request sparked the first of many confrontations regarding proper leadership. Conrad considered himself eminently qualified
to lead allied contingents and indeed commanded the vast majority of
troops presently deployed on the eastern front. German military leaders,
however, adamantly refused to place their troops under foreign command. Conrad's dismissal of numerous generals following the disastrous
1914 opening campaigns increased Germany's lack of confidence in his
leadership. Nevertheless, at this juncture, the German High Command
feared the collapse of its ally's army. In mid-September 1914, hastily sum-
moned allied meetings resulted in a promise of additional German contingents to be transferred to the eastern front. Although Conrad's main
concern was to have the allied front united to initiate cooperative military operations, the bulk of these new formations, designated the
Ninth Army, would be deployed to Upper Silesia to protect the major

German industrial center, rather than to Conrad's requested Fortress Kraków area.

The Habsburg forces withdrew 150 kilometers to West Galicia and into the Carpathian Mountains. The defeated army rapidly became disorganized as it crowded onto the few traversable routes, which spread chaos and panic through the surviving ranks. On September 11, tsarist army units advanced into the enlarging gap between the First and Fourth Armies only to find that the First Army had already initiated its retreat a day earlier, on September 10.

The Habsburg Second and Third Armies also retreated into western Galicia, resulting in a seemingly endless stream of defeated and apathetic troops appearing before Fortress Przemyśl. The difficult, hilly terrain, enduring inclement fall weather, and excessive troop and wagon traffic in the area of Fortress Przemyśl severely impeded any possibility for an organized retreat from the San River. Four weeks of unrelenting rain, cold temperatures, and heavy military wagon traffic transformed the already poor and narrow Galician roadways into a treacherous obstacle course. Other natural passageways proved either too steep or too muddy to traverse safely. Rapidly fleeing supply train columns became hopelessly intertwined, exacerbating the chaotic conditions around the fortress.

General Conrad visited the front lines on September 10, one of the few occasions he did so during the entire time of his active duty. He departed Fortress Przemyśl at 8:20 a.m., initially to visit Third Army headquarters, and returned at 3 p.m. On the same day, Habsburg First Army right flank troops were attacked, hurled back, and forced to retreat. The retrograde movement had only three possible retreat routes through the swampy Tarnov region, impeding the movement of troops who were already exhausted.[16]

Habsburg Third Army supply trains had to pass through the Fortress Przemyśl environs as continuous rainfall caused terrible terrain conditions on the perimeter. The muddy morass quickly bogged down XI Corps to the north and III Corps to the south; ultimately, Third Army supply trains were forced to pass through the citadel, wreaking havoc and chaos on the bulwark's streets.[17] Thousands of wounded soldiers and horses were abandoned in the fortress during the army's passage through it. The Habsburg retreat on September 11 created panic in the ranks, which was exacerbated by the inexperienced and multinational troops. Nevertheless, the retreat saved the Habsburg forces from annihilation.

Conrad's neglect of defensive warfare planning and subsequent training in the prewar period resulted in total chaos at the commencement of and during the completely unprepared and unplanned September retreat. Exhausted soldiers collapsed unnoticed along the retreat routes, often abandoned to be captured by the enemy. The weary troops slogged through incessant rainfall, and regiments originally composed of one hundred officers and over four thousand infantry troops had been reduced to 10 percent of their original numbers.

On September 12, the battle plan assumed that the Germans would deploy nine divisions north of Fortress Kraków, while the Habsburg First, Fourth, and Third Armies would be deployed on the general line along the Biała River. As the retreat commenced, Conrad grouped his armies at the southwest San River line, whereupon the First and Fourth Armies launched offensives against the tsarist forces ensconced at the west San River bank. Thus, the Third Army had to halt Russian progress to the west toward the Fortress Przemyśl and Jaroslau area, while the Second Army's main mission was to halt the Russians pressing forward south of the fortress. The First Army had to defend and provide security at the San River line until the Fourth and Third Armies had crossed that waterway. Meanwhile, Habsburg Supreme Command headquarters had to depart Fortress Przemyśl, as it was now threatened with isolation and siege.

Habsburg Supreme Command evacuated Fortress Przemyśl on September 12 at noon.[18] The Fourth Army command transferred troop units to the San River bridgeheads at Jaroslau and Sieniava to protect the approaches to Fortress Przemyśl, while Habsburg field army forces withdrew behind the San River. Before leaving the fortress, General Conrad ordered his armies to protect the San River area, emphasizing that they had to unconditionally defend the middle Galicia region. The poor physical condition of retreating Habsburg troops remained a major concern, as did the necessity to continue the retreat. However, Conrad's concern relative to the necessity for rapid German military assistance proved decisive. The farther west the Habsburg retreat progressed, the more vital German military assistance became. The recent German military victories at Tannenberg and the Masurian Lakes signified that their military assistance should be available soon.[19]

German Chief of the General Staff General Moltke determined that the first two Eighth Army corps should be transferred to Prussia-Silesia, although the prewar Conrad-Moltke agreements determined that the allied forces should advance to Siedliska to meet allied Austro-Hungarian forces. However, because of the radical change in the Habsburg military situation on September 11, Conrad immediately requested that allied assistance be deployed to Fortress Kraków, although it ultimately arrived too late.[20]

The Russians had attempted to separate the three eastern Habsburg armies (Fourth, Third, and Second) from their connecting supply lines to western Galicia and the hinterland while their numerous reinforcements overwhelmed the exposed Habsburg troops. As the First Army retreated, seven or eight tsarist divisions threatened the Fourth Army's weak northern flank positions, resulting in military catastrophe. The increasingly unfavorable situation forced the Habsburg armies to initiate their retreat, regroup, and rehabilitate over several weeks.[21]

Habsburg troops, however, initially had to stymie enemy progress and prevent or at least slow the advancing tsarist forces from crossing the San River. As it continued its difficult retreat, the Fourth Army's main forces deployed behind the river stretch at the key crossing to the Jaroslau bridgehead, north of Fortress Przemyśl. Eleven infantry battalions initially defended the Jaroslau position, but the number rapidly increased to forty-three.[22] On September 14, the 23rd Honvéd Infantry Division and the 97th Landsturm Infantry Brigade reported to the fortress to strengthen its troop stand.

Given the terrible Habsburg military situation, German command determined to transfer four army corps and a cavalry division to Fortress Kraków's northern flank area. The action threatened the Russian troops assembled beyond Fortress Kraków on the northern Vistula River plain. If the Germans had launched an offensive into that Vistula River area, they would have had the opportunity to sever tsarist northwest front contact to the Austro-Hungarian front.[23]

On September 12, Conrad had to determine whether to deploy allied German troops at Fortress Kraków or Prussian Silesia. If the German troops deployed to the Fortress Kraków area, they would provide immediate relief to the battered allied troops there, which General Conrad considered critical. Deploying German troops to Prussian Silesia, on the other hand, would relieve enemy pressure there and prevent the Russians from launching an offensive into that critical area. Conrad's decision, however, also had to take into account the German military situation, which was less than ideal. Their troops encountered serious supply problems and troop exhaustion following the initial Tannenberg and Masurian Lakes campaigns, and they still possessed inferior troop numbers compared to the Russians.

Meanwhile, the unanticipated Habsburg retreat raised questions concerning Romania's neutral stance. Vienna offered Bucharest the Suczava territory if it actively entered the war on the Austro-Hungarian side. General Conrad still firmly believed that a Romanian offensive in conjunction with his forces launched against Russia would result in a tsarist defeat. In any event, Conrad understood that the Habsburg armies required a decisive victory against their Russian foe to prevent Romania from entering the war against the Dual Monarchy, while neighboring Bulgaria also continued to determine its stance based solely on the outcome of battlefield events.[24]

General Conrad initially grouped his defeated army southwest of the San River, where the Third Army received the mission to defend the Fortress Przemyśl–Jaroslau area. Thus, its XI Corps deployed north of the fortress environs and III Corps south of it. The First and Fourth Armies received orders to attack tsarist troops when they attempted to cross the San River, while the Second Army deployed its troops south of the citadel. Meanwhile, the second Balkan front offensive commenced against Serbia.

The Habsburg Third Army had retreated to the northern Przemyśl area as far as Nizankovice, while the Second Army deployed south of the Third Army in the area of Dobromil-Chyrov; both had the mission to halt the Russian advance toward the fortress. As the first Habsburg units marched through Fortress Przemyśl, citadel officers who had served with some of the retreating units asked about the fate of their former comrades: "Where is so and so?" The answer inevitably was that the individual had been killed or badly wounded. The retreating troops presented a frightening sight, covered with so much mud that one could not distinguish the color of their uniforms. Many no longer possessed hats or guns and wore dirty, blood-stained bandages on their bodies. Multiple units had only a small number of surviving troops. Questions about what happened to the defeated troops received responses with mere tired hand movements and a fatalistic reply: "All is lost."

The Habsburg retreat continued until September 13, with troops marching through the nights on secondary roads and over difficult routes because no decent road connections existed in the Carpathian Mountains. As the retrograde movement progressed, the conditions of the supply train columns worsened, retarding all movement. This resulted partially from the exhaustion and malnourishment of the vital horses, but the incessant rain and deteriorating road conditions also forced multiple transport delays. Many horses had almost starved to death or suffered from exposure, but hundreds simply had been driven to death or were captured by the Russians. When the Third Army abandoned four thousand horses within the fortress, two thousand found immediate work and proved invaluable by transporting ammunition to gun placements, providing crucial movement for mobile artillery and shells and performing other important tasks.

In the Fortress Przemyśl area, coins quickly disappeared, leaving only paper money in circulation. When troops arrived in the vicinity of a village or hamlet, prices quickly increased, as did theft of common commodities required for normal village life such as petroleum, salt, sugar, and soap, because such supplies could no longer be transported by railroad. If a battle took place near a village, violent crimes and abuses became even more rampant. The advancing Russians ransacked villages caught in the path of the early September Habsburg retreat, plundering shops and houses for anything they could seize. Massed rifle, machine gun, and artillery fire frightened villagers as tsarist troops crossed the Vistula River.

The retreating Habsburg troops discarded enormous quantities of food and equipment and surrendered hundreds of kilometers of railroad track, a hundred locomotives, and fifteen thousand train cars to the enemy.[25] Railroad service along the important Chyrov-Przemyśl route had to be terminated, leading to the abandonment of significant quantities of railroad rolling stock and supplies as well as sick and wounded Habsburg soldiers. Within the fortress, streets became jammed with wagons four abreast attempting to pass through the citadel, which promptly obstructed all traffic attempting to travel in the opposite direction. Third Army units remained in the citadel area for several days, creating chaos everywhere.

In his interesting book *Bollwerk am San*, Hermann Heiden vividly described the miserable retreat march. Every few hundred meters wagon columns had to halt for hours on end. At jammed road crossings, only energetic leadership allowed any forward movement. Light rainfall soon gave way to heavy downpours, which extended the delays. As the soldiers' boots and the horses' hooves sank into the mud, Cossack troops broke through gaps in the Fourth Army retreat lines on the second day of the withdrawal. Enemy artillery continued to target Fourth Army side column formations, forcing those that reached the Jaroslau area onto the Third Army supply lines leading into the fortress.[26] The Fourth Army had to wage rearguard battles during the difficult retreat to protect its supply trains, but its first duty became to save the troops; therefore commanders received orders to abandon their supply wagons.[27] The horrendous conditions made the movement of heavy ammunition vehicles particularly difficult. However, even tsarist units had to pause because of their losses and the effects of the strenuous battle.[28] As mounted Cossack divisions advanced into critical Habsburg terrain, the victorious tsarist troops paused to rehabilitate, resupply, and receive reinforcements before they continued their forward movement, saving the retreating Habsburg troops from possible destruction.

The fleeing troops lost their cohesiveness as they rushed through dense woods and marshy terrain along the few passable routes available to them. Thoroughly exhausted and suffering from acute hunger, most of the soldiers had reached their physical limits, and their spirits were completely broken. As inexperienced reserve officers replaced the many professional officer casualties, the overall military situation worsened even further. The Habsburg army had deteriorated into what the official Austrian history termed "a skeleton army." Providing March Brigade replacement troops partially offset the initial devastating losses, but often these inadequately trained and ill-equipped Ersatz replacement soldiers were hurled into battle as combat units in an attempt to fill the huge gaps in the front lines partially caused by the lack of available reserve formations.

The initial Galician campaign (the two battles of Lemberg) expended a catastrophic amount of professional and reserve soldiers. Habsburg troop numbers fell to 477,000 field soldiers and 26,800 cavalry troops, along with 1,578 artillery pieces, which contrasted sharply from the million-man-plus fighting force and 2,068 artillery pieces originally deployed during August 1914.[29] Infantry units suffered 40 percent casualties, including the large numbers of professional soldiers. The opening campaign abruptly and dramatically destroyed any possibility of winning a short war, and the Habsburg army never fully recovered from the disastrous Lemberg battles and concomitant losses.

On September 14, as chaos continued to reign within Fortress Przemyśl, Russian units advanced to the Dukla Pass and prepared to launch an invasion into Hungary. Fortress Przemyśl retarded rapid enemy forward progress, but the tsarist soldiers nevertheless attacked the San River bridgeheads protecting Fortress Przemyśl's northern flank approach area. General Conrad sought to avoid serious contact with enemy forces to provide sufficient time for the rehabilitation of his defeated armies and then launch an allied offensive with German divisions from the area of Fortress Kraków. Meanwhile, the Habsburg retreat continued back to the Dunajec River.[30] While Third Army troops trudged through the Fortress Przemyśl environs for three days and two nights without pause, General Kusmanek dispatched two thousand wagons to Jaroslau to recoup some of the retreating troops' abandoned supplies. The wagon column stretched eighteen kilometers, but retreating field army supply trains crisscrossed the path of the fortress wagon recovery column, splitting it into three segments. The initial eight hundred fortress wagons went astray, never to reach their destination. However, the remaining twelve hundred successfully transported supplies back to the fortress on September 15.[31]

Apart from the weather conditions, Third Army units experienced no serious complications during the first retreat day. However, on

September 13 and 14, the combination of inclement weather, the chaos and problems created by the waterlogged roads, and heightened enemy activity quickly transformed this picture. Multiple kilometer-long wagon columns jostled each other along the few passable routes.[32] The mass of fleeing people and animals soon blocked all north-south roads, as well as other routes, leading to the fortress. Discipline within the ranks had all but vanished. The delayed Russian army pursuit allowed the mass of the Habsburg northern armies some relatively quiet days as they retreated west from the San River. Between September 14 and 16, the only serious battle occurred in the wooded terrain south of the San River.[33]

On September 14, General Conrad requested that German Eighth Army troops in transport be placed under Austro-Hungarian command, but Emperor Wilhelm denied the request. The decision left the allied armies under the command of their own General Staffs. Although they promised to cooperate with each other, no organizational apparatus forced them to do so. General Conrad soon accused the Germans of attempting to dominate the alliance to further their own interests and regarded the negative German response, relative to the allied command request, as a personal affront and a sign of a lack of faith in the capabilities of Austro-Hungarian military commanders and troops.

Also on that day, Archduke Friedrich, nominal commander of the Austro-Hungarian forces fighting Russia, telegraphed Emperor Wilhelm concerning the failure of German troops to launch an offensive toward Siedlice. The German High Command replied that German forces were already in transit to aid their ally.[34] Meanwhile, the German eastern front commander, General Paul von Hindenburg, recognized that the Habsburg army required immediate German assistance. Thus, General Erich von Ludendorff approached the German High Command and suggested that they deploy not just two corps to assist the ally, but possibly the entire German Eighth Army, which would launch a new offensive operation.[35] That evening at 9:15 p.m. the announcement arrived that the entire German Eighth Army, consisting of four corps and one cavalry division, would be utilized to create a new Ninth Army with General Ludendorff as its chief of staff. In addition, two further corps would follow to be deployed on the Silesian and Polish frontier.[36]

The initiation of a renewed allied offensive depended upon the German ally, whose supporting troops required eighteen days to become operationally ready. On September 16, all bridges between Fortress Przemyśl and Jaroslau had to be destroyed, while the First Army received orders to delay any Russian advance over the San River and the Fourth Army regrouped its battered troops. On September 14, as Third Army Command entered Fortress Przemyśl, Fourth Army units covered that army's rapid retreat across the San River.[37] Both armies had crossed the hundred-kilometer-long San River stretch, while to the north the First Army continued its retreat movements.[38] The badly weakened defending Habsburg troops could only hold the San River line for a few days, during which time General Conrad feared that the Russians would launch a double envelopment assault along the river line to entrap his forces.

Meanwhile, Conrad contemplated transferring nine infantry divisions to the Fortress Kraków area to participate in the forthcoming allied offensive with First, Fourth, and Third Armies eventually occupying the general line of the Biala-Dunajec Rivers to the Vistula River. The First Army crossed the San River on September 13, while initially only weak tsarist forces pursued it. The Third and Fourth Armies had to be deployed behind the San River on September 14, and the First Army on September13. The First Army could not retreat any farther until Habsburg troops had been rehabilitated. Fortunately, the enemy pursued them cautiously.[39]

When the Second Army redeployed behind the forward Carpathian Mountain ridges south of Fortress Przemyśl, a defensive force consisting of six March (replacement) battalions, twenty-two Landsturm (third-line territorial) battalions, and three artillery batteries received the mission to halt enemy egress along the extended mountain front from the Uzsok to the Jablonica Pass. These hastily assembled second-line troops were unprepared for combat and incapable of defending the Carpathian Mountain front against regular tsarist forces. Fortunately, the Russians, also badly mauled during the initial military campaign, did not pressure this portion of the front.[40]

General Conrad's pleas for immediate German assistance commenced just as the decisive battle of the Marne on the western front concluded and German troops simultaneously battled against superior enemy numbers in East Prussia and on the western front. Conrad became frantic and frustrated because his army had sustained such enormous casualties and catastrophic defeat, which he blamed on the German forces' failure to launch an offensive into Poland. Conrad initially requested the immediate deployment of at least two German corps to the Fortress Przemyśl area, emphasizing that the Russians could easily replace their casualties, but he could not. Since he possessed no reserve units, his armies could not launch an offensive in their present state and required German assistance to do so. On September 15, the German High Command announced the formation of its new Ninth Army and preparations to assist its hard-pressed Habsburg ally. Its military objective became to entice the Russians to transfer large troop numbers from the Austro-Hungarian front to counter the new German threat, thus relieving pressure on their ally.

The question of neutral European nations remained at the forefront of allied discussions. General Conrad continued to believe that he had to win a decisive military victory over the Russians to persuade Romania to fulfill its prewar treaty obligations, or merely to remain neutral. The Romanians could have entered the conflict at any moment depending on which side achieved a decisive battlefield success. A major Habsburg victory might also have influenced Bulgaria, or perhaps even Italy, to join the Central Powers. On the Balkan front, when the Serbian troops crossed the Drina River on September 15, it raised concern in Viennese military circles, while Habsburg armies continued to retreat on the Russian front. By September 17, 1914, Romania's threatening conduct raised the question whether Habsburg troops should be deployed in Transylvania.[41]

The Habsburg First Army continued to retreat slowly under tsarist Ninth Army pressure, while the enemy Fourth Army deployed a battalion of troops across the San River at Krzeszov close to Fortress Przemyśl. The tsarist Fifth Army had advanced toward Jaroslau (north of Fortress Przemyśl). Meanwhile, tsarist general Nikolai Ivanov and his chief of staff, Mihail Vasilev Alexejew, concentrated on besieging the fortress at the earliest possible date.

On September 16, General Conrad's main concern remained that his northernmost First Army not be pushed too far south.[42] That same day, tsarist Third Army infantry and artillery units appeared at the Fortress Przemyśl eastern front.[43] In the interim, General Kusmanek remained concerned about the fortress's southeast front defensive lines at Defensive District VI, which remained closer to the inner city than the other districts, so that enemy artillery fire could strike the city and San River bridges. The resulting improvements at that sector extended the Habsburg perimeter lines forward through the high terrain at Pod Mazurami to Helicha two to three kilometers forward of the fortress ring onto the opposing high terrain. Four garrison infantry battalions occupied these new positions after they had been rapidly fortified. This forced the Russians to move their siege lines rearward, which required additional troop units to man the new lines. Meanwhile, enemy Fourth and Fifth Armies crossed the San River north of the fortress, while the Eighth Army advanced south of it into the Carpathian Mountains to protect what would soon be siege armies from a flank attack through the mountains.[44]

First Army, which had to defend a hundred-kilometer stretch on the San River line, became threatened with encirclement because of its extensive front. Nevertheless, the army received orders to delay the Russians from crossing the river. The disposition for the troop deployments for September 16 included the order for the First Army to maintain its present positions on September 16 and 17 if possible without becoming involved in serious battle. The Second, Third, and Fourth Armies continued their reassembly of forces.

Meanwhile, reports from Bucharest regarding the battlefield results on the western and eastern fronts indicated that Romania would not join the Central Powers. To the contrary, it seemed likely to intervene against Austria-Hungary in the war. Even its king, Carol, reported the battlefield situation to be very unfavorable. By the next day, the question arose of a Romanian threat to Transylvania.[45]

Between September 17 and 19, the Russian Third and Eighth Armies approached the fortress and commenced a siege. The Russian Third Army and additional forces received the mission to protect the siege troops by deploying along the north Wisloka River–Rzeszów–Dynow and south of the fortress extending from Chyrov to Sambor. The mission of the Russian armies encompassed the Russian Third Army attacking the Habsburg front in the area of Radymno, encircling the fortress from the north and south, while the Eighth Army attacked the front extending from that army's flank to protect the tsarist Third Army from the south and the roads leading to Lemberg. The Fifth Army had to drive the enemy from the right bank of the San River, cooperating with the Fourth Army to take the Jaroslau bridgehead, and then break the communications lines between the fortress and the left flank positions. After that, it would seize the surrounding area and protect the flank positions of the Fifth Army as it approached the San River. Meanwhile, the Ninth Army would take the area along the Wisloka River, covering the right flank of the entire tsarist front while it also secured the Vistula River line and the San River bridges.

Emperor Wilhelm again contacted Archduke Friedrich on September 17, informing him that General Hindenburg would command the new German Ninth Army consisting of five army corps. The remaining weakened German Eighth Army forces had the mission to defend East Prussia while the new offensive operations unfolded on the Austro-Hungarian front.[46] In the meantime, Habsburg Supreme Command continued to worry that the enemy could outflank its First Army positions; therefore, that army had to retreat to the west and southwest. The Fourth, Third, and Second Armies received orders to delay any retrograde movement from the San River, while the bridgeheads protecting Fortress Przemyśl had to be defended as long as possible. A day earlier General Conrad had ordered his armies to withdraw from the San River line and avoid decisive battle. The Second Army had to retreat to the Dukla Pass area. The other three armies prepared defensive positions behind the Biala and Dunajec Rivers. The First Army encountered strong enemy cavalry forces, which pressed its troops back toward the lower Wisloka River.

General Conrad and German general Ludendorff met on September 18 at Neu Sandec to discuss allied strategy for a joint October campaign against their opponent.[47] It was agreed that everything depended on enemy action. General Ludendorff determined to launch the German Ninth Army forces against the Russian west flank positions situated along the Vistula River if they approached Fortress Kraków; such an action would expose the tsarist northern flank troop formations on the

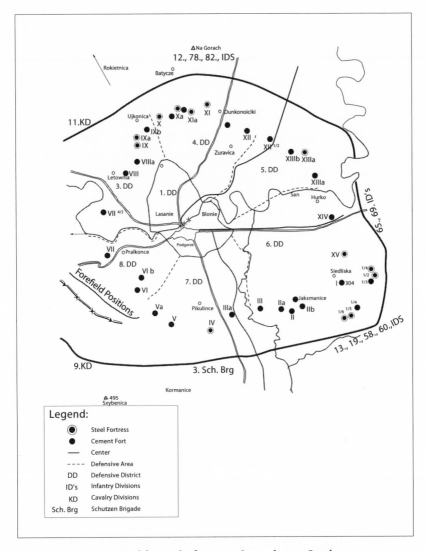

Map 2.3. Fortress Przemyśl during the first siege, September 18–October 9, 1914.

right Vistula River front. At the meeting, General Ludendorff raised an interesting question of transferring the Habsburg Second Army from the Carpathian Mountain region into the area north of Fortress Kraków to increase the troop numbers on that portion of the unprotected 180-kilometer-wide German front.[48] He also suggested moving the First Army over the Vistula River against the flank of the tsarist troops deployed along the San River. However, inadequate troop numbers and ammunition meant that this potentially decisive strategy could not succeed.

Conrad hoped to regain the initiative against his foe, but he had no clue about Russian intentions. The Russians continued to press westward, eventually deploying troops in the Carpathian Mountain region. General Ludendorff, aware of large numbers of Russian troops now established at the middle Vistula River area, deployed the German Ninth Army north of Fortress Kraków. The decision provided an extended position from which to attack tsarist northern defensive flank forces. For General Conrad, it was imperative that Habsburg forces remain close to allied German troops in order to launch a rapid offensive on the Vistula River front. Meanwhile, the Habsburg Second Army launched an attack from its Carpathian Mountain positions to envelop the Russian forces before it.[49]

The ensuing German operation at the middle Vistula River area almost developed into a "thrust into the air," but it drew immediate Russian attention and concern. The German Ninth Army deployed, as promised, between Galicia and the middle Vistula River area to relieve the battered Habsburg forces by drawing tsarist troops from them to counter the new German threat. Conrad had long wanted to launch a Habsburg offensive over the San and Vistula Rivers, but the terrible condition of his recovering troops left him unable to do so without German assistance. The October operation, which was the first combined allied effort of the war, thus occurred in west Galicia and west of the Vistula River because Conrad's offensive plans did not seek to extend battle into the Carpathian Mountains.[50]

Also on September 18, the two-year-old railroad bridge at Radymno had to be destroyed because of the looming tsarist threat to the critical Chyrov-Sambor railroad line.[51] The decision caused concern in Fortress Przemyśl because seven missing railroad tanker cars filled with gasoline had not been returned to the citadel. Luckily, the tankers eventually reappeared. Meanwhile, railroad officials attempted to ensure that a twenty-two-tanker-car train could be returned to the fortress before all bridges had to be destroyed. Cossack troops threatened to capture the train, but it managed to depart for the bulwark just before explosives were set off to cripple the railroad crossings behind it.[52] Enemy troops soon reached the Dynov area, the end station of a subsidiary railroad line to the fortress, where earlier infantry ammunition had been transported into the citadel. A garrison infantry battalion located and successfully rescued an automobile column that had been halted at Dynov and attempted to return to the fortress.

On September 19 and 20, as the Habsburg armies continued their retrograde troop movements, and although terrible road conditions resulted in multiple march stoppages, the pursuing Russians did not press them.[53] Meanwhile, on the Balkan front, heavy battle continued along the lower Drina River. Systematic tsarist artillery barrages commenced against the fortress inner city and the San River bridges as the Russian Fourth and Fifth Armies rapidly approached the fortress's northern and eastern perimeter regions. A major Russian objective became to seize the two-track railroad line leading to the fortress and to methodically destroy all rail lines to the citadel as they progressed.

Vanguard Russian units crossed the San River at the significant Radymno and Jaroslau locations. North of Fortress Przemyśl at Walawa, the Russians could be observed crossing the river and approaching the citadel's northern front. The tsarist Eighth Army and portions of the Third Army shifted their troop concentrations to the citadel's south and southwest front, while two cavalry divisions completed the encirclement of the fortress's western front by September 24.[54]

In Fortress Przemyśl, Slavic Ruthenian citizens and soldiers increasingly found themselves accused of treasonous activities for reputedly pinpointing Habsburg troop and artillery battery positions for the enemy. During the earlier Habsburg retreat, fleeing troops often took out their frustration over the catastrophic situation on the local peasants. Dozens were hanged and hundreds shot. Some suspected pro-Russian sympathizers arrested on September 14 were massacred while being escorted to confinement. Their remains were transferred to the main Przemyśl cemetery in 1922.[55] Many local peasants also became involuntary recruits for military service, having to leave their families to fend for themselves. Garrison troops meanwhile requisitioned peasant crops, paying for them with paper money, which rapidly lost value. Soldiers, particularly Hungarian troops, who considered themselves to be in enemy (Slavic) territory often robbed or committed even more heinous crimes against the civilian population. In one specific instance, a group of Magyar Hussars (cavalry troops) attacked and killed some helpless villagers for no particular reason, then galloped away.

Hostages were sometimes taken for minor reputed transgressions that the troops, not the villagers, had committed. Some were even shot. In the meantime, because of the military activity in the area, much of the land remained untilled, creating shortages of food, clothing, and shelter for the villagers. Thus, misery became widespread. In addition to recruiting young male peasants, the military also requisitioned their oxen and horses, leaving those who remained with no way to till the fields. Rationing had to be instituted so that the villagers would not starve to death. Farmers attempted to conceal food, because if the army bought it, the price paid was below the production cost. However, by hiding crops such as rye, much was wasted or spoiled, which made food supplies even scarcer. The lack of an adequate number of farmhands resulted in famine for some villagers.

Troop movements and battle also created enormous devastation in the countryside, while contagious diseases and epidemics, among them dysentery, typhoid, influenza, and a type of skin inflammation, became common. Bodies had to be piled in heaps, as village cemeteries soon became full; almost every day one would observe a burial party progressing down a road. Thousands of acres of forest had been set on fire, either on purpose by soldiers, by artillery and rifle fire, or while trenches were being dug.

Russian Third Army troops besieged Fortress Przemyśl, while those of the newly formed Eleventh Army, composed of second-line divisions and militia brigades, surrounded the fortress. They eventually replaced the Third and Eighth Army first-line blockading soldiers. Their first mission after they reached the San River was to isolate Fortress Przemyśl and occupy the key Carpathian Mountain crossing locations at Sanok, Sambor, and Chyrov.[56] On September 17, the first rifle shot and fortress artillery fired at a Russian cavalry patrol before the Siedliska Fort Work (Werk) I/5 position. On September 21, the main 280,000 Russian forces crossed the San River. The fortress utilized long-range artillery fire and small breakout efforts (sorties) to disturb the ensuing Russian siege efforts as much as possible. Habsburg soldiers deployed at the Jaroslau and Sieniava bridgeheads received orders to hold their positions unconditionally until otherwise directed.[57]

The Third Army continued to retreat west of the fortress, and the Fourth Army to the southwest of Rzeszov. The Russians pursued the retreating troops but did not press them.[58] However, they deployed strong forces east of the fortress. The threatening fortress situation quickly interrupted the transport of wounded soldiers to rear echelon areas and delayed the arrival of units marching toward the fortress. Some lightly wounded troops and field hospital personnel fled as enemy forces approached. The commotion subsided to some degree on September 16, when Third Army troops received a much-needed rest day. On the next day, the army retreat movement recommenced just as the first enemy artillery shells struck the fortress walls. As the last Habsburg field troops abandoned the fortress area, they spotted the first enemy patrols to the north and east of the fortress walls.

The retreat of the hard-pressed Habsburg armies raised the question of the fortress's future role and mission. Previously, its main objective had been to prevent the loss of the citadel, because the fortified San River line, especially at Fortress Przemyśl, temporarily blocked enemy pursuit of the retreating Habsburg field armies. On September 16, Habsburg Supreme Command evacuated the fortress; General Conrad, after driving for hours in the rain, arrived at Neu Sandec and ordered the fortress commander to "hold out to the very end."[59] The relocation of Habsburg headquarters from Fortress Przemyśl became necessary due to the serious threat of the enemy interrupting communications networks.[60] Neu Sandec contained sufficient buildings and railroad connections behind the middle of the Habsburg army front, which facilitated contact with army commanders and the front lines. It would also be the scene of heavy fighting during the early December Limanova-Lapanov battle.

The fortress's new mission remained to bind as many enemy units as possible to prevent their deployment against the retreating field armies. Unless it was liberated in the interim, the fortress was expected to remain active for at least three months, as it reputedly contained sufficient food and ammunition stores for that length of time. Whether the fortress could actually accomplish this was questionable. The citadel's resistance strength could not be highly regarded, since most of the forts were at least twenty or thirty years old and armed with obsolete cannons, some dating back as far as 1861.[61] Momentarily, however, Fortress Przemyśl had provided desperately needed breathing space for the Habsburg troops by delaying a rapid enemy pursuit against them. The Habsburg retreat from the San River area thus made the fortress an indispensable military asset.

During the night of September 16, all bridges between Jaroslau and the fortress were dynamited. The Second Army continued to retreat southwest of the Dukla Pass, maneuvering into the higher middle Carpathian Mountain terrain. The remaining Habsburg armies held their positions behind the Biala-Dunajec River line. Regardless of their location, all Habsburg forces suffered from the inclement fall weather conditions. The heavy rain transformed the already deficient roadways into a muddy morass of potholes, which placed enormous strain on soldiers, horses, and supply trains.[62]

On September 17, Second Army Command reported that its retrograde movement had been delayed and that its troops required a one- to two-day rest in their present positions; thus, the army could not attain its ordered positions until September 20 to 22. Third and Fourth Army activity also experienced serious delays. Fortress Przemyśl reported that it possessed a mobile troop stand of fifth-seven and a quarter infantry battalions, four field cannon batteries, three cavalry squadrons, and seven sapper companies, excluding the 108th Landsturm Infantry Brigade formations.[63]

Before the Russian siege of Fortress Przemyśl commenced, General Conrad ordered reinforcements to the citadel because he feared that it could not provide an adequate defense, creating a dangerous situation as the enemy approached it. These new citadel troops, totaling forty-three battalions, had to be oriented regarding the fortification's special defensive requirements.[64] The newly assigned troop entities deployed into their positions in separate groups rather than in their compact units, which hindered defensive preparations and hurt unit cohesion while the soldiers required additional training in fortress warfare. To delay enemy egress toward the fortress, forefield vanguard positions were established forward of the citadel perimeter on higher terrain whenever possible.

The reinforcing k.k. 111th Landsturm Infantry Brigade consisted of ten battalions, a Hungarian March Regiment containing three battalions, twelve k.u. (Hungarian) 97th Landsturm Infantry Brigade battalions, and six battalions of two Hungarian March regiments. General Conrad also added the k.k. 108th and k.k. 93rd Landsturm Infantry Brigades. Of these new units, the 108th Landsturm Infantry Brigade had the weakest troop stands. For example, a full-strength regiment consisted of about 4,600 troops, but Infantry Regiment 20 contained only 1,930 soldiers, and Regiment 21 only 1,094. The 97th Landsturm Infantry Brigade had lost 123 officers and 4,400 soldiers in battle.[65] Originally, the brigade was to be transferred to the hinterland, but it then received orders to proceed to the fortress. The Habsburg retreat had, in the interim, removed all Habsburg espionage agents from behind enemy lines, which deprived the army of one of its best sources of information about the enemy. The initial fortress sortie was launched from Defensive District VI (Siedliska) toward Dusowce. Its five infantry battalions and two artillery batteries succeeded in achieving surprise and denting the tsarist siege line between Medyka and Bykov. The Russians hurriedly transferred two infantry divisions to that area to restore the military situation.

The sortie resulted in a thousand Habsburg fortress casualties and was proclaimed to be a success. As would occur so often in the future, the order for the garrison troops to retreat into the bulwark signified defeat to the participating troops. Fortress personnel observing the silent troop columns returning from the mission lost hope for the citadel's rapid liberation. Meanwhile, Honvéd Infantry Regiment 5 had unsuccessfully attacked toward Na Gorach to reconquer surrendered forward positions, which proved impossible after the Russians seized the Jaroslau bridgehead.[66] Under enemy artillery fire, the Honvéd Infantry Regiment reached a railroad line, whereupon patrols confirmed that many Cossack troops and enemy infantry units had been redeployed from there. Just before noon the regiment received orders to retreat from the Na Gorach heights because two enemy regiments threatened Honvéd Infantry Regiment 7's left flank positions. Defensive fortress artillery fire, meanwhile, inflicted heavy tsarist losses.

The second fortress sortie launched on September 20 consisted of twelve to fourteen infantry battalions and an artillery battery. Both sorties resulted from intelligence reports indicating that tsarist troop formations continued westward. Reacting to these initial fortress efforts, tsarist troops advanced with far greater caution than they had before. Following the ensuing three-day battle, General Kusmanek determined to maintain his garrison strength, which had just sustained two thousand casualties. He also decided that Ruthenian troops should not be deployed separately in the fortress works. Honvéd soldiers had to be intermixed with them.[67]

As Habsburg Third Army units retreated from the western fortress perimeter area, enemy Cossack and infantry reconnaissance units approached the fortress. When tsarist troops crossed the San River at Walawa, this movement threatened Fortress Przemyśl's contact and connections with the bridgeheads at Jaroslau and Radymno. By 5:30 p.m., tsarist artillery and troop units dispersed into several positions before Defensive District VI at Siedliska. Meanwhile, the tsarist Third Army's slow crossing of the San River briefly delayed the complete siege of Fortress Przemyśl.[68]

Beginning on September 23, the enemy hastily constructed a railroad line around the entire fortress environs, which significantly limited citadel military efforts, because the Russians could now rapidly transport reinforcements to any threatened area at the citadel. That same day, General Ivanov ordered the tsarist Third and Eighth Armies to advance to Radymno-Przemyśl-Chyrov. General Aleksei Brusilov's Eighth Army had to defend the Carpathian Mountain passes. Further north, the tsarist Fifth Army attacked through Jaroslau-Przeworsk toward Dynov–Fortress Przemyśl. The Russian Fourth and Ninth Armies had to seize the area around Rzeszov and the lower Wisloka River. Already on September 16, five and one-half cavalry divisions had been deployed to secure the northern Vistula River area and perform reconnaissance missions in the extensive region between Czenstochau and Fortress Kraków. The new enemy advance commenced on September 22.[69]

The critical question quickly arose of whether and when to evacuate the Jaroslau and Sieniava bridgehead positions. They initially had to be defended so that the Habsburg Fourth Army retreat could continue undisturbed. The Fourth Army received orders to unconditionally defend the Sieniava bridgehead until the evening of September 19, when it could be evacuated, but by 3:15 p.m. heavy tsarist mortar fire had already devastated the fortified defensive positions while enemy infantry units advanced to within close range of the defensive position. By 5:30 p.m., the Russians had seized both the Jaroslau and Sieniava bridgeheads, the last defensive positions before the fortress, while initially the units in Sieniava had retreated to Jaroslau with enemy troops in rapid pursuit. All nonmobile artillery pieces were rendered nonoperable, and then the bridge over the San was blown up.[70]

Heavy tsarist artillery fire had already commenced northeast of the Jaroslau positions during the morning hours before Russian infantry approached to within nine hundred paces of the defensive entrenchments. The bridgehead received heavy artillery fire during the afternoon of September 20, while Fortress Przemyśl troops observed strong Russian infantry forces approaching the citadel's eastern perimeter. During the night of September 21, the Habsburg bridgehead garrison retreated; some troops marched back into the fortress, others to join the First Army.[71] The Russians had to neutralize the two bridgeheads before they could unleash their full forces on Fortress Przemyśl. Habsburg forces continued their retreat on September 20, but the terrible road conditions caused many supply train stoppages, and soldiers increasingly suffered from dysentery. Fortress Przemyśl personnel reported that small enemy detachments had crossed the San River. According to intelligence estimates, up to fifty-two tsarist divisions opposed Habsburg field armies, and six or more of those prepared to besiege Fortress Przemyśl. Habsburg forces consisted of thirty-seven and one-half understrength divisions (plus two German divisions), while the German Ninth Army (ten divisions) opposed forty-nine and one-half tsarist units.[72]

Meanwhile, Third Army troops deployed west of Fortress Przemyśl after their departure from the citadel, while the Fourth Army deployed west of Rzeszov. Pursuing tsarist forces did not immediately press the Habsburg troops but merely maintained contact with them.[73] As

Romanov troops encircled the fortress, they blew up the crucial Nizankovice railroad bridge on September 19, severing the main railroad
supply line to the fortress. The rebuilding of this structure became a key
element in resupplying the citadel after its liberation from the Russians
in early October 1914 and before its subsequent re-encirclement in early
November.

At an allied meeting at Breslau convened between September 19 and
20, it was agreed that the German Ninth Army would be ready for action
near Fortress Kraków by September 30. Cavalry forces would shield the
forthcoming deployment for the offensive. During September, only local
military actions occurred at the three northernmost fortress defensive
districts. These districts required reinforcements from the fortress's
main manpower reserve pool to initiate any effective military action of
their own. When the Jaroslau bridgehead position capitulated, small
enemy detachments advanced closer to the fortress in the area of Sosnica-
Dusowce-Walawa on September 20. Other troop units immediately
approached from the Radymno position after that bridgehead had surrendered.[74] When the first enemy troops crossed the San River, they
encountered only Habsburg patrols. Defensive District V artillery fire
assisted similar efforts from Forts XII/1, XII/2, and XIII against enemy
units crossing the river.

When enemy troops quickly occupied the opposing northern fortress front, they squandered significant time by instituting overly cautious security measures as they approached the fortress. Their generally
sluggish and cautious pursuit of the retreating Habsburg armies had not
only spared the latter from annihilation but also given the fortress invaluable time to complete additional defensive measures and assisted the
field armies in rapidly preparing to launch another offensive in conjunction with allied German troops in early October. Meanwhile, the situation
on the Balkan front had reversed, and preparations commenced to transport the German troops by railroad to the Habsburg front at Fortress
Kraków.

As early as September 21, significant Russian forces had deployed in
the fortress area. Battle soon commenced as Russian troops attacked
the southern and southwestern fortress perimeters after major forces

had crossed the San River. Heavy battle ensued at fortress forefield positions between September 21 and 25. Habsburg troops had to abandon many of these forward positions, which enemy troops rapidly seized and occupied.

The Russian Fifth Army crossed the San River north of the fortress and advanced on September 22 and 23, while neighboring Third Army flank units advanced to the areas north and south of the fortress.[75] Soon the Russians could cross the San River toward Fortress Przemyśl at will, significantly increasing the military threat to it. Defensive District V reported that enemy troops had already occupied the southern perimeter area of Walawa. Meanwhile, fortress artillery targeted enemy artillery units and returned their barrages. On September 22, tsarist cavalry troops besieged the western fortress area as other units advanced north and south of the fortress.[76] Defensive District IV artillery fired at approaching enemy patrols while their forces established forward positions north of Batycze in forested terrain. When a fortress detachment deployed toward Na Gorach to counter the enemy activity, its western flank positions quickly became threatened with encirclement.[77]

The fortress continued emergency preparations for an anticipated major enemy attack. General Kusmanek emphasized constructing additional field gun emplacements, better securing the fortress walls, and establishing mobile and heavy artillery units to counter anticipated Russian assaults. These efforts closed some gaps between various infantry positions, while new construction covered approaches to the battlefield area and established telephone lines to artillery units. A shortage of manpower had previously prevented such an ambitious building program, but the improvements could no longer be delayed given the impending enemy threat.

Construction began on the high ground of Pod Mazurami–Helicha beyond Defensive District VIII forefield positions even as enemy troops approached the area. At Defensive District VII positions, the Russians maneuvered in the open, where defenders could easily observe the terrain in the area of Nizankowice. Tsarist forces became quite active before Defensive District VIII because the thickly forested terrain provided excellent cover that camouflaged them. The fortress commander intended to launch a sortie from the Pod Mazurami–Helicha area if construction of the new positions was completed by September 26.

Elsewhere, garrison intelligence detachments conducted long-range reconnaissance missions before the fortress's southern and southwestern fronts, where it could be anticipated that the Russians would initiate their first serious military efforts. They continued these operations until the enemy forced them to retreat.[78] The Russians then launched an overwhelming attack with artillery support on September 22, which the older and weary Landsturm troops could not halt until reinforcements arrived. In the meantime, two Russian corps (IX and X) deployed against the southeast fortress perimeter, while the tsarist Fifth Army (V and XVII Corps) crossed the San River stretch at Jaroslau to prepare to attack the fortress.[79] On September 23, General Kusmanek ordered his troops to hurl tsarist troops back across the San River and to prevent any future crossing attempts. Defensive Districts IV and V supported these efforts with artillery fire.

On September 24, the tsarist commander decided to halt the westward advance of his armies until the siege of Fortress Przemyśl had been completed. His Fourth Army had the mission to complete the siege of the fortress within six days after marching to the area, while the Third Army besieged the fortress. The other Russian armies received orders relative to their fronts. The Eighth Army would deploy in the region between Chyrov and Sambor.

During the first siege, the exact amount of mail that accumulated in the fortress environs could not be determined, but much remained there. Following the October liberation of the fortress, for the first and only time troops could relate their actual experience in the mail now being sent out. Goods transported into the bulwark following the liberation of the fortress included newspapers, which were among the first items to arrive by automobile. Officers read them to the troops because of the short supply. Soldiers were well aware that mail service had been suspended and would be restarted on October 14. The siege disrupted all communications on the Habsburg front, including in Galicia and the Bukovina. Meanwhile, Russian planes encircled the fortress and dropped bombs on a regular basis, hurting garrison morale and spooking the troops.

Meanwhile, the Russians established positions three to six kilometers from the southern fortress front and deployed portions of four infantry divisions before fortress Defensive Districts VI and VII. The 42nd, 5th, 9th, and 31st Infantry Divisions established themselves from tsarist IX and X Corps at the southeast fortress perimeter. Other major units were reputedly deployed in the Nizankovice area, in addition to a portion of the tsarist VII Corps (9th, 31st, and 60th Reserve Infantry Divisions). Yet Russian intentions remained a mystery, a problem that plagued Habsburg Supreme Command throughout the war.

The Russians planned to complete their siege of the fortress swiftly and sever all its connections to the outside world. General Kusmanek anticipated that they would proceed rapidly against Defensive District VIII to protect their deployed cavalry flank positions in the San River valley. A fortress civilian remarked, "The Russians are in no hurry, they slowly advance toward the fortress." In fact, their activity quickly interrupted railroad traffic and blockaded roads in the northern fortress sector. The civilian, a woman, went on to reveal: "It is still hard to understand that the greater portion of the old fortress works still stand. They are severely damaged from powerful cracks and fissures with many openings. However it holds." Meanwhile, fortress inhabitants heard the sounds of battle raging around them. In a September 23 diary entry, the same woman wrote: "It rains-rains-rains and the thunder of the guns has let up, the night before last and yesterday artillery fire continued almost till dawn. . . . Last night you could hear the gunfire until midnight."[80]

She lamented the fact that blocking mail delivery to the fortress had a very negative effect on morale for both civilians and military personnel. On September 17, the last fortress mail was officially collected and dispatched. However, mail delivery may have continued beyond that time. She stated, "Thus, today we learn from several sources that for a few days a gap existed in the siege lines, through which mail could be delivered by automobile." On September 21, she noted that "today's the third day without mail delivery or newspapers. To my great surprise some automobiles arrived this morning to pick up mail, including a letter to my mother."[81] A letter from an officer, Felix Holzer, confirmed this; on September 23, he stated that he had written to his wife that afternoon in haste, because "an automobile is here so this must go immediately."

That same day, Cossack units entered the San River valley. Habsburg troops attempted to reach Dynov by automobile, about forty kilometers west of the fortress, to pick up mail and ammunition. This twenty-four-hour mission culminated in the safe arrival of a mail vehicle. Then, on September 28, a Red Cross worker stated, "Still no post!—at least letters can be delivered by automobile from Sanok. We will also find out today if we will be receiving additional mail."[82] Meanwhile, on September 24, two tsarist cavalry divisions commenced their siege of the western fortress front.[83]

As late as early October, a fortress civilian wrote that "the [Habsburg] army had been expected to approach the fortress for several days" and noted that "it is even more significant that the road stretch Dynov can be utilized, so the field post can once again be delivered by automobile. That is a great joy." Bruno Wolfgang, author of *Przemyśl 1914–1915,* also noted that the road "stretch to Dynov, being repaired by our engineers, allows us to receive the first post."[84] The following conveys the negative effect on troops of not receiving mail: "It's a terrible feeling to be totally isolated, no letters and no newspapers. We have no idea what is occurring in the world." Many soldiers felt fortunate that they received correspondence from their loved ones, but when soldiers did not receive mail (which occurred much too often due to erratic deliveries), it had the opposite effect. Letters served to assure the troops that their loved ones supported them, and through the written word "spoke person-to-person." When troops returned from their field posts in the evening, they immediately wanted to know if they had received any letters; if not, "they succumbed to a feeling of hopelessness."[85] Each field soldier and specific unit had its own field or post office. A familiar complaint often heard on the city streets in the center of the citadel concerned the lack of mail or newspapers: "We are standing in the midst as enormous history is being made, but we know nothing about it."[86] The fortress had a daily newspaper printed in German, Hungarian, and Polish, but it supplied only the "official, or allowed," interpretation of military events. Fortress inhabitants, nevertheless, scoured each issue daily for any sign of the possibility of the fortress being liberated soon.

A further civilian diary entry noted that "the day before yesterday, cannon fire against the villages of Malkovice and Novosiolki caused them to burst into flames." Apparently, garrison troops destroyed additional villages every day, mostly toward the Medyka area, to prevent the enemy from procuring the advantage of valuable cover for its troops as they approached the fortress. Farmers from the burned villages later appeared with their families in the city portion of the fortress carrying assorted household goods. Everything else they owned had been destroyed.[87]

By September 23, the fortress had been completely encircled with very little Habsburg resistance. Fortress Przemyśl's contact with the field armies had finally been severed. Because the German front still received precedence for heavy artillery units, the tsarist siege troops continued to lack the necessary heavy caliber guns that could have destroyed the obsolete fortress walls. By September 26, nine Russian infantry divisions and two cavalry divisions blockaded the fortress, thus the citadel fulfilled its mission of binding significant enemy forces. Two Russian armies and four reserve divisions contained a total of 280,000 troops, more than twice the number of the 131,000 besieged Habsburg garrison troops.

Fortress Przemyśl, although ill prepared for its imposing challenges, successfully resisted enemy efforts to conquer it for almost six months despite being besieged in late September and again during early November. This defensive success proved important in thwarting Russian plans to initiate an offensive against Fortress Kraków, situated only two hundred kilometers to the north. Habsburg troops launched numerous offensive thrusts (sorties) from the fortress in an attempt to keep the enemy off balance and bind as many of its troops as possible to prevent their deployment against their field armies. Each effort, however, inevitably culminated in a retreat into the citadel, as any initial military successes ultimately produced troop exhaustion, serious casualty numbers, and the inevitable demoralizing withdrawal into the fortress. The troops also had to struggle against icy autumn storms. Listening posts situated outside the citadel's perimeter in the forefields lay in mud and wet clay during heavy downpours, and in ice during colder conditions, negatively affecting the troops' health and morale.

General Conrad was determined to initiate an allied offensive operation somewhere in the Fortress Kraków area, because the Habsburg
army desperately required allied support to conduct an offensive, and it
provided a convenient location because of its railroad connections. The
newly formed German Ninth Army launched a two-corps thrust from
north of that fortress area on September 28, while its Eighth Army advanced from East Prussia and north of the Vistula River to cooperate
with the Austro-Hungarian army forces and draw enemy troops from
the Habsburg front. In the interim, vanguard units of the German IV
Army Corps arrived north of Fortress Kraków on September 22, while
the Russians prepared to launch a major offensive to invade Germany
from west of the Vistula River. The Habsburg units launched an offensive
on October 3 between the Carpathian Mountains and the Vistula River
with the mission to encircle the enemy forces pressing their troops. The
Habsburg Second Army would also eventually advance to halt enemy
progress along the southern Carpathian Mountain ridgelines below Fortress Przemyśl.

When advancing Russian field armies attained the San River stretch
at Jaroslau-Radymno close to the Fortress Przemyśl eastern front, General Kusmanek reacted by hurling an infantry column through Dobromil
toward the Uzsok Pass.[88] Eventually, three of the eight Russian armies
(the Third, Eighth, and Eleventh) participated in the siege of the Galician
fortress. Meanwhile, at the fortress's Defensive District III, major forces
could be observed moving to the west. By September 23, the Russians
had occupied a large area of the San valley. In the days that followed,
Russian cavalry units dispatched patrols forward into the forested zone
before the western fortress front Defensive District III forefields. This
forced the removal of intelligence detachments from the heights of Kijov,
which became an objective for future fortress sorties.

On September 24, a battalion of Honvéd Infantry Regiment 7 advanced toward Radymno to intercept and try to delay enemy forces
pressing from the north and northeast. General Kusmanek also deployed
garrison troops in the areas of Sosnica-Dusowce-Walawa near Radymno.
Ensuing battles that developed before the fortress's northern front perimeter area proved to be only enemy demonstrations rather than major
offensive efforts. Few details exist today concerning these encounters,

but numerous enemy units, such as the 78th Infantry Division, had deployed along the northern fortress front. A Reserve Infantry Division at Sosnica and the 11th Infantry Division in the Radymno area alongside tsarist vanguard units advanced toward Walawa. Behind those units stood the deployed Russian XI and XXI Corps, consisting partially of the 35th, the 44th, and the 69th Reserve Infantry Divisions, while Russian cavalry divisions continued to deploy in the San River valley. Fortress reconnaissance and security units repeatedly attempted to disrupt the advancing enemy forces.

When battle ebbed on September 24, forward Russian troop units had reached the lower Wisloka River area ready to advance to Fortress Przemyśl's eastern front. The next day, additional tsarist cavalry forces crossed the river.[89] Then the fortress launched a sortie, consisting of over six infantry battalions with two M 75 9-centimeter field cannons from Defensive District VI. The objective entailed advancing to seize the weakly held area forward of the siege line Medyka-Wielki and bind enemy forces.

On September 25, the Russians launched an overpowering attack against Defensive District VI (Siedliska) utilizing IX Corps' 42nd and 5th and X Corps' 9th and 31st Infantry Divisions. General Kusmanek reacted by launching three separate sortie efforts. The first major one moved in a southerly direction because tsarist troops had crossed the San River there. Some right flank Habsburg defensive forces retreated, but then launched a counterattack despite the fact that two battalions of reinforcements from Defensive District VI/3 had not arrived. General Kusmanek also launched a one-battalion sortie toward Olszany and Cisova to provide left flank security for the above missions. In the meantime, General Conrad requested that the Germans transfer twenty-four divisions to the vicinity of Fortress Kraków to cooperate in the approaching allied campaign in the Carpathian Mountain theater, which had become increasingly significant to both the Austro-Hungarian and Russian military leadership.

The major sortie commenced, representing the first time that the citadel utilized any of its main troop reserves for a major action in the fortress forefields. On September 24 and 25, intelligence reports indicated that four Russian infantry divisions had been deployed between the San and Wiar Rivers, which was confirmed a few days later. The 23rd Honvéd Infantry Division's 46th Honvéd Brigade's Infantry Regiments 7 and 8, as well as Honvéd Infantry Regiment 4, Honvéd Hussar (cavalry) regiments, and four Honvéd field cannon batteries, participated in the next sortie. Ten and one-half infantry battalions and four artillery batteries advanced from Defensive District VII. On September 25 garrison troops also prepared to march to the heights of Helicha to establish new defensive positions forward of the fortress perimeter. On the following day, 46th Honvéd Infantry Brigade troops advanced toward the heights of Szybenica to launch the major sortie effort. Honvéd Infantry Cannon Regiment 2 provided artillery support for the operation.

Honvéd Infantry Regiment 3 launched one and a half battalions toward the heights of Helicha; cavalry attachments provided the liaison between the advancing Honvéd units. To provide additional security to Defensive District VII's eastern flank area, troops deployed into the forefield area, but insufficient fortress artillery support ensured that this did not provide any particular advantage. Extremely thick undergrowth and forested terrain slowed 46th Honvéd Infantry Brigade's forward momentum, then it encountered heavy and effective enemy artillery fire against its right flank and frontal positions. Meanwhile, heavy Russian artillery fire forced a battalion of Honvéd March Regiment 4 to retreat. Tsarist units then assaulted the heights of Szybenica, while attacking Habsburg troops approaching Cisova encountered effective enemy artillery fire. The sortie units received an order to retreat at 3 p.m. after General Kusmanek thought the enemy had attacked garrison positions from multiple directions. He nevertheless claimed that the sortie mission had been a success. The retreat began at 10 p.m., but the enemy did not press the retreating troops, who had to march through woods, water, and mud. Some of these Habsburg troops were temporarily deployed at the fortress forefield perimeter as rearguard protection until the other units had successfully entered the fortress.

The fortress sortie operation initially surprised the Russians, particularly when the envelopment maneuver toward Medyka proved successful. This hurled forward Russian security positions rearward and overwhelmed tsarist soldiers immediately before the attacking garrison troops. Defensive District VI artillery and mobile 9-centimeter field cannon batteries supported the Habsburg troops. Habsburg guns could not neutralize Russian artillery fire, as they could not locate their positions. This resulted in numerous Habsburg casualties. Russian reinforcements then arrived on the battlefield, supported by intensifying artillery fire support. Effective fortress artillery fire in this instance caused multiple Russian casualties but could not turn the tide of battle. The southern flank forces' advance also soon halted. Landsturm Infantry Regiment 18 launched a counterattack, but Russian artillery fire quickly halted any forward progress. Two enemy battalions and two or three machine gun squads then smashed into them. When darkness fell, the unit retreated.

The attacking garrison troops lost only about a hundred soldiers, but Russian forward positions had been temporarily captured, with the enemy defenders sustaining serious losses, mainly resulting from fortress artillery fire barrages against the high terrain at Medyka. The four-hour operation caused an estimated 10 percent Russian casualty rate, or thirty-two hundred fatalities, at the fortress's Defensive District VI forward area (Siedliska group).

The Russians then realigned their units and shifted their main attack focus to the Siedliska northern perimeter area. General Kusmanek, anticipating a powerful enemy attack there, had extended the forefield positions in that area, an extremely fortunate action, although initially he could not be certain where the Russians would concentrate their assault. Colonel Hans Schwalb, commander of the fortress's Genie (engineering) Department, claimed that during this first September siege of the fortress, the Russians had exact orientation about events in Fortress Przemyśl and appeared familiar with the most favorable directions from which to attack the fortress, specifically Defensive District VI. There, the fortress positions jutted outward from the fortress perimeter, which the enemy could easily encircle utilizing the favorable terrain to approach the citadel. In addition, tsarist forces had the advantage of being able to transport siege equipment on the railroad line to Mosciska, close to the fortress.

Initially, it appeared that the Russians might launch their major assault against Defensive District VIII because of the favorable forested terrain that extended almost to the fortress ring area; thus they could easily launch a surprise attack against the defending troops. General

Kusmanek correctly assumed that the enemy targeted the Defensive District VI ring position, but the Russians also hurled troops against Defensive District VIII because of its forward positions at Tarnawce–Pod Mazurami–Helicha. Defensive District VI troops retreated over three kilometers to the fortress ring because of the enemy threat. The Russians also continued to move large troop entities to the west, particularly after they had seized the Habsburg Jaroslau and Sieniava bridgeheads.

Honvéd Infantry Regiment 7 participated in four separate firefights before being transferred to the southwest fortress front on September 26 to participate in the sortie launched toward the heights of Szybenica. According to existing evidence, the Honvéd Infantry Regiment again launched an attack from the heights of Na Gorach toward the area of Dusowce-Sosnica, as a day earlier an artillery reconnaissance patrol had encountered strong enemy fire. Just before noon, the regiment received orders to retreat from the heights of Na Gorach because the two enemy regiments threatened the Honvéd's left flank position. The ensuing regiment retreat transpired under heavy enemy artillery and infantry fire, but the troops suffered few casualties. A fortress infantry battalion was also deployed toward Mackovice as large tsarist units advanced from the Rokietnica area over the next few days.

The Russian Third Army had now completely encircled the fortress without encountering serious Habsburg resistance. Simultaneously, the tsarist Fifth and Eighth Armies established their positions for the siege of the citadel from the north and south fortress perimeter.[90] Meanwhile, General Ivanov, commander of the tsarist front, continued to move his troops west of the San River and to the eastern Vistula River bank to protect the main river crossing locations. On the German front, Stavka (the Russian high command) accelerated preparations to launch a major invasion into Germany. A slow, three-week redeployment of thirty infantry divisions commenced for the campaign. The time lapse provided the Central Powers with time to institute their own military endeavors.

However, on September 25, German troops had to retreat to their frontier. This produced a dilemma for the Russian strategists: they could not attempt to seize Fortress Kraków until they had conquered Fortress Przemyśl, which Habsburg troops would liberate on October 9, 1914.

The Third and Second Habsburg Armies reached their march goals on September 26, just as the German Ninth Army arrived north of Fortress Kraków and northeast of Czenstochau. The Habsburg First Army provided liaison and deployed beside the German army for the operation launched on September 28.[91]

On September 28, in the midst of all the military activity, Fortress Przemyśl civilian complaints about the absence of mail continued. One woman's diary entry also deplored the fact that hopelessly wounded soldiers had filled all the available hospital rooms. Then, on September 30, she wrote that these wounded had serious trouble communicating with their nurses because many spoke only Polish. Troops who had lost their limbs in battle wondered what occupation they could perform or even obtain once the war ended and they could return home. The writer specifically mentioned one wounded soldier who had a wife and three children, and was expecting a fourth. He worried about informing his wife about his present physical condition.[92]

Intercepted Russian radio messages revealed that tsarist troops continued to cross the San and Vistula Rivers, but Habsburg air reconnaissance missions could not be launched to verify enemy activity because of the inclement weather conditions.[93] On September 29, General Kusmanek learned that considerable tsarist units had advanced along the fortress's southern perimeter area and responded by launching a sortie consisting of twelve to fourteen 23rd Honvéd Infantry Division battalions to intercept them.

Following the September fortress sortie efforts, advancing tsarist troops proceeded with far greater caution than before. During the last week of September, only tsarist artillery fire disturbed the fortress. Turning to the German front, the Ninth Army soon attempted to encircle the Russian northern flank military positions, while a strong supporting Habsburg First Army was deployed north of the Vistula River to launch the first allied offensive of the war. On September 23, General Conrad had promised to transfer five or six infantry divisions to the northern Vistula River theater from his front. He refused a request to deploy additional troops in that theater because many Russian forces remained ensconced south of the river. Thus, the Habsburg First Army prepared for battle north of the Vistula River in the area of the Dunajec River mouth–Nida River line by September 30. On October 1, four Habsburg armies initiated their own endeavor.[94] These maneuvers did not receive a major enemy response, but a tsarist threat loomed from the areas of Fortress Ivangorod and Warsaw. No significant progress had been reported on the Balkan front either.

Generals Conrad, Hindenburg, and Ludendorff believed that Russia could be driven out of the war if they could deploy sufficient troop numbers on the eastern front.[95] General Eric von Falkenhayn, however, firmly believed that victory could be obtained only on the western front, thus the eastern front commanders could not anticipate receiving major reinforcements. The western front "Race to the Sea" and the subsequent battle at Ypres were the priority.

By the end of September, Habsburg troops had been pressed into the Carpathian Mountains and behind the Dunajec River following their earlier, serious defeats. The Russians had advanced to within twelve kilometers of Fortress Kraków, and battle soon erupted in that area as well. They also prepared to storm Fortress Przemyśl before relieving Habsburg troops could launch an offensive to liberate it. Early October would witness a renewed Austro-Hungarian offensive that hoped to turn the extreme tsarist left flank positions and liberate the fortress. German troops supported the operation to ensure that their battered ally's army did not collapse. As September drew to a close, it remained unclear which plan, the allied operation or the tsarist mass attacks to seize Fortress Przemyśl, would prove successful. The events that decided the fate of these operations would unfold during early October.

3

✠ ✠ ✠

Siege and Liberation

OCTOBER 1914

OCTOBER 1914 MARKED THE BEGINNING OF A VERY EVENTFUL period for Fortress Przemyśl. After besieging the San River bastion in late September, Russian forces sought to capture the fortress before an anticipated Habsburg liberation attempt could be made. When their bloody storm assaults failed, Russian troops hastily retreated from all but the eastern bulwark perimeter areas. Overwhelming supply challenges stymied Habsburg efforts to liberate the fortress and pursue the retreating Russians. Heavy supply wagon traffic, combined with weeks of inclement weather, rendered the inadequate Galician roadways nearly impassable, thus thwarting the Habsburg objective to rapidly relieve the fortress. The ensuing October, late November, and December campaigns revealed just how excruciatingly difficult it could be to wage war over mountain terrain during the depths of winter.

On October 1, a military aircraft flew from Habsburg Supreme Command headquarters in Neu Sandec into the fortress with new orders. It flew back on October 6 carrying one hundred field postcards with messages from staff personnel. The plane, struck by enemy fire, crash-landed about thirty miles from Neu Sandec. The postcards were then transported by car to the headquarters. Habsburg offensive efforts began on October 1, 1914, and extended the Third Army front some ninety miles from its major railroad depot. This left many Habsburg troop units without sufficient food or ammunition as they advanced toward the bulwark. In addition, once liberated, the fortress became a food and supply depot for the victorious field armies' troops, which created further strain on the already limited citadel resources. Dwindling supplies and appalling weather conditions also resulted in widespread cholera, which killed hundreds of soldiers. Dysentery and typhus were rampant, and some soldiers resorted to self-mutilation to escape the horrific situation. Once field army troops departed the fortress, the bastion was cleansed to prevent the spread of further disease.

Major battle erupted as Habsburg First Army troops reached the Russian fortress at Ivangorod along the Vistula River. Allied High Commands initially ordered the German Ninth Army and the Habsburg First Army to maintain their positions at the fortress, but after Russian troops crossed the Vistula River, the First Army received orders to withdraw. After a significant number of tsarist troops completed the crossing, the First Army received orders to attack them. However, the defeat of the Germans on the battlefield at Warsaw exposed the Habsburg First Army's flank, forcing it to retreat.

Meanwhile, in early October, the plans evolved to launch the Austro-Hungarian offensive that would encircle left flank tsarist forces, liberate Fortress Przemyśl, and allow troops to march to the San River. General Conrad hastily launched the operation for fear that the fortress would be incapable of repulsing mass tsarist attacks. The Germans simultaneously advanced from East Prussia to the area northeast of Fortress Kraków with the allied objective of reaching the San-Vistula River line. The Habsburg First Army advanced northward into Russian Poland and, in conjunction with German forces, attacked the enemy near Ivangorod. The plan illuminated serious discord among the Central Power military leaders regarding a unified command structure for eastern front operations. As was common throughout most of the war, neither side proved willing to relinquish power, ultimately to the detriment of both.

Between October 1 and 10, advancing Habsburg troops successfully purged the wooded Carpathian Mountain region of enemy troops, temporarily neutralizing the threat of a Russian invasion of Hungary. By October 4, Second Army units reached the Dukla Pass, advancing toward their major objectives. This brought the war to the foothills of the Carpathian Mountains and the Romanian frontier. Habsburg units repulsed the few tsarist troops that had penetrated into Hungary and the wooded mountain terrain. Then, between October 2 and 7, the Second

Army deployed a strong right flank force, traversing the Carpathian Mountains south of Fortress Przemyśl.

By October 1, the Russian Third Army had established its siege of Fortress Przemyśl, as its neighboring Fifth Army bivouacked in the mountain terrain to the west. Five new infantry and two artillery divisions deployed close to the bulwark. The renewed Habsburg offensive campaign to recapture Fortress Przemyśl and attain the San River line depended on allied German forces maintaining the northern Vistula River line to protect its northern flank. The Russians accelerated their timetable to attempt to capture the fortress before Habsburg forces could liberate it. The heavy rain produced a morass of mud and meter-deep potholes on the difficult mountain terrain, which sorely delayed the attacking soldiers and their supplies. The tsarist strategy for conquering the fortress involved attacking the most important and strongest position at its perimeter, the Defensive District VI (Siedliska) series of six forts while launching diversionary attacks at other citadel positions. The western fortress perimeter walls were not as well armed and provided the Russian siege forces with greater promise of successfully blocking a Habsburg retreat from the fortress if it became necessary. Habsburg forces remained only a three- to four-day march from the fortress, which the Russians had to consider before they attempted to capture the bulwark. The initial tsarist offensive demonstrations were intended to divert citadel attention and draw reserve forces away from their intended target. They then launched their major offensive effort against the northwest and southeast citadel fronts.[1]

The Habsburg Third Army had destroyed railroad lines and bridges in the wake of its September retreat, just as the Russians had done during the new Third Army offensive and their retrograde movement. Ironically, these were crucial for the October offensive operation's success.

The fortress commander learned that some enemy troops were already evacuating the fortress area.[2] A new siege army, later designated the Russian Eleventh Army, replaced Russian Third Army divisions that had besieged the bulwark. The Habsburg Third Army marched toward the citadel as Russian intentions to attack the fortress became evident. General Brusilov sought to hasten the attack amid allegations that some garrison units had become increasingly unreliable. However, he also realized that Fortress Przemyśl lacked serious defensive strength and that a renewed Austro-Hungarian offensive would soon follow. Thus, General Brusilov rapidly prepared his troops to attack the fortress.

Renewed tsarist military strikes against the bulwark required the continuous shifting of Habsburg garrison reserve troops to stem the latest threat. Such frantic and exhausting efforts usually occurred when the enemy attempted to sap troops closer to the fortress at night. Nonstop Russian artillery barrages pounded the citadel's defensive barbed wire emplacements. Then, enemy troops assaulted the fortress walls, but powerful defensive artillery fire halted their efforts. Enemy artillery interfered with post-battle repair work on the fortress environs, forcing the work to be done at night. On twenty-four-hour alert, the garrison troops had no time to rest. Repairing trenches, telephone lines, barbed wire, emplacements, and damaged fortress walls took priority. Habsburg troops had to remove the Russian corpses to the bastion perimeter to prevent the spread of disease, but tsarist artillery efforts made it impossible to do so.

By the end of September 1914, Germany found itself in a highly unfavorable military situation. The fatal defeat at the Marne signified that it could not keep its prewar promise to transfer major forces to the eastern front in a timely manner. It also represented the failure of the Schlieffen Plan. German High Command now faced a second serious crisis on the Russian front. By mid-September 1914, it had become obvious that the Austro-Hungarian army desperately required assistance to prevent its collapse.

Initially, the Germans planned to transfer two army corps to Silesia to serve as the cadre of a new army. These numbers, however, would not be sufficient, since Habsburg forces had suffered a more serious defeat than originally thought. German troops had to be deployed north of Fortress Kraków to support the tottering ally, while the newly designated German Ninth Army marched to the Vistula River to deflect enemy attention from the reeling Austro-Hungarian army. The Ninth Army's mission was intended to shore up Habsburg forces and prevent Russian attempts to regain the initiative.

The German advance on September 29 reached the area east of Lodz and achieved its objective. The enemy began shifting major troop numbers to the north Vistula River front to meet the new threat, relieving tsarist pressure from the Habsburg front. Enemy radio messages described Russian intentions to use their large concentration of forces to outflank the German Ninth Army in the vicinity of Warsaw, their major railroad and communication junction. This release of enemy pressure on the Austro-Hungarian front proved critical in liberating Fortress Przemyśl by October 9.

Aware that the enemy had transferred large troop numbers north of the Vistula River, Habsburg forces' objective was to prevent them from crossing the river. The German Ninth Army and the Habsburg First Army maneuvered between the northern San River area and Warsaw.[3] Then the Germans discovered the plan for the Russian Vistula River offensive campaign on the body of a dead Russian officer, which alerted them to the enormous threat. Meanwhile, heavy rains deterred German attempts to entrench in the saturated and flooded Vistula lowland terrain.

The Habsburg offensive campaign began in early October when Fourth Army units advanced toward the San River area from north of Fortress Przemyśl. The offensive objective, launched through a broad portion of the Carpathian Mountains, had the Second and Third Armies liberating Fortress Przemyśl. Garrison troops would then join the Third Army's battle east of the fortress front. It began with the Second Army maneuvering south and southeast of the Third Army between the Carpathian Mountain passes Lupkov, Uzsok, and Dukla and south of Fortress Przemyśl; its IV Corps endeavored to encircle the retreating Russian troops at the Stary Sambor railroad junction. During this operation, the fortress served as a major supply depot and rallying point for Habsburg troops and cemented its front lines. The crisis of supplying the advancing field armies with food, artillery pieces and shells, and other vital equipment forced the Fortress Przemyśl garrison to surrender a significant portion of its food stores and ammunition (particularly artillery shells) to the field armies. Russian Eighth Army counterattacks against the Second Army forward lines at Chyrov halted that army's offensive effort, but

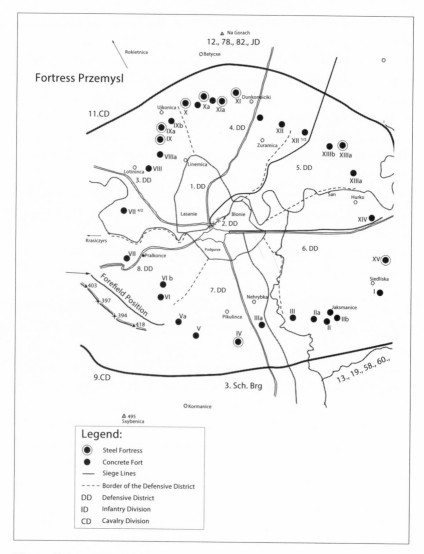

Map 3.1. Fortress Przemyśl, 1914.

not before the fortress had relinquished a nineteen-day food supply and a twenty-six-day supply of oats to the advancing Habsburg field armies.[4]

Terrain and weather conditions continued to hinder supply of even the most basic necessities to the Habsburg offensive forces.[5] As a result, the field armies commandeered many lighter fortress supply wagons to replace their heavier, obsolete models, nearly half of which were never returned. On October 9, the Third Army received a thousand fortress wagons, and the Second Army an additional three hundred.[6]

Initially, only one tsarist cavalry division (the 9th) served as a siege force on the northwestern and western fortress fronts. On October 2, tsarist artillery ceased firing as a parliamentarian approached Fort XI Dunowiczki waving a white flag and conveying a request that the fortress surrender. General Kusmanek firmly replied, "Herr Kommandant, your ridiculous suggestion does not warrant the favor of a reply." Habsburg troops proceeded to blindfold the Russian emissary and took him by auto on a three-hour trip to fortress headquarters. There they sought to convince him that an entire army occupied the fortress, even going so far as to include signs on the doors identifying the location of Army Operation Bureau and other army departments.[7]

Habsburg Supreme Command dispatched an airplane to the fortress to inform the commandant of the forthcoming Austro-Hungarian offensive operation, as well as ancillary details.[8] The Albatross double-decker airplane landed in the fortress amid heavy tsarist artillery barrages, an unprecedented event. A General Staff captain provided General Kusmanek with details about the planned allied offensive as the Russians launched an attack against the fortress with the support of intense artillery fire. However, the majority of the tsarist guns remained too distant from the fortress to support a sudden, overwhelming attack.[9] General Brusilov rushed reinforcements (XII Corps' 12th and 19th Infantry Divisions, 68th Reserve Infantry Division, three heavy cannon and three mortar divisions, and the 3rd Schützen Brigade) to the front as the Russians prepared to launch a powerful attack against the citadel on October 5.[10] The only outside contact with the encircled garrison came from radio traffic and aircraft.

Nine and one-half infantry and two cavalry divisions (150 battalions, 48 cavalry squadrons, and 800 artillery pieces) comprised the tsarist offensive force (the entire Eleventh and Third Armies and parts of the Eighth). Russian light and medium artillery units and forty 18- and 21-centimeter field howitzer artillery barrages initially concentrated on the fortress's Defensive District VI area. From October 3 through October 6, they launched increasingly powerful storm attacks against Fortress Werk I/1 of that defensive district in preparation for the main assault. Simultaneously, tsarist maneuvers supported by heavy artillery barrages began along the northern fortress perimeter, but Habsburg defenders quickly recognized the timing of the enemy's artillery fire and reacted accordingly.[11]

Meanwhile, the Russian Third Army prepared to launch a major attack against Fortress Przemyśl, but tsarist units had to sap forward four to five kilometers from the fortress before they could storm the citadel. General Brusilov ordered the commander of the siege forces on the San River right bank, to launch a massive attack against the fortress. However, there was not enough time to sufficiently prepare for such a powerful assault.[12] Inadequate planning was a major factor in the preceding tsarist failures.

From October 6 to 9, garrison troops endured unrelenting battle consisting of waves of artillery barrages and infantry storm attacks. Each tsarist assault produced horrendous casualties for both sides and brought the attacking troops closer to the fortress perimeter areas. One would have expected the old forts to be badly damaged by the enemy artillery, but Russian shells exploded too rapidly. While individual works sustained many direct hits, they suffered only minor damage and would be repaired during nighttime hours.

Tsarist artillery fire did, however, largely destroy the infantry defensive positions between the various interval fortress works, barbed wire emplacements, and trenches. Fortress reserve formations deployed in the open fields directly behind the fortress walls. With no overhead protective cover, the men became easy targets for enemy shrapnel shells. Telephone communications quickly broke down, raising the question of whether the defensive positions could be held under the constant artillery fire. In the meantime, the weather worsened; snow began to fall, and heavy cloud cover continued to negatively affect artillery fire and air reconnaissance missions.

Enemy infantry troops sapped closer to the fortress walls as small units rapidly traversed the terrain 100 to 150 paces at a time. The soldiers then dropped to the ground seeking momentary shelter, dug in, and repeated the maneuver to rapidly approach the fortress walls. The Russians utilized the nearby Radymno-Rokietnica railroad line to move supplies rapidly for their storm attacks. Meanwhile, on the other side of the fortress, the Habsburg Third Army encountered no serious tsarist resistance as it advanced. Habsburg Supreme Command Daily Report (AOK Operation Nr. 2870) indicated that tsarist troops continued to maneuver toward the area north of the fortress and east of the San River in preparation for the battle to occur along the eastern Vistula River front.[13]

During these early October days, efforts were undertaken to improve the fortress's defensive strength throughout the citadel area. Telephone connections were extended to the perimeter and forefield positions, while infantry blocking sites also expanded outward between six and thirty meters. Patrols outside the citadel walls doubled at night, while thick clouds often ruled out air reconnaissance missions. The few intelligence reports indicated that the enemy continued to shift troops around the Fortress Przemyśl perimeter.

On October 3, under enemy artillery fire, fortress troops observed small Russian infantry and cavalry units approaching the western and southwestern fortress perimeter areas and continuous troop movements east of the San River. The fortress dispatched five Honvéd battalions to Walawa and Dusowce, as reconnaissance missions confirmed that tsarist Eleventh Army troops had replaced Third Army troops at the siege lines. Heavy tsarist artillery fire commenced against the citadel forts at the northern, eastern, and southern fronts, while large troop units shifted forward and advanced north of the bulwark. Four or five enemy infantry divisions advanced to the southern and eastern citadel areas.[14] Meanwhile, tsarist troops had been transferred from the fortress area to participate in the developing battle along the eastern Vistula River front. As Russian forces continued to sap toward the citadel, they sustained heavy casualties from defensive artillery fire. Nevertheless, the enemy acted with uncharacteristic speed, intensifying artillery barrages against the fortress walls. Siedliska (Defensive District VI) continued to bear the brunt of the assaults, but Defensive District IV also sustained increased enemy cannon fire.[15]

As Habsburg Second Army troops advanced toward the fortress through the Dukla Pass, General Kusmanek reported that Russian columns had been observed in the vicinity of the bulwark from Radymno toward Rokietnica. In retaliation, he launched a sortie with a twelve-infantry battalion, four field cannon, and three 15-centimeter howitzer batteries in the direction of Rokietnica. To prevent tsarist troops from withdrawing from the bulwark area, the Habsburg Third Army launched its offensive toward the fortress. Sortie units encountered strong enemy forces and heavy artillery fire. This forced them to retreat into the fortress after dark with some captured prisoners of war and war materiel. General Kusmanek proclaimed the sortie a success because it had supposedly disturbed Russian troop movements.

Reconnaissance reports indicated massive tsarist troop movements on the right San River bank region. Enemy cannon fire against the fortress's Defensive District IV intensified after dusk. General Kusmanek launched a mission toward Dusowce with five infantry battalions of Honvéd Infantry Regiment 5 and artillery support from the fortress's Defensive District XIII, while a small troop contingent maneuvered along the railroad tracks at Defensive District XII. At the same time, large numbers of tsarist troops reportedly advanced toward Malkovice, but inclement weather conditions delayed the launch of the proposed fortress operation.

On October 4, following a Russian diversionary strike, the first serious fortress battle commenced. The action was intended to lure General Kusmanek into diverting major reserve formations to that area away from their major storm attack objective. Russian artillery bombardment against the citadel doubled in intensity, introducing the bogus attack. Then, tsarist troops unleashed their main assault against the north and southwest garrison perimeters. Russian generals reasoned that if their forces quickly captured the fortress, the siege troops would be free to join the armies battling in the Carpathian Mountains. In early October, the entire Russian Third Army (IX, X, XI, and XXI Corps), part of the Eighth Army (XII Corps and portions of VII Corps), and three additional rifle brigades remained at the fortress front. Tsarist generals postulated from Habsburg prisoner of war testimony that troop morale was low and that the defending garrison forces consisted of only five regiments and eight Landsturm companies.[16] Allegedly, the fortress's Habsburg defenders had slept very little and would surrender at the first opportunity. October 4 reconnaissance reports reconfirmed earlier indications of the northward deployment of enemy units.[17] Consequently, the Russians were determined to quickly overpower the fortress.

To support their frantic efforts, the Russians deployed the 78th heavy howitzer battery in the wooded region north of the Siedliska Defensive District VI front, the main assault area, to fire against Forts Hurko, Borek, and Siedliska. The northern battery group deployed six to seven kilometers from Forts Borek and Siedliska, while the 1st and 2nd heavy howitzer batteries were positioned six to eight kilometers from the Siedliska battle zone (Defensive District VI forts I/1–5). The tsarist 4th and 5th heavy howitzer batteries fired from positions five to seven kilometers from the fortress front. All possible guns targeted Defensive District VI Fortress Siedliska positions. Russian commanders postulated that the lack of heavy artillery pieces presupposed that their artillery fire could be effective against the fortress only in concentrated barrages.[18]

Russian artillery bombardment intensified with great ferocity. During the night of October 5, powerful assault units rapidly approached the fortress in an attempt at a hand strike against the six Siedliska forts. Under cover of the sustained artillery barrages, more than seven and one-half infantry divisions, three rifle brigades, and additional supporting units, totaling 117 battalions, twenty-four cavalry squadrons, and 483 artillery pieces, participated in the initial tsarist efforts.[19] The artillery complement included forty field howitzer and field cannons, while 24-centimeter howitzers, their heaviest guns, fired from multiple positions on the high terrain at Magiera against the forward Siedliska positions.[20] Three infantry divisions launched an attack at 8 a.m. with a 1,000-officer and 92,000-man strong force against the Siedliska group of forts, initiating seventy-two hours of bloody battle.[21] The tsarist first-day mission encompassed hurling back Habsburg forward defensive positions as supporting artillery fire intensified its already heavy barrages, now utilizing additional 10-centimeter field cannon and 15- and 21-centimeter batteries.

Severe weather and terrain conditions continued to frustrate both the Habsburg Third Army efforts to liberate Fortress Przemyśl and the tsarist attempts to seize it. Second Army units traversed the Carpathian Mountain ridges over a broad front and launched a three-pronged attack from their right flank positions toward Dobromil and Sambor in an attempt to encircle tsarist troops in the San River area. However, because of troop exhaustion resulting from the adverse march conditions, the operation did not begin until the next morning.[22] Although inclement weather conditions caused severe problems, the Second Army's XII and VII Corps encountered no serious resistance from the defending tsarist cavalry, which retreated without opposition.[23] Habsburg infantry had to battle without artillery support because the guns lagged far behind the frontline troops. This, coupled with the inadequate training of replacement troops in the army ranks, caused casualty numbers to soar. On October 5, Second Army troops advanced in an attempt to encircle the Russian forces pressing into Chyrov through the important Uzsok Pass, with some units also traversing the middle Lupkov Pass saddle and the left flank of the Dukla Pass.[24] Tsarist VII Corps troops halted the effort, allowing Russian forces to cover the critical Stary Sambor-Lisko-Sanok siege line. Severe weather, coupled with a limited number of supply routes, slowed Habsburg support efforts, creating significant deficiencies in the timely transport of food, ammunition, and artillery shells to the advancing Habsburg troops.

On the next day, October 6, cold and rainy conditions continued to cause nearly insurmountable delays in supply traffic. The constant rainfall commencing in mid-September prevented units from attaining their march goals and made any movement extremely difficult. Habsburg Second and Third Armies nevertheless advanced slowly toward their objectives of Bircza and Nizankovice located close to Fortress Przemyśl. The Second Army continued its attempt to encircle tsarist forces deployed east of the fortress from a southerly direction.[25]

Tsarist command deployed three infantry divisions against the forts' Defensive Districts Xa and XII on the northern front, half a division at the southern front, two cavalry divisions at the western and southwestern fronts, and six divisions to launch the attacks at the eastern and southeastern fortress fronts. As the three tsarist infantry divisions stormed the Siedliska Group forts I/1–6 at 7:00 a.m., they concentrated shrapnel fire at Fortress I/1, while troops and sappers reconnoitered the fortress minefield and barbed wire defensive emplacements. The enemy troops sought to destroy these obstacles, while a tsarist division unsuccessfully attacked Forts I/5 and I/6. Between October 5 and 7, large numbers of

Russian forces continued to cross the north Vistula River. Habsburg Third Army units meanwhile approached Fortress Przemyśl, impeded by thousands of horse cadavers littering the sides of the heavily trafficked roadways. The farther field army troops advanced from their far rearward railroad depots, the more difficult the maintenance of the supply situation became. Meanwhile, gunfire could be heard from the western fortress perimeter, indicating to the inhabitants that help would soon arrive.[26]

The Russians then attacked the Defensive District IV ring and simultaneously launched storm attacks against Defensive Districts VI and VII. Tsarist soldiers pressed the furthest Habsburg infantry outposts rearward, drawing ever closer to the citadel. Russian artillery fire targeted fortress artillery units and defensive obstacles.[27] Habsburg fortress troop commanders tried to determine where the main enemy effort would ultimately strike. Terrain obstacles eliminated the northwestern, northern, and southern fortress fronts. The weakest citadel defensive position, the southwestern, held promise for tsarist success because the forested terrain could conceal troop movement almost to the perimeter walls. The hilly terrain and poor roadways, however, made it extremely difficult for the Russians to transport their artillery forward to assist their offensive operation.

As General Kusmanek correctly calculated, based on the amount of enemy artillery fire, the massive major enemy storm attack occurred at the southeastern fortress front against the inviting Siedliska Defensive District VI situated between the San and Wiar Rivers. The jutting portions of terrain resulting from the elliptical shapes of the northern and southern Siedliska fortress ring attracted enemy flanking fire, while their troops could deploy in the wooded terrain undetected. Under cover of artillery fire, tsarist troops also approached the northern Forts X to XII, southeast I/1–6 (Siedliska), and IV and V on the southern front.[28] Much of the preparation took place at night, while secondary assaults continued to be utilized as diversionary strokes against other perimeter positions, particularly at the northern citadel front. Because the Siedliska forts proved especially inviting, the Russians advanced to within five hundred meters of Forts I/1–3, but their supporting artillery fire failed to suppress the infantry defensive lines or defensive artillery fire at any of the six Siedliska forts.[29]

Realizing the imminent danger to the Defensive District VI front, General Kusmanek reinforced the eleven battalions defending that critical area. Fourteen additional infantry battalions were rushed forward with 350 23th Honvéd Infantry Division artillery pieces (twenty-five batteries), including some that quickly unleashed flanking fire against the attacking enemy forces at the threatened Forts I/1 and I/2.[30] Overpowering defensive fire halted most mass enemy storm attacks against the Siedliska positions, but, nevertheless, some of the forward defensive positions had to be abandoned. The fortress commander ordered the strengthening of all citadel perimeter areas that the enemy artillery targeted. Defensive artillery fire inflicted enormous casualties on the attacking troops.

In the meantime, the Habsburg field armies faced their own significant challenges. During the September Habsburg retreat, the armies destroyed numerous railroad lines and bridges, and the Russians had followed suit during their retreat. The damage proved a significant hindrance to Habsburg offensive efforts; it would eventually require three weeks to repair the lines and place them back into service after the fortress was liberated. In the meantime, however, wagon supply trains had to transport the Third Army's eight-hundred-ton-per-day supply requirements from the rearward echelon railhead to the front along the few muddy and eroded roadways, a journey that often stretched up to ninety kilometers.[31]

In late October, the bridges were reconstructed and made operational, but this also stretched the Habsburg railroad traffic and resupply efforts between the northern and southern flanks, as no rail line led directly to the rear of the fortress. This shortcoming hampered the mobility of troops and supplies, and proved especially disastrous to resupply efforts after the fortress was liberated. General Conrad estimated that his field armies would reach the fortress by October 10, but the consistent supply problems signified that soldiers received only a quarter of their normal food rations.[32] Transport had become completely limited to the smaller Galician *panja* wagons and horses bearing light loads as the cumbersome army-issue wagons became bogged down in the muck, making them unusable.

The Third Army's offensive objectives directed it northward toward Radymno and Nizankovice, along the Bircza-Nizankovice road, and then on to the fortress. Two Second Army corps were ordered to march to the strategic area at Chyrov and its key railroad station by October 10, and another group to Stary-Sambor. The two armies were to cooperate to liberate Fortress Przemyśl.

Second Army units deployed south of Fortress Przemyśl in the Carpathian Mountains battled harsh weather and inadequate supply lines. Only one road led to the army's left flank forces. Artillery and supply wagons suffered serious delays, and some never reached their destination, casting doubt on whether the army could achieve its objectives.[33] Exacerbating the situation, seven Second Army divisions entered a narrow pass at Chyrov where it proved almost impossible to maneuver, and instead of meeting weak enemy forces as anticipated, the Second Army encountered the entire Russian Eighth Army.

Russian troops at Fortress Przemyśl had hastily prepared their offensive to seize the fortress; however, as they lacked heavy caliber artillery weapons, these last-ditch efforts failed. At the same time, tsarist light artillery on the fortress front concentrated their most intense firepower, 21-centimeter caliber guns, against Habsburg trenches and artillery batteries, aiming specifically at the positions jutting out of the Siedliska Fortress. The Russian barrages, however, failed to destroy or even badly damage the fortress walls, and the attacking troops again sustained severe losses.

During the morning, portions of the Russian 19th Infantry Division rapidly advanced four to five kilometers to within eighty to five hundred meters of fortress defensive positions, less than one kilometer from the northern Siedliska fortress rings. However, defensive flanking firepower wrought heavy casualties and forced the Russians to retreat.[34] At the same time, a concentrated tsarist attack targeted Werk I/4, while comparable action proved unsuccessful at Werk I/5.[35] The three-infantry division enemy storm column failed to take advantage of the approaching darkness to reach the Habsburg defensive barbed wire.

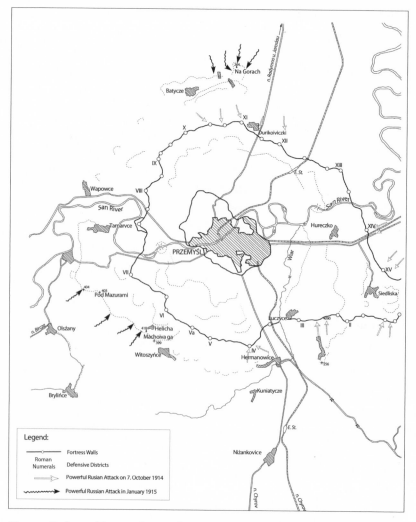

Map 3.2. Defense of Fortress Przemyśl, 1914–1915.

At the fortress walls, two meters of concrete protected defensive artillery positions from tsarist artillery shells and prevented serious damage to the major positions. Nonetheless, nightfall brought no rest to the weary Habsburg troops. Continuous shelling, the urgent need to transport shells to the fortress walls, and repairing the damaged ramparts left no time for sleep. Between 12:00 noon and 2:00 p.m., tsarist artillery barrages against the fortress walls recommenced. The fortress defenders' nerves cracked in the wake of utter helplessness and exhaustion. Garrison troops placed sandbags to fill in large gaps along the fortress walls, while the infantry deployed in the interval positions faced the enemy onslaught with no protection from its artillery fire. With the telephone cables destroyed, Habsburg commanders had to resort to delivering orders on horseback. Once tsarist artillery barrages halted, the sudden silence wreaked havoc on the garrison troops' psyche. Russian sappers advanced until they had reached the bulwark's walls.[36] Battle alarms were followed by gunfire and screaming as enemy troops approached. As the Russians attacked Fortress I/1 fore-field positions, neighboring fortress works fired shrapnel shells at that specific position, producing what eyewitnesses likened to "the sound of hell."

During the ongoing enemy efforts, the 23rd Honvéd Infantry Division units' artillery targeted enemy infantry flank positions. The Russian 19th Infantry Division and Infantry Regiment 76, the main attack units against Werk I/1, reportedly sacrificed three thousand men in their attack. The Russians also launched a strong assault against the fortress's Defensive District IV, which received Defensive District IX and X supporting artillery flanking fire against the attacking enemy forces. The enemy attack collapsed. A tsarist retreat movement reportedly commenced at Defensive Districts IV, VI, and VII as enemy artillery barrages subsided in intensity.

The Russians also launched their 58thInfantry Division, as well as a brigade of the 69th Reserve Infantry Division in addition to 19th Infantry Division forces, against the east and southeast front along the Grodek roads' Defensive Districts XV (Hurko) and VI (Siedliska), supported by continuous artillery support. A Reserve Infantry Division brigade assaulted the villages of Popowice-Siedliska. The tsarist 60th Reserve Infantry Division stormed the area from the south, while 12th, 78th, and 82nd Reserve Infantry Divisions with the 11th and 12th Mortar Divisions attacked the Batycze-Malkovice front. The failed Russian storm attacks produced further significant bloodshed.[37]

The tsarist 78th and 82nd Reserve Infantry Divisions plus the 3rd Schützen Brigade positioned at the left flank attacked the fortress's southeast sector front at Grochawce, supported by twenty-four artillery pieces. Flanking fortress artillery fire from Fort Hurko prevented the Russians from receiving any substantial additional reinforcements. When the attack bogged down at the northern fortress front, only three hundred paces from the defensive lines, some assaulting troops had almost attained their objectives along the extensive four-kilometer front.[38] However, fortress defensive fire had not been subdued or even weakened, as the armored cupolas withstood all tsarist artillery barrages.

The Russians concentrated artillery fire against the Siedliska group in the early morning hours of October 7. Between 3:00 and 4:00 a.m., tsarist troop masses again stormed the fortress on a broad front from the southeast until 6:00 a.m., still intending to capture the Siedliska positions before Habsburg relieving troops arrived. Meanwhile, the tsarist Eighth Army reported that advancing Habsburg forces had reached the Carpathian Mountain passes. The failure of that first assault against the Siedliska positions, a result of intense defensive machine gun and artillery fire, was followed by a second bloody onslaught at 9:00 a.m., which the defenders also repulsed with severe enemy losses. The Russians failed to get closer than a thousand paces to the fortress walls. Only a few brave troops reached the barbed wire entanglements. Despite the continuing deadly defensive artillery fire, the third attack occurred at 2:00 p.m.[39] Smaller assaults targeted other fortress positions, but the heaviest enemy artillery concentrations continued to focus on the most important fortress Defensive District VI front resistance points. By daybreak, a battalion of tsarist Infantry Regiment 76 (19th Infantry Division) succeeded in penetrating the Fort I/1 infantry defensive zone unnoticed, having overrun the protective barbed wire given the absence of fortress lighting in that area.[40] Infantry Regiment 73 troops also utilized the light from mortar fire to reach the fortress barbed wire lines and forward infantry positions without the assistance of artillery support or reserve units. Tsarist troops then overran forward Habsburg defending infantry positions and barbed wire emplacements. Some even scaled the fortress walls and penetrated Fort I through deadly defensive machine gun fire. This produced utter chaos as two tsarist infantry companies, in bloody hand-to-hand combat, pushed the few Habsburg defenders into the interior of Fort I. Battle continued until 9:00 a.m the following day. A company of Hungarian troops from Landsturm Infantry Regiment 18 rushed to counterattack the tsarist troops. The disorderly tsarist storm attacks would ultimately be halted when major Habsburg field army troops approached the fortress from the west.[41] Meanwhile, tsarist infantry troops, consisting of an infantry battalion and one sapper squad, had advanced from elevated terrain against Forts I/1 and I/2 in cold, stormy conditions with assistance from the 19th Artillery Brigade's forty-eight gun tubes.

Tsarist Infantry Regiment 75, meanwhile, launched a storm attack against Fort I/2. The attack evolved from two directions in an attempt to encircle the fort at both flanks. A frontal attack ensued between 4:00 and 5:00 a.m., but by daybreak it became obvious that the concentrated tsarist artillery fire had again caused no serious damage to the main fortress structure. Nor had the barbed wire and flanking infantry positions been destroyed; therefore, the regiment had to retreat to await artillery support.

Any tsarist troops caught between the firing zones and minefields became prisoners of war.[42] The Russians, however, failed to reach the barbed wire entanglements in front of several forts (Xa, XIa, XI, and XII). Additional tsarist assaults occurred against Forts XIV, XV (Hurko), I/2 through I/6, and IV, I/1.[43]

The Russians resumed offensive efforts, attempting to launch a surprise attack during the night of October 8 despite the failures of the previous day. Repeated powerful assaults against Defensive Districts IV and VI again brought tsarist troops forward to the defensive obstacles. Their artillery barrages, however, pounded Defensive Districts III and VII to no avail. The tsarist Third Army began to retreat to the right bank of the San River to defend the river line, while a snowstorm delayed enemy supply train movement. As the Habsburg field armies finally approached the fortress environs, the besieging tsarist cavalry divisions retreated from the citadel's western front in the early morning hours. A relentless assault was unleashed over the forefields in an attempt to seize the Siedliska positions at noon on that bright, sunny day. The fortress troops expected another attack during the morning hours against Forts I/1 and I/5, and they successfully repulsed it. Waving Red Cross flags, Honvéd troops attempted to collect the dead and wounded in the midst of battle, but the Russians ignored the flags and fired on them anyway.[44]

When the storm attacks finally ended, thousands of dead and seriously wounded tsarist troops lay in the open at the Siedliska position,
but their own artillery fire prevented them from tending to their
wounded until nightfall. A mass grave was dug the following night close
to the fortress walls, but some tsarist units could not retreat until the
following day because their attack positions remained too close to the
fortress. After seventy-two hours of bloody battle lasting from October
6 to 9, 1914, the tsarist attack ended in failure. Meanwhile, Habsburg
Third Army troops approached the fortress from south of Dynov, where
they initially encountered no enemy troops. The only tsarist unit in that
area, the tsarist 10th Cavalry Division, deployed in the Bircza area. As
the Habsburg Third Army IX Corps reached that same region, enemy
infantry and cavalry units retreated from the west, then northwest, fortress fronts to the east. Some friendly troop units moved into the terrain
south of the San River; the III Corps moved into the San valley.

Temperatures dropped as cold rain, fog, and the first snowstorms of
the season commenced. The inclement weather led to growing concerns
about the maintenance of Habsburg field armies' supply routes as Third
Army supply trains continued to lag far behind the advancing combat
troops. In addition, the troops deployed along the seventy-kilometer
front suffered from complete exhaustion.[45] Neither the Second nor the
Third Army encountered serious enemy resistance as they continued
their advance toward the citadel, but the poor weather conditions prevented air reconnaissance activity, producing uncertainty about the prevailing enemy situation and intentions.

Some Habsburg sources listed Russian casualties in the unsuccessful attempt to capture Fortress Przemyśl at seventy thousand, but the
actual number was probably close to ten thousand. Some four thousand
died, and three times that number were probably wounded or captured.
The tsarist 19th Infantry Division alone lost forty-four officers and thirty-
four hundred soldiers, 25 percent of its original stand. Russian corpses
reputedly could be seen stacked a meter deep on the ground surrounding
the fortress, though this estimate is probably exaggerated. Fortress defenders had repulsed nine tsarist divisions and inflicted enormous casualties on the Russian foe.[46] General Brusilov initially intended to launch
another major attack the next day, but his left flank positions had be-

come exposed when the tsarist Fourth, Fifth, and Ninth Armies (ten corps) marched to the Vistula River front to prepare for an overpowering invasion of German Silesia.[47] Moreover, Stavka would not allow another storm attack at any price. Thus, large troop concentrations deployed west of the Vistula River in the area of Fortress Kraków were shifted to provide flank security for their Austro-Hungarian front operations.[48] The Tsarist Third and Eleventh armies received orders to retreat across the San River, but because their assault troops remained in close proximity to the fortress walls, they could not retreat until the night to October 9.

The Russian October storm attacks failed for multiple reasons. The designated offensive troops had already been exhausted, having endured a two- to three-day approach march in rainy and muddy conditions and arriving at the fortress siege lines just prior to launching the assaults. Furthermore, the hastily prepared offensive plans proved flawed, neglecting many crucial details. Faulty intelligence reports suggesting that fortress troop morale had sunk so low that the citadel garrison would capitulate if pressured contributed to the failed plan of attack. No tsarist reconnaissance missions occurred at the fortress prior to the attack; they were undertaken only when the offensive operation commenced. Although tsarist infantry troops received new weapons such as hand grenades and wire cutters before their storm assaults, they had not been properly trained in how to use them. Technical details for the operation had also been neglected. For example, of the Russian siege army's 483 artillery pieces, only about 6.5 percent of that complement consisted of heavy guns capable of destroying the bulwark's perimeter walls. In addition, tsarist artillery failed to adequately support the attacking infantry by neutralizing the defensive artillery throughout the storm attacks. A shortage of experienced combat officers and serious supply difficulties stemming from the inclement weather and hazardous terrain conditions also took their toll. Night attacks, which were originally planned, would probably have allowed the Russian troops to attain the opposing barbed wire entanglements. Unfortunately for the Russians, a confused command structure initiated the storm attacks after dawn. These Russian mishaps, combined with devastating defensive fortress fire, particularly in the major Siedliska battle area, proved decisive during the operation. Multiple tsarist assaults were routinely halted at the first major defensive obstacles, while mounting casualties wreaked havoc on the attacking troops' morale.[49]

General Conrad planned to launch a double envelopment offensive against tsarist forces in middle Galicia by October 12, in particular, to roll up the Russian front from south of Fortress Przemyśl.[50] The Habsburg First Army had to attack toward the lower San-Vistula River area at Zawichost, while the Fourth Army supported them by aiding with their river crossing and providing flank protection to the east toward Lemberg.

On October 8, strong Third Army forces marched north to the area of Radymno and the critical railroad bridge at Nizankovice, but the tsarist Eighth Army blocked the positions at Bircza. The Russians ultimately evacuated Nizankovice and Chyrov, but previously destroyed railroad bridges had to be rebuilt, delaying Third Army progress; the mass of III Corps entered the San Valley to approach the fortress north of Jaroslau. On October 9, the Fourth Army advanced to the San River stretch near Rzeszóv, with the Second Army's VII and XII Corps following the next day. There they would prepare to ford the lower San and Vistula Rivers and open the approaches to the fortress and Radymno.[51] Yet, despite multiple hindrances, intelligence reports indicated that the Russians had terminated their siege of the fortress in the area west and southwest of the citadel.

The Habsburg Fourth Army pressed forward toward Jaroslau-Krzeszóv between October 8 and 11, but the continuous rains halted its progress. The army's XVII Corps advanced to the hilly terrain south of the Wisloka River while the II Corps and XIV Corps protected the army's northern front area. A corps followed to protect the army's left flank positions. The 2nd and 6th Cavalry Divisions commenced reconnaissance to the northeast toward the San River, while 10th Cavalry Division protected the army's northern flank. On October 8, Fourth Army command reported that the II and XVII Corps encountered strong resistance allegedly consisting of five to six Russian divisions. Its XIV Corps advanced to the southeast in an attempt to cut off the enemy retreat from the Fortress Przemyśl area to behind the San River. However, General Conrad's attempted double encirclement failed because Russian Third

Army units west of the river had promptly evacuated their positions during the night of October 9.[52]

Third Army Command initially assumed that tsarist forces would defend all approaches to the fortress extending from the area of Dynov, close to the citadel, with equally strong forces deployed along both sides of the San River. As the Third Army prepared to counter the threat, damaged bridges along the advance route, which could not be repaired until at least October 10, delayed their movement. The area east of the San River at Dynov lacked the resources necessary to conduct major operations, limiting deployments to smaller troop units. Thus, south of the San River, only Group Tschurtschenthaler and the 6th Infantry Division from III Corps advanced. North of the river, the mass of III Corps (22nd and 28th Infantry Divisions) advanced to the San River Valley roads leading to the fortress from Rokietnica. Third Army forces crossed the high waters of the San River and moved some troops toward Bircza, where they encountered no enemy troops on the area's elevated banks. The Fourth Army's left flank units north of the San River approached the fortress and the Radymno area, encountering strong enemy resistance. On the same day, Habsburg Supreme Command ordered a general attack against enemy forces in the fortress area.[53] As usual, the overall enemy military situation remained unclear.

The major field army battle scene now shifted to the Habsburg Second Army eastern flank positions, where the first phase of the battles of Fortress Przemyśl and Chyrov occurred. The enemy's destruction of numerous bridges delayed the arrival of two Second Army corps to the two major railroad stations and junctions at Lisko and Sanok overlooking the San River. These locations became significant military objectives during the early 1915 Carpathian Mountain Winter War campaigns. The Second Army had sought to advance through the narrow confines at Chyrov between October 8 and 10, but, on the first day, the effective defensive efforts of the tsarist Eighth Army halted its northern and middle flank movements.

Enemy troops at the northern and southern siege lines finally displayed indications that they too might retreat, while troops on the southeastern and eastern fronts remained at their positions. As Habsburg field army forces approached the fortress, the besieging Eleventh Army withdrew to just east of the citadel with its XXIX Corps initially covering the evacuation of its Jaroslau bridgehead positions at the San River. Battle commenced there on October 10 and ended with the tsarist army retreating. Yet Habsburg forces progressed slowly. The Russian Third Army established a cavalry screen at the San River as its main units retreated across it to establish defensive positions given the flank threat from the north. Strong forces (four corps) covered the tsarist Third Army's southern flank retreat through Radymno-Jaroslau-Sieniava. The effect of battle on the German front at the Warsaw-Ivangorod area suddenly threatened the tsarist position on the Habsburg Galician front, particularly at the San River. Russian Ninth Army radio transmissions revealed that three tsarist armies were being redeployed to the Vistula River line south of Warsaw. This represented a serious weakening of tsarist troop numbers on the Habsburg front and brought about a significant battle at Ivangorod.

At about noon on October 9, a Habsburg Second Army XII Corps Hussar cavalry patrol reached the outer perimeter of the western fortress at Fort Pralkovce, after being delayed for days by the difficult terrain and unrelenting weather. Fortress observers rejoiced at the sight of friendly forces. Infantry units followed the cavalry formations, and the field armies finally liberated the fortress. Three Russian corps retreated behind the San River, including the tsarist siege troops, which offered little resistance to the Habsburg troops at the northern fortress front. However, tsarist forces established strong defensive lines within artillery range of the fortress's eastern and southeastern fronts at the San River and a major stronghold on the Magiera Heights, which soon became the scene of fierce, bloody battle. Strong forces had to protect the movement of supplies from the Jaroslau area; two corps also guarded the San River crossings as the Russians created a defensive line along the river east of Fortress Przemyśl.[54]

Third Army troops battled some of the retreating enemy flank units. However, IX Corps troops (northern army flank) again met strong enemy resistance on unfavorable terrain. As the enemy conducted a scorched earth withdrawal, Habsburg forces reached the San River without serious resistance.[55] The war expanded into the Carpathian Mountains and spread to the Romanian frontier.

Habsburg army ranks contained ill-trained replacement troops that lacked ammunition and artillery shells, which resulted in sustaining excessive casualties. During the night of October 10, Habsburg Fourth Army units approached the San River, focusing on pursuing enemy forces at the Sieniava bridgehead, while one corps advanced in the area of Jaroslau and another at Radymno. Tsarist Third and Eighth Army forces, however, successfully blocked the Fourth Army's attempts to cross the San River. The Habsburg army encountered strong enemy forces covering the tsarist retreat, and attempts to advance the Fourth Army's right flank failed. In the interim, General Conrad ordered the army to encircle tsarist forces west of the San River. The Third Army attacked south of Jaroslau as its main forces advanced to the fortress, but met strong enemy numbers at the San River.[56]

Fortress Przemyśl quickly became a major strong point on Austria-Hungary's eastern front battlefield. During the tsarist retreat, repair work commenced on the damaged citadel walls. In addition, new fore-field positions were reestablished forward of the fortress at the northwest and southern citadel perimeters. However, the condition of roads and railroad bridges prevented any major food or ammunition supply deliveries to the fortress immediately after its liberation. Furthermore, evacuation of sick and wounded soldiers could not be completed, leaving seven thousand wounded in the bulwark when Habsburg troops eventually had to retreat again.

The main fortress offensive unit, the 23rd Honvéd Infantry Division, rejoined the Third Army to assist in the pursuit of the retreating Russians and participated in the bloody battle at the heights of Magiera from October 10 to 14. Meanwhile, General Conrad briefly considered transferring Habsburg Supreme Command headquarters back to the fortress. However, his chief of telegraph services convinced him that the present communications system would be seriously hindered because the Russians had destroyed all fortress wire connections and removed telegraph and telephone poles during their siege. It would require some time to restore such services, so Conrad dropped the idea.[57]

On October 10, General Conrad ordered the launching of a general offensive against the enemy troops remaining in the fortress environs. He insisted on maintaining the initiative and planned to roll up the tsarist Vistula German front from the south, disregarding the serious losses his troops had sustained during the initial war operations. While no notable progress had occurred on the Habsburg Balkan front, preparations commenced to cross the lower San and Vistula Rivers. One Habsburg corps advanced toward Bircza, then Nizankovice, against strong enemy defensive positions east of the fortress. First Army mission became to seize the San River area that stretched to the lower San River area at the Vistula River Zawichost location.[58] The German Ninth Army's left flank units marched toward the lower Pilica River and then on to Warsaw, partly to protect the present northern Habsburg flank.[59]

On October 10, the northern deployed Russian Ninth and Fifth Armies threatened Habsburg positions at the gap between the San River and the Carpathian Mountains, while additional troop units initially would launch a major offensive, the infamous Dampfwalze (steamroller), into Germany.[60] The presence of such a large enemy force threatening to cross the Vistula River between the mouth of the San River and the fortresses in Poland created a serious military crisis for the Central Powers.[61]

During the night of October 11, strong tsarist rearguard units finally evacuated their last positions at Fortress Przemyśl. Then, Fourth Army southern flank forces advanced simultaneously with the neighboring Third Army left flank units (III Corps) to pursue the enemy to Radymno. Tsarist defensive positions at Jaroslau were attacked from the south, west, and northwest, but enemy resistance hardened at Sosnica and Radymno. Third Army IX Corps seized bridges while the Jaroslau bridgehead positions remained at the front combat zone as tsarist forces retreated from the citadel's eastern and southern perimeter. The Fourth Army, meanwhile, had finally made contact with First Army units at the San River and subsequently received orders to cross the San and Vistula Rivers.

General Conrad, having no indication of Russian intentions, ordered his troops to maintain constant contact with the enemy to ascertain if they would continue to retreat. The Russians, however, merely intended to protect their artillery units, which were slowly withdrawing toward Lemberg, and established a defensive bridgehead at Sosnica on the western San River bank. The Habsburg Third Army could not launch its intended operation toward Radymno until October 12 because of the terrible weather and terrain conditions. Twenty-two fortress infantry battalions and twenty-seven artillery batteries participated in the field army battle, while tsarist forces tenaciously defended key San River crossing points. Widespread troop exhaustion, lack of protection against the elements, and hunger placed Habsburg troops in an unenviable situation. Many horses abandoned by the field armies during the September 1914 retreat assisted Third Army resupply efforts.[62]

Overpowering tsarist troop numbers regularly attacked Habsburg soldiers. Many such attacks ended in deadly hand-to-hand combat. The horrendous conditions resulted in many soldiers simply never waking up. Transporting artillery shells to the front lines caused particular problems. The destruction of railroads in middle Galicia had limited traffic to only four stations, which significantly and negatively affected all military operations south of the San River. In addition, Habsburg units lacked bridge-crossing materials to traverse the San.[63] Meanwhile, Third Army vanguard troops entered the area of Bircza without battle, but the northern flank IX Corps encountered strong Russian resistance. The unfavorable conditions continued to prevent Habsburg units from attaining their assigned march goals.

Third Army X Corps initially seized the Jaroslau bridgehead, which partially utilized fortress artillery for its defense. On the following day, October 11, Habsburg troops pursuing retreating tsarist formations attempted to achieve a double encirclement in the Jaroslau area, initially against weak enemy resistance.

As Russian troops retreated, they destroyed roads, bridges, and key railroad lines essential to supplying the advancing Habsburg armies. It became imperative that the railroads and bridges be rebuilt as quickly as possible, since the Habsburg armies sequestered a twenty-one-day food supply from the fortress, as well as artillery, artillery shells, and other material needs. Thus, the fortress became a major supply depot for the field armies, but the armies were then expected to replace or return the food, artillery units, and unexpended shells to Fortress Przemyśl.

The Russians finally evacuated the left San River bank at Radymno, leaving cavalry forces as rearguard protection, and established new positions on the right San River bank. When they abandoned their locations at the eastern and southern fortress perimeter areas, they established their new defensive positions on the San River line where the Dniester River flowed out of the Carpathian Mountains in the Stary Sambor area. Their flank and rear echelon positions thus had protection from the Dniester River swamps, and they dominated all approach routes to their new positions. The Habsburg Third Army's commander had entered the fortress as his troops intercepted enemy forces at Rokietnica and seized Jaroslau and its bridgeheads before commencing an advance toward Radymno. Progress proved slow given the flooded conditions and enormous casualties sustained when they encountered Russian rearguard troops at Sosnica and Radymno.

On October 11 and 12, a fortress sortie was launched in unrelenting rain northward toward Sosnica to cooperate with Habsburg Third Army III Corps, advancing toward Radymno and the southern San River line. The attempt would hurl the enemy across the San River. Third Army III Corps troops and a mobile 9-centimeter cannon battery protected the left flank of the sortie units against two enemy corps. The Third and Fourth Armies advanced to the San River, but, because of the unfavorable conditions, could not cross, delaying the offensive for several days. Other major hindrances to further forward movement involved the lack of bridge-crossing equipment and sheer exhaustion of Habsburg troops. The enemy had also constructed strong positions across the river. General Conrad ordered the Fourth Army to cross the river on October 14, but that action would be delayed until October 17 because the army could not penetrate the strong tsarist defensive positions, and vital bridge-crossing equipment still had not reached the army.[64] Conrad's order to cross the San River assumed that the Russians had retreated from the river line, leaving only rear echelon defensive units to protect it. The Fourth Army thus expected to encounter no serious resistance, but heavy Russian artillery fire halted its units attempting to cross the river, resulting in numerous casualties.[65]

Although Russian forces had occupied the vital river crossing points after destroying all the pertinent bridges, tsarist defensive efforts represented only part of the problems facing Habsburg forces. Supply efforts in the midst of heavy rainstorms exhausted the soldiers, as the mud rendered the wagons virtually unmovable. The deteriorating supply situation gave Third Army officers and soldiers an excuse to plunder the fortress food supplies.[66]

On October 11, south of the fortress, Third Army right flank units battled the Russian XII Corps but failed to seize strong defensive positions such as the high terrain of Magiera and Tyskovice. The First Army's situation worsened at the crossing of the lower San River, where they discovered that the approach routes consisted of deep mud. Despite the unfavorable terrain and supply conditions, they were compelled to cross the river on October 12.[67] For the next few days, Conrad ordered the Fourth and Third Armies to pursue the retreating enemy. The Third and Second Armies were ordered to hinder the tsarist retreat movement of its siege artillery and other war materiel. Habsburg forces had to seize the various San River crossing points, causing as much damage to the enemy as possible. Relentless rain flooded the entire region between the San and Vistula Rivers, turning the terrain into a large swamp and preventing the forward transportation of heavy bridge-crossing equipment. Following time-consuming attempts to prepare to cross the river on October 11, the Habsburg offensive ground to a halt.

On October 12, the Second Army's VII and XII Corps received orders to attack Russian forces, the majority of which were deployed east of Chyrov, but its commanders reported that accelerating the troops' movements would neutralize their battle worth.[68]

Over the next twenty-four hours, troublesome reports arrived from the German Vistula River Ivangorod battlefield. Defeat there could threaten the entire northern Habsburg flank positions, as the adverse conditions there left little chance of First Army traversing the San River even after seizing its crossing points.[69] Meanwhile, the war's first significant mountain battle erupted at Magiera—one of the bloodiest encounters on the eastern front. On October 17, the offensive operation against Radymno also failed, forcing the Fourth Army into a defensive stance along the line between the San River inlet to Fortress Przemyśl.

The perpetual supply crisis was a critical aspect of the Fortress Przemyśl saga. Providing the Habsburg field armies with food supplies during the early October fortress liberation campaign remained difficult. This was the case not only because of terrible weather and terrain conditions, but also because the railroad connection to the attacking troops remained almost a hundred kilometers from the fortress. Although not published in the historical accounts, on October 4, General Conrad ordered fortress bakeries to prepare a four-day supply of bread rations and straw to feed the equivalent of four field army division troops and horses, or fifty-six battalions (88,000 portions), which required 61,600 kilograms of bread.[70] Unbeknown to the general, this would be the initial step toward the downfall of the fortress and its garrison of 120,000 troops on March 22, 1915. For the first time in history, a citadel under siege for many weeks and preparing for a new enemy attack against it received orders to bake bread for an approaching field army.[71]

The bread was to be delivered to the Third Army, but upon entering the fortress, starving Third Army soldiers plundered the garrison's food stores. One postwar source estimated that in a period of about a month, between September 19 and October 22, the Third Army and the fortress garrison consumed a seventy-nine-day supply of bread, forty-two days' worth of vegetables, eighty-eight days' worth of meat, and 230 days' worth of hay. The Third Army also abandoned thousands of sick and wounded soldiers in the fortress when it retreated, raising that total to fifteen thousand. The fortress had also provided necessary food supplies for the October 9–12 Third Army offensive efforts in its environs.[72]

Although several historical accounts make note of the Third Army's "provisioning" at Fortress Przemyśl's expense, none of them point out that the citadel supply command also provided four division days of R rations to the Second Army and three division days of N rations, bread, rusk, and hay to the Fourth Army on October 5. Furthermore, on October 12, Logistics Command approved the transport of ten division day supplies of bread, or rusk, preserved meat, vegetables, and oats to the Fourth Army. On October 18, the fortress provided thirteen division days of N rations and five days of R rations to the Third Army. The Logistics Command then forbade further supplies from being removed from the fortress.[73] Austrian postwar writings have conveniently ignored these factors, as well as the following information.

The Third Army seized a four-day food supply to nourish its two hundred thousand troops and fifty thousand horses. Fortress food supplies thus provided at least nineteen days of food and twenty-six days of hay to the field armies. Given the extent of unsanctioned plundering of the food stores, however, the actual total may have been significantly higher. It is reasonable to question whether the fortress would have had to surrender on March 22, 1915, if such quantities of supplies had not been removed during the October 1914 fortress liberation campaign and immediately afterward.

In the meantime, to resupply its plundered warehouses, Fortress Przemyśl desperately needed to repair the railroad bridges that the enemy had destroyed during its retreat. On October 27, the critical railroad line between Chyrov and Nizankovice reopened, while October 28 finally witnessed the arrival of some resupply services to the fortress following the repair of the Nizankovice railroad bridge. One hundred locomotives, hundreds of rail cars, and many railroad personnel participated during the short resupply efforts. Habsburg Supreme Command had requested the construction of a railroad line to the rear of the citadel since 1902 to no avail. After the war, General Kusmanek and Habsburg General Staff officers faced an investigation committee that inquired why no railroad line extended to the rear Fortress Przemyśl area. The investigation ultimately determined that the railroad had not been constructed because of the lack of funding.

To its disadvantage, the Habsburg military could not utilize the local Karl Ludwig railroad line because its close proximity to enemy lines placed it within artillery range of Radymno and Jaroslau. Fortress resupply efforts continued until 7:00 a.m. on November 4, when the field armies again retreated from the citadel and destroyed the Nizankovice Bridge to prevent it from falling into enemy hands. If the Chyrov railroad link had been restored a week earlier, far more supplies could have been delivered to the fortress, and it might not have had to surrender on March 22, 1915.[74] The resupply efforts, however, lasted for only six days. On November 5, Russian troops again besieged the fortress.

Statistics relating to the fortress resupply effort are complicated. Most Austrian sources give the amounts necessary to supply a prewar planned fortress garrison of 85,000 troops, 3,700 horses, 18,000 civilians, and 20,000 prisoners. However, the October fortress garrison average stood at 128,000 troops, 14,500 horses, and 18,000 civilians. Thus, although Austrian statistics claimed that the resupply effort provided 172 days of bread portions, 214 of vegetables, 111 of meat, and 510 of oats, since the actual garrison numbers were larger, the supply numbers decline to a 111-day supply of bread, 139 of vegetables, 72 of meat, and 90 of oats.[75]

A Habsburg Supreme Command memorandum dispatched to Emperor Franz Joseph's Military Chancellery, dated April 13, 1915, claimed that during the six days of railroad resupply activity, 128 trains arrived at the fortress, which was an undoubted exaggeration to protect General Conrad's reputation.[76] Loading supplies onto a fortress horse-drawn field railroad line and unloading them in the citadel proved an extremely time-consuming process. Fortress troops, in the interim, managed to forage a twenty-one-day supply of vegetables from the fields outside the fortress perimeter. General Conrad halted efforts to commandeer additional supplies destined for the fortress.[77] Anticipating the enormous transport problems with the citadel resupply effort, General Kusmanek, on his own initiative, ordered the construction of the horse-drawn railroad line, which extended from Nizankovice over the Wiar River to the fortress. While this supply line expedited the transfer of goods from the restored railroad bridge, it still proved time-consuming. It also required a large number of horse teams to transport the supplies.[78]

The horse railroad field line required eight to ten days to construct, and despite the repairs, the railroad lines and bridges still proved insufficient for the fortress resupply efforts. Making matters worse, the reconstruction and constant maintenance of the bridges, combined with the need to also equip the Second and Third Armies, proved time-consuming and costly. It would be claimed that four and a half months of food supplies, or sufficient quantities to last until the second half of March, had been delivered to the fortress, but this was a serious exaggeration. The destroyed railroad bridges could not be repaired while enemy siege troops remained along the southwest and southern fortress perimeters. Furthermore, much of the renewed rail traffic occurred at night, with only a few trains originating from the hinterland.[79]

The Railroad Bureau reportedly dispatched 213 supply trains to the Carpathian Mountain front, which also carried some wounded Fortress Przemyśl troops on the return trip. Although thousands of wounded soldiers as well as eight thousand civilians were evacuated from the fortress, another seven thousand wounded and eighteen thousand civilians remained when the Russians renewed their siege. According to Habsburg Supreme Command, 128 of these trains reached Fortress Przemyśl, while the other 85 continued to the field armies. Another official report claimed that nine of the trains transported replacement troops, fifteen ammunition, eighteen material and armaments, fourteen medical supplies, fifty-five food items, and nine hay.[80] The fortress ammunition magazines and supply depots were reportedly refilled to one-half capacity. Military authorities' claims that the garrison now possessed sufficient provisions for a long siege did not fit the facts. For example, the field army and fortress troops did not receive desperately needed winter uniforms and equipment, so they had to continue to wear summer-issue uniforms through the January 23 to mid-April 1915 Carpathian Mountain Winter War campaign. Thus, frostbite ran rampant, particularly for troops deployed at fortress perimeter outpost positions.[81]

Returning to the field armies, the troops participating in the Austro-Hungarian offensive campaign in early October sustained enormous casualties, particularly when the Third Army fought at the bloody battle of Magiera between October 11 and 15. On October 11, 23rd Honvéd Infantry Division soldiers, supported by Third Army troops, stormed the newly constructed Russian bridgehead at Sosnica, rapidly driving tsarist siege troops from the northern and southern fortress fronts back across the San River. During the hasty retreat, the bridges at Sosnice collapsed and numerous San River bridges were destroyed, resulting in the drowning of many Russian soldiers.

The enemy had besieged Fortress Przemyśl for three weeks, but the fortress had persevered through the numerous storm attacks and achieved its main mission of binding enemy forces. General Kusmanek thanked the garrison troops for their bravery and sacrificial duty during that episode. Meanwhile, a lack of artillery shells increasingly retarded Habsburg field army efforts, while the Russian Eighth Army had retreated to the elevated terrain southeast of the fortress in the area of

Chyrov-Sanok. The tsarist Third Army remained a respectable distance from the fortress's eastern front.

Fourth Army movement proved possible only on side roads. On the San River's east bank (toward Fortress Przemyśl) strong tsarist forces prepared to recross the river.[82] Tsarist positions were protected by the flooding San River, and the main Habsburg forces now deployed in the small area south of the river's mouth with troops that desperately required rehabilitation.

Then, on October 14, Russian artillery barrages increased against the Chyrov battlefield as their troops prepared to launch a strong attack toward Habsburg positions. The tsarist Eighth Army XXIV and VII Corps troops counterattacked the Habsburg Second Army deployed south of the fortress to protect and secure their southern flank positions.[83] Meanwhile, the temporary battle lull at the fortress allowed emergency repairs to continue on the damaged perimeter positions under more peaceful conditions, while the tediously slow unloading of supply trains at the end of the month produced additional delays for food and ammunition transports. Harassing tsarist artillery fire did not prevent the construction of additional forward fortress defensive positions, which commenced on October 9, particularly on the northern citadel sector.[84] The forward extension of perimeter positions to Na Gorach–Batycze served to neutralize Russian artillery fire against the exposed San River Bridge and central city area. Meanwhile, vegetables, hay, and wood continued to be foraged far beyond the fortress forefields, although few wagons were available to transport the recovered goods.

Emperor Franz Joseph congratulated the fortress garrison for resisting the enemy storm assaults despite the terrible conditions. The Third Army prepared to advance forward of the fortress eastern front again, while the most difficult problem remained a sufficient supply of field howitzer shells.[85] Between October 14 and 18, battle continued at Ivangorod on the German front. The Habsburg First Army had advanced to the San River and attempted to cross it, as well as the Vistula River line at Zawichost. However, the unsatisfactory road conditions, in conjunction with the well-conducted Russian retreat movements, dashed any possibility that the latter could be forced into battle west of the Vistula River. Russian forces originally retreated to Ivangorod, one of the two major Vistula River crossings along a ninety-mile front, while forming a new Second Army to defend the Warsaw depot and communications center. When the German Ninth Army forces advanced toward Warsaw, the Russians launched a major attack from the city against its left flank positions. The German army found itself in a vulnerable position after tsarist forces crossed the Vistula River and had to rely on Habsburg forces to bind enemy forces west of the river.

On October 15, Habsburg First Army attacked the Russian forces as they attempted to cross the Vistula River at Ivangorod. At Warsaw, the enemy extended its flank positions further west to increase pressure on the opposing German lines. The enormous Russian numerical superiority eventually forced a German retreat on October 20, but the Vistula River offensive operation successfully disrupted tsarist plans to launch a major invasion of Germany. The San-Vistula River line developed into a crucial Russian defensive front. A combination of accurate aerial reconnaissance and the capture of documents from a dead Russian officer apprised German High Command that they were suddenly confronting vastly superior enemy troop numbers. Retreat soon became inevitable.

After mid-October, much of the fighting in the Fortress Przemyśl area occurred at the east and southeast forefield positions, while battle raged along the San River east of Nizankovice. Enemy resistance proved strongest against the southeast fortress works and at Magiera. On October 16, Conrad transferred four infantry divisions to his First Army to strengthen its operations against the Russian flank positions. He hoped to obtain a military success at Ivangorod. Tsarist forces, however, had already crossed the Vistula River at that location, forcing the Habsburg Fourth Army to initiate flank security along the San River extending to the Vistula's mouth. The Germans had debouched their troops on the west bank of the Vistula River, while General August von Mackensen's three corps moved toward Warsaw. Further south, Conrad intended to cross the San River and advance toward Lemberg, the provincial capital.[86]

He planned to launch an attack by Third Army III Corps that would extend from Radymno across the river against the tsarist Eleventh Army siege flank positions from the south. The goal was to cut off enemy supply lines and isolate the formerly besieging army. Second Army right flank units would support the assault, but again the Russians intervened and circumvented Conrad's operational plan as pressure continued to increase steadily against Habsburg forces. The Third Army, lacking sufficient artillery support, remained preoccupied in the mountains at Magiera southeast of the fortress. Offensive activity had to be halted and a defensive posture established because of the lack of artillery shells and terrible supply route conditions. The preliminary railroad supply movements commenced again on October 18. A week later, the first train departed from the key Chyrov station; however, it was not until October 28, when the bridge at Nizankovice had finally been repaired and become operationally ready, that transports actually reached the fortress in numbers.[87]

Costly victories at Magiera and Tyszkovice proved of great significance for fortress resupply efforts. Tsarist forces had previously been able to fire unmolested artillery barrages from these elevated locations at approaching Habsburg supply trains. With the capture of these two positions, train traffic could proceed more smoothly and without the danger of interruption.

Meanwhile, a dangerous eighty-mile gap opened between the Habsburg Third and Fourth Armies. The First Army deployed five divisions to the north, as the Russians advanced at the northern Vistula River, forcing that army's northern flank to retreat from its San River positions. Reinforcements arrived at the Second Army battlefield, where that army fought in uninterrupted battle. The troops held their lines, but reinforced enemy attacks targeted their east flank positions at the high terrain south of Stary Sambor extending to the heights of Medyka near the fortress. The Russians also attacked the former Habsburg bridgehead at Jaroslau. General Kusmanek received orders to launch a sortie to the heights at Szechynic, followed by an energetic attack against enemy positions at Medyka.

Also, on October 18, the Russian Third Army crossed the San River at various locations and launched an attack to relieve the Habsburg pressure against their Eleventh Army and Eighth Army in the Carpathian Mountains. Habsburg Supreme Command then ordered that the Russian troops that had crossed the San River be destroyed by October 20.[88] However, increasing tsarist pressure became so strong that it prevented the Third Army's IX Corps from advancing south of the fortress and its X Corps from moving north of its positions. The Habsburgs could not progress anywhere, and the battle southeast of the bulwark area developed into a bloody position struggle. A tsarist Eighth Army counterattack forced Habsburg troops to provide better flank protection before launching an offensive from the area south of Fortress Przemyśl.

The Habsburgs failed on many attempts to cross the San River and pursue the Russians. The Fourth Army's failure on October 17, for example, resulted from massive Russian defensive artillery fire, which caused serious losses and halted the operation almost immediately. The Russians, however, successfully crossed the river at four different locations, which forced the Habsburg Third and Fourth Armies into a defensive stance.[89] A shortage of artillery shells compelled the Habsburgs to allocate their diminishing artillery resources against enemy attacks that the infantry could not repulse. Third Army's III Corps commandeered three 15-centimeter howitzer batteries, and XI Corps three fortress March battalions, whereas III and XI Corps also divided a 9-centimeter M 75 artillery battery. A major detriment to the shortage of artillery shells was the lack of Dual Monarchy industrial capacity, which failed to produce vital military materiel.[90] The enormous loss of horses also seriously slowed maneuverability, while Fourth Army troops' negative psychological and physical condition hampered effective action.[91]

As the Russians launched their steamroller offensive with their Second, Fourth, Fifth, and Ninth Armies on the German north Vistula front, they hurled additional forces against the Habsburg Second Army, which constantly fought to maintain its lines. The Fourth Army estimated that nine to ten tsarist divisions had been deployed between Jarsolau and the mouth of the San River; thus their counterattacks failed. At Fortress Przemyśl, several enemy regiments had occupied the high terrain opposite Siedliska (Defensive District VI). Great concern mounted relative to replacing the food stores from the citadel.

On October 19, Third Army efforts to advance again proved unsuccessful against defending tsarist rearguard forces. Fortress Przemyśl Artillery Battery Number 5 and mobile reserve guns, in conjunction with Siedliska Defensive District VI support and some Honvéd units, assisted a garrison demonstration launched toward Medyka and the higher terrain opposite that location. Enemy attacks continued against the Habsburg Second and Third Armies.[92] That same day, substantial numbers of Russian troops crossed the San River and launched a major offensive.[93]

On October 20, General Hindenburg commenced a new German offensive operation, moving his troops northward to avoid encirclement.[94] Earlier, on October 18, Ludendorff had secretly ordered a German retreat. The German High Command hoped that the Habsburg First Army would be successful at the battle at Ivangorod, because as long as that army maintained its position, the Germans could launch an offensive across the Pilica River toward Warsaw.[95] On October 23, Hindenburg informed the Habsburg First Army command that his troops would retreat. As the German military situation at Warsaw rapidly deteriorated, it became increasingly doubtful that the Habsburg First Army could maintain its positions at the Ivangorod Vistula River crossing after the Russians launched their own offensive there. As the German troops recoiled from their Warsaw campaign, the Russians also launched an offensive into Galicia, both events forcing a general Habsburg retreat into the Carpathian Mountains when their central and flank positions could not halt the enemy pressure. General Conrad had once again overestimated his armies' capabilities against superior Russian troop numbers. In addition, enemy artillery remained superior to the Habsburgs' in every category, and Conrad did not possess sufficient reinforcements to improve the outcome of the present battle.[96]

The Russian offensive smashed the badly shaken Habsburg First Army. That army's Ivangorod offensive operation was a total failure, costing fifty thousand casualties and resulting in the survivors retreating to the Fortress Kraków area. The unanticipated German retreat, caused by an overwhelming Russian attack, opened First Army positions to an enemy-flanking maneuver. This endangered Habsburg positions along the Vistula River front and exposed the Habsburg Third and Second Army's flank positions at Fortress Przemyśl and Chyrov. Following mutual allied recriminations and allied mistrust resulting from the retreats, the troops withdrew to their original positions by the end of October.[97] The Germans, however, rapidly regrouped their forces to launch yet another offensive, while Habsburg troops withdrew slowly to enable resupply efforts to continue as long as possible at Fortress Przemyśl.

Conrad could not allow his armies to retreat west of the San River's mouth area because it would cause the entire river defensive line to collapse and leave Fortress Przemyśl vulnerable to attack.

On October 22, Conrad ordered the Third Army to hurl the advancing enemy troops from their positions at Radymno and then encircle them to enable the Galician operation to resume. However, tsarist troops prevented the Habsburg Second Army's right flank forces from progressing south of Fortress Przemyśl, and Second Army units had to retreat. This prevented a Habsburg victory south of Fortress Przemyśl. The Second Army also was ordered to halt the enemy advance across the upper Dniester River, which could threaten the fortress. General Conrad argued on October 24 that if his First Army retreated behind the San River, it would become incapable of defending that important river line, and Fortress Przemyśl would again be under siege. When German High Command requested that General Conrad shift more of his forces from the Galician to the Russian Polish front, he declined. He reasoned that shifting troops to that battle area would prevent the decisive success he desired at the southeast Fortress Przemyśl front.[98]

The Habsburg First Army, however, could not maintain its lines much longer because of the major Russian attack hurled against its left flank positions on October 25, which threatened it with encirclement. By that point, significant tsarist forces had obtained a foothold on the other side of the Vistula River.[99] On October 26, Habsburg troops retreated from the enemy forces advancing along the northern Vistula River bank, which effectively neutralized Conrad's offensive plans. Despite its low ammunition supply, the Third Army was ordered to launch an attack near the fortress. The attack failed due in part to the lack of artillery support.[100] The Russians held the strong bridgehead position at Radymno and roads and railroad at Jaroslau, blocking Fortress Przemyśl. Under such circumstances, Habsburg troops had no choice but to retreat. At the same time, the Russians encircled the Second Army XII Corps from the south and attempted to roll up its flank.

Fully operational railroads would be crucial to resupplying the citadel, but the area surrounding Fortress Przemyśl also lacked sufficient railroad connections to maintain such large Habsburg troop numbers. The few connections it did possess were much too small to accommodate the citadel's supply demands. Resupply efforts were also dependent on field army success. Habsburg planners assumed that the Fourth Army would maintain its San River positions, but it could only do so provided that the First Army maintained its positions. Consequently, the entire supply chain threatened to collapse when the First Army had to retreat, but here again, the Russians did not press their advantage.[101]

October 27 marked a very important day for Fortress Przemyśl. Three weeks after its liberation, the railroad line connecting Chyrov to Nizankovice reopened briefly before closing again on November 4. Multiple trains accumulated at the Sanok railroad station to travel across the Zagorz Bridge to the citadel. However, after the reconstruction of the railroad bridges, many had to be further materially reinforced, losing additional valuable time. One in particular, the bridge at Ustrzyki, required seven hours of repair. Even when the railroad bridges had been rebuilt, they could not operate at full capacity, which was necessary to resupply the bulwark. The situation was exacerbated by enemy artillery fire aimed at the various bridges and railroad lines, which reportedly halted railroad traffic and eventually forced traffic along the southern route through Chyrov.

By the end of October, the Habsburg First Army was outmanned and outgunned along the Vistula River front, while the Russians hurled strong units across the San River toward Prussian Silesia. If the First Army had to retreat, it was not a viable option, as it would endanger Habsburg Vistula River positions and expose Third and Second Army flank positions at Fortress Przemyśl and Chyrov. The German military situation west of Warsaw also became increasingly threatened. The events ultimately forced the Habsburg First Army to retreat north of the upper Vistula River, where General Conrad ordered it to hold its lines. Under no conditions or circumstances would it be permitted to retreat. The military situation, however, had become so ominous that it was questionable whether the army could protect even the Nida River line if it had to retreat. The Third and Fourth Armies, meanwhile, held their positions at the San River lowlands and hills south of Fortress Przemyśl.[102]

Traffic conditions in the fortress area proved catastrophic during the last week of October.[103] The few serviceable roads and the hilly terrain surrounding Fortress Przemyśl forced Third Army troops to fight in unfavorable circumstances in late October. Thus, following two days of particularly heavy fighting (by October 28), the Russians hurled back the depleted Habsburg ranks. The Second and Third Armies had to relinquish their strategically important positions, which then became their primary military objectives during the remainder of the year and during the early 1915 Carpathian Mountain Winter War campaigns. The First Army retreated to establish new positions north of Fortress Kraków, and Conrad ordered them to hold those positions as long as possible to facilitate fortress resupply efforts. Unrelenting Russian attacks, however, forced Conrad to allow the First Army to retreat even further back.[104] The retreat, however, threatened to compromise the entire San River line and leave Fortress Przemyśl vulnerable to siege once again.

On October 31, the Russian Third Army crossed the San and the Ninth Army crossed the Vistula. General Ivanov ordered tsarist troops to defeat the Habsburg armies deployed along the San River line. Conrad's armies were now in full retreat mode. He had launched his October offensive in great haste, largely because of his concern that Fortress Przemyśl could not repulse a mass enemy attack. The swift Habsburg retreat from the citadel in late October and early November proved far-reaching and marked the second time that Conrad allowed the fortress to dictate his military operations. The detrimental physical and psychological effects of the harsh troop conditions and poor supply efforts had become painfully obvious during the fall 1914 mountain campaigns. General Conrad nevertheless continued to launch offensives in the Carpathian Mountains in early 1915, even worse conditions than during the October campaign.

By the last day of October, the First Army had completed a rapid, four-day march to its new resistance lines. Its commander raised serious concerns, having reported to General Conrad on October 28 uncertainty about whether his army could defend the ninety-kilometer line extending from the San River mouth with insufficient troop numbers. Two significant problems included the slow supply of ammunition, particularly artillery shells, and whether the troops, in their present condition, could defend their new positions for at least three days.[105]

That persistent enemy pressure forced the First Army to retreat north of the upper Vistula River and the Second Army south of Fortress

Przemyśl to avoid encirclement and major defeat. Third Army units re-treated through the Dukla hollow into northern Hungary, and the Fourth Army defended the Dunajec River front. By the end of the month, the Central Powers' offensive had failed, and their troops were in full retreat. The Russians, already enjoying numerical superiority, deployed approximately two million troops at the Vistula River bend in prepara-tion for a massive Dampfwalze invasion of Germany.

Russian military leaders realized that Fortress Przemyśl had become a significant political and morale symbol, as well as the major Habsburg bulwark. Thus, its capture assumed increasing strategic and psycho-logical implications. General Conrad believed that he could not sur-render the citadel on military, political, and morale grounds. Conrad allowed these factors to overshadow the fact that, after its first siege, Fortress Przemyśl lost much of its strategic significance. In early November 1914, additional factors compelled Conrad not to surrender the fortress, particularly the issue of neutral Italy and Romania.[106] He also had to consider hinterland morale, the effect of the fortress's capitulation on enemy and ally alike, and increasing diplomatic and political concerns, including maintaining Polish sympathy in Galicia. He harbored serious concerns about potential criticism of the Habsburg Supreme Command and the fact that the Austro-Hungarian army con-tinually suffered significant battlefield defeats. Furthermore, the sur-render of the fortress would destroy any possibility for future offensive operations directed to the north to liberate the bulwark, as well as pos-sibly precluding any further Balkan front offensive operations. Consider-ing the fortress's present military situation, General Conrad desperately requested that additional German units deploy to the eastern front to launch a decisive offensive against Russia—the only means by which the fortress could now be liberated.

During early November, before the Russians besieged the fortress again, Third Army commander General Svetozar von Bojna Boroević and the Fortress Przemyśl chief of staff recommended that the fortress be abandoned to its fate. The futile attempts to raise the second enemy siege in November resulted in enormous bloodletting and suffering for the fortress garrison and Habsburg field troops. During the month of November, the Russians temporarily shifted their major operations from the Galician to the northern Polish front to launch their massive invasion of Germany. This removed one of Fortress Przemyśl's major raisons d'être—to protect retreating Habsburg armies and serve as a major Stutzpunkt or military base at the front lines. Furthermore, subsequent claims that the besieged fortress continued to bind significant enemy units were simply untrue. By the end of October, the tsarist Eleventh Army siege forces consisted solely of reserve and third-line units, which proved adequate to neutralize the fortress. Moreover, the October military operations revealed that rapid liberation of the fortress had become highly unlikely.

Once Habsburg troops had recaptured the fortress in early October, Russian soldiers entrenched themselves only a few kilometers east of the citadel walls. South of the fortress, enemy artillery fired at the bulwark railroad lines, and all attempts to drive the enemy back ended in failure. The Russians' possession at Magiera had a significant effect on attempted repairs on the major railroad bridge at Nizankovice. Meanwhile, garrison troops hoped that they would not be besieged again and that the fort remained a strong point (Stutzpunkt) on the Habsburg eastern front. Then fortress inhabitants noticed that dead horses, broken wagons, and vast amounts of equipment covered much of the terrain west of the citadel. Increasingly, large supply trains moved westward, followed by long troop columns moving rapidly away from the fortress. Once again the fortress streets grew empty and silent.

The October 1914 Fortress Przemyśl saga unfolded in phases. During its first siege in late September and early October, the fortress achieved its main mission of binding significant enemy troop numbers, which prevented their deployment against the reeling Habsburg field armies and significantly delayed tsarist pursuits. Immediately upon its liberation from the Russian siege in early October, the fortress bastion became the "solid anchor" for Habsburg eastern front battle. The eleven tsarist siege divisions could have been deployed against Habsburg field armies, but the Russians could not ignore a 130,000-man garrison situated behind their forward lines because it posed a serious threat to their rearward transportation and supply connections. If it had maintained its offensive capabilities, the fortress could also have actively assisted field army operations to a greater extent. Following the early

November siege, attempts to liberate the fortress continued to detrimentally influence Habsburg military operations, just as they had during the first encirclement.

The month had opened with a Habsburg offensive hurling the besieging Russian troops back and liberating Fortress Przemyśl, but the tsarist numerical superiority and massive Dual Monarchy casualties quickly turned the battlefield odds in the enemy's favor. Austro-Hungarian forces could not achieve a military victory even though the Russians had redeployed their Second, Fourth, Fifth, and Ninth Armies (ten corps) to the Vistula River front against Germany, which left only the Third, Eighth, and Eleventh Armies to counter the Dual Monarchy. By the end of October, Fortress Przemyśl faced another siege, as the Habsburg armies again retreated. What would the month of November have in store for Habsburg armed forces? More pertinently, what fate awaited Fortress Przemyśl?

4

✠ ✠ ✠

The Second Siege

NOVEMBER 1914

THE SECOND SIEGE OF FORTRESS PRZEMYŚL OCCURRED IN November as the arrival of cold weather further exacerbated the Habsburg military situation. The Russians threatened to cross the Carpathian Mountains and invade Hungary, a move that very well might have ended the war. The retreat of the Habsburg forces, however, granted the Habsburg Supreme Command some operational freedom.[1] A major battle erupted near Fortress Kraków between November 16 and November 20, as well as on the German front. Once the Habsburg field army had completely evacuated the Fortress Przemyśl area by November 4, the Russians again encircled the San River bastion. Thus commenced the second siege of Fortress Przemyśl, which endured until its final surrender on March 22, 1915.

In early November, Habsburg Supreme Command transferred a large contingent of Second Army units deployed south of the fortress to the German front to assist in safeguarding the vital industrial region of Silesia. This left a weakened Habsburg army to defend the Carpathian Mountain battle zone southeast of Fortress Kraków. Predictably, the Russians immediately sought to take advantage of the new situation.

Throughout early November, the Habsburg military crisis continued. The First and Fourth Armies battled north of Fortress Kraków, while the Second and Third Armies fought below the Vistula River line. Fierce and sustained battle and rampant illness produced enormous Third Army casualties and left the surviving troops utterly exhausted. Between October 29 and November 2, the Russians undertook their second major offensive operation and pushed across the San River. The tsarist Third and Eighth Armies launched an offensive along the vast front extending from Kraków to the Carpathian Mountains, covering hundreds of miles of territory.

Deciphered Russian communications revealed enemy intentions at critical times throughout the war, which often allowed General Conrad to neutralize potentially disastrous situations. For example, Habsburg command learned that the tsarist Fourth Army suffered from supply difficulties and could not rapidly pursue retreating Habsburg troops, particularly lessening the threat to the Fourth Army's left flank forces. Enemy armies pursued the retreating Austro-Hungarian soldiers and hurled seven corps against the Habsburg forces, two to three of them against the First Army's left flank positions. That army, having already sustained severe casualties at the battle at Ivangorod, now also lacked artillery shells to support its hard-pressed troops.

The numerous attempts to liberate Fortress Przemyśl following the renewed tsarist siege on November 4 proved futile. Paradoxically, the October campaign had sealed the fortress's fate. Throughout November, the eastern front gained significance in the overall war picture. The deteriorating Central Powers military situation in that theater and the German failure to achieve victory at the first battle of Ypres in Flanders forced General Erich von Falkenhayn to reassess his options. He determined that the eastern allies had to counter the Russian advance north of the Vistula River; meanwhile, Habsburg Supreme Command established defensive positions at the Fortress Kraków left flank area. Fortress Kraków had become critical for Habsburg operations because it provided an undisturbed crossing of the Vistula River for the planned Fourth Army intervention on that front. It also served as the hinge for the entire Habsburg front.

Turkey also joined the Central Powers in November, which bound Russian troops on the new Caucasus front, but neither factor immediately lessened the Austro-Hungarian army's burden. The Habsburg army launched November offensives despite the enormous logistical difficulties once Central Powers troops regrouped for renewed offensive operations. Army Group Pflanzer-Baltin continued to defend the southern Carpathian Mountain passes, and the Third Army remained deployed in those mountains further north.

By October 29, the tsarist general Ivanov had made considerable territorial gains north and southeast of Fortress Kraków. His four-corps Ninth Army crossed the Vistula River and deployed north of the fortress, while his Third Army, also consisting of four corps, crossed the San River in an attempt to cut off the fortress connections from the south. The Russian Eighth Army, consisting of two corps, advanced westward, applying added pressure from the Carpathian Mountain area. In the interim, the Habsburg army faced multiple difficulties in an effort to avoid retreating southward, which would have severed contact with allied German forces.

On October 27, four tsarist armies pursued the retreating Habsburg forces.[2] By October 31, Conrad's armies were in full retreat. Despite achieving indecisive military success at the San River and in the area south of Fortress Przemyśl in mid-October, Habsburg forces found it impossible to drive the enemy out of its well-fortified defensive positions east of the fortress. On the German front, overwhelming enemy troop numbers had attacked the Habsburg First and German Ninth Armies southwest of Warsaw and at Ivangorod, which forced the First Army to withdraw to the lower Nida River without serious battle.[3] Meanwhile, the subsequent German retreat from the area south of Warsaw also caused the Habsburg Fourth, Third, and Second Armies to initiate a retrograde movement because the German action bared the northern flank of the Austro-Hungarian armies. All Habsburg units desperately required reinforcements to replace casualties and replenish ammunition stores, particularly artillery shells and damaged equipment. In addition, they did not possess sufficient reserve formations, and their troops suffered from extreme exhaustion; thus they required rest and rehabilitation to recover from the recent battles.

The Habsburg First Army, almost encircled by vastly numerically superior tsarist forces, had to retreat, but it could not reach the Nida River before the tsarist Ninth Army attacked its main forces and the enemy Fourth Army units advanced to strike its flank positions. The threatened Habsburg First Army's left flank forces rapidly withdrew to the heights of Fortress Kraków—an area its troops received orders to unconditionally defend. The First Army's retreat movement bared the neighboring Fourth Army's left flank positions, while First Army

Command reported it could not halt a potential enemy night attack because it lacked sufficient reserve units. The army required several days before it would again be combat-ready. As Habsburg Second Army troops approached the Dniester valley and swung north to attack Russian flank positions south of Sambor, they struck new enemy resistance when Russian forces stood fast and halted the Second Army's advance at Stary Sambor.[4]

Meanwhile, the Second and Third Habsburg Armies had originally advanced in unison, but the Second Army immediately had to retreat to establish new resistance lines because the Russians had received reinforcements at the heights of Stary Sambor. The army thus withdrew into the Carpathian Mountains without serious enemy pressure.

The Habsburg First and German Ninth Armies' retreat threatened to break contact between the allied armies in early November. Neither could overcome the enemy's double numerical superiority, and German High Command could not anticipate receiving reinforcements from the western front because of the serious battle situation at Ypres in Flanders. The First Army initially received thirty thousand replacement troops to replenish its ranks. The retrograde movements, as mentioned, isolated Fortress Przemyśl before all the food, artillery shells, and ammunition had been restored from the field armies' looting during the October campaign. A November 1 fortress report revealed that the citadel's bread supplies would last only fifty-six days, meat twenty-five, and vegetables ninety-two. The fortress received one and one-half infantry divisions as reinforcements before the field army retreat commenced from the fortress area, which included the k.u.k. 85th Landwehr Infantry Brigade and the 111th Landsturm Infantry Brigade, as well as Air Flight (Flik) Company 11. Meanwhile, Third Army contingents cleared the fortress perimeter of fifteen thousand bloated Russian corpses.[5]

On November 1, 1914, Archduke Karl Franz Joseph visited the fortress just before the new Russian offensive commenced. Fortress leadership ordered a forcible evacuation of nonessential citadel residents; artisans, restaurant owners, doctors, and the like were allowed to stay. The 23rd Honvéd Infantry Division, assigned again to the citadel as its major offensive force, contained half of its battle stand since its recent battle at the heights at Magiera near the fortress. It had been determined that a reinforcing infantry brigade would be insufficient to replace the recent bulwark losses; therefore, General Kusmanek requested a full infantry division as reinforcements and return of the 23rd Honvéd Infantry Division to its mid-September battle strength and its full complement of artillery and ammunition.

The fortress commander reported on November 2 that fortress food supplies remained inadequate. Much of the available straw and hay originally intended to feed the horses was used to transport ill and wounded soldiers. Kusmanek also complained that nearly all garrison troops still wore their summer-issue uniforms, which were entirely insufficient against the harsh winter weather. Of the seventeen thousand military laborers, half still wore defective summer uniforms and boots.[6]

Because of the renewed threat to Fortress Przemyśl, General Conrad transferred Habsburg Supreme Command headquarters farther behind the front to Neu Sandec. Although a November 1 Habsburg offensive temporarily halted the Russian advance, the army could not obtain a decisive victory because of the enemy's continued numerical superiority. General Conrad lamented the lack of German reinforcements and the failure of the German High Command to place more emphasis on the eastern front, where he believed that a major victory over Russia could be achieved if his ally would transfer significant combat forces there.

General Falkenhayn, however, argued that he could not transfer reinforcements to the eastern front because a military decision in France had to be resolved through an attack against Ypres. Therefore, the eastern front remained a secondary theater, but he suggested that perhaps in six weeks reinforcements could be sent from the west. When those troops finally did arrive, they consisted of only three cavalry divisions.[7]

General Conrad briefed General Kusmanek about the recent Habsburg retreat, explaining that the numerically superior enemy had launched an offensive against the allied German Ninth and Habsburg First Armies west of the Vistula River in Poland. This forced the First Army to retreat behind the Nida River on November 2. The action removed any chance for a decisive Habsburg success at Fortress Przemyśl; therefore, the Fourth, Third, and Second Armies joined the retreat to the west. The Third Army had to remove itself from enemy contact by early November 5. It had advanced a day's march east of Fortress Przemyśl when it encountered strong Russian opposition in strong, dug-in positions after the enemy received reinforcements in the Medyka area. When the Third Army's eastern flank group failed to conquer the high terrain before it, its forces retreated to the Carpathian Mountain Dukla Pass hollow to attempt to prevent a Russian invasion of northern Hungary. The general Habsburg retreat signified that its troops had to surrender their defensive positions at the San River and south of Fortress Przemyśl, which they had conquered earlier at such great human cost.[8]

Fortress Przemyśl retained the same mission as during the first siege. Habsburg field troops received orders to return the previously requisitioned heavy artillery batteries to the fortress. Railroad traffic had to be extended as long as possible before the railroad bridge at Nizankovice was destroyed, while Fortress Przemyśl utilized its military labor sections as infantry troops for future defense of the fortress.

General Conrad hoped that the second citadel defense would be as successful as the first and that the fortress would be capable of repelling all enemy attacks and draw significant tsarist troop numbers to it. If the Russians deployed only weak siege forces this time, the fortress needed to initiate active military measures against their supply and communications connections and rear echelon areas.[9]

While the First Army's left flank units retreated to the Fortress Kraków area to defend the fortress's northern girdle positions, Third Army units passed through Fortress Przemyśl before moving southward. General Conrad refused the First Army's initial request to withdraw further and ordered it to renew resistance at the Nida River, not retreat to the Vistula River, so that the recently initiated resupply of Fortress Przemyśl could continue.

The Russians launched their attack across the San River on November 2, which foiled the Second Army's attempts to encircle the Russian southern flank positions.[10] On November 3, the Habsburg armies retreated behind the Nida and Dunajec Rivers and into the Carpathian Mountains while German Ninth Army troops marched to their designated railroad stations for their next mission. The Fourth Army received orders to prevent the enemy from shifting significant troop numbers against Fortress Przemyśl and to prepare to launch an attack against the enemy's flank positions. This required the army to cross the northern

Vistula River to ensure cooperation with the First Army and German forces deployed west of that river. The Habsburg military situation remained extremely tenuous while major battles simultaneously raged at Ypres in Flanders on the western front and in Prussian Silesia on the German front.

The German Ninth Army, preparing to launch a new offensive endeavor, hurled three rapidly railroad-transported corps toward Thorn, concentrating its main forces between Posen and Thorn at the Vistula and Warta Rivers to attack advancing Russian northern flank formations. The rapid transfer of German troops provided the advantage of surprise when they successfully attacked and temporarily halted the Russian offensive plans on that front. The Germans denuded East Prussia and Silesia of troops to deploy every available soldier against the Russian right flank positions at Lodz-Warsaw and to launch a giant pincer movement to crush the Russian Second Army and any other tsarist forces deployed along the riverfront.

While German troops boarded their trains for their new mission, Habsburg forces retreated from the Fortress Przemyśl area. Between November 11 and 25, General Hindenburg, without waiting for reinforcements from the western front, regrouped the German Ninth Army to launch an attack against the inner flank of the two Russian armies deployed at the northern Vistula River flank. Hindenburg concentrated his attack against the larger enemy assemblage, hoping to drive a wedge between the Russian First and Second Armies near Lodz. The Ninth Army almost annihilated the tsarist First Army and drove the Second Army eighty miles back to Warsaw, claiming to have captured 136,000 Russian prisoners of war.

General Conrad devised a new offensive envelopment plan calling for allied troops to advance between the lower Vistula River and the Carpathian Mountains, similar to his 1914 plans.[11] He sought to support the German operation against Thorn by also commencing a Habsburg assault. He ordered his Third and Fourth Armies to advance between the Dunajec and Wisloka Rivers, cross the Vistula River, and join the First Army's battle. Meanwhile, the Second Army prepared to transfer its major troop formations from the Carpathian Mountains to Silesia by November 5.[12] Thus, the designated troops had to break off battle, and the remaining Second Army troops retreated without sustaining excessive casualties because the enemy did not press them. General Conrad agreed to redeploy the Second Army to the German front to help defend industrial Silesia because of the existing and dangerous 180-kilometer gap in the front lines that invited a tsarist attack. This, however, also opened a large space in Habsburg lines where those Second Army troops had been deployed, which encouraged a Russian offensive thrust into the Carpathian Mountains, particularly after they received sufficient reinforcements.

The neighboring Habsburg Third Army advanced northward to attack and attempt to encircle the advancing enemy troops at Jaroslau and create favorable defensive positions at the San River to provide flank security for its forces. Third Army rearguard units meanwhile retreated from the area southeast of Fortress Przemyśl to the Bircza area. Second Army troops not ordered to be redeployed to the German front occupied key Carpathian Mountain ridgelines near Chyrov, thus its VII Corps had the mission to thwart enemy forces advancing westward from the region below Fortress Przemyśl. Farther south, Army Group Pflanzer-Baltin's mission remained to defend the higher east Carpathian Mountain crossing points and the province of the Bukovina near the neutral Romanian frontier.

The First Army meanwhile received orders to counter the Russian troops advancing south of the Vistula River. If the enemy deployed large troop numbers at the San River and Carpathian Mountain front, the remaining Second Army forces had to attack them south of the mountain ridges. If Russian units retreated, the Third Army had to maintain its position to attack enemy flank locations as they advanced from the area south of Fortress Przemyśl.

Third Army troops retreated on a wide front southeast of Fortress Przemyśl, positioning rearguard troops to prevent or at least delay enemy units from crossing the Carpathian Mountain forelands.[13] Meanwhile, on the Balkan front, General Oskar Potiorek launched a third offensive with the goal of achieving a decisive victory over the pesky Serbian neighbor and gaining revenge for the two embarrassing earlier failed offensive campaigns.

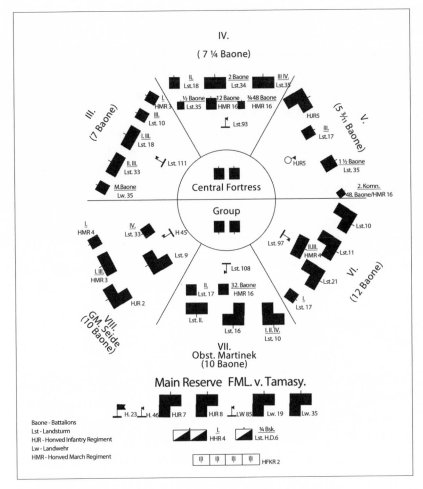

Map 4.1. Situation at the beginning of the second siege, November 1914.

General Kusmanek ordered his garrison troops to write their last letters home because the citadel would soon be besieged and mail delivery halted. On November 5, a fortress inhabitant's diary entry stated that "tonight the post went out and probably for the last time." Two days later, an automobile loaded with mail was stopped by a tsarist cavalry patrol fifteen miles west of the fortress, which forced the driver to return to the citadel. Radio transmissions again became the fortress's only means of contact with the outer world because the enemy quickly severed all telegraph and telephone lines. Aircraft delivered Habsburg Supreme Command orders and some mail to the fortress even as tsarist planes continued to bomb the fortress area.[14] The weather continued to negatively affect battle, and Habsburg forces suffered from a severe lack of regular army officers because of accelerating combat losses.

General Conrad again requested the transfer of German troops from the western front to assist in overcoming the new eastern front military crisis. Because the first battle of Ypres still preoccupied General Falkenhayn, Conrad received a negative reply. In the interim, Conrad intended to contain the Russian advance, but the First Army unfortunately had to extend its retreat to the lower Nida River. When overwhelming enemy numbers also attacked a Fourth Army division, that army had to withdraw as well.

German Ninth Army Command, meanwhile, harbored grave concerns that the Habsburg First Army could not defend its Nida River positions, which in turn would directly threaten their forces. Therefore, they inquired whether Habsburg forces could defend the northern Fortress Kraków area before undertaking a new Vistula River offensive operation. The Habsburg armies had to maintain their present positions for the Germans to have a chance to achieve success, thus they insisted that a Habsburg retreat could occur only in a worst-case scenario and then could not extend west of the Vistula River.[15]

Three Russian armies meanwhile forced Habsburg troops to retreat from the San River line back to Fortress Kraków when they again besieged Fortress Przemyśl. General Ivanov now began to plan a tsarist advance into the Carpathian Mountains to invade Hungary.[16] In the fortress, the fear of an outbreak of epidemics and plague intensified, but a rapid immunization program controlled the number of cases. Many burials continued to be conducted at the fortress, but fewer deaths were attributed to hunger. A large amount of straw and hay had to be utilized to transport the wounded, to the detriment of feeding the horses. When deciding whether to ship artillery shells and ammunition or food to the fortress, Emperor Franz Joseph chose the latter.[17]

The fortress supply effort terminated on November 4, leaving its magazines and depots only half full. Bread supplies would reportedly last for 172 days, vegetables for 214, meat supplies for 111, and hay for 150.

General Conrad's report to the Emperor's Military Chancellery stated that ammunition, technical material, sanitation goods, and fuel supplies now stood far above the required amount. This claim, however, was only partially true because the statistics he cited applied to the original planned number of fortress troops, or 85,000 soldiers and 3,700 horses. The fortress garrison actually stood at 130,000 troops, and between 18,000 and 30,000 civilians and 21,500 horses.[18] If calculated on the actual garrison numbers, the bread supply would last not 111 days but 98 days; vegetables 122 days, not 139; and meat 63 days rather than 72. In addition, no winter uniforms had been supplied, and the troops still wore the field jackets received during the August mobilization period.[19]

Fortress Przemyśl also required the replacement of the multiple artillery pieces that Third Army had removed from the bulwark and utilized for battle, particularly at the bloody battle of Magiera.[20] The fifty-five offensive infantry battalions within the fortress numbered 34,700 troops when the 23rd Honvéd Infantry Division returned to garrison army duty after the liberation of the fortress. General Conrad's prime concern remained resupplying the fortress.[21] The November 4 Habsburg retrograde movement reached the main Carpathian Mountain ridges at the Dukla, Lupkov, and Uzsok Passes to block the key crossing points as Russian units advanced slowly, not pressing the retreating troops.

On November 4, the German undersecretary of state, Arthur Zimmermann approached the Habsburg ambassador, Prince Gottfried Hohenlohe, and suggested the creation of a unified Central Powers command for the eastern front. The German Military Chancellery recommended that Habsburg Archduke Friedrich, nominal commander of the Austro-Hungarian army, become the honorary allied commander, while German general Erich Ludendorff assumed the duties of chief of the Allied General Staffs. This would ensure that General Ludendorff would make the major decisions relative to allied military strategy and operations. General Conrad would remain as commander of Austro-Hungarian forces. Archduke Friedrich favored a unified command structure, but not with a German chief of the General Staff.[22] Conrad, ever sensitive to such German proposals, threatened to resign, perceiving his ally's mistrust in his military leadership and a German attempt to destroy Habsburg military independence.[23] He used every strategy he could conceive of to retain his position as chief of the General Staff, conveniently ignoring that his glaring errors during the July 1914 mobilization and opening campaign had resulted in a disastrous military defeat on the Russian front. Emperor Franz Joseph eventually relented and informed Conrad that he had his full support to remain in his position. The vital question of a unified Central Powers command would be resuscitated numerous times, but it remained unresolved until late 1916, albeit momentarily, to the detriment of allied military fortunes.

On November 5, the last twenty-seven trains arrived at Fortress Przemyśl carrying desperately required ammunition and food. Meat supplies, however, fell far below the expected amount, and were calculated to last only thirty-five days. Even worse, only vanguard units remained deployed south of the citadel after defending troops had been hurled back at Rokietnica. Second Army units received orders to advance as rapidly as possible to the northeast to relieve enemy pressure on the Third Army and to cooperate with it as it retreated south of the fortress.[24]

The next day, Fourth Army units retreated, but saddled with the mission to delay the Russian advance and create a defensive line at the Wisloka River so that the other armies' retreat movements remained unmolested until they could cross the San River. Fortunately, the Russians advanced slowly as their Third and Eighth Armies again moved to encircle Fortress Przemyśl.[25] The Third Army, meanwhile, received multiple and often conflicting orders to regroup, advance to the north, attack the enemy flank units moving west of Jaroslau, and even create a resistance line behind the San River to provide security to the east. The hard-pressed army could not fulfill all of these missions, as its corps troop numbers had dropped to division-size units.

While defending the Nida River line, First Army lines were flanked and sustained numerous casualties, forcing an entire corps to retreat. When the Second Army retreated, it initially deployed its troops east of Chyrov to defend against strong Russian Eighth Army units. After traversing the Carpathian Mountain ridges, the army was forced to retreat even farther because of the arrival of tsarist reinforcements. VII Corps defended the Dukla Pass while IV Corps' main forces maneuvered to the north and northeast to defend the Uzsok Pass. The remaining IV Corps units stretched along the Lisko and Sanok roads to protect the strategic Carpathian Mountain passes and ridgelines to halt further enemy egress to the west. Excessive casualties reduced Habsburg troop numbers to little more than fifty soldiers per infantry company, far below normal unit strength.

Meanwhile, General Kusmanek utilized the available time prior to the renewed siege of Fortress Przemyśl to improve and extend the citadel's outer perimeter lines. In particular, he ordered a new series of completely earthen works constructed at the western and northern fortress positions, increasing the defensive strength of those areas. In addition, thousands of enemy corpses had to be disposed of to prevent the spread of disease, and damaged fortress defensive positions had to be rapidly repaired. General Kusmanek repeated his earlier request to Conrad that the fortress receive no further Ruthenian units because of the fear of treasonous activity on their part.[26] Small units dispatched outside perimeter walls collected supplies and material that the field army abandoned when they retreated.

The fortress's precarious military situation became a major political and morale factor for the Dual Monarchy's armed forces and civilians. The definitive fortress orders not to surrender without serious resistance became somewhat suspect, particularly when the field armies failed to defend the citadel. Once the field army units retreated from the fortress environs, the bulwark's mission remained to repel enemy offensive efforts, disrupt its rear echelon and communications lines, and bind as many troops as possible. Because tsarist offensive storm tactics had failed in October, General Conrad surmised that the enemy would now besiege the citadel with fewer troops and not attempt to seize it by force. While General Kusmanek prepared the citadel for its renewed siege, the Fourth Army successfully battled advancing Russian troops in the Jaroslau-Wisloka River area, which assisted its retreat movement and forced some tsarist units back across the San River. The Russians then established defensive positions along the river, providing security to the east. Major Russian forces also cautiously advanced south of the Vistula River.[27]

On November 5, as the field armies withdrew from the Fortress Przemyśl area, 85th Landwehr Infantry Brigade's Infantry Regiments 19 and 35 entered the fortress to replace 23rd Honvéd Infantry Division losses sustained during the bloody battle of Magiera. For almost a month, the fortress had served as a major bastion on the eastern front. General Conrad meanwhile became concerned about which tsarist units remained to besiege the fortress, because major troop numbers had been reputedly transferred to the Carpathian Mountain front. Fortress reconnaissance missions confirmed that the tsarist XXVIII Corps—consisting of the 58th, 60th, 69th, and 82nd, as well as one-fourth of the 78th Reserve Infantry and the 12th, 15th, 19th, and 31st Infantry Divisions—now besieged the bulwark.[28] Various historical sources, however, disagree on the exact Russian siege troop dispositions during this time period because of the various enemy units diverted into the Carpathian Mountains for the attempt to invade Hungary.

The renewed encirclement of Fortress Przemyśl, initially at the eastern and southeastern fronts, dealt a major blow to Habsburg army prestige. General Conrad allowed the fate of the fortress to exert increasing influence on overall Habsburg eastern front military strategy. Therefore, he reasoned that every means possible must be attempted to liberate the fortress before it would be forced to capitulate. At the same time, tsarist general Ivanov ordered his armies to continue to advance west from the Dunajec River area between the Vistula River and the Carpathian Mountain forelands to penetrate the major mountain ridgelines. Thus, the Russian Eighth Army advanced and proceeded to occupy critical positions in the mountain approaches, particularly at Bircza, Sanok, and Chyrov. General Ivanov planned to launch a major offensive on his front even though Stavka had prioritized a major invasion into German Silesia for Russian armed forces.[29] Meanwhile, Third and Eighth Russian Army troops encircled the fortress while deploying some other forces into the mountains. General Ivanov ordered the Eleventh Army to surround the fortress and release the earlier siege troops, while the XX and VII Corps and 9th and 11th Cavalry Divisions advanced to the eastern, southern, and western fronts of the fortress. The tsarist XII Corps deployed at Bircza near the blockading forces, while half of the XXIX Corps mobilized at the northern fortress front. Then the two Russian armies advanced toward the Dunajec River and the Carpathian Mountains.

November witnessed significant inclement weather, which had a negative effect not only on the fortress civilians and the garrison but also on the pilots who flew mail, Habsburg Supreme Command orders, and medicine to and from the fort. The airmail service had originally been established to increase fortress morale, but it was also one of the few supply sources that remained open. The same pilots performed reconnaissance missions whenever weather conditions allowed it, but also at times when it proved extremely dangerous to fly. During several days in November, no such flights could even be attempted (for example, November 9, 11, 12, 14, 15, and 17).[30] Despite the dangers, reconnaissance flights proved vital to strategic planning. Key surveillance targets included the area between Radymno and Nizankovice, the critical railroad bridge location near Fortress Przemyśl, and the Russian artillery battalions deployed near Medyka. Flights also extended from Tarnov to Fortress Kraków.

Weather conditions were consistently unfavorable and included snowstorms, fog, low-lying clouds, shifting crosswinds, and sleet. Compasses did not function in fog, and the winds constantly varied in direction. Counterwinds toward the homeland made flights especially dangerous. Landing aircraft at the fortress was a difficult task, and turbulent winds made it challenging to simply gain altitude once in the air. Enemy antiaircraft fire made the unfavorable conditions even more deadly. Fortress airplanes lacked spare parts, and their Mercedes engines proved overly sensitive to cold temperatures, which caused them to freeze in midair. Pilots claimed that their earlier aircraft had been better. Despite the continuous difficulties, the pilots continued to cling to their motto: "We fly in any weather."

On November 3, Flick (airplane) Company 14 was redeployed from the fortress to the airfield at Jaslo, while Flick Company 11 replaced it at the fortress. No airplane units had been deployed in the fortress during the first siege. One reconnaissance mission located two thousand Russian supply wagons in several separate supply trains, which was immediately reported to army headquarters.[31] That particular flight covered the area of Sadova-Sambor and Chyrov before returning to the fortress. During the mission, enemy artillery attempted to shoot the plane down. In the meantime, Habsburg field army supply trains began to retreat, the plane flights helping to distract tsarist forces and camouflage the retrograde activity.

On November 4, a new airfield was constructed at Iworksi at the eastern perimeter of Fortress Przemyśl. The location had the advantage of being concealed from enemy sight and protected from direct tsarist artillery fire. Another airfield at Zuravica was located in the northern fortress area. During the next several days, pilots continued to encounter numerous hindrances owing to the weather, particularly the constantly shifting winds. Although a three-hour reconnaissance flight managed to scout the Russian front on November 7, poor conditions grounded many planes or forced them to return to the airfield shortly after takeoff.[32]

The weather worsened on November 20, blanketing the fortress environs in snow and making flights even more hazardous. A strong sortie was launched from the fortress's southwest front on that day, the main force advancing toward Cisova while a secondary force moved toward Krzywcza and the high terrain at Zubenica. The action proved inconclusive, serving to do little more than expose the garrison troops to the starving inhabitants of villages in the surrounding area. Soldiers took to scavenging the fortress forefield areas for potatoes, beets, and fruit as the temperature plummeted. By November 23, the temperature had reached $-7°C$.

Stavka's plans to invade Silesia required the continuation of its offensive operations south of the Vistula River against Habsburg forces. Meanwhile, with its main forces situated west of the fortress, the Habsburg Third Army's mission became to defend the Carpathian Mountain invasion routes to the Hungarian plains through the Dukla and Lupkov passes. The mass of that army deployed at the northern base of the mountains, whereas west of the fortress environs it had to establish new positions. Tsarist troops routed the Third Army's rear echelon detachments at Rokietnica and swiftly occupied key positions to complete the siege of the bulwark.[33] Though inclement weather and terrain conditions, poor communications, and insufficient resources ensured that the mission would be extremely difficult, a tsarist invasion of Hungary had to be prevented at all costs. The Third Army and the remnants of the neighboring Second Army were given the dual mission of preventing an enemy advance into western Galicia while defending the Carpathian Mountain main crossing points—neither task an easy one. This proved particularly difficult once the Second Army had transferred major units to the German front, thus seriously weakening the Carpathian Mountain area.

Enemy intentions, meanwhile, remained a mystery to Habsburg Supreme Command.

When General Ivanov ordered the Eleventh Army to besiege Fortress Przemyśl, Second Army Command proposed to General Conrad that its army launch a powerful attack against the advancing left flank Russian forces. While the plan might have provided a military victory, it would have had little effect on the overall Habsburg military situation. General Eduard von Böhm-Ermolli then suggested that a portion of his army be transferred to the German front.[34] When the Second Army received the orders to transfer some of its troop formations to the German front, it also received new missions for both operational theaters. On the German front, it had to defend against an enemy invasion toward Silesia through the enormous gap in the front. In the Carpathian Mountains, the remaining army troops had to defend the mountain ridges to prevent a tsarist invasion of Hungary while its designated units transferred to the German front. In conjunction with Third Army forces, which now had to extend their front lines from the Carpathian Mountain forelands to the upper Dunajec basin, remaining Second Army units had to secure the critical crossing points between the Dukla and Uzsok Passes.[35]

The Habsburg army troops' deteriorating conditions and chronic absence of reserve formations raised serious concerns about the declining morale and inadequate training of replacement troops who were deployed immediately to the front, where they became cannon fodder. Because of the severe shortage of rifles, wooden stocks had to be substituted for the weapons during the recruits' basic training. Not surprisingly, the combat preparedness of replacement troops declined precipitously. Training time continued to decrease owing to the constant need to replace the severe casualties, and many howitzers now lay silent on the battlefield because of the lack of shells.[36] The loss of professional officers, noncommissioned officers, and regular troops continued at an alarming rate, leaving Fortress Przemyśl with only 34,700 offensive troops at its disposal. Although the fortress's main offensive unit, the 23rd Honvéd Infantry Division, now totaled 11,200 troops, it was supported by 93rd Landsturm Infantry Brigade (3,000 troops), 97th Landwehr Infantry Brigade (6,000), 111th Landsturm Infantry Brigade (3,000), 108th Landsturm

Infantry Brigade (3,085), 85th Landsturm Infantry Brigade (4,000), and a March Regiment (1,500).[37]

A fortress sortie attempted to ascertain the composition of the enemy siege forces, while small excursion parties continued to search for equipment and food stores outside fortress perimeters that the retreating field armies had discarded. Citadel inhabitants could only pray for peace. They recognized that the field armies could not liberate the bulwark in the near future because of the unusually cold temperatures and deep snow. Many soldiers questioned how they could survive and lost all hope for survival. By November, horses were being slaughtered to provide more food for the troops. In the meantime, the lack of straw and surrogate mixtures to feed the unfortunate animals had rendered them little more than skin and bone. The garrison had almost no potatoes, vegetables, salt, sugar, coffee, tea, bread, or matches available. Smoking had become costly, but alcohol and sauerkraut supplies still remained in stock. In the interim, the enemy continued to fire shrapnel shells into the fortress.

As Habsburg field armies continued their retreat movements, Fortress Przemyśl lay farther and farther from the front lines. The Russians therefore conducted a slow, systematic siege with the goal of starving the garrison into submission, the opposite of the speedy offensive military action they conducted during the first siege. In the interim, the Russians deployed strong infantry forces at the key Galician railroad junctions while pursuing the retreating Habsburg forces. Once their troops attained the area of Radymno-Jaroslau, they established an effective siege of the fortress and advanced troops into the Carpathian Mountains and to the Dunajec River.[38]

On November 5, tsarist forces attacked First Army left flank positions, which neutralized its resistance. The army withdrew its troops from the Nida River area, sacrificing one-third of its troop numbers while lacking adequate ammunition supplies for its combat missions.[39] Meanwhile, the Russians threatened to encircle the army's northern flank positions, which might sever their retreat routes. Conrad ordered the Habsburg armies to avoid major battle until the First Army had retreated far enough that the Russian offensive either slackened or halted because of ensuing supply difficulties.

During the late afternoon of November 5, the Russians pressed toward Chyrov while Habsburg Third Army Group Karg and Second Army's VII Corps protected the assembly and transfer of Second Army troops designated for deployment to the German front.[40] Simultaneously, the mass of Third Army, III, IX, and XI Corps, retreated into the Carpathian Mountain northern forelands, partly because of the lack of indication of enemy intentions. It remained unclear if the Russians would rapidly launch an offensive or if their present weakness, resulting from mounting casualties, an outbreak of cholera in their ranks, and the extraordinary sacrificial efforts from earlier operations, would force them into a defensive posture.

Meanwhile, the Habsburg liaison officer to the German Command headquarters, reported that the German Reserve Corps that had been protecting the First Army's left flank positions would be transferred to protect the Silesian frontier on November 6. Thus, early on November 5, Conrad ordered the First Army to retreat to the high terrain at Fortress Kraków. He also ordered Fourth Army to rapidly march to the First Army area and deploy troops at the Vistula River stretch extending from the Dunajec River mouth to protect the area between the two armies.

On November 6, tsarist troops reached the high terrain at Tyszkovce, while three regiments approached Nizankovic. Strong enemy infantry units besieged Fortress Przemyśl, while daily patrols were dispatched north of Mackovice. These and other troops attempted to salvage automobiles and telephone equipment from Dynov. The enemy had advanced quite far west, indicating that the siege had occurred much more rapidly than anticipated.

Also on November 6, Habsburg Fourth Army IX Corps received orders to protect the Third Army northern flank as it continued its retreat. Fourth Army troops had already retreated behind the Wisloka River. The next day, intelligence reports indicated that tsarist troops had shifted toward the Nizankovice area of Fortress Przemyśl.[41] Meanwhile, Second Army's Command Staff, IV and XII Corps troops, and a cavalry regiment deployed at the Carpathian Mountain extreme left flank area began their march to railroad boarding stations for their transfer to the German Vistula River front at Silesia. This action vastly increased the

threat of a successful Russian invasion into the Carpathian Mountains
and onto the Hungarian plains, but protection of Silesia now received
priority in the Central Powers' calculations because they could not surrender it to the Russians. When it became evident that the Second Army
would transfer troops from the Carpathian Mountain front, tsarist forces
sought to take advantage of the opportunity by attacking this weakened
section of the Habsburg front. Third Army troops had to fill the ensuing
gap in the Habsburg army's front lines and extend its already thin front
lines resulting from the Second Army's redeployment. The Second Army
transfer also signified that the major Central Powers eastern front military decision would occur in Russian Poland.

Habsburg railroad bureau officials originally estimated that it would
require ten days to transfer the designated troops to the German front,
but this proved overly optimistic. Repeated delays and stoppages along
the railways significantly slowed the transfer, adding multiple days to the
original estimate.[42] The remaining Carpathian Mountain Second Army
units established defensive positions at the crossings between the Uzsok
and Dukla Passes, which assisted the Third Army's difficult mission to
protect those key positions against tsarist attack.

The Third Army's November 7 mission became to slow the enemy
advance along both sides of Fortress Przemyśl and then westward into
the mountainous terrain. If enemy pressure there became too great, the
army had to retreat to the southwest, but if the Russians advanced into
the mountains, the Third Army had to neutralize them.[43]

Two days after the field armies retreated from the bulwark, and the
first day of the second siege, the fortress launched an infantry regiment
sortie toward the Nizankovice area that reached the forward Russian
lines at Batycze before enemy reinforcements neutralized the effort.[44]
The next day, the Fourth Army received orders to deploy to the Fortress
Kraków area once it had reached the Dunajec River. By November 9,
security measures allowed the troops to assemble at the army's new positions near that fortress. The Fourth Army passed through the Fortress
Kraków zone to attempt to cross the Vistula River.[45] Third Army forces
meanwhile established defensive positions to secure the key railroad connections to the Uzsok Pass and important Mezölaborcz communications
and railroad center while cooperating with Army Group Pflanzer-Baltin,

which still defended the eastern (southern) Carpathian Mountain passes and had the mission to bind enemy troops on that front.

The Russian Third Army had meanwhile advanced to both sides of Rzeszov from Dynov by November 8.[46] The Eleventh Army, with half of the XXIX Corps, deployed north of the fortress, while XXVIII Corps and 9th Cavalry Division encircled the fortress from the east, south, and west. The Russian XII Corps deployed in the area of Bircza near the blockade army, while Eighth Army units marched into the Carpathian Mountains. During early November, the tsarist 65th Reserve Infantry and 12th Siberian Schützen Divisions reinforced the Eleventh Army.

Tsarist forces completed their encirclement of the citadel between November 8 and November 11, utilizing the inclement weather conditions to sever all rail and road access to the fortress. The Russians remained generally passive during the month, satisfied with starving the garrison into submission. The new tsarist Eleventh Army, consisting of four to five reserve divisions and the 19th Infantry Division (XII Corps), became the main siege forces of Fortress Przemyśl.

Along the southern fortress perimeter, General Kusmanek fortified his defensive lines and established new forward outposts and resistance lines, which expanded the bulwark's maneuver area to launch future sorties at the key sections at Na Gorach, Batycze, Helicha, and Pod Mazurami. Massive defensive artillery barrages thwarted enemy efforts to approach the fortress perimeter.

General Kusmanek could not immediately confirm which tsarist units had deployed behind the forward siege lines. He had reason to believe, however, that his Russian counterparts knew the layout of Fortress Przemyśl. At one point during the siege, a pilot, Nicolaus Wagner-Florheim, showed him the photographic reproduction of a secret map of the citadel that had been confiscated from a dead Russian captain. The map revealed all of the permanent works, strong points, and interval artillery battery locations to be constructed in case of war. Kusmanek believed that all tsarist company commanders possessed a copy of this reproduction, reputedly as clear as the original map.[47]

The Habsburg offensive continued on the Balkan front, with the Sixth Army achieving some battle success. On November 8, Conrad traveled to the Neu Sandec headquarters in a car through pouring rain.

The Neu Sandec headquarters proved equally temporary, however, and would be relocated to Teschen in early December.[48] In the interim, the main Habsburg Third Army forces deployed at the Dukla Pass, while the Russians maintained close contact with the Third and Fourth Armies between the Uzsok and Dukla Passes. Positions at Turka, which protected the approaches to the Uzsok Pass, had to be defended as long as possible, otherwise all Habsburg right flank units would be forced to immediately retreat into the rearward Carpathian Mountain ridges. VII Corps troops continued to occupy San River crossings to protect Second Army units preparing for their rail transport to the German front during the next two days. Increasing enemy XXIV Corps troop numbers soon crossed the river, however, forcing another Habsburg VII Corps retreat.[49]

The tsarist 71st and 78th Reserve Infantry Divisions, along with other units, were transferred to the upper San River area to be deployed near the Uzsok Pass. General Ivanov anticipated that the obsolete fortress could not hold out very long, whereas General Conrad continued to predicate his plans on Fortress Przemyśl to the great disadvantage of Habsburg field army operations. Thus, hundreds of thousands of lives would be sacrificed on both sides of the battlefield in futile rescue attempts, the fortress's so-called Schuldkonto guilt.[50]

The decision to maintain a larger than necessary garrison at Fortress Przemyśl behind enemy lines with no means to quickly lift the siege would later haunt General Conrad. Although recent battles and disease had reduced the garrison combat strength by 20,000 soldiers, the garrison numbers remained close to 130,000 soldiers and 21,500 horses.[51] Approximately 30,000 civilians (10,000 more than Austrian sources often claim) also remained in the fortress, 18,000 of whom the military had to feed, further depleting the citadel's food supplies. Within the fortress, troops accumulated goods and supplies by scavenging through shops deserted by their owners. The search for food also extended to abandoned private dwellings, though officers typically did not partake in these efforts. A fortress inhabitant's diary entry revealed that officers with one-hundred kronen notes went to the back entrances of bakeries and received closed boxes of goods. No one knew the contents of the smuggled packages.[52]

The Russian Eighth Army seized strategic Carpathian Mountain passes, particularly the forelands of Dukla Pass, while the tsarist Third Army pressed the Habsburg Third Army back into the Carpathian Mountain passes between the Vistula River and mountain forelands between November 10 and 19. The German Ninth Army retreated from Silesia to concentrate its forces between Posen and Thorn at the Vistula and Warta Rivers in preparation for a new offensive operation. By November 19, the Russians had seized the Uzok Pass and important railroad connections at Cisna and Lupkov. The Habsburg General Staff realized that it had to restore its battered reputation, especially relative to Italy and Romania (Italy because Vienna refused to yield to its repeated territorial demands for compensation), but its troops suffered from widespread battle fatigue and questionable fitness for actual combat.

Meanwhile, the First Army finally broke contact with the enemy and arrived at its new resistance lines northwest of Fortress Kraków. Its commander informed General Conrad that his army was in no condition to launch an attack against the Russians and that he did not know how long he could hold his new positions, in part because the artillery, supply trains, and other necessary units protecting the armies' left flank positions had not arrived. The army anticipated an overpowering Russian attack against its unfortified defensive lines, ultimately forcing it to have to retreat. It remained questionable whether the First Army could halt new enemy attacks from the numerically superior enemy before the Fourth Army launched its ordered offensive. Even if it managed to do so, the Fourth Army's ability to launch a rapid flank attack from the Fortress Kraków area was severely limited due to the effects of strenuous marches and casualties from earlier battles.[53]

Habsburg calculations on November 9 placed General Selivanov's besieging Eleventh Army at four infantry divisions and half a cavalry division, or barely one-half the number of troops used in the first siege. Fortress Przemyśl's role, therefore, had been seriously diminished, effectively rendering it a secondary military theater. General Kusmanek still had no knowledge regarding which tsarist units had been deployed behind the closest siege troops.[54]

Specific defensive positions had to be maintained as long as possible before Third Army right flank units could retreat into the Carpathian

Mountains.[55] Strong enemy forces attacked the Third Army's left flank positions when the Russians advanced slowly to the west.

Fortress Przemyśl sorties continued to be launched whenever the besieging enemy forces remained passive in an attempt to prevent the transfer of siege troops to the main battlefield and disrupt their transport movement. Fortress Kraków's role for military operations north of the Vistula River became increasingly significant. Meanwhile, Fourth Army formations attacked advancing Russian troops as Second Army IV and XII Corps troops boarded trains for their transport to redeploy in Silesia.[56]

The deteriorating Central Powers eastern front military situation forced General Falkenhayn to review his options while he continued the Flanders Ypres offensive following the western front "Race to the Sea." He informed Conrad that if the Ypres offensive did not achieve the long-sought victory, he could possibly transfer four to five army corps to the eastern front.[57] General Conrad, meanwhile, prepared his First and Fourth Armies to launch a new offensive.

The Fourth Army assembled its XVII Corps at the Dunajec River on November 10 with strong security forces deployed along the Vistula River stretch that extended from the mouth of the Dunajec River to the west. During the night, the remaining Habsburg forces at Fortress Kraków prepared to attack the Russian forces approaching from the south.[58]

On November 11 and 12, Russian activity increased along Fortress Przemyśl's northern perimeter as part of its Vistula River operations, while Habsburg air reconnaissance flights reported long tsarist infantry and supply columns marching west and southwest of the fortress perimeter, indicating the possibility of an enemy retreat. General Kusmanek wanted to ascertain the tsarist units participating in the siege and thus ordered that prisoners be taken. It was discovered that the tsarist 82nd Reserve Infantry Division to the northwest of Defensive District III and the Russian 9th Cavalry Division had deployed to besiege the western perimeter of the fort. The sortie troops scavenged for food during their missions.

The First Army had to maintain its present positions northwest of Fortress Kraków. The Fourth Army, also deployed in that area and west of the fortress, would utilize the citadel flank protection for security and then, in turn, attempt to attack enemy flank positions. However, the threat remained that the Russians could advance into the 180-kilometer gap that existed between the allied armies on the German front.[59]

During the early days of the second fortress siege, garrison units scavenged for food outside the citadel's perimeter as the Russians tightened the siege operation. The previous defensive improvements initiated at Pod Mazurami–Helica offered better protection for Defensive District VIII. The new forward troop deployment lines extended north to the Na Gorach–Batycze and Radymno positions and toward Rokietnica to protect the approach roads and fortress city from enemy artillery barrages. Fortress artillery fire continued to halt Russian attempts to rapidly approach the fortress perimeter, but enemy forces nevertheless somewhat improved their positions.[60]

Also, on November 11, the German Ninth Army assembled to launch a new offensive between the Warta and Vistula Rivers. Habsburg Supreme Command continued to have no indication of enemy intentions, but assumed that tsarist commanders planned to continue to advance in a western direction as the Russian Third Army advanced slowly into western Galicia. The Habsburg Third Army had retreated to the Carpathian Mountain ridges to establish several protracted defense lines, particularly at the Dukla depression, but also the Uzsok Pass and Cisna railroad center. The neighboring Fourth Army deployed units south of the Vistula River toward Fortress Kraków. Third Army corps units divided into two groups, the III and IX to the Dukla Pass depression, and the XI to the Gorlice area to cross the Vistula River and attack the Russians.[61]

Between November 10 and 19, the Third Army's mission entailed protecting the approach to the Uzsok Pass by creating several lines of defense while simultaneously being hard pressed by the enemy and then forced to retreat. During that frantic activity, the Fourth Army conducted intensive reconnaissance missions northeast of Fortress Kraków, where serious battle soon erupted. The army had just completed eight exhausting days of forced marches, finally resting on November 10.[62] On the Balkan front, the Habsburg offensive continued with Serbian forces in full retreat.

General Ivanov ordered his Third Army to advance to the Dunajec River; tsarist troops had surrounded Fortress Przemyśl and traversed into the Carpathian Mountains. His Eighth Army's mission remained to hurl the Habsburg defenders behind the northern Carpathian Mountain passes. The Tsarist Eleventh Army continued to besiege the fortress, while other Russian troop units threatened to capture the Uzsok Pass. General Ivanov determined to launch a major offensive on November 12 where the main tsarist concern entailed the dangerous flank threat emanating from the northern Carpathian Mountain front.[63]

The tsarist advances to the main Carpathian Mountain ridges, which forced numerous Habsburg retreats, led General Ivanov to detect the possibility of obtaining a major military victory at this "point of least resistance" along the Hungarian frontier. However, an operation of this magnitude would require reinforcements, which could only be obtained from the tsarist German front. Ivanov planned to encircle the Habsburg right flank troop concentrations to enable the launching of a Russian invasion of Hungary to end the war.

The Habsburg First Army prepared to launch an offensive from its southern flank area when the Fourth Army initiated its northern Vistula River bank offensive to attempt to push to the northeast to hurl the tsarist flank positions back. But as the attack commenced, the Russians launched their own offensive against the First Army. The Germans had prepared to attack on November 12, but Conrad wanted to wait until reinforcements arrived from the western front, and the Second Army had already deployed in Silesia before his troops joined the effort.[64] Meanwhile, the Russian army had attacked on the German front, threatening to invade Prussian Silesia.

Also on November 12, General Kusmanek launched a sortie toward Nizankovice to disturb tsarist supply movements because air reconnaissance discovered long troop columns and numerous supply trains moving west toward the sortie area.[65] General Kusmanek launched the sortie with Honvéd Infantry Regiments 7 and 8 (six battalions) and Landsturm Infantry Regiments 19 and 35 (six battalions and four artillery batteries) from the 85th Landwehr Infantry Brigade to intercept and disrupt enemy troop movements shifting toward Rokietnica. The operation also sought to protect Third Army eastern flank forces by drawing as many troops as possible from them as they advanced toward the fortress from the area of Radymno. Launched in three columns, the sortie ultimately compromised seventeen infantry battalions and eight to ten artillery batteries. The action surprised the enemy, which had initially pushed its forward fortified positions back to Rokietnica, prompting the Russians to rapidly dispatch reinforcements from east of the San River to contain the breakout attempt. This made any further garrison effort senseless; thus, the troops retreated into the fortress after dark, having sustained only minor losses.[66] A fortress inhabitant's diary entry on that day revealed that sixteen villages had been burning for a week; evening skies appeared blood-red from the flames. The troops destroyed the hamlets to prevent the enemy from utilizing them. Most peasants returned to the villages confused and distraught as they watched their homes burning. Habsburg officers often left the villages with children wrapped in their greatcoats. In one case, a three-year-old child was deposited in an orphanage that was already full because so many children had become lost when their parents fled rapidly from their burning homes. The diary also mentioned the transport of wounded children to the fortress hospital.[67]

Meanwhile, Defensive District VII Command reported that the tsarist 81st Reserve Infantry Division had replaced the 12th Infantry Division in the siege lines. At Defensive District III, in an attempt to prevent additional tsarist troops from crossing the San River, a detachment attempted to seize the high terrain at Kijov as Russian units crossed the San River and advanced to the south.[68]

The Russians meanwhile launched their November 12 offensive on the German Silesian front while continuing their operations in the southern Vistula River area.[69] Russian Third Army units struck key Habsburg positions, while the army's VII and XII Corps supported the siege of Fortress Przemyśl. Tsarist forces, which had already launched a broad attack against the key Turka positions on November 10, forced a Habsburg retreat from that key position that they did not disturb. Turka was the key to possessing the Uzsok Pass.

On November 12 and 13, Habsburg decoders intercepted numerous tsarist wireless messages, which revealed that the Russians planned to launch their Ninth, Fourth, and Fifth Armies toward Fortress Kraków on November 15. General Conrad, nevertheless, renewed his army's offensive efforts even though the enemy pressed his troops along their entire front. His strategy entailed the First and Fourth Armies attempting to roll up the Russian front at Fortress Kraków while providing the necessary security to the east. The long-range operation failed, however, resulting in a Habsburg retreat to the area of Limanova, where the Russians pressed over the Dunajec River toward Neu Sandec. Fighting recurred in this area until mid-December, forcing Habsburg Supreme Command to transfer its headquarters to Teschen. Meanwhile, a Habsburg Third Army counterattack drove the Russian Third Army back to the transportation center at Gorlice.

General Conrad also planned for the Fourth Army, opposed by an equal number of enemy troops, to launch an attack to liberate Fortress Przemyśl after any Third Army battle success.[70] The Third Army's main objective became to seize the major railroad centers at Lisko and Sanok, which became the Carpathian Mountain winter campaign objectives in 1915 when unsuccessful earlier. Fortress Przemyśl launched a supporting sortie in that direction to assist Third Army offensive efforts. Air reconnaissance reported the shifting of tsarist troops to the west and southwest, which resulted in the sortie being launched toward Rokietnica on November 17–20. However, a Russian counterattack against Third Army right flank offensive units and the concentration of Russian units close to the fortress forced the sortie troops to retreat into the citadel and the Third Army to terminate relief efforts. The Third Army offensive operations collapsed as the attacking Russians also defeated the opposing Habsburg First and Fourth Army offensive from the Fortress Kraków area.

On November 14, General Kusmanek reported that two Russian frontline divisions (the 15th and the 31st) had been transferred from the southern citadel front. At Defensive District III, a sortie was launched to seize the high terrain at Kijov to prevent the Russians from crossing the San River to the south and another one toward Rokietnica to protect the troops' left flank positions. For the moment, Russian forces did not pressure Habsburg units in the area, but continued their threatening advances to conquer the key Carpathian Mountain crossing points.[71] Meanwhile, winter weather had settled in the Carpathian Mountains, and heavy snow fell on November 19. Frigid weather conditions ravaged the ill-provisioned soldiers, many still forced to wear their summer-issue uniforms. Fortress perimeter forefield listening post troops continued to suffer greatly as frostbite took an enormous toll on them.

During mid-November, only tsarist reserve troops besieged the fortress—the 82nd Reserve Infantry Division on the north and northwest fortress fronts, the 81st on the southwest, and the 59th, 60th and 69th on the south and southeastern fronts. The 9th Cavalry Division still deployed along both sides of the San River at the western fortress front, while the 74th and half of the 78th Reserve Infantry Division had reputedly established positions at the northeastern perimeter area. Meanwhile, during the next few days, the first major battles erupted in the Carpathian Mountain passes.[72]

Battle raged around Fortress Kraków as well. The Russians had launched their major offensive operation in the Vistula River region. They also reached the key Dukla Pass in the Carpathian Mountains while threatening Lupkov and Uzsok Pass positions. During the second half of the month, conquering the Dukla Pass region remained the tsarist goal.

On the German front, the Ninth Army succeeded in driving a wedge into the Russian left flank at Lodz, completely surprising the enemy defenders. When five German corps broke through tsarist lines, the opposing tsarist First Army again narrowly escaped annihilation while the Second Army retreated to Warsaw. Faced with potential military disaster on this front, Stavka canceled its plans for an offensive into Silesia. Instead, its Second and Fifth Armies had to transfer troops to relieve the battered First and Second Armies, which retreated toward their major supply center at Lodz. During the ensuing battle (November 16–25), the German Ninth Army barely escaped defeat. Two weeks later, however, reinforced by four infantry corps transferred from the western front, the Germans finally seized Lodz, but then struck a mass of Russian reserves that outnumbered their troops two to one. Seven tsarist corps awaited the German advance around the perimeter of Lodz.[73]

As battle raged at Lodz, the Habsburg armies again teetered on the brink of disaster. On November 16, the Russian Ninth Army pressed the Habsburg Fourth Army back to Fortress Kraków, while the tsarist Third and Eighth Armies advanced into the Bukovina. The ensuing battle at Kraków lasted from November 16 to November 22. A more than 100-kilometer gap now separated the Habsburg Fourth and Third Armies; thus the Russian attack threatened to hurl Habsburg forces back through the Carpathian Mountain passes into Hungary. Only Russian command ineptitude and the arrival of the full-strength German 47th Reserve Infantry Division stemmed the tsarist tide in early December at the battle of Limanova-Lapanov, discussed in the next chapter.

Also on November 16, General Conrad learned that German rein-forcements from the western front would be redeployed to the east on November 22, assuming no military problems occurred there in the in-terim. The following day, in an attempt to force a more precise commit-ment from General Falkenhayn, Conrad reiterated that Austro-Hungarian armed forces had borne the brunt of the Russian 1914 offensive efforts launched by a numerically superior force of fifty Russian divisions. He complained that the longer the delay in transferring reinforcements east, the greater the likelihood of a Russian invasion of Hungary. Habsburg forces at Fortress Kraków meanwhile had the mission to delay the Rus-sian westward march, as additional tsarist troops continued to deploy into the Carpathian Mountains. Habsburg Third Army forces reentered the Carpathian Mountains badly weakened, in dire need of reinforce-ments and rehabilitation, and bloodied from months of difficult offensive and defensive battle to prevent a tsarist advance beyond the Hungarian frontier. The Third Army could not defeat the two opposing tsarist armies, but it continued efforts to halt the enemy Eighth Army despite having to retreat.

The Russian Eighth Army unleashed an attack on November 17 toward the Dukla and Uzsok Passes, while General Conrad launched a surprise assault against the flank and rear of the Russian VIII and XXIV Corps. The Habsburg Fourth Army's eight divisions advanced against the enemy right flank positions with one unit moving against the flank and rear of the two tsarist units.[74] Conrad became increasingly con-cerned when the tsarist Eighth Army advanced through the Carpathian Mountains against the weakened Third Army at the key Uzsok, Beskid, and Dukla Passes. The enemy Third Army also hurled three corps toward the area between Gorlice and Tarnov. The situation at Fortress Przemyśl, however, remained unchanged.

General Conrad contemplated launching a new Fourth Army offensive operation to strike the Russian lines of communication east of Fortress Kraków leading toward the Carpathian Mountain crests. The Fourth Army aimed to cripple the Russian southern flank formations advancing from the Vistula River line. Railroads transported Group Roth (XIV Corps), and the German 47th Reserve Infantry Division prepared to launch a surprise attack into the gap that separated the Russian Third and Eighth Armies in the Carpathian Mountains as soon as military success could be achieved north of Fortress Kraków. This maneuver would also take pressure off Fortress Przemyśl to the south. However, Russia's numerical superiority continued to overwhelm the struggling Habsburg armies. Third Army corps numbers had declined steadily until they equaled mere infantry division stands. Meanwhile, the tsarist Third Army swung toward Fortress Kraków after recently passing north of it.

Major battle continued on the northern Vistula River front on November 18 as the German Ninth Army (nine infantry divisions) continued to advance toward Lodz against the tsarist Second and Fifth Armies. On the Balkan front, the enemy reportedly had commenced a full retreat; the Habsburg Fifth Army XV Corps had attained the crucial Kolubara area, and XVI Corps secured Valjevo, both key offensive objectives.

The Habsburg Third Army's hundred-kilometer separation from the Fourth Army created a tense situation because of the danger that the Russian Third and Eighth Armies might advance into the gap toward the Hungarian frontier. Meanwhile, a major portion of Second Army troop units continued their delayed railroad transport to the German front. General Conrad determined to transfer some Habsburg Fourth Army units to the southern Vistula River area to halt the increasing Russian pressure. The Fourth Army launched an attack to roll up the opposing enemy flank forces where Habsburg troop numbers had been greatly reduced because of the major battle that raged on the Russian-Polish front. Fortress Kraków continued to block tsarist forces from invading Austrian provinces as well as German Silesia, as battle and reconnaissance reports indicated that the enemy now prepared to unleash another major offensive in Russian Poland.[75]

The Russian Third and Eighth Army offensives launched along the entire front between Kraków and the Bukovina now extended into the Carpathian Mountains. Tsarist forces seized the Lupkov and Dukla Passes as their Eighth Army increased pressure against the isolated Habsburg Third Army, still struggling to defend the main Carpathian Mountain ridge lines.[76] The Russians, halted at the Dukla depression, because the farther west they progressed, the more vulnerable their northern flank positions became to counteraction from Habsburg and German forces.

Tsarist efforts to advance security troops closer to Fortress Przemyśl's southern perimeter failed, resulting in the enemy siege forces sustaining serious losses. Still, the overall Habsburg military situation worsened when Russian forces continued their westward advance. For the Habsburg forces, military success on that portion of the front was critical. The Russian Third Army continued toward Gorlice, the major transportation hub in that area. General Falkenhayn pressured Conrad to launch an offensive into the northeast corner of Serbia to open the Danube River for supply transit to the new Turkish ally, but Conrad replied that he had no available troops for such an operation and emphasized that it would give Romania an excuse to enter the war. He also insisted that the allies required Bulgarian assistance for such an undertaking.[77]

As battle intensified toward the end of the month, Conrad deployed some troop units previously positioned southeast of Fortress Kraków into the Carpathian Mountains. Since multiple Second Army units had been transferred to the German front, the Third Army's eleven infantry divisions, the remaining Second Army troops, the Fortress Przemyśl garrison, and Army Group Pflanzer-Baltin's irregular forces had the mission to defend the Carpathian Mountain crossings, which extended for hundreds of kilometers. When tsarist generals convened at Siedlice, General Ivanov advocated launching a major offensive into the Carpathian Mountains. Stavka reluctantly accepted his proposal, which entailed its four Ninth Army corps advancing north of Fortress Przemyśl close to a major Habsburg Fourth Army defensive position. The tsarist Third Army would attack the fortress after obtaining a victory at Gorlice. The Habsburg Third Army battled in a snowstorm without winter-issue uniforms, resulting in increased numbers of troops suffering and dying from cold-related illnesses, frostbite, and exposure.[78] The army remained tasked with several difficult missions. It still had to prevent a Russian invasion of Hungary while simultaneously binding enemy forces at the northern Vistula River area to halt their westward advance.

Further indications of tsarist troop movement prompted another Fortress Przemyśl sortie consisting of six infantry battalions and three artillery batteries from Honvéd Infantry Regiments 7 and 8 and Landsturm Infantry Regiments 19 and 35. A total of fourteen battalions, one cavalry squadron, and seven artillery batteries ultimately participated in the operation, which received support from Defensive District VIII artillery. Group Letay, consisting of eight infantry battalions and three artillery batteries, moved north toward Cisova between the San River and the local roads. A Group Komma (six battalions and one artillery battery) and an additional detachment had the mission to both secure the sortie troops' northern flank and seize the high ground at Kijov to prevent additional Russian units from crossing the San River.

Troops in fortress forefield positions had no oil and therefore no light during the long, cold winter nights, and could not sleep because of the unrelenting artillery fire. The pressure and tension had become so pervasive that they could not adequately perform their assigned military duties; many of them became apathetic. Starving, marching soldiers could not pause for even a second for fear of freezing to death. They even had to carry wood from the forests because of the lack of draft animals. One soldier came within one hundred meters of his position while doing so, sat down, and died. Not surprisingly, desertions also increased.[79]

Fortress patrols heard distant artillery fire, which raised hope for the garrison troops. Rumors spread throughout the citadel that an offensive had been launched to liberate the fortress by Christmas. The sound of cannon fire remained the only connection between the fortress and the outside world. Thus, everyone cheered when the cannon fire sounded close but sank into apathy when it became distant. Official fortress reports, however, contained no information about Habsburg field armies approaching the fortress. During one period, after artillery fire was heard for three days, it became silent. When the thunder of salvos vanished, so too did any hope of liberation. Artillery fire and optimism went hand in hand, building and destroying hope with the ebb and flow of battle. On

New Year's Eve cannon fire could again be heard, but it quickly dissipated as the internal fortress situation continued to worsen.[80]

On November 20, as the first snow fell, Fortress Przemyśl troops
launched a powerful sortie, with the main offensive force advancing
toward Cisova, ultimately consisting of eighteen infantry battalions and
eleven artillery batteries. A secondary attack group advanced into the
San River valley toward the important Nizankovice rail junction. The
enemy momentarily retreated, incurring considerable casualties at its
western and southern flank positions as its forward siege lines were
pushed back to the heights of Krzwcza.[81] This, however, did not prevent
the enemy from transferring three divisions (the 12th and 19th Regular
and the 81st Reserve Infantry Divisions) from the siege army to the
Carpathian Mountains in the Dukla Pass area. The besieging Eleventh
Army now consisted of only six infantry and one cavalry division composed almost entirely of reserve troops. Such caliber units did not pose
a significant military threat to the garrison but nevertheless proved
sufficient to maintain the siege. Assured that time remained on his side,
the tsarist siege commander remained passive at Fortress Przemyśl
during much of November, although artillery duels erupted late in the
month. Third-line territorial formations, in turn, replaced tsarist siege
reserve divisions. Thus, by the end of the month, Russian blockade troop
numbers had diminished, having transferred numerous units to other
fronts elsewhere, because Fortress Przemyśl had decreased in military
importance.[82]

Disregarding the unfavorable conditions, a flight arrived at the fortress carrying badly needed medicine. The extreme cold weather of the
next few days (dropping as low as −7°C) prevented any flights from departing the fortress, but an incoming plane braved a snowstorm to deliver mail on November 23. Two Aviatik aircraft arrived on November 26
to reinforce the aerial units at the fortress, but the winter conditions and
the thick fog cover in the San River area continued to prove unfavorable
for flight. Any flights to and from the fortress were risky, even for experienced pilots. The windy conditions made it difficult to gain an altitude
higher than seven hundred meters and forced most planes to fly as low
as one to two hundred meters for long durations. Flight operations were
further hampered by the lack of spare parts for aircraft.

Despite these challenges, fortress aircraft did conduct a number of successful reconnaissance missions. The most critical involved the surveillance of the area between Radymno and Nizankovice. The vital railroad bridge near Nizankovice was an essential supply line that the fortress could not afford to lose. Aircraft reconnaissance missions also searched for enemy positions, particularly artillery battery locations. Several scouting flights also extended from Tarnov to Fortress Kraków.

By November 21, the Habsburg front stagnated as supply efforts continued to be bogged down. Temperatures plummeted to −13°C, and the troops increasingly suffered from frostbite. In the interim, the four-corps-strong Russian Third Army advanced westward toward Limanova, preceded by strong cavalry forces along the Dunajec River route beginning at Neu Sandec.

Third Army Command ordered that stiff defensive measures be established on all mountain routes leading into Hungary until there was a military decision in the Fortress Kraków area. The newly formed 200th and 201st Honvéd Infantry Brigades provided fresh impulse to the army right flank positions, where reinforcements were most desperately required to halt the advancing tsarist forces.[83] However, the Third Army's right flank Group Krautwald had to retreat before these reinforcements arrived at the front.

On the same day, Stavka launched counterattacks on the German front, creating a crisis by threatening German Ninth Army rear echelon positions. German reinforcements arriving from the western front remained too few and arrived too late to positively affect the battle. The northern Vistula River Lodz campaign now provided little possibility for success because of the Russians' numerical superiority. Increased Russian pressure on the Habsburg front also encountered little resistance as the military situation worsened south of Fortress Kraków. An overpowering Russian Third Army attack soon dislodged weak Habsburg covering troops defending their portion of the fortress front.

By November 22, it had become obvious that any further Habsburg offensive operations could only result in disaster. This was particularly true for the Third Army, whose extreme troop exhaustion affected its capability to fight effectively. Third Army troops rapidly retreated as fierce battle erupted north of the Fortress Kraków area. Recent enemy successes forced General Conrad to revise his plans. The tsarist Eighth Army's swift advance necessitated the deployment of additional troops to defend the Carpathian Mountain passes to protect Hungary from tsarist invasion; his Third Army proved too weak to accomplish that mission. Supply efforts remained tenuous, temperatures plummeted, and snowstorms and frostbite continued to ravage the field armies. Although Habsburg troops had reached the extreme boundaries of their physical capabilities, they still received orders to hold their positions!

Russian forces unleashed a major offensive in the Beskid Pass area between November 22 and December 2. Thus, the Habsburg Carpathian Mountain military situation worsened just when the Germans momentarily appeared to be gaining a decisive victory at Lodz. Habsburg VII Corps retreated in great haste after launching a brief counterattack when Russian columns broke through its lines and forced it back to the Dukla Pass. The intermixed units of four different infantry divisions defended the southern mountain ridges, the Lupkov Pass, and the heights west of that area.[84] General Boroević ordered his Third Army IX Corps to retreat during late November 22 when VII Corps failed to hold the frontier heights at the critical Laborcza valley. The defensive lines on the steep Lupkov-Beskid Pass ridges could no longer be defended while the XXIV Russian Corps right flank formations advanced to the Lupkov Pass.

When tsarist forces reached the vital upper Laborcza River area, they forced the Habsburg VII Corps rearward toward the key transportation and communications center at Mezőlaborza. The threat increased that a Russian battlefield victory could prevent a Habsburg retreat through their rearward connections to the homeland. Faced with the dangerous possibility of being cut off from potential retrograde routes, the exhausted and intermingled corps troops (20th Honvéd and 17th Infantry Divisions) received orders to counterattack the advancing enemy regardless of their present military situation.

Meanwhile, Conrad redeployed an infantry division from the north Fortress Kraków front to its southern perimeter area to launch a surprise attack into the gap that separated the Russian Third and Eighth Armies. This served as the background to the early December Limanova-Lapanov battle. The Habsburg Third Army, its front overextended and troop stands weakening, nevertheless had to continue to bind the Russian Eighth Army on the Carpathian Mountain front.[85] Conrad's armies countered the eleven-division-strong Russian Eighth and Third Army infantry and cavalry forces. The Habsburg Third Army's severely weakened III, VII, and IX Corps forces had retreated on November 23. Habsburg and Russian troops crisscrossed the mountainous terrain, which soon after would be drenched with the blood of innumerable soldiers during the 1915 Carpathian Mountain winter campaigns (January 23 to mid-April).

The Habsburg military situation at Fortress Kraków worsened as the Russian Eighth Army simultaneously hurled weak Habsburg covering troops back to the mountain regions that protected Hungary. Between November 24 and 28, Habsburg forces surrendered the critical Dukla, Lupkov, and Beskid Passes to the numerically superior enemy. The Habsburg Fourth Army battled against the enemy's eight-division Fourth Army and fourteen to fifteen divisions of the Russian Ninth Army. North of that battle zone, the Habsburg First Army continued to suffer serious losses in its continuing battle, while the situation at Fortress Przemyśl remained unchanged. In the midst of the Habsburg military crisis, General Falkenhayn again suggested the launching of a Habsburg offensive against Serbia.[86] Unfortunately, General Conrad did not possess the troop numbers necessary for such an operation, as his troops remained threatened on the Russian front.

Enemy forces attacked the Habsburg positions on the Uzsok Pass on November 25, where fighting continued throughout December. Then, on November 26, Habsburg units on the north Vistula River front had to retreat. The German 47th Reserve Infantry Division, with its full component of troops, deployed where General Conrad now envisioned launching a surprise offensive. By attacking from south of Fortress Kraków, Conrad could utilize the reinforcing German division to relieve pressure on his Third Army, while halting enemy progress toward the Hungarian frontier. Accordingly, the Fourth Army's XIV Corps received orders to advance to the Fortress Kraków area even as Russian armies continued to press that army's eastern flank forces rearward. Conrad countered this enemy movement by launching a surprise encircling maneuver with three Fourth Army divisions attempting to envelop the enemy positions south of the Vistula River to halt their westward drive toward Fortress Kraków. The Habsburg First Army, after receiving critically needed reinforcements, had to unconditionally defend its front area northwest of that fortress, a critical factor in Conrad's planning.[87] The Russian Third Army meanwhile shifted some of its troop units northward toward the fortress to attempt to turn the Austro-Hungarian right flank positions, sever General Conrad's potential retreat route, and further isolate Fortress Przemyśl.

The Fourth Army's XIV Corps, later designated Group Roth, expanded to eight infantry and three cavalry divisions and became the main offensive force against the enemy flank and rear echelon positions. Major battle commenced in the Fortress Kraków area during late November, which again brought significant battle into the Carpathian Mountain region. Since Fortress Kraków presently served as the hinge of the entire Austro-Hungarian eastern front, it had to be unconditionally defended and tsarist pressure neutralized. As four Habsburg corps redeployed in preparation for the new offensive operation, the Third Army retreated again after another heavy tsarist attack. During the night of November 27, two and a half Russian corps smashed into the Third Army's weakened three corps' defensive lines, threatening to pierce the defending army's front. The Third Army's situation became increasingly critical as its exhausted troops sustained excessive casualties. A severe shortage of ammunition, particularly artillery shells, as well as other necessities such as winter uniforms, added to the soldiers' misery and misfortune.

As battle raged in the Carpathian Mountains, Habsburg VII Corps barely maintained its defensive positions just as tsarist troops prepared to attempt to encircle Third Army left flank units. The nearly crippled Third Army found it extremely difficult to halt the incessant Russian attacks. Hungry, cold, and exposed, the Habsburg troops suffered enormous losses from frostbite, freezing to death, and illness.

Although the Fortress Przemyśl situation remained generally static, the Russians strengthened their defensive siege positions against any renewed sortie attempts. Available tsarist heavy artillery pieces were transported to the Fortress Kraków area to participate in the escalating battle.[88] Also on November 27, strong Russian Reichswehr (third line troops) formations deployed at the fortress perimeter launched an attack against the often-targeted Na Gorach-Batycze positions. Fortress artillery fired barrages from Na Gorach against the Radymno railroad and roads, as well as toward Rokietnica and Sosnica.

As an example of the condition of troop formations, Infantry Regiment 74 reported temperatures at $-15°C$, with brutal winds battering its exhausted soldiers. The regiment had not received food provisions for four days, while battalion strength had sunk to 200 to 250 rifles, instead of the usual 1,000, and those few troops defended front lines that stretched eight hundred to two thousand paces. Such small troop numbers prevented the creation of reserve formations and resulted in gaps forming in the front lines. The Russians skillfully utilized the terrain features and unfavorable weather conditions to camouflage their frequent nighttime attacks against Habsburg positions. One such tsarist attack captured an entire regimental staff, resulting in a unit retreat.[89]

At this point, the Austrian official history of the war states that the replacement Czech troops arriving at the front had been poisoned by antimilitary and dynastic propaganda. Allegedly, Czech troops also could not stomach the demands of the winter mountain warfare, and many reportedly surrendered to the enemy and became prisoners of war.[90] Meanwhile, under horrendous conditions, Habsburg forces deployed at the upper Laborcza valley and Dukla Pass could no longer halt the irresistible Russian pressure.

On November 28, the enemy assaulted the fortified Fortress Przemyśl positions at Batycze, Na Gorach, and Helicha–Pod Mazurami, again utilizing the inclement weather conditions to achieve surprise when they stormed the defenders. Four tsarist battalions attacked Na Gorach positions, but fortress artillery barrages halted the attack about a thousand meters from the defenders' positions during the early morning hours. Tsarist artillery fire inevitably halted at dusk to camouflage their battery positions. Enemy losses proved significant. Fortress troops launched a counterattack two days later, and by the end of the month the Fortress Przemyśl situation had returned to normal.

During the night of November 28, a tsarist attack commenced against VII, and then spread to III Corps positions before attacking other Third Army units, which quickly found themselves in an extremely difficult military situation in the Mezölaborcza area. The Dukla Pass defensive area remained threatened from its rearward positions as VII and III Corps retreated. The Third Army had the mission to prevent the transfer of enemy forces from the Carpathian Mountains to the Galician front while still defending the mountain crossings into Hungary. However, the army could not accomplish this mission because its III, VII, and IX Corps, all in overall terrible conditions, had become involved in serious battle, and as a result of extreme tsarist pressure that rolled up the front, the troops had to retreat.[91] Unrelenting tsarist pressure to seize the key Carpathian Mountain passes stemmed partly from the Russians' determination to secure their left flank positions in preparation for a major invasion of Silesia. Likewise, tsarist attacks to the southwest of Fortress Kraków endeavored to seize the key mountain passes in that region. This enabled tsarist forces to advance further toward the Przemyśl bulwark. Favorable battlefield reports from the Balkan theater encouraged troops fighting in the Carpathian Mountains to continue their efforts regardless of their condition.

Fortunately, the Russians halted their pursuit of the Third Army's units, but they maintained serious pressure against its IX Corps positions. If IX Corps could not maintain these positions along the important invasion routes, Third Army left flank positions could be enveloped. It remained unclear whether the badly battered Habsburg troops could halt another Russian attack, particularly given IX Corps' extremely unfavorable situation and its troop conditions.

No special events occurred on November 29. Both sides utilized the time to technically improve their defensive positions. General Conrad, however, realized that the Third Army desperately required reinforcements to replace its disastrous losses. When the Russians commenced withdrawing troops from the Fortress Przemyśl area, General Kusmanek launched a sortie on November 30 from Defensive District IV at Baty-cze–Na Gorach, which introduced the bloodiest and most active month of the second siege. The operation, which the 85th Landwehr Infantry Brigade's Regiments 19 and 35 (six battalions) reinforced, did not achieve its objective to halt tsarist troops pressing against their fortified positions at the forefield position east of Makovice despite great human sacrifice.

Following the battle, the surviving troops returned to the fortress after ascertaining opposing enemy dispositions.[92]

By November 29, General Ivanov had achieved considerable progress on the Fortress Kraków front. His Third Army had advanced to attempt to isolate the fortress from the south. The Eighth Army simultaneously increased pressure on the Carpathian Mountain region as tsarist troops pursued the rapidly retreating Habsburg Third Army. To his astonishment, General Boroević soon received orders to occupy the main Carpathian Mountain passes and deploy his main troop entities rapidly toward Fortress Kraków while continuing to assure protection of his army's left flank positions.[93]

The newly created Fourth Army Group Roth, initially composed of the 2nd, 8th, 13th, and German 47th Reserve Infantry Divisions, received orders to launch an offensive on December 2. As the month of November ended on a negative note for the Austro-Hungarian army, there was great concern about what fate December had in store for the unfavorable Habsburg military situation. Could the unrelenting Russian pressure be halted after the numerous Habsburg battlefield defeats, and could Fortress Przemyśl survive much longer? Could the Fourth Army finally halt the steady enemy advances and force them to retreat from the Fortress Kraków area? The month of November had been a pivotal time for Habsburg military fortunes. Fortress Przemyśl had been besieged again and Habsburg troops forced back into the Carpathian Mountains.

What fate awaited the Austro-Hungarian military efforts in December?

5

✠ ✠ ✠

Limanova-Lapanov and Defeat

DECEMBER 1914

IN EARLY DECEMBER 1914, THE HABSBURG ARMY HAD THE MIS-
sion to halt the relentless Russian westward pressure. Though the influx
of tsarist troops into the Carpathian Mountain passes posed a critical
military threat as they became more active, the Austro-Hungarian army
simply lacked sufficient troop numbers to counter them. Furthermore,
three and one-half months of continuous fighting and marching had seriously weakened its forces. Division strengths had been reduced from
12,000–15,000 soldiers to 2,000–3,000, and Slavic national replacement
troops reputedly proved unreliable in battle, a foreboding sign that undermined Austro-Hungarian troop morale on the Carpathian Mountain
front. There were serious deficiencies in transporting artillery shells,
which steadily worsened, while Fortress Przemyśl artillery capabilities
also began to decline rapidly. Gun tubes deteriorated and could not be
replaced, thus effective artillery range dropped precipitously. Shells had
to be conserved, and certain caliber rounds had already been depleted,
placing multiple guns out of action.[1] How long the fortress could endure
its siege depended to a great extent on the number of horses available for
duty to provide artillery maneuverability and sortie efforts. Nevertheless, General Conrad remained fixated on his military objectives—to
liberate Galicia and Fortress Przemyśl by outflanking tsarist extreme left
flank positions, despite the fact that the prewar-trained k.u.k. Armee had
all but disappeared on the bloody battlefields. On December 1, at a conference in Posen, General Ludendorff argued that he must receive reinforcements on the eastern front to prevent Austria-Hungary from being
defeated.

Given the deplorable battle and supply conditions and the transfer of much of the Habsburg Second Army troop components to the German front, postponing further offensive efforts until spring seemed plausible, but General Conrad desperately needed a major victory against the Russians to restore the damaged Habsburg military reputation after so many battlefield defeats. In early December, the Dual Monarchy was gravely embarrassed by the defeat on the Balkan front, creating an extremely unfavorable military situation in that war theater and destroying any remaining Habsburg prestige in the Balkan Peninsula. The German military command pressured General Conrad to rectify that inglorious defeat, but the primary motivation for his launching a Habsburg offensive in the Carpathian Mountains stemmed from the threat of neutral Italy and Romania entering the war (partly because the Habsburg government had refused Italy's demand for territorial concessions to maintain its neutrality). Both countries sought to obtain irredenta lands from the Dual Monarchy, but awaited definitive battlefield results against Austro-Hungarian forces before entering the conflict to assure easy seizure of these desired territories. As a result, a decisive change in the unfavorable Habsburg military situation appeared unlikely in the near future. The perilous frontline gap between Fortress Kraków and the Carpathian Mountain ranges continued to widen while Russian Third Army troops maneuvered from the Fortress Przemyśl environs. Meanwhile, the Galician and Polish fronts settled into a semi-trench line.

By December it had become evident that the Russians' numerical superiority, combined with unfavorable terrain and weather conditions, would negatively affect any attempts to liberate Fortress Przemyśl. However, the declining fortress food supply and worsening troop conditions demanded rapid action. An effective offensive operation to liberate the citadel could be launched only from the Carpathian Mountains, about eighty kilometers from the fortress.

December thus introduced an especially difficult and eventful month for Habsburg military fortunes. Fortress Przemyśl continued to launch costly sorties, while the exhausted and demoralized Third Army continued its efforts to liberate the fortress. Mounting casualties and the chronic shortage of troop numbers, including a lack of reinforcement and replacement troops, posed a serious problem. The declining Habsburg troop numbers also resulted in a series of daily military crises. Unrelenting battle, long marches, sickness, and frostbite claimed many lives. In addition, the campaign region's lack of suitable roadways and its reliance on a single-track, small-capacity railroad line made the rapid transport of any available troops, supplies, and reinforcements an enormously difficult task.

The Habsburg retreat into the Carpathian Mountain range in early December left the major mountain crossings unprotected, and pitched battle soon erupted at the critical Laborcza valley railroad center at Mezölaborcz. Military action in this region continued until the loss of Mezölaborcz in February 1915, which proved detrimental to all efforts to liberate Fortress Przemyśl, as its two-track railroad line was absolutely necessary for such an operation.

Despite these hardships, the battle of Limanova-Lapanov, fought between December 2 and 11, finally produced the first major Habsburg military victory over previously undefeated tsarist forces. The objective of the offensive focused on driving tsarist troops back across the Vistula River. During the ensuing battle and the resulting fifty-kilometer enemy retreat, the Russian Eighth Army suffered 70 percent casualties, and the effort succeeded in momentarily thwarting the threat of a tsarist invasion of Hungary. The Russians also had to abandon their efforts to invade Germany because of a serious threat to their right flank positions, a threat caused by their previous defeat and retreat. Consequently, Habsburg forces temporarily regained the initiative and extended their front to Gorlice, where major east-west railroads intersected and a successful Central Powers offensive ensued in early May 1915 after the 1915 Carpathian Winter War debacle.

The Russians had recently seized the critical Dukla Pass and constructed a defensive line, which extended to the Uzsok Pass. Habsburg post-battle reports emphasized the enormous losses sustained during recent battles and the extraordinary troop efforts expended under the harsh weather and terrain conditions. The troops suffered enormous hardships while fighting twenty-four-hour battles with no protective cover from enemy artillery fire and no regular meals and supplies. A continuing loss of active duty officers, noncommissioned officers, and soldiers led to declining battlefield effectiveness and slackened discipline in the ranks. The ever-present extreme exhaustion also accelerated troop apathy. War weariness took root, particularly in Vienna, and refugees continued to flee from Galicia, the Bukovina, and Poland into the Habsburg homeland.

The early December Limanova-Lapanov campaign, which had a major effect on Fortress Przemyśl, involved thirteen Habsburg infantry and four cavalry divisions (90,000 troops) attacking eleven to thirteen Russian infantry divisions (100,000–120,000 soldiers). On December 1, Habsburg eastern front forces totaled only 303,000 troops, having sacrificed almost a million soldiers since the initial August 1914 campaigns. On December 1 and 2, the Russians launched heavy forays at the Carpathian Mountain Beskid Pass, while the Habsburg Third Army, having sustained enormous casualties and teetering on the brink of exhaustion following its three-week November campaign, enjoyed a short rehabilitation period between December 2 and 7.

The Fourth Army's XIV Corps, Group Roth, received reinforcements on December 1, and the German 47th Reserve Infantry Division, en route, arrived within a few days. The Fourth Army launched an offensive on December 3 with a strong right flank against the opposing tsarist Third Army's southern flank forces.

But even at the onset of the ten-day Limanova-Lapanov campaign, the surviving soldiers of the Third Army had lost much of their will to fight. Technically, III Corps no longer existed after being reduced to less than half the number of an infantry division stand. IX Corps' battle worthiness had also been decimated. Following eleven days of marching and thirty-five in combat, the army received an order to intervene in the ensuing Limanova-Lapanov battle. In their weakened physical condition, Third Army troops marched only fifteen kilometers a day toward the Fourth Army battlefield.

At Fortress Przemyśl, the worsening food shortage prompted the slaughter of thousands of horses, which increased the meat supply, added fat for cooking purposes, and helped alleviate the scarcity of straw and hay. With rationing and the slaughter of horses, estimates had the fortress's food supplies lasting until early March. Troops foraged outside the fortress walls for frozen vegetables, while requisition commissions confiscated food from civilians on several occasions. Horse meat, originally a despised commodity, became a delicacy.[2] Water had to be boiled because it was germ-infested due to the contamination of most wells. Bread portions, however, were reduced, as were vegetable and meat rations, including horse meat.

December 2 proved decisive for Third Army fortunes because the Russians removed at least three army corps from that army's front, allowing the Third Army several days of rest and rehabilitation.[3] The month heralded the commencement of significant Russian military activity at Fortress Przemyśl. On December 1, strong tsarist assaults renewed against the critical fortress Defensive District VI perimeter position at Na Gorach. General Kusmanek immediately launched a sortie against the enemy group's left flank position that forced an enemy retreat. Nevertheless, the Russians continued their assaults against this sensitive forefield position.[4]

Fortress operations assumed greater significance with the commencement of the battle of Limanova-Lapanov on December 3. To bind the siege troops, General Kusmanek launched a sortie composed of eighteen and three-quarters infantry battalions and fourteen artillery batteries in coordination with the field army's new offensive effort to liberate the citadel. Several smaller efforts were initiated from other sectors of the fortress as well.

Utilizing the cover of early morning fog on December 8, Russian troops overran the key Na Gorach blocking positions' forward defensive lines. Meanwhile, General Kusmanek learned that a powerful Russian counteroffensive had forced Third Army Group Krautwald, entrusted with liberating the besieged citadel, to retreat. This disheartening report coincided with the setback at Na Gorach. Unbeknownst to the garrison troops, they had just experienced their next to last major sortie effort until the disastrous fortress breakthrough attempt on March 19, 1915, on the eve of its March 22 capitulation. Throughout this period, the distance separating the fortress and the field armies proved too great for field army success, and thus all attempts to liberate Fortress Przemyśl failed.

The Germans attempted to force the Russians behind the Vistula River in their Lodz campaign, while Habsburg forces received the minimum mission to bind opposing tsarist formations so that the Russians could not shift sizable troop numbers against the advancing German forces.

On December 3 and 4, tsarist troops cautiously approached Third Army positions along the ice- and snow-covered Carpathian Mountain ridgelines, particularly near the critical Dukla and Uzsok Passes. If the Russians had completely captured the entire Dukla and Uszok Pass territory, Habsburg forces would have lost their main defensive flank position. The Third Army, having suffered multiple defeats in the Carpathian Mountains in November, now lingered on the verge of a fatal collapse from battle exhaustion. The troops suffered from cholera and typhus in the snow- and ice-covered mountains 120 kilometers from the evolving Fourth Army battle.

Fourth Army Group Roth (XIV Corps) launched its major offensive effort, consisting of three infantry divisions, northward toward Limanova against advancing enemy forces on December 3. They targeted the Russians' most vulnerable position: a sixty-kilometer gap between their Third and Eighth Armies that offered the greatest opportunity for Habsburg victory. Tsarist troops, however, successfully countered Group Roth's offensive efforts. At the same time, a Habsburg defensive group, having encountered forward units of the Russian Eighth Army's VIII and XXIV Corps, was forced back to Limanova, a small village located at the Russians' flank position. A race commenced on both sides of the front in the general direction of the town of Neu Sandec, and Group Roth deployed small cavalry forces to probe the roads in that direction.

Habsburg Supreme Command ordered its weakened and exhausted ten-division-strong Third Army to prepare to support the new Fourth Army offensive, although it remained over one hundred kilometers from the main battlefield. Then, on December 4, the Russians perceived the danger posed by the Habsburg Fourth Army offensive operation and quickly began to reinforce their threatened flank positions. Russia, like Austria-Hungary, had to obtain a major battlefield success, otherwise Italy, Romania, and Bulgaria might be swayed to forgo their neutrality and enter the conflict on the opposing side, which both opponents mistakenly believed could decide the course of the war. On the Balkan front, the Serbian defeat of Habsburg forces followed an initial capture of Belgrade on December 2. News of the capture of Belgrade improved Habsburg civilian and army morale incredibly, sweeping aside the negativity caused by the November Carpathian Mountain battlefield events. Emperor Franz Joseph could now appear momentarily in public again. Belgrade had to be evacuated after a successful Serbian counterattack against the overextended Habsburg Sixth Army. This embarrassing defeat placed additional pressure on the tenuous situation at the Habsburg eastern front.

The three humiliating 1914 Serbian battlefield defeats—in August and September, but particularly the December fiasco—also seriously affected other future Habsburg military operations. The German Foreign Office and High Command urged General Conrad to participate in an allied offensive to conquer the Negotine (northeastern) sector of Serbia, which would restore Habsburg military honor and prestige while simultaneously opening a secure supply route to provide necessary ammunition and equipment to their new Turkish ally. A Balkan victory could also serve to convince Bulgaria to finally join the Central Powers; however, General Falkenhayn informed Conrad that he could not transfer additional German troops from the hotly contested western front for the proposed Habsburg operation. Conrad replied that he could not provide Habsburg soldiers for a Balkan campaign either, because his troops were currently tied down on the Russian front.[5]

General Falkenhayn's eastern front strategy entailed hurling the Russians behind the San-Vistula River lines and reducing their offensive capabilities. Meanwhile, the German Ninth Army gained additional territory with its victory at Lodz against the ten-division-strong Russian Fifth Army. On the Habsburg front, the Third Army mission became to bind Russian Eighth Army troops, sever the last major tsarist supply and transportation artery behind its front, and block their potential retreat route. However, an unanticipated Russian counterattack briefly ended those plans and forced Third Army troops back into the mountains.

By December 4, the Habsburg Fourth Army's Limanova-Lapanov operation had conquered considerable terrain. Group Roth advanced after shifting northward and initially encountering only weak tsarist cavalry forces, but then enemy resistance steadily increased. Meanwhile, unknown to either Conrad or Roth, the tsarist VIII and XXIV Corps began approaching the critical area of Neu Sandec, as their Third and Eighth Armies threatened Habsburg flank positions. By December 5, the only chance for a major military success was dependent upon the immediate reinforcement of Group Roth's XIV Corps, because it lacked sufficient reserve formations. Since the enemy steadily received reinforcements, time was of the essence; the Fourth Army had to advance before additional large numbers of tsarist troops arrived at the front. Most immediately, Habsburg troops had to halt tsarist forces advancing toward Neu Sandec, which later became the distant Third Army's new mission objective.[6] Thus, General Conrad, on December 6, ordered the Third Army to commence forced marches from the west and northwest to reach the Fourth Army battle zone to prevent the consolidation of the tsarist Eighth Army's VIII and XXIV Corps positions.

On that same day, Habsburg reconnaissance missions revealed that strong enemy forces were maneuvering toward Neu Sandec, which was a weakly held area. Concern mounted when deciphered Russian radio transmissions revealed details regarding the tsarist forces' advance toward the town and the eighty-kilometer gap between the Habsburg Third and Fourth Armies and Group Roth's attack forces. Thus reinforcements had to be deployed to Neu Sandec to secure the Fourth Army's right flank positions. Strong tsarist resistance could now be felt all along the Fourth Army front.[7] The enemy's reinforcements and deployment of reserve forces endangered the Fourth Army main attack group and its entire operation. Additional units would be transferred from other Habsburg armies to this main battle area as quickly as possible as tsarist resistance halted all forward progress.

In the meantime, the newly arrived, full-strength 47th German Reserve Infantry Division had advanced twenty-five kilometers from its detraining area into the wooded Carpathian Mountain terrain, where vision proved severely restricted. Unfortunately, its troops were unaccustomed to winter mountain conditions and possessed no mountain equipment. Making matters worse, the early arrival of snow and ice proved detrimental to overall Habsburg offensive efforts. The 47th Reserve Infantry Division encountered delays in its marches to its assembly area, and then achieved only limited progress. The infantry

division, on the eastern flank of the northern Habsburg offensive operation, opened a ten-mile gap between the Habsburg forces protecting
New Sandec.

As early as November 1914, as noted, the Russian southwest front
commander, General Ivanov, had issued secret instructions to prepare
to invade Hungary. His particular attention focused on the significant
problem of providing regular supply transport into the difficult Carpathian Mountain terrain, calculating that his preparations to launch an offensive could be completed within fourteen to eighteen days.[8] General
Ivanov pressed Stavka to reinforce his southwest front against a reputed
German threat to his left flank positions, although there was no evidence
of excessive German activity on that front or the threat of the liberation
of Fortress Przemyśl. Ivanov's pet project, the invasion of Hungary, required the conquest of the Carpathian Mountain front; he also fully
recognized the great political significance of his proposed invasion while
maintaining the siege of Fortress Przemyśl.

General Ivanov's arguments convinced Stavka to transfer the XII
Corps and five to six mountain artillery batteries from the German front
to the southwest front, because regular field artillery proved ineffective
on the mountainous winter terrain.

On December 6, 1914, thirteen Habsburg First Army divisions battled fourteen to fifteen Russian Ninth Army divisions in standing battle
in the Pilica River area northwest of Fortress Kraków and the major
Fourth Army operation. Russian Third Army troops maneuvered northeast of the fortress to the Vistula River, threatening Neu Sandec and
attacking the German 47th Reserve Infantry Division. Other tsarist
units from other fronts were deployed toward Neu Sandec.

Realizing their dangerous situation, the Russians deployed troops
south of Fortress Kraków to attack Habsburg flank positions.[9] This
forced the Habsburg Fourth Army to shift from an attempt to encircle
the enemy forces to a frontal assault toward Limanova and west of Boch-
nia. Meanwhile, on the East Prussian front, seven German Eighth Army
divisions battled sixteen tsarist Tenth Army units on the northern flank
of an attempted tsarist invasion of Silesia. The Russians retreated to
the river line at Warsaw terminating the earlier major tsarist offensive
against Germany.

Group Roth continued its assault. As tsarist advances continued to threaten Group Roth's eastern flank positions and connections to its rear echelon area, the situation could not be ignored. Habsburg Supreme Command ordered that reinforcements be deployed to the Fourth Army to enable Group Roth to continue its attempt to encircle the opposing forces. Third Army units prepared to launch an attack against tsarist VIII Corps units in the critical area of Neu Sandec in an attempt to halt the Russian advance and achieve victory. As sickness, battle, and dwindling troop numbers weakened Fourth Army efforts, the Third Army's intervention became an absolute necessity to assure obtaining an ultimate victory by preventing the Russian Eighth Army, deployed in the Carpathian Mountains, from intervening.[10]

A Russian counterattack in the area of Limanova endangered the success of the Fourth Army offensive as both sides desperately sought reinforcements to continue their offensive efforts. A tsarist VIII Corps attack pressed hard against Group Roth's flank and rear connections. That serious threat increased the pressure for the Habsburg Third Army to intervene in the battle as soon as possible.[11]

As news began arriving of the unfortunate battle results on the Balkan front, Conrad worried that any further setbacks would sway Italy, Bulgaria, and Romania to intervene militarily against the Dual Monarchy. Conrad desperately sought to achieve a victory against the Russians, while Premier Istvan Tisza of Hungary demanded that enemy advances into Hungarian territory be halted. Conrad turned his attention to his Third Army to order it to intervene in the Fourth Army's battle by deploying troops toward Neu Sandec.

The Russian Eighth Army pinned the Habsburg Third Army along the length of the Carpathian Mountains. The Russian Third Army slowly closed in on Kraków, the primary objective. Conrad recognized the possibility of turning the Russian Third Army's flank as two Russian corps became increasingly exposed. Third Army units attacked Bartfeld, then proceeded to Neu Sandec. Group Roth attempted to prevent the Russians from pulling back to safety by shifting additional troops to its eastern flank position.

The situation became critical on December 7 when Russian Eighth Army units began to advance toward Habsburg Fourth Army positions at Limanova. The tsarist VIII Corps had already entered the battle, and the XXIV Corps also threatened to do so. By evening, the situation had become tense as the entire tsarist Third Army attacked Fourth Army positions. The Habsburg Third Army's mission remained to ensure that the sixty-kilometer gap continued to separate tsarist Third and Eighth Army forces. Only minimal Fourth Army troop numbers were deployed at Limanova, where the enemy now advanced with strong forces. If Habsburg Third Army units rapidly reached the area of Neu Sandec as ordered, that could disrupt the tsarist corps' rear echelon area, which threatened Fourth Army efforts. However, Third Army troops had to advance through difficult wooded terrain, encountering serious delays and problems as they attempted to move forward, while individual Landsturm troop units began to disintegrate because of their increasing casualty numbers.[12] The lack of Habsburg reinforcements and inadequate frontline troop numbers intensified the crisis posed by the tsarist threat to Limanova. Heavy fighting raged for several days, extending from Lapanov north to Limanova.

On that same day, other Third Army (VII Corps) vanguard units on the other Carpathian Mountain front also attained the Dukla Pass, while X Corps entered Mezölaborcza on December 11 as they attempted to reach and liberate Fortress Przemyśl. General Kusmanek launched a powerful sortie on December 9 consisting of nineteen infantry battalions and fourteen artillery batteries to hinder any tsarist troop withdrawal of siege troops and confirm their troop numbers. The main sortie, cloaked by several smaller efforts, continued to bind Russian troops on the citadel's southeastern perimeter flank on December 9 and 10.[13]

In an often-repeated scenario, Honvéd troops reached forward Russian positions but lacked sufficient troop numbers to pierce the strong enemy lines. Thus, additional offensive efforts proved fruitless because the Russians rapidly realigned their forces to neutralize any subsequent actions. The notorious inaccuracy of Habsburg artillery fire and accompanying short rounds had characterized the first siege, but at that time field commanders had blamed inadequate troop training for the failure. It must be mentioned that much of the fortress artillery was obsolete and that the gun tubes had begun to wear out. Nevertheless, on December 10, after two days of fierce fighting, the exhausted surviving soldiers withdrew into the fortress. Honvéd infantry regiment troops captured some prisoners of war and booty, but the effort proved inconsequential.

Spy paranoia, meanwhile, swept the fortress and resulted in widespread rumors of espionage within the citadel. Ruthenian peasants reportedly signaled Habsburg positions to the enemy by telephone, light signals, and messages placed in bottles and dropped in the San River, which merely increased the garrison's spy hysteria and resulted in the shooting and hanging of hundreds of Ruthenians. The heavy, intermittent battle (and concomitant casualties) between December 9 and 28 significantly reduced the garrison's offensive strength. General Kusmanek launched sorties on December 9, 10, and 13 and between December 15 and 18, producing heavy clashes before the fortress perimeter and particularly significant officer and veteran combat fortress troop casualties.

Meanwhile, Habsburg Third Army eastern flank forces advanced toward the fortress in an attempt to liberate it. Other Third Army units, in the meantime, had commenced marching over one hundred kilometers through snow-covered Carpathian Mountain passes and valleys to the Fourth Army battlefield. On December 8, those troops received orders to advance toward Neu Sandec as rapidly and with as many troops as possible. Meanwhile, between December 1 and 10, the Russians continued to transfer reinforcements from their north Vistula River and Carpathian Mountain theaters to the battle area. These additional enemy forces helped halt the Habsburg Fourth Army progress by launching a counterattack. The Russians regained the initiative as they smashed into Group Roth's open flank position and pushed its troops back. The entire tsarist Third Army, reinforced by two corps, participated in the attack. In the meantime, the Fourth Army's offensive had shifted from the attempted envelopment of tsarist forces, as mentioned, to a frontal battle in the Limanova area. Russian VIII Corps troops continued to attack the Fourth Army's flank and rearward connections along the Neu Sandec railroad stretch.

Some Third Army troops marched to within a mere twenty kilometers of Neu Sandec, while its IX Corps made its way to the major transportation center at Gorlice. A Fourth Army force of five infantry and one cavalry division defended the high ground south and north of Limanova against the tsarist VIII Corps attack, having to utilize nonbattle troops for combat to continue the fight. As a result of accelerating casualties, its division numbers had shrunk from 12,000–15,000 soldiers to only 2,000–3,000, while the Third Army's average division numbers dropped to only 2,000 troops. Its 3rd Infantry Division, for example, had been reduced to 900 troops by December 10.[14]

Third Army right flank Group Krautwald forces, still attempting to liberate Fortress Przemyśl, advanced to within fifty kilometers of the citadel while garrison troops in forward perimeter positions listened to the sounds of that battle. The mentioned fortress sortie objective became to bind tsarist troops from interfering with Group Krautwald's effort.[15]

As air reconnaissance efforts were interrupted by inclement weather conditions, they failed to discover significant tsarist troop movements. Meanwhile, the Fourth Army crisis intensified as the Russians increased pressure on their eastern and rear flank positions from the south. A tsarist counteroffensive on the northern front threatened to break through Fourth Army lines and forced Habsburg troops onto the defensive, while the poor handling of railroad traffic continued to hamper the transportation of reinforcements. The Third Army's Group Szurmay 38th *Honvéd* Infantry Division and a combined division advanced toward Neu Sandec, finally initiating its decisive appearance on the Fourth Army's battlefield, striking tsarist vanguard units along a broad front. The next day, Habsburg Third Army troops compelled the enemy to retreat by driving decisively through the gap between the two enemy armies, consummating the Limanova-Lapanov victory.

In the meantime, the First Army's XVIII Corps continued its delayed rail transport to the Third Army eastern flank area to reinforce it and provide sufficient impulse to the Third Army attempt to liberate Fortress Przemyśl, but the low-capacity mountain railroad lines seriously retarded arrival timetables. Third Army detachments fanned northward toward the strategically important area encompassing Dukla-Zmigrod-Gorlice on December 11. The remainder of the Third Army troops had resolutely marched toward the critical Neu Sandec region to positively affect the Fourth Army's Limanova-Lapanov battle.

The Russian assaults against the German 47th Reserve Infantry Division had, meanwhile, failed. As the Third Army continued its advance,

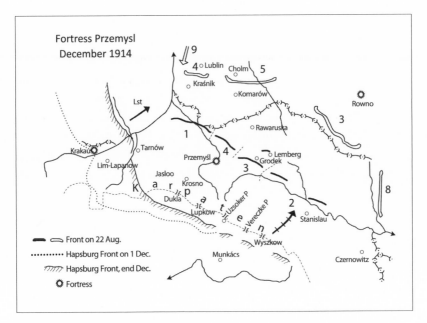

Map 5.1. Fortress Przemyśl, December 1914.

it encountered only Russian rearguard units and thus could shift its left flank units toward Neu Sandec. To support Fourth Army efforts, the 106th Landsturm Infantry Division launched a sortie from Fortress Kraków to bind tsarist troops deployed at the citadel.[16]

On December 11, Third Army's IX Corps had attained the area of Gorlice, severing the important enemy's east-west transportation link and forcing their troops to begin to withdraw, which proved significant for the Limanova-Lapanov operation's success. The Third Army's advance placed it in the gap between the Russian Third and Eighth Armies' southern flank and rearward connections. This prevented the tsarist XXIV corps from intervening in the main battle and ultimately forced the Russian retreat. The victory at Limanova-Lapanov received invaluable aid from the full-strength German 47th Reserve Infantry Division, which possessed more troop numbers than several participating Habsburg divisions combined.

The turning point in the fight for Limanova-Lapanov occurred on December 12, when Habsburg Third Army units decisively intervened in the Fourth Army's battle, forcing the tsarist VIII Corps from the Neu

Sandec area while its IX Corps pushed the enemy's XXIV Corps rear-ward, advancing into Neu Sandec and forcing the tsarist retreat.

On the Carpathian Mountain front, the Third Army's VII Corps seized the Uzsok Pass on December 17; thus, Group Krautwald on the army's eastern flank advanced to the east in an attempt to sever the key enemy railroad supply line and retreat route at Lisko-Sanok, then on to attain the San River lines and liberate Fortress Przemyśl.[17] However, all subsequent Habsburg December efforts to liberate the fortress proved futile. Excessive casualties and the lack of reserve formations to replenish depleted Third Army ranks proved decisive in preventing the forcing of tsarist troops back across the Vistula River. In addition, the overutiliza-tion of Habsburg railroads seriously retarded the transport of troops and supplies, resulting in traffic chaos.[18]

The tsarist objective, on the other hand, entailed occupying and fortifying key Carpathian Mountain crossings to secure the Russian southwest flank position, an absolute necessity before attempting to launch another invasion of Germany. General Ivanov concentrated his forces around the Mezölaborcz railroad and communications center, soon to be the scene of major battle during the first Carpathian Moun-tain winter offensive campaign in late January and early February 1915.

Fortunes fluctuated daily during the battle, but it ultimately pro-duced the first significant Dual Monarchy battlefield victory against Russia. Nevertheless, it came at a heavy cost, and Habsburg officers had to counter the increasing apathy that permeated their troop ranks. Poor troop morale made it difficult to maintain discipline in the ranks during the campaign. The majority of the exhausted troops par-ticipated in almost constant battle, which seriously hindered the rapid pursuit of enemy forces that Conrad ordered following the significant battlefield victory.

Habsburg forces defeated the numerically superior tsarist units by skillfully utilizing maneuver tactics and their interior lines to their ad-vantage. General Conrad also succeeded in momentarily overcoming the increasing criticism of his command leadership.[19] The Third Army, in the interim, attempted to achieve a major victory on its right flank by inserting the in-transport X and XVIII Corps to pursue and encircle the retreating enemy forces in the area close to Fortress Przemyśl. Ice-covered roads, however, severely retarded the transport of those troops. The Russians, meanwhile, deployed strong forces to protect their threatened Third and Eighth Army inner flank positions. Excessive Habsburg troop exhaustion and excellent Russian retrograde movements prevented major tsarist territorial losses and seriously hindered Habsburg efforts to effectively pursue defeated enemy troops.

Allied Austro-Hungarian and German forces had finally halted the heretofore unstoppable Russian steamroller pressing into Galicia. They prevented the enemy from successfully traversing the Carpathian Mountains to invade Hungary and forced them to abandon plans to seek a major military decision against the Germans because of the sudden threat to their southern flank positions on the southwest front. The threat to Fortress Kraków ended, and the Habsburg front momentarily had stabilized.

During the decisive phase of the battle, Army Group Pflanzer-Baltin protected the extreme Habsburg eastern flank position along the major ridgelines in the Carpathian Mountains against Russian units almost double its size. In early December, the Army Group had been forced to extend its front lines to close the gap in its lines resulting from the Third Army's westward deployment shift, caused by the redeployment of some Second Army units to the Polish front. The stubborn Army Group commander steadfastly refused to surrender any of his several-hundred-kilometer front, now extending from southern Galicia to the Bukovina.

On the German front, the Russian First, Second, and Fifth Armies now defended Warsaw, the transportation and depot center along the right Vistula River bank area. On their southwest front the tsarist armies retreated along the Vistula River to prepare to launch new military operations. The tsarist Eighth Army's slow Carpathian Mountain retrograde movement delayed the Habsburg Third Army's pursuit of the enemy's retreating forces around Fortress Przemyśl by destroying the San River bridges as they withdrew. The Eleventh Army maintained its siege of Fortress Przemyśl and prevented garrison troops from advancing to the Jaroslau area (north of the fortress) and Third Army eastern flank forces from liberating the citadel. Habsburg Third Army forces desperately, but unsuccessfully, attempted to attain the critical Lisko-Sanok railroad junctions that would remain the Habsburg operational objectives throughout the 1915 Carpathian Mountain winter campaign. The Third Army lacked sufficient troop numbers to reach Jaroslau, Przemyśl, and Chyrov. Tsarist troops remained ensconced behind their strong defensive positions before the San River in the area of Fortress Przemyśl.

At the same time, the tsarist 19th Infantry Division, redeployed from the Fortress Przemyśl siege front in mid-December, was replaced by three reserve infantry divisions. Due to foggy conditions, Habsburg air reconnaissance failed to detect not only this movement but other major enemy activities as well. Then, a fortress air reconnaissance mission finally spotted large Russian troop and supply columns moving eastward, leading General Conrad to assume that any present tsarist military action served merely to gain time because of their recent defeat.[20] Conrad planned to capitalize on the Limanova-Lapanov campaign by launching a relentless pursuit action to encircle retreating enemy soldiers, mainly with his Third Army eastern flank units, although his battle-weary troops continued to desperately require rest and rehabilitation. Meanwhile, the Russians assembled strong forces in preparation to commence their own major offensive operation, which rapidly stifled all further Habsburg offensive efforts.

On December 14, Fortress Przemyśl garrison units cooperated with Third Army right flank Group Krautwald's attempts to liberate the bulwark. In the meantime, tsarist units had retreated to east of the Vistula River. The entire Russian front commenced a general retrograde movement. The tsarist troops destroyed all bridges and established individual vanguard position resistance. The Habsburg pursuit continued on December 15 and 16. The Habsburg Third and Fourth Armies encountered tenacious Russian rearguard defensive efforts, which attempted to delay the pursuing Habsburg troops as long as possible in the area of the Biala and Dunajec Rivers. The Third Army's mission, after advancing, entailed disrupting the Carpathian railroads in the latter area. In addition, the question of negotiating a separate peace with Russia arose, but St. Petersburg vetoed such efforts as the Entente powers signed a pact agreeing not to negotiate a separate peace with the Central Powers.[21] Rumors spread on December 14 that the Germans sought a separate peace with Russia. Conrad approached Leopold von Berchtold in opposition of such a notion.[22] General Falkenhayn had come to the conclusion that the Central Powers could not defeat the combined Entente forces.[23]

In the interim, on December 14, Habsburg field armies had renewed their offensive, and Third Army flank Group Krautwald forces pursued the enemy toward the fortress through the Dukla Pass to Sanok (about fifty kilometers from the bulwark). This force threatened the rear echelon connections of the tsarist front, providing perhaps the opportunity for a decisive advance to liberate the citadel. Group Krautwald encountered and battled three Russian divisions. As a result, Third Army units had to retreat to their defensive lines, encountering serious attacks on their rearguard positions as they did. The fortress sortie launched on December 15 expanded to between twenty-three and twenty-five infantry battalions, fifteen artillery batteries, and eight and one-half cavalry squadrons. These forces advanced toward Bircza and Krzywcza, which initiated the four-day battle between December 15 and December 18. Initially, the operation produced a string of uninterrupted victories, hurling enemy troops back from numerous forward strongly fortified tsarist defensive lines. But when the fortress offensive units reached strong Russian forward defensive positions, the attackers lacked sufficient troop numbers to breach the enemy's main well-prepared defensive lines while receiving neither sufficient nor effective artillery support. The terrain also favored the tsarist forces, which regrouped and neutralized any further Habsburg assaults.

The Third Army received orders to renew its right flank offensive efforts on December 15, but it immediately encountered strong tsarist defensive measures and effective artillery fire. The San River gave the Third Army's northern flank some protection for its advance.[24] The Third Army's objective encompassed attaining the areas of Sanok-Krosno-Jaslo, but its intended eastern offensive flank units required the previously mentioned X and XVIII Corps reinforcements to enable it to advance further toward Jaroslau- Przemyśl-Chyrov to liberate the fortress. General Conrad desired to force the San River crossings and then drive east to liberate Fortress Przemyśl, but he feared that the Russians would be able to retreat behind the river undisturbed. Group Krautwald meanwhile attacked toward Lisko, but those efforts failed. The Habsburg Fourth Army pursued the fleeing tsarist troops along the entire course of the San River, but the enemy destroyed all the bridges to delay any forward pursuit.

Unrelenting inclement weather and extremely poor road conditions caused perpetual delays in Habsburg troop and supply column movement. The Russians could more easily replace their casualties and thus speedily recovered from the German front Lodz and Habsburg Limanova-Lapanov battles. Sickness, extraordinary physical activity, and battle losses steadily decreased Habsburg numbers, while the troops' physical condition, combined with the lack of equipment, artillery shells, and food, took an increasingly enormous toll. The troops still lacked winter uniforms.

The month of December also witnessed the largest fortress sorties being launched. One operation succeeded in advancing eighteen kilometers into tsarist defensive positions, but the subsequent battle losses strongly reduced the bulwark's offensive capabilities. Troop morale plunged as the possibility of liberation appeared to vanish by the end of 1914. From then on, the fortress received weeklong enemy artillery barrages on a regular basis.

Fortress Przemyśl garrison troops, however, still had to cooperate with the Third Army attempts to liberate the bulwark by launching a major sortie, which briefly raised the morale of the citadel because military personnel and civilians now anticipated the rapid liberation of the fortress.[25] During the December 15 fortress action, garrison troops had to traverse rugged and forested mountain terrain, including a long, torturous 500-meter-high ravine, under poor visibility conditions.

The failure of Third Army troops to advance as anticipated decided the fate of the fortress sortie. For the garrison sortie to have had any chance of success, during both sieges, field army troops had to advance to the proximity of the fortress. Fortress troops had just disregarded their serious casualties in the hope that the fortress would soon be liberated. Garrison soldiers realized that they lacked the necessary troop numbers to achieve a major military success, which in turn depended on achieving surprise and launching a rapid offensive to deny the enemy valuable time to effectively react and initiate effective counteractions. Success was closely correlated with the Third Army's proximity to the fortress, because sortie troops anticipated a rapid tsarist counterattack.

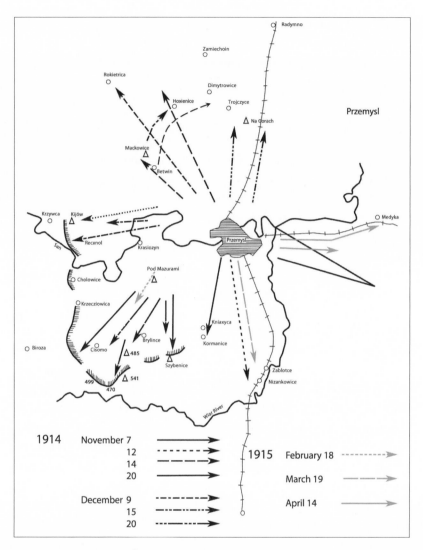

Map 5.2. Fortress Przemyśl sorties.

However, the three-day drama, as with all sortie efforts, produced the same results: some conquered enemy terrain gained with much human sacrifice soon had to be surrendered. A hasty retreat inevitably followed, with the concomitant loss of garrison troop morale. The attack commenced at 5:00 a.m. on December 15 with nineteen infantry battalions and twelve artillery batteries toward the high terrain at Cisova.

Third Army command radioed the fortress to inform them that the Russians had begun to retreat. Thus, they requested that garrison units bind enemy troops at its front and launch a sortie to join the Habsburg forces halfway to cooperate in hurling enemy forces behind the San River, or, at a minimum, neutralize their present efforts. By December 17, enemy resistance had solidified considerably, and Fortress Przemyśl garrison sortie setbacks had become more serious. Grave difficulties continued during attempts to transport artillery and supply trains on the miserable mountain routes. The fortress troops could not reach the Third Army lines once its lead forces had been defeated, eliminating a major opportunity to liberate the fortress. This news destroyed any lingering hope that the bulwark could be liberated and struck a serious blow to the inhabitants' morale.

Fortress casualties between December 15 and 18 included a thousand dead and wounded, and 232 additional prisoners of war were captured. Three thousand casualties were sustained between December 15 and 21, mostly in the fighting at Na Gorach. Meanwhile, thousands of corpses covered the battlefield.[26]

As early as December 16, the Third Army encountered stubborn enemy resistance on the main battlefield. The Russians masterfully utilized their inner line advantage during their retreat and deployed strong forces against the Third Army right flank positions before the Habsburg reinforcements (X and XVIII Corps) could arrive. As weather conditions deteriorated, the extreme eastern flank X Corps had to halt enemy progress and repulse tsarist thrusts near Lisko. Army Group Pflanzer-Baltin received orders to prepare a twenty-battalion, nine-battery assault force against the strategic Uzsok Pass on December 20.

The fatal combination of insufficient troop numbers, overextended front lines, unfavorable weather conditions, and impassable terrain made it difficult to defend new positions once the exhausted Habsburg troops' forward progress ended and the Russians launched a counterattack. The continuing lack of reserves also did not bode well for battlefield success. Sickness, excessive physical exertion, and large numbers lost as prisoners of war or and stragglers removed many troops from action by mid-December.

Thus, by December 18, after the failure of the four-day fortress sortie in the area between Cisova and Bircza, the Habsburg effort initially repulsed forward enemy positions, captured several machine guns, and seized control of the Bircza roads south of Cisova. Neighboring units, however, could not advance rapidly enough, so the Honvéds ultimately had to sacrifice the captured high terrain.

The entire Habsburg Third Army quickly terminated its pursuit efforts between December 18 and 20, while the seemingly endless supply of Russian reinforcements enabled the enemy to launch a series of counteroffensives that ruptured the weak and fragile Habsburg defensive positions anywhere on the front they selected. Tsarist occupation of key Carpathian Mountain ridges provided the necessary security for their troops besieging Fortress Przemyśl, while it also offered an opportunity to soon launch a decisive offensive into the heartland of Hungary. The enemy also enjoyed the major advantage of shorter, more direct railroad and road transport routes for its supplies and reinforcements, as Habsburg units were ensconced in the higher mountain terrain; thus, their reinforcements had to be rail transported over a much wider area, extending from Fortress Kraków to Mezölaborcz and Takczany. Dual Monarchy troops then had to march considerable distances over rugged mountain terrain to attain their deployment area.

While the Habsburg Fourth Army maintained its positions along the confluence of the Dunajec and Vistula Rivers, Third Army troops surrendered several crucial mountain passes to irresistible Russian frontal assaults and then retreated twenty kilometers on December 18. A new defensive line ten to twelve kilometers south of the lost passes was established between the mountain ridges and the important Ung valley. Encountering particularly strong Fourth Army enemy defensive positions, its commander determined to transfer numerous infantry divisions to the Third Army rather than launch an attack himself, a practice that would continue throughout the 1915 Carpathian Winter War campaign.

During the latter half of December, the military initiative at the fortress and on the Carpathian Mountain battlefield reverted to Russian favor as Habsburg military setbacks continued unabated. Enemy troops hurled Third Army units from the Carpathian Mountain forelands back to several major ridges with enormous losses.

By December 19, it became evident that the precarious Third Army eastern flank forces needed to be strengthened with the in-transit X and XVIII Corps. An attempt to encircle the opposing tsarist forces and liberate Fortress Przemyśl required significantly more troop numbers. The Third Army had the mission to bind the opposing Russian Third and Eighth Army troops until the arrival of the two reinforcing corps. Conrad continued to attempt to convince General Falkenhayn that military success against Russia would lead to the defeat of France and Serbia. Conrad, however, also recognized that without German assistance he would be unable to extend the Habsburg front east of Fortress Przemyśl, which made his overall chances of success minimal at best. With tragic consequences for the Austro-Hungarian army, General Conrad's strategic planning became based primarily on liberating the fortress. This would have catastrophic results and nearly annihilate the Habsburg army during the 1915 Carpathian Mountain Winter War campaign.

On December 17, an alarming internal fortress report indicated that the fortress could sustain itself only until early January 1915 because of the rapidly depleting food supplies.[27] General Kusmanek, considering the calculations too conservative, established a commission of inquiry to further investigate the matter. As the situation became increasingly desperate, widespread corruption spread throughout the bulwark.

The Germans were determined to continue their operation in the middle Vistula River area, thus General Falkenhayn invited General Conrad to discuss further allied military objectives with him.[28] Conrad finally realized that his exhausted troops, now at their breaking point, had been "pumped dry." During the past five months, Habsburg troops had launched three offensives against the Russians but had been forced to retreat after the first two operations while sustaining almost a million casualties. During the ensuing retrograde movements, the field armies abandoned enormous amounts of irreplaceable equipment and food supplies. On December 21, Conrad reported to the Emperor's Military Chancellery that "the best officers and non-commissioned officers had died or been removed from service," as well as the professional corps of the rank-and-file troops. He also described Habsburg reserve or replacement troops as "being of poor quality and partly young, partly older men." The 1914 eastern front campaign had almost eliminated the

Habsburg army as a viable fighting force. The final casualty toll included 189,000 dead, 500,000 wounded, and 280,000 taken as prisoners of war. Officer casualties alone reached 26,500. In December 1914, the Dual Monarchy could deploy only 303,000 combatants against the numerically superior tsarist enemy, but few had the capability to liberate Fortress Przemyśl. German liaison observers at Habsburg headquarters noted that General Conrad had lost faith in his own troops and that a dangerous fatalism now permeated Habsburg Supreme Command. Conrad also complained about his secret enemies, the Germans and the German emperor, whom he described as a comedian.[29] Conrad resented the German expressions of superiority over his troops, their snide comments, and the fact that they represented the stronger ally.

On December 20, General Kusmanek launched another sortie toward the Na Gorach ridge to press enemy troops back, while Defensive District VIII launched a distraction effort to cloak the location of the main action.[30] Meanwhile, on December 22, the sortie troops retreated into the fortress.

As battle raged before the Fortress Przemyśl perimeter, General Kusmanek convened the previously mentioned commission of inquiry on December 20 to investigate the dwindling fortress food supply. The next day, the fortress quartermaster reported that the horse fodder reserve would last only until January 1915, but when the commission results were completed on December 28, the new calculations extended the supply of horse feed until February 18 and fodder until March 7.[31] The commission demanded that ten thousand horses be immediately slaughtered to provide additional sustenance for the starving garrison troops. Habsburg Supreme Command accepted the commission's findings but continued to be alarmed by exaggerated fortress claims. Subsequent reports extended food supplies until March 23. However, these findings proved misleading, as the commission ignored calculations based on fewer garrison troops, horses, and civilian numbers than the fortress actually housed.

On the main battlefield, Habsburg Supreme Command remained completely unaware of whether Stavka now intended to order a retreat behind the San River or, conversely, to launch an offensive. The Russians could not immediately launch an attack to protect their retreating troops, but the windy, icy mountain terrain also retarded any rapid Habsburg pursuit of them. The pursuing troops' exhaustion and excellent tsarist retreat tactics prevented a disaster for the defeated enemy forces.

On December 20, Conrad announced directions for continuing Habsburg military operations, returning to his 1914 concept of a double envelopment launched from East Prussia and Galicia. Third Army eastern flank forces must liberate Fortress Przemyśl and also create a dependable defensive security system for the Carpathian Mountains. The other Habsburg armies must maintain their earlier positions and attack the enemy only if it attempted to transfer forces to another front. However, in the meantime, the enemy amassed enormous troop numbers at the endangered Third Army right flank area; this increased tsarist presence ultimately terminated any attempts to advance or to liberate Fortress Przemyśl.

Between December 20 and 24, the Russians launched a decisive counteroffensive along the entire Galician front. Utilizing the cover of heavy snowfall and fog, the Russians initiated fierce battle and seized the major Carpathian Mountain ridgelines, neutralizing any potential Habsburg military threat from that direction. The tsarist objective remained to cross the easily accessible Dukla Pass to traverse the remaining Carpathian Mountain ridges to invade Hungary and to capture Budapest. On December 20, the vulnerable Habsburg nine-division army crumbled under the twelve-division Russian counterattack. Continued Russian military successes also raised the specter of neutral Italy and Romania entering the war against the Central Powers. When Habsburg Third Army units had to retreat into the mountains, this also forced the neighboring Fourth Army right flank units to initiate their own retrograde movement to the Dunajec River. Habsburg military operations south of the Vistula River had reached their turning point. All Habsburg counterattacks to the enemy assaults launched between December 20 and 22 failed, but Third Army command nevertheless continued to plan further offensive efforts, hoping that once X and XVIII Corps troops arrived at its right flank deployment areas, it could turn the tide of the battle in their favor.[32] The major Russian counterstroke, however, ultimately neutralized those efforts.

The Habsburg field army now faced a seemingly insurmountable obstacle with its rapidly declining troop numbers. For example, III Corps' three divisions now consisted of only 10,200 men, while IX Corps' numbers were equally low.[33] On December 22, the Third Army's VII Corps was suddenly faced with encirclement and defeat at the Dukla Pass, because it could not resist the major enemy assault. Its present positions had to be maintained to enable Third Army Command to insert the still en route X and XVIII Corps at the designated army's right flank to relaunch its offensive. Thus, the unexpected gap that opened between III and VII Corps positions created a dangerous situation that portended disaster for any future Habsburg offensive efforts.

When Habsburg XVIII and X Corps units finally began arriving in strength, VII Corps had been hurled out of the Dukla Pass, also prompting the retreat of the neighboring III Corps. The Russians consistently battered III and VII Corps positions, VII Corps bearing the brunt of their incessant attacks. The few corps reserves could not turn the tide of battle, forcing VII Corps to retreat to the high terrain south and southeast of the Dukla Pass, removing the cornerstone positions vital for the arriving X Corps deployment. The limited capacity and stoppages on the small-gauge mountain railroads had seriously delayed the troops' arrival. The undaunted tsarist Eighth Army continued to smash forward, while other attacks battered Habsburg positions between the Biala and Dunajec Rivers to bind those forces and prevent reinforcements being transferred to the battered Third Army.

Then, on December 22, another major enemy assault threatened to breach the front lines between the Third and Fourth Armies' inner flanks. Their drastically diminishing troop stands raised the question whether either army could halt enemy pressure until the X and XVIII Corps had been fully deployed. Army Group Pflanzer-Baltin received orders to retake the Uzsok Pass to provide some protection for the endangered Third Army flank positions. As the tsarist advance swept forward through December 23, the beleaguered Habsburg troops were again ordered to maintain their lines until the main XVIII Corps units arrived, which could not be anticipated until December 26. However, on December 24, the Russians again smashed into the reeling Habsburg III and VII Corps positions. The dangerous combination of overextended front lines, diminishing troop stands, severe weather, and difficult terrain again created perilous gaps in the Habsburg defensive lines. Battle fatigue had also become universal along the entire Habsburg front, preventing the troops from mustering any serious resistance to enemy offensive efforts at the mountain crossing sites.

Third Army right flank offensive Group Krautwald had initially gained considerable territory, but only because the enemy had concentrated its main military efforts against the VII Corps positions at the critical Dukla Pass. General Josef Freiherr Krautwald attempted to continue his offensive efforts until December 24, but when tsarist troops broke into the VII Corps east flank positions, his group and ultimately the entire Habsburg front had to retreat. Belatedly inserting the late-arriving X Corps units into Third Army right flank positions proved ineffective because the Russians unleashed another surprise attack, abetted by inclement weather conditions, which forced further Habsburg retreat.

At Fortress Przemyśl, Christmas was described as the most tragic event on the entire Habsburg eastern front during the holiday season. The future seemed hopeless for garrison troops as they contemplated perpetual battle followed by death or capture.[34] By December 23, it had become obvious that the Russians had launched a decisive offensive between the San and Vistula Rivers, but Habsburg Supreme Command lacked the necessary troop numbers to halt the tsarist army.

By December 21, fortress inhabitants had already begun preparations for the Christmas holidays. For example, the hospitals detailed men to go into the woods outside the fortress perimeter to cut down and bring trees back to cheer up the patients.[35] On Christmas Eve, a group of the garrison perimeter troops, despite the deep snow, kneeled outside a small chapel to pray. The bulwark garrison unexpectedly enjoyed a brief reprieve as tsarist artillery lay silent until the New Year. However, on December 23, the Russians briefly attempted to seize the forefield positions at Na Gorach–Batycze. Here, undernourished and exhausted perimeter troops remained dangerously close to enemy positions and continued to suffer from the fluctuating bitter winter weather conditions without cover or warmth. Worse, these forward positions lacked adequate protection from enemy artillery fire, and the benumbed soldiers had to perform around-the-clock repair work on them.

On Christmas morning, the fortress's Defensive District VII artillery observers noticed that a large table had been placed outside the fortress walls. Returning garrison patrols also brought back baskets of white bread, other food items, and tobacco. During the holiday season, Russian pilots also halted the bombing of the fortress area.[36]

On Christmas Eve at another location, Russian troops placed a large proclamation on the barbed wire emplacements. At another forefield observation post two Russian officers, displaying a white flag, proclaimed their Christmas wishes, while some tsarist troops presented bread and tobacco to fortress soldiers. Often forward garrison troops found Russian cigarettes left close to their positions. Troops from both sides had developed a form of camaraderie, oftentimes addressing each other by name across the front lines.[37] Neither side fired artillery shells, and gunshots could rarely be heard as both sides honored the unofficial pact until after Christmas. The Russians naturally anticipated the same favor during their Orthodox holidays in two weeks.[38]

On Christmas Day, the Habsburg field armies commenced a general retreat to a shorter defensive line to await replacement troops and sorely needed artillery shells. The Fourth Army's southern flank positions had to be moved back to Gorlice, sustaining heavy losses in the process. Group Pflanzer-Baltin's forces seized the Uzsok Pass after a four-day battle, but the military setbacks at the Dukla Pass and elsewhere rendered it a hollow victory. The Russians again broke through Third Army lines in the Dukla Pass area, creating renewed crisis. The impossibly muddy retreat routes pushed the troops to the brink of their physical and emotional capabilities.[39]

Between December 25 and December 27, the enemy seized the key Beskid Mountain roads and continued their advances, forcing the Third Army further back to the main Carpathian Mountain ridgelines. The continuing chronic lack of reserve forces aggravated the seriously declining troop numbers and created large gaps between defensive positions. An ammunition shortage exacerbated the already dire military situation. Third Army troops continued to endure brutal weather and terrain conditions, while losing irreplaceable numbers of troops, horses, and necessary supplies and equipment during their retrograde maneuvers.

Stronger defensive measures became necessary to halt further enemy egress between Third and Fourth Army inner flank positions, where Habsburg forces sustained heavy losses when forced back to the Gorlice area. With his armies again on the verge of collapse, General Conrad urgently appealed for immediate German military assistance to help maintain his tenuous mountain front, reminding General Falkenhayn of the danger of the neutral powers intervening in the war because of the unfavorable eastern front military situation.

The Russians, meanwhile, replenished their ranks in preparation for renewed offensive operations against the hapless Habsburg Third Army. Utilizing the heavy rain and dense fog conditions to their tactical advantage, the enemy advanced along the vital roadways toward Baligrod, a major Habsburg objective during the forthcoming 1915 Carpathian Mountain Winter War campaign. On December 27, tsarist troops successfully ruptured VII Corps 17th Infantry Division's positions to clear that important high terrain. Given the unrelenting numerical superiority of the enemy forces, the Habsburg ammunition shortage further worsened the critical military crisis. Defending their positions proved to be a monumental task for the weary Habsburg soldiers.

A December 26 Habsburg Supreme Command radio dispatch to General Kusmanek ordered him to launch a sortie to support Third Army attempts to advance. On the next day, he hurled twenty and one-half battalions, two cavalry squadrons, and fifteen artillery batteries against enemy siege positions, but, unbeknownst to Kusmanek, the delayed arrival of the XVIII Corps forced the Third Army to cancel its operation. The fortress order to commence the sortie, however, had already been issued and the operation launched against reinforced tsarist defensive positions. Again, the weary garrison attackers succeeded in reaching the enemy's well-prepared siege lines but could not penetrate them. Then came the customary enemy counterattacks, defeat, and enormous loss of sortie troop morale. The pointless venture ended the next day. With such successive operations, the garrison troops' poor physical condition, along with intense food rationing, left the troops increasingly unable to perform their duties adequately.

Enemy corpses lying before the fortress walls could not be buried because of the tenuous military situation. Lack of sleep, insufficient nourishment, and the harsh winter conditions only accelerated the garrison troops' deteriorating condition. Some soldiers simply collapsed and died, while others deserted to the enemy. Battle reports emphasized the extraordinarily strenuous troop efforts under the horrendous conditions.[40]

Garrison troops had been in constant battle for twelve days with little pause during the fortress efforts. Troop numbers, particularly those of officer rank, had been greatly reduced, which negatively affected military discipline, especially within the inadequately trained Ersatz troops.[41] The slaughter of horses also further reduced mobility and increased troop duties, which negatively affected soldier morale as well, since the troops now had to perform functions that the horses had carried out earlier.

The loss of the province of Galicia in December signified a major reduction in grain supplies, oil, horses, and army recruits for the Dual Monarchy; the loss of the Bukovina province raised concern about Romania entering the war against Austria-Hungary. In the interim, Habsburg field army troops retreated further behind the main Carpathian Mountain ridges to recover and replace the significant troop losses, while simultaneously attempting to halt the enemy advances into the region and a possibly decisive invasion onto the Hungarian plains. The Russians continued to starve Fortress Przemyśl into submission, not anticipating any serious threat to their siege forces from the increasingly weakened garrison troop contingents.

The late December tsarist military successes were tempered only by the winter weather conditions, which delayed their efforts. Meanwhile, a dangerous twenty-kilometer gap between the Dual Monarchy's Third and Fourth Army's inner flanks had to be sealed, but because of inadequate troop numbers, this proved impossible. The Fourth Army's problems increased because of its now endangered southern flank positions, where, for example, the 10th and the arriving 13th Infantry Divisions numbered only six hundred rifles.

The military situation deteriorated further between December 28 and 31 when a Third Army withdrawal along both sides of the important narrow-gauge Lupkov Pass railway became necessary after the Russians attacked along the entire front. On December 28, battle raged at the Dukla, Uzsok and Lupkov Passes and other critically important Carpathian Mountain areas, where the ill-fated 1915 Carpathian Winter War offensives would soon commence. The Habsburg military situation had deteriorated so drastically that General Conrad contemplated redeploying his Second Army to the endangered Carpathian Mountain front from the German Silesian theater.[42] Also, on December 28, a sortie emanated from Defensive District VIII. When the Third Army offensive collapsed, Habsburg Supreme Command ordered a halt to the latest citadel sortie.[43]

During the period December 9–28, significant portions of the Fortress Przemyśl garrison fought outside the citadel against tsarist siege troops. In the process, some of the best fortress troops continued to become casualties, which greatly reduced the bulwark troops' fighting capacities. The lack of sufficient food, along with severe rationing, further negatively affected the health of man and beast. The slaughter of ten thousand horses provided temporary sustenance, but in the process the garrison troops lost much of their mobility and physical capabilities. Running out of artillery shells merely exacerbated the situation.

During the night of December 30, the Russians attacked several Third and Fourth Army front positions, forcing further retreat. As the year wound down, mutual exhaustion forced a brief battle pause on the Carpathian Mountain front.[44]

By late December 1914, the tsarist general Ivanov believed that he could decisively defeat his seriously weakened enemy because of its increasingly worsening critical military situation. He envisioned launching a decisive war-ending offensive into Hungary. General Conrad, after ensuring that the Habsburg army had somewhat recovered and replaced some of its enormous casualties, determined to initiate an offensive operation in the Carpathian Mountains in early 1915. He ignored the numerous valid arguments against launching a winter mountain campaign in such rugged terrain and horrendous inclement weather conditions. Launching an attack on the ice- and snow-covered mountain slopes and ridges with a skeleton or Miliz army would be a fateful gamble.

At the end of the year in Fortress Przemyśl, the combination of mass troop and animal starvation and worsening weather conditions had diminished garrison resistance to disease. Cases of petty crime, embezzlement, and robbery increased. Harsh penalties no longer had any major effect on halting crime, since military authorities themselves had become complicit in accelerating the corruption. Reports surfaced that wounded patients received little medical attention and that many starved to death. Wounded troop numbers had increased enormously with the launching of the December sorties. Morale in the hospital wards remained extremely low, partially because many nurses were untrained and unqualified. When multiple adolescent girls became nurses, it created a life-threatening situation for many sick and wounded soldiers left in their care. Medical supplies had also become depleted, although some were flown into the citadel, while a thousand cases of cholera continued to require quarantine.

The year obviously ended poorly for the Austro-Hungarian army. The three embarrassing Serbian front defeats accompanied severe Habsburg losses and battlefield setbacks on the Russian front until the Limanova-Lapanov victory. That success, however, could not offset the loss of morale after the Balkan front defeats, and Eastern front Habsburg troops found themselves forced on the defensive by December 20. General Conrad realized that he required another major eastern front victory to sway the wavering neutrals, Bulgaria, Romania, and particularly Italy, to retain that status. With the increasing threat of a tsarist invasion of Hungary, the Habsburg army had to block the remaining Carpathian Mountain crossings although suffering numerous recent battlefield setbacks. However, the armies first had to be rehabilitated and resupplied before any major activity could be initiated.

Thus, General Conrad faced several enormous problems at the end of 1914. The hemorrhaging troop losses had to be quickly replaced because of the unrelenting Russian numerical superiority. The crushing Habsburg military defeats at the end of December opened the invasion routes though the Carpathian Mountains, particularly between the Third and Fourth Armies' inner flanks. Nevertheless, the Austro-Hungarian front ultimately stabilized; its defensive lines followed the

course of the Dunajec River, then curved south and east along the Carpathian Mountain crests.

The Russian objective became to push Third Army forces entirely
out of the Carpathian Mountains by securing the main ridges, which
would eliminate the Habsburg military threat there. In addition, besieged Fortress Przemyśl could then be starved into submission without
serious threat of military interference. Moreover, occupation of the main
western Carpathian Mountain ridges provided a favorable starting point
for a 1915 Russian campaign to invade Hungary.

The German Foreign Office and High Command meanwhile urged
General Conrad to cooperate in an offensive effort to conquer the Negotine (northeastern) sector of Serbia to restore Habsburg military
honor and prestige while opening a secure transportation route for sorely
needed ammunition to the Turkish ally to keep it in the war. The operation might also compel Bulgaria to join the Central Powers. However,
General Falkenhayn claimed that no further German troops could be
removed from the hotly contested western front for transfer to the eastern one, and General Conrad certainly could not spare troops for such
a campaign, because of the terrible situation on the Russian front. Only
a skeleton Dual Monarchy force remained by the end of the month. The
enormous losses were partially replaced, but with inadequately trained
reserve troops and officers.

For Fortress Przemyśl, under siege in late September into early October and again in early November, rapidly dwindling food supplies
could force capitulation soon. The late December Habsburg setbacks did
not bode well for the Dual Monarchy's overall military position. To
counter the potential tsarist military threat, General Conrad proposed
to launch the previously mentioned major offensive in the Carpathian
Mountains, its objectives being to defeat the Russian army, protect Hungary, liberate besieged Fortress Przemyśl, and keep the neutral countries
out of the war. The fatal flaw in his strategy was that the Carpathian
Mountain region was unsuitable for the major military campaign he
envisioned for early 1915. The rugged terrain and severe weather conditions had already presented insurmountable obstacles to his armies during late 1914. The sparse and insufficient Galician networks of roads,
trails, and railroad lines severely restricted the maneuverability of large

army formations. Inclement weather conditions and steep mountain terrain made the regular movement of supplies almost impossible to achieve. Under the circumstances, such a campaign would severely jeopardize the troops' well-being and place inhuman demands on them. Furthermore, Habsburg troops had to launch deadly frontal attacks against well-prepared tsarist defensive positions. Moreover, they were compelled to do so under specific time constraints—the fate of Fortress Przemyśl demanded it!

By the end of December, only forty-five thousand infantry troops remained of the original nine hundred thousand that had been deployed during August 1914. The Habsburg army on the Russian front now consisted of only 303,000 combat soldiers in December. Meanwhile, 690,000 March Brigade, or Ersatz replacement, troops had been deployed to the Russian front, but they possessed no machine guns or artillery and lacked adequate mountain warfare equipment and training. In addition to the serious lack of artillery shells, by the end of December infantry losses stood at 85 percent of the troops originally mobilized in 1914.

A further major problem resulted from the continued failure to properly coordinate fortress and field army military efforts, which produced huge casualties for both forces. It remained significant that the Russians never had to withdraw substantial troop numbers from their siege front lines to contain the garrison breakout efforts, this despite the fact that after November 1914 tsarist third-line units served as the siege troops.

Further, serious Honvéd tactical errors have been mentioned, as well as the fact that fortress sorties were launched from the same location, with the same tactical units, and toward the same objectives. Even worse, the sortie missions proved far too ambitious considering the limited number of fortress troops deployed for the operations. Compounding the problem further, the overemphasis on flank security during the various operations proved very disadvantageous, not only because this reduced offensive troop numbers that could have better served with the main attack effort but also because the practice resulted in increased casualties. With the aid of Ruthenian spies, the Russians anticipated all of the fortress military operations and had broken the Habsburg code.

Following the disastrous December events for the Austro-Hungarian army, both opponents faced winter battle on the Carpathian Mountain front and the necessity of winning a decisive battle either to keep the neutral European countries out of the war or gain them as allies. Unfortunately, the only geographical area that General Conrad considered advantageous to launch an offensive that could provide a major victory was the Carpathian Mountains. The next chapter focuses on the Habsburg preparations for the first Carpathian Mountain Winter War in January 1915 and assesses the condition of the participating troops. Was the Habsburg army prepared to launch a major offensive in late January 1915? Were Conrad's offensive plans realistic? Could the field armies liberate Fortress Przemyśl before it had to surrender?

Plate 1. Demolition of a fort at Fortress Przemyśl, March 22, 1915. From *Przemyśl Album*, M. G. Rosenfeld Papierhandlung, [ca. 1915]. Courtesy of the Library of the University of Silesia in Katowice.

Plate 2. Destroyed fort. From *Przemyśl* Album, M. G. Rosenfeld Papierhandlung, [ca. 1915]. Courtesy of the Library of the University of Silesia in Katowice.

Plate 3. Demolished railroad bridge on the San River. From *Przemyśl* Album, M. G. Rosenfeld Papierhandlung, [ca. 1915]. Courtesy of the Library of the University of Silesia in Katowice.

Plate 4. Destroyed armored train. From *Przemyśl* Album, M. G. Rosenfeld Papierhandlung, [ca. 1915]. Courtesy of the Library of the University of Silesia in Katowice.

Plate 5. View of Przemyśl. From *Przemyśl* Album, M. G. Rosenfeld Papierhandlung, [ca. 1915]. Courtesy of the Library of the University of Silesia in Katowice.

Plate 6. Inspection of the Cossacks near Fortress Przemyśl. From *Przemyśl* Album, M. G. Rosenfeld Papierhandlung, [ca. 1915]. Courtesy of the Library of the University of Silesia in Katowice.

Plate 7. Rebuilding train tracks near Fortress Przemyśl. From *Przemyśl* Album, M. G. Rosenfeld Papierhandlung, [ca. 1915]. Courtesy of the Library of the University of Silesia in Katowice.

Plate 8. Removal of barbed wire from train tracks near Fortress Przemyśl. From *Przemyśl* Album, M. G. Rosenfeld Papierhandlung, [ca. 1915]. Courtesy of the Library of the University of Silesia in Katowice.

Plate 9. Presentation of medals to Russian soldiers at Fortress Przemyśl. From *Przemyśl* Album, M. G. Rosenfeld Papierhandlung, [ca. 1915]. Courtesy of the Library of the University of Silesia in Katowice.

Plate 10. Entrance to ammunition dump, present day. Main fortress (Fort No. 1), city of Przemyśl, September 2012. Photograph by author.

Plate 11. View from fortress walls, present day. Main fortress (Fort No. 1), city of Przemyśl, September 2012. Photograph by author.

6

✣ ✣ ✣

The First Two Carpathian Mountain Offensives

JANUARY TO MID-MARCH 1915

THE NOVEMBER AND DECEMBER 1914 BATTLES IN THE CAR-pathian Mountains left both the Russian and Austro-Hungarian combatants exhausted. In January 1915, Habsburg and Romanov commanders attempted to rehabilitate their battered forces, and they initially conducted only local battles to improve frontline positions. Believing that the first side to launch an offensive in the Carpathian Mountains would gain a critical advantage over its enemy, General Conrad planned his offensive operation where he believed the greatest chance existed of achieving a victory over the Russians. He was greatly influenced by the potential action of neutral European powers, following disturbing diplomatic reports suggesting that Italy and Romania might intervene in the war if the Habsburg military situation had not improved by spring. However, the main focus of the offensive was the liberation of besieged Fortress Przemyśl, which lay near the center of the Austro-Hungarian front some 150 miles southeast of Fortress Kraków.

Generals Conrad and Falkenhayn met on December 2, 1914, at Oppeln and again on January 1 at Breslau. The meetings produced no major results, but a prime concern at the conferences was the Fortress Przemyśl situation and the necessity to liberate it before food shortages forced it to surrender. The projected Carpathian Mountain offensive had three main objectives: to prevent the Russians from invading Hungary; to liberate Fortress Przemyśl, under siege for the second time since early November 1914; and to envelop the enemy's extreme left flank mountain positions.

Similar to the December 1914 Habsburg offensive planning, the major effort would emanate from the Habsburg Third Army eastern flank area in an initial attempt to sever tsarist railroad lines, thereby cutting off Russian reinforcements and supply capabilities. Third Army left flank forces and Fourth Army eastern (southern) flank units would at first assume a defensive stance. Army Group Pflanzer-Baltin and South Army, the latter a new allied military entity created in early January 1915 consisting of units from both allied armies, would provide active support in the lower Carpathian Mountain region south of the Third Army's projected operation. For Habsburg Supreme Command, a major impediment to planning such a major offensive involved the continuing lack of reserve units and reinforcements to replenish the already casualty-riddled ranks.

The success of General Conrad's ambitious plan hinged on proper timing, the element of surprise, and maintaining close cooperation between the participating armies. If the offensive succeeded, the Russians would be unable to transfer reinforcements rapidly enough to launch a counterstroke once the action had commenced. Habsburg troops had to traverse the difficult winter Carpathian Mountain terrain to ultimately debouch onto the Galician plains. Conrad's plans, however, failed to consider numerous critical factors that ultimately sabotaged the success of the campaign, including the shortage of railroad lines to the intended offensive operational area. With only four low-capacity railroad lines serving the Carpathian Mountain region, troop and supply movements remained severely limited over the circuitous routes. Providing regular food and ammunition supplies to the troops posed a serious logistical challenge that the Habsburg military never resolved. Furthermore, the earlier 1914 battles and harsh weather and mountain conditions left Austro-Hungarian troops exhausted, benumbed, and demoralized. General Conrad failed to give enough consideration to the inherent difficulties associated with the rugged mountain terrain, especially during winter months.

The Russians, on the other hand, possessed several significant advantages for launching their own campaign in early 1915, including well-constructed defensive positions established on higher terrain than those of their Habsburg counterparts, similar to the German situation on the western front. In addition, tsarist artillery remained far superior to the Habsburgs' because of its greater accuracy and range. Russia's better-developed railroad network also facilitated more-rapid transport of troops and supplies to the mountain front. Most significantly, the Russians' recapture of vital Carpathian Mountain passes and ridges in late December 1914 provided them with a major strategic advantage for any operation on the mountainous terrain early in 1915.

Prior to the fall 1914 Carpathian Mountain military operations, neither the Russian nor the Austro-Hungarian commanders had experienced prolonged mountain winter battles, certainly not in a total war environment. In early January, meanwhile, it appeared to Habsburg Supreme Command that Stavka had reinforced its Carpathian units. The western front had settled into protracted trench warfare in late December 1914 and early 1915, and the Balkan arena remained quiescent after disease and battle decimated the Serbian army following its successful December 1914 campaign against the Austro-Hungarian invaders. These events set the stage for those that would follow.

General Ivanov had already planned to launch a major military operation in the Carpathian Mountains with the objectives of destroying the Habsburg armies, invading Hungary, and persuading neutral Italy and Romania to join the Entente. With their multiple railroad lines in close proximity to their Galician southwest front, the Russians could easily launch an offensive and transport significant supplies, troops, and reinforcements when it became necessary. However, at a meeting in Siedlice on January 17, 1915, Stavka determined that its main 1915 military effort would be to initiate a major offensive against Germany in continuation of its 1914 Vistula River campaign. The Austro-Hungarian front would therefore be relegated to a secondary theater.

As frequently occurred, however, Stavka had divided counsel, which enabled General Ivanov to focus on preparing for an early 1915 Carpathian Mountain campaign.[1] Ivanov requested reinforcements from Stavka, insisting that his weak siege troops at Fortress Przemyśl could not repel a major Habsburg attack or the serious German troop numbers that had recently been deployed against his units. He emphasized that only two cavalry divisions currently defended key tsarist positions in the area between the Uzsok Pass and important Baligrod positions. He further projected that an invasion of Hungary would require additional troops as well as numerous mountain artillery batteries because of the treacherous terrain and inclement weather conditions that negatively affected regular artillery batteries' effectiveness. The tsarist southwest front commander insisted that a major military victory against the Habsburgs was feasible and would simultaneously provide political capital vis-à-vis the neutral powers. Ivanov succeeded in acquiring XII Corps and six mountain artillery batteries as reinforcements on January 26. These reinforcements, originally destined for the projected offensive against Germany, weakened Romanov Tenth Army efforts against the Germans in that campaign and worked to the disadvantage of later tsarist efforts during the second battle of the Masurian Lakes in early February 1915. Meanwhile, General Ivanov finalized his plans on January 20 to launch a frontal assault on the Carpathian Mountain front and invade Hungary to knock the Dual Monarchy out of the war. Neither he nor General Conrad had any idea what a horrible effect this would have on their troops and themselves.

The turning point in the fortress's fate came in 1915 because there was little chance of a timely liberation of the citadel due to the distance and severe winter mountain climate and terrain. Within the fortress itself, hunger and rationing increasingly weakened the troops' physical condition and left them unable to launch any effective major sorties. Battle fatigue, hunger, sickness, and frostbite permeated the ranks, rendering many of the men unfit for military duty altogether. The declining effectiveness of the Habsburg armed forces worried the German High Command; the threat of neutral nations entering the war made it crucial that they provide aid to the floundering Austro-Hungarian army.

Fortress Przemyśl's steadily worsening food situation and the deteriorating condition of its troops placed additional pressure on General Conrad to quickly initiate military action to liberate the citadel as soon as possible. In January, he ordered General Kusmanek to designate a minimal fortress defensive force to protect the bulwark. The remaining garrison troops had to launch an offensive to attempt to break through the Russian encirclement. The defensive force had the mission of destroying any important military objects within the fortress that the enemy could utilize after the bastion's capitulation. With that mission completed, the garrison troops would join their fellow units in the offensive breakthrough attempt. During the latter part of January, General Kusmanek reorganized fortress troops in preparation for the projected efforts.

Meanwhile, General Conrad's German counterpart, General Falkenhayn, began to fear the collapse of the Austro-Hungarian army in early 1915 and thus begrudgingly designated four newly formed strategic German reserve corps, originally destined to participate in a western front offensive operation, to now be deployed in East Prussia to conduct a campaign to support the Habsburg Carpathian Mountain offensive operations. This infusion of German troops resulted in the second battle of the Masurian Lakes in early February, which, despite being a great German tactical success, provided no significant strategic advantage. The 375-kilometer distance between the German and Austro-Hungarian allied fronts also precluded any major positive effect on General Conrad's Carpathian Mountain operation.

Harboring serious reservations concerning Conrad's Carpathian Mountain offensive plans, Falkenhayn initially informed his Habsburg counterpart that he could not spare any additional German troops to support his approaching offensive operation. Furthermore, Entente troops outnumbered his forces by a two-to-one margin on the western front. Falkenhayn cited multiple arguments against General Conrad's plans for launching a January Carpathian Mountain offensive. He contended that the distance separating the allied armies was much too extensive to achieve a major victory.[2] He also cited the critical shortage of traversable roads and high-capacity rail lines as well as the inevitable communications and logistical problems that the army would encounter in winter mountain warfare. Conrad's German counterpart further suggested that he might win a few local victories, simply forcing the Russians back, but not a decisive triumph. He also declared that the operation would not influence Italy and Romania. General Conrad, however, reiterated the necessity of launching the major mountain campaign particularly because of the increasing tsarist military presence in the region and the pressing necessity to liberate Fortress Przemyśl. Falkenhayn further argued that since the Save and Danube Rivers had frozen over, the Balkan front posed no imminent military danger to Austria-Hungary. Claiming that sufficient troop numbers existed to repel a Serbian attack, Conrad rapidly transferred entire corps units from that front to the Carpathian Mountain theater. The Fortress Przemyśl dilemma continued to dictate Conrad's military operations to Habsburg disadvantage for the next several months.

Falkenhayn offered a counter suggestion that Conrad launch an offensive on the Serbian, rather than the Russian, front. He argued that heavy casualties, disease, privations, and material shortages had severely weakened the Serbian army. He also insisted that a military victory over Serbia would help restore lost Habsburg prestige because of the embarrassing 1914 Balkan front defeats. Conrad, in turn, responded that a Balkan campaign was simply not feasible; he simply could not spare any troops from the Russian front and brazenly repeated a request for German reinforcements to be deployed for his offensive endeavor. Falkenhayn's numerous and sound negative arguments failed to deter Conrad from continuously insisting that his ally provide the necessary troops to prevail against Russia on the eastern front. To his utter dismay, Falkenhayn unexpectedly learned that during late December the Habsburg army had retreated fifty kilometers into the Carpathian Mountains.

Habsburg troops were in a most unfavorable situation prior to launching Conrad's major offensive. Combat strength declined at a disturbing rate owing to cold-related casualties and low morale. Troops were not equipped to deal with the severe winter mountain conditions. Discipline had become a problem in several units, and many troops simply lacked the physical strength necessary to mount an effective resistance. Exposure often proved a more serious threat than enemy fire, and the horrendous weather wreaked havoc on operational timetables, especially when vital supplies could not be delivered by rail. Mountain train wrecks halted troop unit efforts in their tracks and disrupted the operational timetables critical for success.

During January 1915, a fortress civilian diarist noted multiple interesting facts. She wrote, "We do not have time to talk because of days of great work on the fortress works." It had become a do-or-die situation for the fortress, but the citadel inhabitants considered their duties ended. Sadly, on January 5, the last great sortie, which strove to attain liberation on New Year's Day, did not have the hoped-for success. Thus, the diarist recorded that it was a "severe blow to the fortress." Earlier New Year's greetings over the radio ended with the exciting words "We are coming!" from the Second and Third Armies. The conviction grew within the *place d'armes* that "we will be freed before the winter is out," but the inhabitants also recognized that, because of the severe winter mountain conditions, it would be almost impossible for any Habsburg advance in the Carpathian Mountains to succeed. In fact, the field armies floundered in the deep snow during the particularly severe winter conditions. Casualty numbers drastically increased from rampant illness and frostbite, and the Third Army, the main offensive force, would sacrifice almost one hundred thousand troops by February 6, 1915.[3]

The diarist also indicated that the Orthodox Christmas (January 7) produced a brief pause in the fighting. Tsarist officers exchanged good wishes with Habsburg officers, trading cigarettes for "sardines and salami. This irony is happily laughed at throughout the fortress." The holiday spirits, however, proved to be short-lived.[4]

A further entry on January 15 explained that horse meat had become more important with each passing day because the military and civilian population now existed almost entirely on it. This presented a problem for the Jewish population, which could not eat the meat, but garrison troops had already been consuming horseflesh for three to four weeks. For variety, cooks prepared it into wurst and goulash and cut it into small pieces to add to rice soup as well. Although it tasted terrible, no alternative existed. Fortress inhabitants even attempted to utilize horse lard to expand their meal contents. In contrast, before the second siege commenced, some officer messes had their own chicken coops, calves, and pigs.[5]

Under the increasingly desperate circumstances, food prices rose sharply. Women farmers brought hens to the market, selling them for twenty kronen or more. People purchased them in spite of the now exorbitant prices, but inflation had left money almost entirely worthless. A piglet now cost five hundred kronen and a cow up to one thousand kronen.

On January 1, a garrison troop stand report did not mention or describe the troops' or horses' physical condition. Many soldiers could not perform forefield duty. The reduction in food rations and the lack of winter equipment or uniforms resulted in ever-increasing exhaustion, illness, frostbite, and freezing to death. Some sources claimed that two hundred soldiers succumbed each day to exhaustion alone, but this has not been confirmed. During the siege, twenty-four thousand men would be listed as incapable of service. At least 4,500 wounded soldiers remained in hospitals and 1,280 were listed as invalids. A sufficient number of horses no longer existed for fortress duties, and the few available animals had been starved and driven to skin and bones. The January 3 pause in battle between the opposing Habsburg and Romanov armies may have spared troops the dangers of combat, but the conditions on the front made day-to-day survival extremely difficult.

A January 15 fortress report calculated that the slaughter of thirty-five hundred additional horses would extend the garrison's food supply until March 7. Recognizing the increasingly dire food situation within the citadel, Russian siege troops joked about how at Troy the warriors rode inside the Trojan horse, while at Fortress Przemyśl the horses ended up in the bellies of the defending troops.[6] Also during January, rutabaga replaced other vegetables for the garrison diet. Desperation led to increasing troop desertions, especially in the case of Slavic troops, particularly Ruthenians who lived within the fortress region. All Slavic soldiers, but particularly Ruthenians, were most unhappy about fighting their Russian cousins.

Crime also became more frequent at all levels of society. Many soldiers, by now dressed in rags, begged for pieces of bread or a bowl of hot soup from civilians. Others risked the death penalty by looting private apartments. Courts martial punished supply officers when they gave away food, but discipline soon collapsed completely. To retain at least some semblance of normalcy, the 23rd Honvéd Infantry Division band performed regularly in the main square for soldiers and civilians alike, while movie theaters showed old films.

The Carpathian Mountain front also remained isolated from other Habsburg operational theaters, while division and corps fronts were spread too thinly on the torturous mountain terrain, making the threat of an enemy breakthrough a constant concern. Relative to troop quality, the Ersatz (replacement troops) were not adequately trained or supplied. They also contained highly unreliable national elements such as the Ruthenians.

On January 5, the first airmail letters left the fortress environs. Three aircraft carried 140 kilograms of postage to the fortress one day later. Also on January 6, Fortress Przemyśl Post Office Number 1 opened and established regular flights between Kraków and Fortress Przemyśl.[7]

The Habsburg Third Army situation in the Carpathian Mountains remained passive. All attempts to advance toward the fortress encountered serious resistance. Additional reports emphasized the shortage of officers and lack of effective artillery support, while heavy snowfall and meter-deep snow hampered visibility, forward movement, and artillery fire accuracy. When General Conrad again requested reinforcements from the Germans, he was promised one division but was refused further requests from early January through February 25 despite the fact that the Carpathian offensive was originally supposed to be reinforced with four to five German divisions.

As the date for launching Conrad's Carpathian Mountain offensive approached, everyone remained well aware that time was running out for the fortress. The food situation required immediate action. To make matters worse, Conrad's Russian counterpart, General Ivanov, planned to attack and seize the Dukla Pass and the Laborcz valley. If Ivanov succeeded, Russian forces would control Mezölaborcz, a vital railroad and communications center. Conrad allowed these circumstances to dictate his strategy, which partially explains the desperate and deadly frontal assaults that were launched.

On January 9, the commander of Fortress Przemyśl issued an order allowing the delivery of citadel mail by paper balloons. All postcards received a special "Balloon Fortress Przemyśl 1915" stamp. The balloons were constructed from varnished wrapping paper to be as light as possible and small enough to avoid easy detection. A load of eight cubic meters of illuminating gas could carry approximately five to six pounds of mail. The balloon then had to ascend into the air and travel about 120 kilometers over the front and enemy-occupied territory.[8]

On January 11, the two chiefs of their General Staffs met at Breslau to agree on future offensive operations.[9] On the next day, the danger of

Romanian intervention increased because the Russians had occupied almost all of the Bukovina near the Transylvanian frontier. The situation had become increasingly unfavorable, and only successful military action could forestall further difficulties. If tsarist troops entered the eastern Dual Monarchy territory, Romania would almost certainly decide to intervene. General Falkenhayn suggested that Viennese leaders buy Bucharest's neutrality through diplomacy by surrendering territory rather than risking another Carpathian Mountain offensive. The Habsburg position, however, held that negotiations would be absolutely worthless; only a military victory could avert the danger.[10]

By 1915, the Austro-Hungarian army bore little resemblance to the proud force that had mobilized during July 1914. The opening August–September and fall 1914 campaigns, as mentioned, had resulted in most professional soldiers becoming casualties. The enormous number of Miliz, or militia troops, had reduced the Habsburg army to an improvised force of reservists. The official Austrian history of the war described the 1915 army as a Volksheer (People's Army) because of the catastrophic battlefield casualties involving professional soldiers, leaving only reserve officers and new recruits to continue the battle. The multivolume publication *Österreich-Ungarns letzter Krieg* (Austria-Hungary's Last War) claims that the Habsburg army sustained 800,000 casualties during the January 23 to mid-April 1915 Carpathian Mountain Winter War campaign, which attempted to break the siege of Fortress Przemyśl and liberate the 130,000-troop garrison. Due to the universal inaccuracy in assessing casualties, the losses could very well have been much greater. Official reports failed to mention that the majority of casualties did not result from combat action; rather, many of the troops succumbed to *der weisse Tod* (the White Death), or froze to death, suffered from frostbite, or succumbed to serious lung or intestinal illness.

The large, hostile Ruthenian (Ukrainian) population that inhabited much of the Carpathian Mountain region was sympathetic to the Russians, with whom they shared religious practices and language. This made the theater even more dangerous for Habsburg soldiers, and the presence of so many Ruthenian troops within the fortress increased the other soldiers' paranoia. Many Ruthenians were found guilty of treason and hanged. In addition, the influx of the supposedly unreliable

Romanian and Czech/Slovak replacement troops on the Habsburg eastern front reputedly resulted in mass troop desertions. According to the Habsburg military High Command, this disturbing trend, especially relative to the Czechs, continued throughout the Carpathian winter campaigns and the remainder of the war, fueled by antimilitary and antidynastic propaganda from the hinterland.[11] This has recently been proven to be largely a myth.

During January 1915, thirty-five Habsburg infantry divisions opposed twenty-nine tsarist units on the Carpathian Mountain front. South of Fortress Przemyśl, a 140-kilometer line led to the Uzsok Pass and then extended another 250 kilometers to the Romanian frontier. The fortress's three-and one-half starving divisions countered four infantry and two cavalry tsarist siege divisions.

Meanwhile, General Conrad commenced transferring troops from the other Habsburg fronts into the Carpathian Mountains in preparation for his January offensive. For example, V Corps, designated to secure the Third Army's weak right flank positions in the offensive effort, arrived from the northern Habsburg First Army front. Troops already deployed on the mountain terrain encountered enormous obstacles, including snowbound roadways that transformed into seas of mud during thaws. At most other times, these areas experienced deep snow and icy conditions. Sleds transported supplies and artillery batteries into the higher elevations, where the transport and emplacement of artillery pieces proved increasingly difficult. Numerous Habsburg artillery batteries were abandoned behind the rearward lower-level mountain ridges. Without this artillery support, attacking troops suffered enormous casualties. Poor visibility (fog and snow) and frigid weather did not deter Russian activity around Fortress Przemyśl. Citing the dwindling food supplies, General Kusmanek inquired of General Conrad whether the fortress would be liberated in the near future or whether he should plan to launch an effort to break through enemy lines to attempt to reach the field armies. Conrad delayed responding to the fortress commander's query to await results from his initial Carpathian Mountain offensive efforts, which commenced on January 23, 1915. Meanwhile, garrison troops continued to forage for food around the fortress perimeter.

General Conrad, increasingly concerned about the fortress's worsening food crisis, ordered General Kusmanek to devise a plan for a major
breakout operation to be launched by mid-February. Meanwhile, the
tsarist troops tightened their siege on the fortress. The New Year brought
even stricter food rationing; bread portions were reduced by one-quarter
and animal feed mixed with food for human consumption to quell
the troops' hunger pangs. The slaughter of horses, despite providing additional sustenance and increasing the supply of oats for human consumption, seriously reduced fortress mobility because of the troops' declining
physical condition.

The fortress commander requested medicine to be delivered to the
bulwark because supplies had run dangerously low by mid-December. On
January 17, 1915, General Kusmanek requisitioned narcotics, chloroform,
camphor, glycerin, insecticide, antidiuretic gastric juice, codeine, castor
oil, and other such supplies. Airplanes flew medicine to the citadel but
were seriously limited by how much weight they could carry. The fortress
had meanwhile run out of important medicinal needs such as aspirin,
codeine, and alcohol by February 1915.

Fortress inhabitants also had to contend with intermittent artillery
and airplane bombardments from Russian siege forces. According to a
January 18 civilian diary entry, the attacks did much to worsen an already
difficult situation: "There were anxious moments during the entire day
as Russian airplanes encircled the fortress. Shrapnel shells fell on numerous occasions, therefore, there was no quiet. Fortress airplanes attempted
to intercept the enemy aircraft and individual soldier rifle fire. The bombings did some damage but the main effect was psychological." Thousands
of windows had been destroyed, while supplies and replacement items
disappeared from store shelves. Many windows were covered with paper
or other material, but observers claimed that the civilian inhabitants
reportedly did not complain.[12]

As the launch of the Habsburg Carpathian Mountain offensive
approached in late January, heavy rain, a change in the weather, turned
road surfaces into rivers of mud. Soldiers struggled to navigate through
the quagmire, supply columns became bogged down, and reconnaissance efforts were severely hampered. Nevertheless, Habsburg troops

had to launch the offensive to break the Russian siege of Fortress Przemyśl.

Reports emanating from the fortress indicated that the enemy had transferred troops from its Uzsok Pass mountain positions and deployed two further divisions in the citadel area. General Conrad commenced his Carpathian Mountain offensive operations during late January, February, and mid-March mainly because the time pressure to liberate Fortress Przemyśl left no alternative. Meanwhile, Russian forces continued to hurl Habsburg defenders back from the critical Dukla Pass region in an effort to seize the key railroad and communications junction at Mezőlaborcz. Its capture in early February crippled all future Habsburg attempts to liberate the fortress.

The Third and South Armies would launch deadly frontal assaults against strong tsarist defensive positions. In the face of steadily deteriorating weather conditions on January 21, twelve Third Army divisions deployed along the 100-kilometer front prepared to commence the offensive operation while some field army units deployed a mere sixty kilometers from the fortress. The stage had been set for history's first protracted mountain warfare in the age of total war.

During the next several months, Generals Ivanov and Conrad doggedly pursued their individual strategies, both disregarding the potentially enormous human cost. Ivanov failed to appreciate the danger for the Russians should major tsarist units be drawn too deeply into the frigid Carpathian Mountain ranges. Moreover, if his forces advanced too far into the mountains, the tsarist northern (German) flank would become exposed. Meanwhile, General Conrad ordered his weakened Third Army to launch the frontal attack along the shortest route to the fortress. As the Russian and Austro-Hungarian commanders prepared to unleash their respective Carpathian Mountain offensives, they did not foresee that eventually two-thirds of the Habsburg armed forces and four Russian armies would become embroiled in the enormous mountain struggle.

From the outset of the offensive, which began on January 23, 1915, the Habsburg army's haste in launching an offensive put the participating troops in a terrible tactical situation. Prior to the attack, unit combat strength had declined at an alarming rate, primarily due to cold-related casualties; subzero temperatures, deep snow, and bitter wind blasted troops still wearing summer uniforms. Lacking regular meals, they suffered from every imaginable form of deprivation, which in turn produced a steep decline in morale, discipline, and physical stamina. There could be no adjusting to the unimaginably brutal winter mountain environment; every day became a struggle for survival.

Once the offensive commenced, supply difficulties not only persisted but grew consistently worse. Destroyed railroad lines and tunnels had to be repaired, damaged bridges had to be rebuilt, and train stations required constant maintenance. The inferior roads in Galicia could be utilized only by lighter (*panja*) Polish wagons. Potholes harassed troop and supply columns but proved even more dangerous for unwary horses. It required a gargantuan effort to maintain the roadways in usable condition. Snow had to be shoveled continually due to the heavy snowstorms. Trees and horse carcasses became temporary expedients to prevent wagons from sinking into the mire up to their axles. The conditions proved a logistical nightmare for moving large military formations, reinforcements, artillery, and basic supplies into the war theater. Mountain slopes and ridgelines often forced advancing columns to make uncoordinated and isolated attacks in the often man-high snow.

Reacting to the time pressure to liberate Fortress Przemyśl, General Conrad gambled that the temporary break in the inclement weather conditions would continue. However, to his troops' misfortune, a sudden blizzard struck the Carpathian Mountain front, causing Habsburg troops to have to battle two fierce adversaries: tenacious Russian soldiers and fearsome weather conditions. Before they could advance, Habsburg troops exhausted themselves either shoveling through the deep snow or hacking their way one step at a time up the ice-covered mountain slopes. Dense fog at higher elevations further exacerbated the difficult situation, frequently shrouding the mountain terrain from view, thus preventing artillery support for the infantry. A pre–main offensive undertaking to recapture the Uzsok Pass, launched on January 22, failed to achieve its objective because the deep snow and dense fog conditions wreaked havoc on the operational timetables so critical for Habsburg success. The horrendous weather, in conjunction with the terrain conditions, often halted the attacking units in their tracks, while frostbite and exposure constantly posed an increasingly greater threat to Habsburg troops than enemy rifle fire. Numerous pack animals also succumbed to the conditions, often faltering on the slippery mountain slopes and falling to their deaths.

Intermittent periods of warming weather often replaced the blizzard conditions, which melted the snow and produced concomitant flooding everywhere, particularly in the valley areas. The horrific turn of events prompted one Habsburg officer to lament, "It's as if heaven is against us!"[13]

The main Habsburg attacking force, the Third Army, had expanded to fifteen infantry and four cavalry divisions for the operation. The newly created neighboring South Army, composed of new German and Austro-Hungarian troop units, would protect the Third Army's right flank area and also attack, but significant mountain terrain features created a major barrier between the two armies. The Third Army's 175,000-man attack force proved far too weak to accomplish its Herculean mission to launch a frontal assault on a one-hundred-kilometer-wide front. South Army would attack along a sixty-kilometer area. The expansive front and insufficient troop numbers also forced many units to attack in single-file formations because of the lack of manpower. Given the circumstances, the offensive operation's dual mission of enveloping the tsarist extreme left flank positions and liberating Fortress Przemyśl proved quite impossible to achieve. A combined twenty and one-half divisions launched the offensive on January 23. Meanwhile, on the entire Galician front, forty-one Habsburg infantry and eight cavalry divisions opposed thirty-eight tsarist infantry and fifteen cavalry divisions, which possessed much larger troop stands.[14]

The artillery movement and placement in the mountain war theater proved to be a monumental hindrance to operational success and would never be adequately resolved during the three Carpathian Mountain winter campaigns. Habsburg Supreme Command had failed to overcome this critical disadvantage during the November and December 1914 campaigns, which should have served as a stark warning of worse things to come once winter weather fully arrived. The often unavoidable and excessive preparation delays encountered before launching the initial effort gave the Russians adequate time to initiate effective countermeasures. In addition, several infantry divisions designated to participate in the offensive did not arrive in a timely manner for the actual launching of the endeavor, a factor that would haunt all Carpathian Mountain operations. These combined factors did not bode well for the initial offensive success intended to liberate Fortress Przemyśl.

The offensive proceeded in stages, but the countless unfavorable conditions impeded that effort. Mountain ridgelines and slopes separated the advancing columns from each other, resulting in uncoordinated, individual, and isolated attack efforts. Furthermore, the Third Army could not advance if the neighboring Fourth and South Armies did not achieve forward progress on their respective fronts because of the resulting serious threat to the Third Army's flank positions. The ice and heavy snow also damaged telegraph and telephone lines, and the lack of reliable wire communications severely hampered operations.

Biting winds exacerbated the terrible conditions; attacking troops achieved only slow, tedious progress through the often man-high snowdrifts. Even if the initial offensive operation had proved successful, the lack of reserve formations signified that the troops could not long maintain attack momentum, particularly at the most crucial portions of the front. As casualties mounted, front lines became overextended, making it impossible for the surviving troops to provide even adequate defensive coverage over the wide frontal area. The major Attack Group Puhallo advanced northward into a forty-kilometer gap in the Russian lines toward Lisko-Sanok south of Fortress Przemyśl on a mission to seize these key occupied tsarist railroad and road connections. This elusive objective remained Conrad's goal throughout the 1915 Carpathian Mountain campaigns. If those key railroad locations could be captured, the enemy could not supply its troops. However, Group Puhallo's attack force lacked sufficient troop numbers to successfully complete this crucial mission. General Conrad failed to concentrate his limited manpower at the main attack, instead allowing excessive troop numbers to provide flank protection for the operation. This resulted in thrusting the few available reinforcements piecemeal into battle to no positive effect.

Soon after the inadequate three-division main Group Puhallo force advanced, a twenty-kilometer gap formed separating its troop formations. Because there were no reserve units, this dangerous situation could not be rectified. Tsarist military leadership quickly recognized the dangerous Habsburg military predicament and, on January 26, 1915, launched a massive counteroffensive: General Ivanov's previously planned offensive. Meanwhile, the horrendous conditions continued along critical supply routes; road maintenance crews found it impossible to complete the arduous task of keeping the roads open. Landsturm and regular army units had to assist in maintaining the travel routes. Efforts to keep snowbound railroad stretches clear faltered as well due to the shortage of labor crews. Heavy snowfall, fog, and deep snowdrifts hampered visibility and artillery transport. Consequently, Habsburg troops also regularly experienced a critical shortage of equipment, ammunition stores, and food supplies. The few defending Russian forces put up fierce resistance before retreating to newly prepared defensive positions, allowing the terrain, heavy snow, and ice to hinder the progress of the attackers. The dangerous cycle of severe casualties and thinning extended troop front lines doomed the surviving Habsburg troops, who had to remain in their positions for weeks without any rest or rehabilitation.

As the major Habsburg offensive commenced, everyday necessities continued to disappear in Fortress Przemyśl. The shortage of leather forced both military and civilian personnel to wear damaged shoes and boots. Boot soles had to be replaced with rags.[15] At the listening posts before the fortress perimeter walls, duty soldiers wore sandals that fit over their boots. Because of the accelerating lack of basic goods, factories were constructed inside the citadel, since the bulwark could not expect any assistance from the homeland. In one factory, they constructed a machine that mixed wood shavings with salt and other substitutes for flour. The factories also produced other products, such as soap, because there had been none available to wash clothes for some time. Anything that could be useful was collected from local farmers and fortress city inhabitants because most raw materials had been consumed. Horse feed became a major problem because of the thousands of animals in the fortress. Many would be slaughtered to feed the troops, which also conserved supplies of oats. Any horse meat not consumed was made into conserves.

The Zündholz question, a burning one in the literal sense of the word, related to the shortage of matches necessary for light, warmth, and food. A fortress commander order demanded that everyone conserve matches and that none be removed from the fortress magazine without permission. This was strongly regulated; each day, two soldiers received one match, with the matches often further divided into two or three pieces. Every morning, the troops passed them around to light cigarettes and pipes, while in the hospitals they were passed from bed to bed. Many troops became specialists at stretching their meager supplies and quickly learned how to conserve valuable items.

The inhabitants of Fortress Przemyśl desperately desired to be informed about efforts to liberate them. Because they were cut off from the outside world, garrison newspapers became very significant even as paper supplies grew scarce. Printed in different colors for each language, the newspapers appeared in German, Hungarian, and Polish. The citadel regularly received radiograms later published under the title of war reports in the daily editions that circulated on the streets. People stood outside their homes, guesthouses, restaurants, and local stores in the morning to receive a copy; everywhere people anticipated receiving the latest news. Young people ran through the city streets delivering the latest edition and, for a brief time, became the most important people in the citadel as they shouted the news throughout the fortress environs. People rushed out of their homes or buildings without hats or coats to stand in the cold to read the latest copy, hands shaking in anticipation. Even wagons traveling through the streets stopped so that their drivers could read the news; people held onto the papers for dear life even in the snow. Specifically, everyone craved reports about the field armies' attempts to liberate the fortress.[16]

On January 24, General Ivanov informed Stavka that reinforced Habsburg troops and numerous German units had attacked his weakly held positions. Further claiming that the Habsburg offensive's ultimate objective remained the relief of Fortress Przemyśl, the general requested four to five infantry divisions as reinforcements so that he could launch his offensive. On January 26, Stavka released the XII Corps and six mountain artillery batteries so that Ivanov could launch a major Carpathian Mountain front offensive to prevent the loss of Fortress Przemyśl. Meanwhile, the attacking Habsburg field army troops, delayed by snowfall and dense fog, encountered multiple difficulties when preparing to continue their advance on January 25, while they futilely attempted to reconquer the main Carpathian Mountain ridgelines that had been surrendered to the Russians during December 1914 battles.

The required Habsburg Third and South Armies' cooperative efforts failed largely because of the rugged mountain terrain that separated the two armies. Neither gained a significant tactical advantage over its opponent or overcame the unfavorable weather and terrain conditions. South Army units, delayed by the necessity of shoveling through chest-deep snow, advanced scarcely ten kilometers. The resulting troop exhaustion further retarded rapid forward movement and lowered troop morale.

Unbeknownst to Habsburg leaders, the Russians had assembled major troop contingents in preparation to initiate their own major counteroffensive. The Habsburg Third Army's efforts to expand its meager right flank military successes proved elusive, while enemy resistance to its left flank efforts forced them back to their starting positions. The main attack group meanwhile proved unable to attain its goals, thus the fierce battle that raged between the Dukla and Uzsok Passes produced a turning point in Habsburg military fortunes.

On January 26 and 27, the Russians attacked Fortress Przemyśl's forefield positions at Pod Mazurami–Helica and advanced their siege lines closer to the fortress perimeter. Citadel observers witnessed Russian reinforcements, as well as artillery units, approaching Defensive District VIII. Reportedly, the entire 81st Russian Reserve Infantry Division had deployed before that area, while tsarist Infantry Regiments 321 and 322 deployed in the San River left flank area.[17]

On January 26, the major tsarist counteroffensive forces smashed into the Third Army's left and middle positions. The already weakened and battered Habsburg troops could not withstand the assault and sustained additional heavy casualties while being forced rearward to their original positions. The tsarist operation preempted the Third Army offensive effort and dashed any possibility of further Habsburg offensive plans in the near future. The tsarist troops skillfully utilized the most direct route to Budapest through the Dukla Pass; as a result, the ensuing battle of attrition produced enormous casualties. On the Habsburg Third

Army front, three corps now protected the key invasion route to Hungary, an expansive seventy-seven-kilometer front that extended between the Dukla and Lupkov Passes.[18]

The Russian objective in entering the strategic Laborcz valley was to sever the main Habsburg railroad connections, effectively driving a wedge between their armies and neutralizing the threat of the major Habsburg attacking force. Success would also terminate any efforts to liberate Fortress Przemyśl. As Habsburg defensive lines along the South and Third Army fronts buckled under the weight of the tsarist onslaught, apathy and battle fatigue wore the troops down. The Austrian official history of the war concedes that the initial territorial gains made during the first Carpathian Mountain offensive did not justify the bloodletting or the physical and moral suffering of the troops. The Habsburg military situation quickly became untenable. the Third Army, having sacrificed nearly 80 percent of its troop stands, including the thirty thousand replacement troops it received, reported that it could no longer conduct offensive action because of the terrible weather conditions, its excessive casualties, and superior enemy troop numbers.

The Russians' frontal assaults in December that enabled them to seize all the important Carpathian Mountain ridges gave General Ivanov a tremendous advantage for his January 1915 offensive plans to capture the remaining key mountain positions needed for an invasion of Hungary. On January 28, Russian assault troops forced the Third Army's left flank III Corps to retreat to its reward positions. The continued enemy pressure also negatively affected Fourth Army southern flank units, which received orders to launch an offensive in the coming days in conjunction with the Third Army's operation. VII Corps also had to retreat when the enemy attacked its 1st Cavalry Division and pushed it to the south, which forced the corps' 2nd and 20th Landwehr Infantry Divisions back even farther. Snow and fog prohibited launching any air reconnaissance missions.

By concentrating their main forces against the Third Army, the Russians suddenly threatened Mezölaborcz.[19] As the main railroad and communications center in the region, Mezölaborcz was critical for any operation hoping to liberate Fortress Przemyśl. General Ivanov recognized that capturing it would stymie all Habsburg efforts to relieve the citadel. On January 29, the Russians launched another major assault into the Laborcz valley with the objective of seizing the city. The campaign would eventually culminate with the surrender of the critical position on February 5 following brutal battle under the worst possible weather conditions.

Weather played a significant role during all three Carpathian Mountain offensives, just as it had during the October to December 1914 campaigns. Moving supply trains and artillery pieces under the prevailing winter weather conditions posed an enormous challenge. Heavy Habsburg ammunition wagons bogged down in the mud. The weather, including persistent cloud cover that enveloped the mountain regions until noon, also stymied reconnaissance efforts; many air reconnaissance missions had to be canceled. The mountainous terrain quickly exhausted the troops as they struggled to advance. Snow had to be shoveled from lengthy stretches of railroad track as well as roadways. Skis and sleds often served as the only viable mode of transporting men and material. Marches and troop deployments experienced serious delays as sudden melting conditions caused flooding in the valleys, sweeping away bridges and inundating troop positions. These factors added significantly to the mental and physical exhaustion of the troops.

The conditions also proved harmful to the health and well-being of the animals. Horses sank to their bellies in the deep snow. Many starved to death due to the lack of feed combined with extreme physical exertion. Horses had proven a critical resource for many aspects of the mountain campaign, and their loss adversely affected supply efforts. The resulting stoppages or slowing of supplies hampered battlefield planning and the implementation of all three Carpathian Mountain offensives.

Meanwhile, fortress personnel raised money for widows and orphans of those who died defending the fortress, including pilots. Everyone donated, even wounded soldiers, officers, and civilians. At the same time, much concern centered on the surviving soldiers, called "poor devils," who desperately sought bread because of the reduced garrison rations. One thousand civilians had to be fed in the area of Wapowa alone. Several reservist troops were accomplished singers, cello players, pianists, and the like. Someone composed a "Kusmanek March," played at every public concert with the usual accompanying patriotic songs. General Kusmanek was supposedly beloved not only by garrison troops but by civilians as well. During the periodic concerts when the "Kusmanek March" was played, everybody stood up and gave him a standing ovation. "*Hoch* Kusmanek, *Heil* Kusmanek! *Zivio*, Eljen Kusmanek, *evviva!*"[20]

On the mountain front, the winter conditions continued to make movement and battle very difficult for the battered, apathetic Habsburg troops. Habsburg troop apathy intensified particularly as a result of the persistent lack of reinforcements and the general fear of the "White Death." Brutally cold temperatures made it too dangerous for the troops to sleep at night. Some soldiers stood up in enemy fire to escape the nightmarish situation. The battle-weary, outnumbered troops received orders to "hold to the last man," a directive repeated so often that it soon lost any meaning. The crisis on the Habsburg front resulted in the questionable practice of hurling inadequately trained, inexperienced Ersatz replacement units into combat under the leadership of reserve officers. The troops rapidly became cannon fodder against the numerically superior enemy. No adequately trained troops could be found to stem the enemy drive. As the Habsburg military situation steadily worsened, the training time of recruits shrank to just a few weeks, ensuring that the newly minted soldiers would prove completely unprepared for the rigors of mountain battle and the concomitant severe weather conditions.[21] This often resulted in their deaths.

On January 30, strong tsarist forces struck the hapless Third Army after initially concentrating their forces on both sides of the Dukla Pass and threatening the critical railroad junction. Accumulated snow made all movement very difficult in that area. On the next day, February 1, Russian artillery fired intense barrages against Habsburg defensive positions at Mezölaborcz and the defending X Corps supply trains. That corps had fought for twelve days in the open without protective cover for its troops.[22] The persistent unfavorable conditions caused the troops to lose their will to fight. On that same day, a combined brigade (Infantry Regiments 81 and 82) began boarding trains to be transferred to reinforce the Third Army in an attempt to hold this critical area.

By the end of January, Russian soldiers had pursued the retreating Austro-Hungarian troops behind the main Carpathian Mountain ridges critical to preventing an invasion of Hungary. Meanwhile, it had become obvious that the weakened VII Corps troops could not maintain possession of the Dukla Pass. The increasingly dangerous, unfavorable military situation raised the question of transferring the Habsburg VIII Corps from the Balkan front to this critical portion of the Russian front.[23] Something had to be done quickly to continue the so far unsuccessful attempts to reach Fortress Przemyśl.

Although resulting in a tactical victory, the German battle of Masurian Lakes failed in its intent to draw a large number of Russian troops from the Carpathian Mountain front. The battle produced no significant strategic results and had little impact on the Habsburg front. Fortress Przemyśl remained besieged.

On February 1, General Kusmanek received intelligence reports indicating that a number of tsarist siege troop units had been transferred to the Carpathian Mountain front. An airplane landed at Fortress Przemyśl carrying orders for the fortress commander to form combat-ready divisions from his garrison troops. In a worst-case scenario, a skeletal garrison force would remain in the citadel, while the other units launched a breakout effort to pierce the enemy siege lines and attempt to join the field armies. On the same day, a Habsburg airplane was shot down and the pilot and copilot captured by the enemy and shipped to a prisoner-of-war camp in Siberia.[24]

As Habsburg field army troops retreated, the Russians did not disturb their movement. Exhausted reinforcing soldiers marched all night in an attempt to help attain and secure the critical Mezölaborcz-Lupkov railroad line. Most infantry companies counted only thirty to forty men remaining in their ranks.

Because of the Third Army's difficult eastern flank situation, General Conrad ordered one Fourth Army division and two and one-half additional divisions from other deployment locations to be transported by railroad to the Mezölaborcz area to strengthen that buckling army's troops. VIII Corps would then be transferred from the Balkan theater to launch what Conrad hoped would be a decisive counteraction between

February 7 and 8. Until then, the Third Army had to defend its threatened positions, which also protected the exposed South Army flanks.

On February 2, as troops fought in the snow-covered mountain forests and cold temperatures, the extreme conditions hastened their exhaustion. Thus, they offered little resistance to the enemy. The nights remained deadly, as bitter winds chilled the soldiers to the bone and snow and ice crusted their eyes. The virtually zero visibility led to many getting lost when marching, while compasses did not function in the higher elevations. Frostbite cases became rampant along the entire front.[25] The number of frozen bodies encountered horrified all observers.

After twelve days of battle with no shelter in the abysmal weather, troops had become almost completely ineffective and faced catastrophe if they did not retreat soon and receive rehabilitation. X Corps' commander reported to General Conrad that neither of his divisions could possibly halt an enemy night attack, while a serious gap had formed between III and VII Corps' positions. The Russians continued to hammer the armies' thin lines as the battered troops attempted to retreat.

The troops, also desperately requiring new boots, could not attack fortified enemy positions because of the deep snow and ice on the higher ridges. The soldiers, unable to find cover on the frozen terrain, could fire their rifles only while standing up. As the temperature dipped to −18°C, the extremely cold nights caused many troops to fall ill and suffer from frostbite and lung disease. Only troops on skis could move forward.[26]

Also on February 2, concern mounted about the continuing X and VII Corps retreat, which endangered the entire Habsburg eastern front military situation. The continually extended front lines endangered the overall situation. All units repeatedly received orders to unconditionally defend their positions, but the troops had suffered enormous hardships during the almost two weeks of constant battle. Hurling reinforcements piecemeal into the front line inferno to fill the multiple gaps in the front seriously worsened the military situation, because they should have been utilized as solid troop entities for launching counterattacks.[27]

Habsburg field commanders could no longer guarantee that their troops could maintain their positions, especially since the enemy closely pursued the retreating troops. In the meantime, the Balkan front VIII

Corps did not arrive at the threatened mountain front area until February 9 or 10, far too late to significantly affect the battle at Mezölaborcz. On February 2, Habsburg newspapers reported that any further mail delivery to Fortress Przemyśl had been banned. Nevertheless, many people continued to write letters to their relatives and close ones besieged in the fortress, as news of the ban produced a shocked reaction throughout the Dual Monarchy. Meanwhile, the Etappen High Commander announced that the wagonloads of accumulated mail simply could not be delivered.[28]

In Fortress Przemyśl, according to Lieutenant Colonel Molnar, commander of Honvéd Infantry Regiment 7, one of the best circulating garrison jokes had the Russians besieging the fortress, but the garrison had to pay a great deal of money to prevent them from retreating. Meanwhile, one of his fellow officers, a captain, was arrested once again because his mistress sold canned food and fed her pigs hardtack he gave her.[29] A further entry in Molnar's diary related that until February, apart from individual artillery duels and skirmishes, the fortress had remained relatively undisturbed. But on February 9, Russian activity increased, particularly artillery fire partially aimed at various fortress strong points. As tsarist troops sapped forward, they increased the number of their bombing flights to demoralize the garrison and the civilian population. He also mentioned the arrival of Habsburg Aviatik 317 and Albatross HP 100 double-decker planes to conduct reconnaissance missions over enemy positions and supply routes as well as the established air courier service initiated between Fortresses Kraków and Przemyśl. Aviation Company (Flik) Number 11 had been stationed at Fortress Przemyśl, and Flik Number 10 at Kraków. These aircraft also maintained contact with the homeland in addition to conducting reconnaissance missions. They also delivered military orders, documents, mail, chemicals, and medicine to the fortress, but the weight of their cargo was seriously limited due to space.[30]

In February, as hunger intensified in the fortress, requisition committees raided apartments and homes seeking extra food and warm clothes. Soldiers' rations, already at starvation levels, were further reduced. Troops now received only 8.8 ounces of bread daily, 2.1 cups of watery soup without any fat, and a spoonful of rice. Black, sugarless coffee supplemented the meager rations at dinner. Birch bark was ground with flour for baking and accounted for 20 percent of the citadel's bread content. Even as conditions within the fortress deteriorated, however, the inhabitants clung stubbornly to the faint hope of rescue, as shown by a February 4 civilian diary entry:

> Again the fortress is filled with rumors, one has a strong Austro-Hungarian army of fresh troops advancing in the Carpathian Mountains and heading toward the fortress. It is heartrending how everybody grasps the smallest ray of hope, even the pessimists. Every one hopes that the citadel will be liberated because they cannot last much longer and know that February would be a difficult time for all concerned. Officers and troops eat very little, they receive only the most necessary food, "we must persevere!"[31]

An air reconnaissance mission revealed that a seven-kilometer-long tsarist infantry and artillery column had moved toward Sanok and Bircza.[32] February 3 events intensified the Habsburg crisis as the Russians continued to hammer the Habsburg VII and X Corps in the Mezölaborcz area. The Third Army received orders to gradually retreat until reinforcements could arrive to support it. Conrad expected Third Army left flank units to halt the Russian advances with the arrival of the in-transit Fourth Army reinforcements. However, during the night the enemy broke through several positions that had no reserve units or reinforcements available to assist them, baring their flanks and causing X Corps' 2nd and VII Corps' 20th Infantry Divisions to retreat as far as three kilometers to the south.[33] The unfavorable events sharpened the developing personal friction between General Conrad and the Third Army commander, General Boroević. Weather conditions continued to negatively influence battle activity, causing half the casualties and making further retreat necessary with the cumulative severe losses, troop exhaustion, and insufficient available reserve troops. These factors worsened the already dismal chances of liberating Fortress Przemyśl.

The Russians finally entered Mezölaborcz, initiating hand-to-hand combat during a raging snowstorm. Habsburg defenders momentarily halted the attacking Russians at the only major Carpathian Mountain two-track railroad station, while enemy artillery barrages continued to pound Habsburg defensive positions and retreating supply columns. Defending X Corps' 2nd Infantry Division now consisted of only a thousand soldiers.[34] Meanwhile, Russian swarm lines hurled the defending Third Army left flank forces back into the city, where they pierced the center of two infantry divisions.

When the 2nd Infantry Division flank position troops suddenly retreated, it exposed other units' flank and rear echelon areas. In the ensuing retreat, many of the exhausted soldiers simply remained in their positions to be captured.[35] The retreat occurred in extremely cold temperatures and deep snow in a densely wooded area. This time, the Russians pursued their tottering enemy relentlessly. Numerous Habsburg units were outflanked and surrounded before they could retreat, which explained the large number of prisoners of war that fell into tsarist hands. For three days, the exhausted soldiers had no regular food or supplies and suffered from increasingly numerous cases of frostbite.[36] Both sides sacrificed huge numbers of troops.

General Conrad quickly conceived a plan to launch a counterstrike against the enemy utilizing the Fourth Army's XVII Corps to commence on February 7. The five infantry and one cavalry division attack force would initiate an offensive at the Third Army's left flank area, but the failure of that army's units to hold their lines there temporarily negated such plans.[37] Conrad then ordered the unconditional defense of Mezőlaborcz while he rushed the cited combined corps to that front to fill the dangerous gap that had appeared between III and VII Corps, which threatened to result in a tsarist breakthrough of Habsburg lines.[38]

The retreat of these two corps seriously worsened the already desperate Habsburg military situation; both corps lost their resistance power while awaiting the arrival of reinforcements. The continued snowfall required daily shoveling of positions, drastically hindering the operational situation.[39]

Fighting on its one-hundred-kilometer front, with no reserve forces, hampered Third Army efforts to liberate Fortress Przemyśl. The VII and X Corps had been battered in continuous combat, but frostbite accounted for many of the corps' troop losses. Yet the reeling army received orders to recapture Mezőlaborcz. X Corps had to hold its lines until XVII Corps arrived and counterattacked to relieve the pressure on them, but two of the X Corps divisions had already retreated. The critical Third

Army situation now required the Fourth Army to launch an attack; but as a precondition, Third Army's left flank forces had to maintain their present position, as it appeared likely that the Fourth Army could suffer heavy losses if they launched an offensive. Group Kritek (XVII Corps) had to transport heavy artillery pieces to the front for infantry support before they could initiate their assault.[40]

General Conrad originally planned to insert the in-transit VIII Corps as a unified force into the raging battle in an attempt to turn the tide and deploy the Fourth Army's XVII Corps against the advancing Russians. As the Habsburg battlefield situation worsened, many of X Corps' 2nd Infantry Division troops were captured by the enemy, but even more suffered from frostbite. Because the corps possessed no reserve forces, it retreated, its few remaining troops manning a thirty-kilometer front (twenty-five kilometers for VII Corps). General Conrad, when ordering Third Army to maintain its positions, insisted that the enemy did not possess superior numbers.[41] The military crisis had reached its high point as the outmanned and outgunned Third Army's position worsened by the hour. Its continuing retrograde movements threatened the entire army front.

The Russian Eighth Army continued its overpowering assault against the Third Army's left flank and middle areas on February 6 as the Third Army's offensive efforts stalled. It rapidly became obvious that the Third Army, lacking sufficient reserve formations, could not halt the Russian advance, which commenced at the Dukla Pass and now threatened the possession of the Laborcz valley. The three decimated X Corps divisions continued to retreat. A combined offensive of the Third Army right flank forces and neighboring South Army units now provided the only hope for Fortress Przemyśl's liberation. On February 6, continuous gunfire also erupted at the fortress's extended Pod Mazurami forefield positions.[42]

By February 7, any tsarist attack could easily achieve success on any of Third Army's front sectors. X Corps' commander dispatched a personal letter to General Conrad explaining that his corps was in a catastrophic situation and could no longer conduct any offensive action. The inclement weather, terrain conditions, sickness and frostbite, and small troop stands could easily cause the entire operation to collapse.

Large numbers of VII Corps casualties occurred because of the great extension of the battlefront (twenty-five kilometers), which resulted in poor communication between individual units in an almost completely forested area. Snow created further difficulties, as did the poor visibility, which limited necessary supporting artillery fire. In addition, the few available reserve units were not inserted into battle rapidly enough, yet VII Corps received orders to save the offensive operation by unconditionally hurling the numerically superior enemy forces back.[43] If the Fourth Army's southern flank troops had to launch a supporting attack to reduce the pressure on the Third Army, it would occur under extremely difficult circumstances, because they would be attacking strongly fortified enemy positions. The troops would also have to shovel through one and a half to two meters of snow before they could launch an attack. And even if the Fourth Army operation succeeded, they would certainly suffer enormous losses. The lack of artillery shells also proved detrimental to the infantry.[44] Meanwhile, the Lupkov Pass had been surrendered, while a Russian night attack, launched on February 7, produced further heavy Habsburg losses. XIX Corps also had to retreat after its front lines were broken through by a strong Russian assault.

On February 8, a sudden warming trend produced melting snow and flooding conditions, hindering military operations and worsening the already desperate supply problem. Once VIII Corps units arrived, the reinforced Third Army western flank forces attempted to repel the advancing enemy forces coming out of the Dukla and Lupkov Passes. The army's eastern flank assumed a defensive posture until the reinforced Habsburg Second Army, to be transferred back to the Carpathian Mountains from Germany, could be inserted into the front lines. This led to the division of Third Army forces, some to be transferred to the soon-to-arrive Second Army. A second major offensive would eventually be launched toward the earlier objectives of Lisko-Stary-Sambor.[45] The unrelenting Third Army setbacks in the Mezölaborcz area also enhanced the danger of the enemy capturing other areas vital for supplying the Habsburg army. At Fortress Przemyśl between February 8 and 10, various Honvéd units would be transferred into the city or forefield positions at Batyce. A battalion of Honvéd Infantry Regiment 7 marched toward Pod Mazurami, while further east the fourth battalion of Honvéd

Infantry Regiment 8 marched to Helica. On February 7, to raise morale, many fortress inhabitants gathered at the market square to attend a concert.[46]

On February 9, General Boroević ordered the arriving XVII and VIII Corps to launch an attack. Two additional Fourth Army divisions received orders to transfer into the Carpathian Mountain front to help stem the tsarist tide, while the Third and Fourth Armies were to attempt to launch a cooperative offensive effort at their inner flank positions. Meanwhile, Third Army eastern flank units continued to receive the brunt of heavy Russian attacks.

According to a fortress civilian, February 9 witnessed the first true winter weather; morning temperatures dropped from −8°C to −12°C. The diarist proceeded to deplore troop conditions: "Our poor soldiers in the forefields have a difficult time, in spite of the fact that the great cold was natural and daily." Many suffered from frostbite and would be trundled to a fortress hospital. Further, "for many weeks they have not eaten much food, their bodies no longer have the resistance power to counteract the frost and cold weather." Reputedly, no soldiers wanted to report to sick call. At one guard post the duty officer inquired, "Are you all right, can you continue?" The soldier replied, "I can do it!" Half an hour later he collapsed and was hurried to the hospital the next day.[47]

Increasing casualties resulted from overexhaustion. Some field watch posts situated only three hundred paces from enemy positions could be relieved from duty only at night. Patrols dispatched from the forefield positions, many lasting for multiple hours, surrendered to the enemy because of the horrendous conditions and uncertainty about the future destiny of the fortress. Ruthenians comprised the majority of the deserters whose homes and families resided behind the siege lines. Czech, Romanian, and Hungarian troops also deserted, but the Landwehr Infantry Regiment 35 Ruthenians, who proved untrustworthy in battle, exemplified the most notable dereliction of duty.

The Russians also increased the number of bombing flights over the fortress to demoralize the civilian population, while the citadel airplane courier service continued between Fortresses Przemyśl and Kraków. Thus Habsburg Supreme Command orders, other documents, mail, and medicine continued to be delivered to the bulwark. One fortress diary entry deplored the effect the extreme tension had on the soldiers' nerves: "Thus the people burn like a candle that is lit on both ends." Relative to the dwindling food situation during the last several days, the food portions for the troops had improved, but for the past ten days the troops received horse meat only twice; on the other days, they ate frozen flesh and meat conserves.[48]

Tsarist artillery fire had been relatively quiet around the fortress environs for days, but this changed when enemy troops advanced closer to the fortress lines. Then, during the morning of February 11, enemy artillery fire intensified against the fortress, the Russians concentrating on the southern fortress perimeter with their heaviest caliber guns. Many citadel inhabitants expected the enemy to initiate storm attacks against the bulwark as enemy troops sapped closer to portions of the fortress perimeter. That day, pilots reported that long wagon columns with supplies waited to deliver food, including beer, to the fortress. There had been no beer or other basic necessities available for three months. "We learn how to live without them," a diarist observed. The besieged troops and civilians hoped that their ordeal would end soon. They had recently been informed that the Habsburg offensive in the Bukovina and the Carpathian Mountain fronts progressed well despite the deep snow and cold weather conditions. Exhausted garrison troops perked up when they believed that the fortress would soon be liberated.[49]

Bread for the troops had to be prepared without milk, eggs, and yeast because only sugar, water, flour, and some sourdough were still available. The "potato catastrophe" occurred when potatoes became the only food available for meals. The civilian population ate mainly rice, potatoes, and local Polish foods. Despite this, a diarist insisted that one did not hear complaints: "Everyone thanked God if there's food to eat at all!" In contradiction to most historical sources, that writer reported: "We are restocked more than during the first siege. During the three weeks between the first and second siege many new guns and ammunition arrived." Radiograms reached the fortress addressed to "the heroes of Przemyśl." "Many have heard nothing from the Hinterland for many months, thus they have no idea what is happening in the world."[50]

The Habsburg Carpathian Mountain offensive efforts, however, failed largely because of the severe weather and terrain conditions and the enemy's ability to rapidly reinforce its frontline formations. Powerful Russian attacks greatly diminished Habsburg Third Army resistance capabilities, but specifically made any further attempts to launch an offensive senseless before the Second Army could launch the next major effort to liberate Fortress Przemyśl.[51]

On February 12, General Conrad apprised the Emperor's Military Chancellery of the present situation of the fortress. He stated that the second siege had now lasted for more than three months (since November 6), during which time the Russians had not seriously threatened the fortress. Thus, it could be assumed that the unsuccessful but powerful tsarist storm attacks of early October 1914 had convinced Stavka to await the arrival of heavy artillery batteries before again initiating serious military action against the citadel. Intelligence sources indicated that heavier caliber tsarist artillery had begun to arrive near the fortress. A January 27 fortress daily report mentioned the commencement of tsarist artillery barrages, which intensified in early February. The fortress could not launch a decisive sortie because of the troops' worsening physical condition, while citadel food supplies would reportedly run out on March 7 if the fortress was not liberated by then. General Conrad ordered that any troops not absolutely essential on other Habsburg fronts be transferred to the Carpathian Mountain theater to enable the Habsburg armies to advance.[52] It is unclear why this had not been done earlier to enhance offensive efforts. Field unit reports increasingly described their troops as apathetic and no longer capable of defending their positions and, by February 12, also emphasized the effect of the shortage of rifles and the inadequate training of Ersatz units.

On February 13, a soldier of the 23th Honvéd Infantry Division noted in his diary that fortress horses had become useless for combat service, continued to die from hunger, and could not lie down at night because the stables had stone floors but no hay or straw to cover them. He complained that everyone talked about the fort being liberated, but he did not believe it would happen. He also revealed that troops now ate rutabaga because nothing else remained; thus it became an additive for bread. But this and other fillers often proved indigestible, sometimes even resulting in troops becoming sick. After stating that the Russians had barraged the fortress Helica position with 21-centimeter shells, destroying one bunker, he lamented the fact that the fortress situation now appeared hopeless; he believed that he would never get out alive. On the next day, he wrote that garrison morale kept sinking and that every day produced new reports of officers committing fraud and theft. Even senior sergeants had become corrupted because everybody knew the end of the ordeal approached.[53]

The February 14 Third Army left flank position events proved discouraging; thus, one could not expect to achieve any positive or decisive military results on that portion of the front. Third Army troops suffered from increasingly severe battle fatigue, thus attempts to initiate effective military activity proved impossible to achieve. The Habsburg field army desperately needed replacement troops to fill the gaping holes in its front lines. Only the most critical supplies could be transported to the front lines because all routes remained impassable and a perpetual shortage of road maintenance crews continued; numerous artillery pieces still remained in rear echelon valleys.[54]

On February 15, Archduke Friedrich, nominal commander of the Habsburg army, received an order from the Emperor's Military Chancellery that every means possible had to be utilized to prevent Fortress Przemyśl's capitulation.[55] Meanwhile, General Conrad had determined that he had to launch a new offensive, this time with the Second Army, to liberate Fortress Przemyśl. Two weeks later, he launched sixteen Habsburg infantry divisions against seven to eight similar enemy units on a twelve-kilometer front. Despite the hasty preplanning and deployment, the operation could not be initiated by the ordered launch date. Thirteen of the sixteen designated Austro-Hungarian divisions eventually attacked. As plans progressed toward this second major Carpathian Mountain offensive, 24-centimeter Fortress Przemyśl Defensive District VIII mortars fired against the Russians advancing toward the heights of Helica. Nine-centimeter field cannons recently deployed from the citadel artillery reserve raised the total number of defensive district artillery pieces to over one hundred. Tsarist airplanes continued to fly over the fortress city, observing garrison troop movements and dropping bombs.[56] Machine gun fire could be heard from the direction of Lipowica. Then the persistent cold spell broke; rapid melting conditions quickly swamped roads and made bridges unusable.

Almost every day, village farm women came to the fortress market with geese, ducks, and chickens, but charged steep prices. One egg cost 1 to 1.2 kronen. A liter of fresh milk cost 2 Kronen, while other necessities were not available. Military cooks mixed dry with fresh milk, while the troops' breakfast continued to consist of black coffee or rice soup. The major troop complaint arose from the deficiency of bread; troop units received only a quarter loaf of bread per man each day. The civilian population received none. One local woman provided a frank assessment of the grim food situation: "If you do not have flour, you have no bread."[57]

On the same day, a Honvéd officer criticized General Kusmanek, claiming that he never visited his troop units and conversed only with Hungarian officers. He also complained that Kusmanek had begged for Hungarian soldiers for the fortress garrison before the siege commenced but no longer appreciated their service. The next day he described the fortress commander's behavior as inappropriate. Instead of showing true concern for the troops' conditions, he constantly strolled around the main street demanding that everyone salute him. He also reputedly never visited the wounded in the hospital, where an unbelievable number of soldiers died from inadequate dressings, surgeries, and lack of hygiene. The diarist also claimed that every third wounded soldier died from blood poisoning and that only a few horses remained for the entire 23rd Honvéd Infantry Division. General Kusmanek, meanwhile, rode in a coach while "our beautiful horses are being slaughtered."[58]

Meanwhile, on the Carpathian Mountain front, XIX Corps and the 29th Infantry Division retreated soon after launching an attack. These units, critical for any future Habsburg operations to liberate the fortress, now required reinforcements merely to maintain their present positions. The Russians unleashed more than seven infantry divisions against the weakly defended Lupkov Pass and other important nearby positions. The defending Habsburg troops found themselves in desperate straits, partly because the Russians continued to receive plentiful reinforcements, while they did not.

In addition, a serious lack of cooperation existed between Habsburg field commanders and their units, resulting in the launching of repeated, uncoordinated, and isolated battles, partly a result of poor planning. Fortunately for the Habsburgs, their enemy did not usually follow up its battlefield successes with a serious pursuit. Habsburg infantry units continued to receive inadequate artillery support partly because multiple gun batteries had recently been transferred behind the mountain ridgelines due to of a lack of shells, but also because of the recurring enormous difficulties encountered in positioning the guns. General Conrad berated the Third Army's commander, General Boroević, for his lack of success, whereupon the latter replied that Conrad should instead blame the inclement weather conditions, lack of support units, and effective tsarist troop tactics for the ultimate operational failure. Nevertheless, pressured by the increasingly critical Fortress Przemyśl situation, Conrad ordered the army to halt its retreat and launch an attack.

The weather improved briefly in mid-February but immediately reverted to the normal ice and snow, particularly on the mountain terrain, followed by melting and rainy conditions. This made supply routes impassable again. On February 16, wagons sank to their axles in mud, while one meter of snow remained on the higher mountain terrain. The Habsburg military objective continued to focus on the liberation of Fortress Przemyśl and the seizure of key tsarist railroad terminals at Lisko-Sanok. All nonessential railroad cars were rerouted south of the mountains to alleviate some of the rail chaos. Despite the enormous and sacrificial efforts to maintain continuous wagon movement, the flow of supplies to the front lines remained extremely erratic. The inclement weather conditions and significant casualties also continued to negatively affect major battle conducted between February 17 and 22. Soldiers sank to their knees in the mud, making it extremely difficult to even move, as they quickly exhausted themselves.

As Fortress Przemyśl troop numbers continued to decline from disease and exhaustion, a major fortress sortie was launched nevertheless. In preparation for the effort, defensive district artillery fired at enemy positions for several days as the Honvéd units launched the sortie in an attempt to join the field armies, which simultaneously launched their own operation to liberate the fortress.

Fortress Przemyśl Defense District VIII artillery fire had forced enemy units to retreat, but tsarist forces immediately received reinforcements and threatened to encircle the Honvéd Infantry Regiment 5

sortie troops that retreated to Pod Mazurami. The Russians then attacked the forefield positions again at midnight, supported by continuous artillery fire. Barbed wire emplacements failed to protect the field
positions during the battles.[59] Defensive District III troops, with the
main column of Landsturm Regiment 18 on the right flank, moved forward, supported by 3-centimeter heavy howitzer batteries, but little maneuvering room could be found at the forefield positions. A demonstration launched from Defensive District IV protected the right flank
garrison troops, but the Honvéd formations encountered heavy enemy
infantry and artillery fire during their flank movements. The sortie failed
dismally, and the troops retreated to the fortress. An active citadel defensive strategy was no longer possible because of the troops' worsened
physical condition. Their duties had to be reduced just as the Russians
became more active by seizing forefield positions at the fortress perimeters and capturing patrols. Daily artillery fire continued, but tsarist
battery positions remained a mystery. Through the light created by mortar fire, garrison defenders could observe entire rows of tsarist soldiers
advancing as their gunfire intensified. Habsburg troops occupied the
forward forefield positions that the Russians had earlier used to fire artillery barrages into the city.

Fortress troops, exhausted and traumatized, had by that point endured
a nearly five-month ordeal. Soldiers in perimeter forefield positions
rarely received anything to eat, and their morale sank as they continued
to suffer from the cold weather and chilling dampness of their earthen
bulwarks: "Thus everyone waits from day to day, from week to week, from
month to month . . . wait, wait."[60]

In the interim, fortress coffeehouses had served only tea for a month
with just a small amount of sugar to accompany it. A pilot periodically
delivered a newspaper from the homeland, so people read it and then
wrote down its contents to share with others.[61]

On February 16, Russian troops advanced against the northwest and
western fortress fronts. To counter such efforts, all artillery batteries of
the targeted defensive districts fired barrages into the enemy positions
while Honvéd Infantry Regiment 2 troops deployed to the Pod Mazurami defensive lines.[62] Russian soldiers also approached the southwest

fortress perimeter on February 18. During the night of February 19, a tsarist regiment attacked the Pod Mazurami and Helicha forefield positions. The attackers sustained bloody losses and left behind 140 prisoners of war, but they nevertheless continued their efforts.

At 6 a.m., the initial heavy fortress artillery fire opened against enemy troop assembly areas. By 9 a.m., 30.5 mm mortars commenced firing into the adjacent wooded area, forcing the enemy troops to retreat with heavy losses. Meanwhile, Landsturm Infantry Regiment 18 suffered from a murderous attack, which caused numerous casualties. The Russians then launched a concentrated two-regiment attack against the fortress perimeter. Reportedly, the ultimate disaster for the defending Habsburg units occurred because of insufficient security measures at its left flank positions, inadequate training, an insufficient number of machine guns, and the lack of offensive spirit, all of which combined to produce bloody losses. The Russians cut through the defensive barbed wire at three different positions and then penetrated them in an attempt to overpower the position. Reinforcements were rushed to Defensive District VIII for the Pod Mazurami action and a nearby strong point. Four hundred fifty prisoners of war were seized, while the number of tsarist dead and wounded could not be calculated because the enemy carried the bodies away during the night. Nevertheless, over 230 rifles and forty Russian corpses remained at the scene of battle. Later, tsarist prisoners of war stated that the Russians lost one thousand troops. During the battle, soldiers could not tell friend from foe in the darkness because orientation proved very difficult. Then, having sustained enormous casualties, the Russians finally retreated. At 3:45 p.m., the garrison regiment also retreated on a broad front, its losses including 5 officers dead, 211 troops and 7 officers wounded, and 200 missing in action.[63]

The next day, it was presumed that the enemy would launch a night attack against the fortress because Landsturm Infantry Regiment 18 troops were mentally and physically exhausted. This regiment was regarded as one of the best Slavic Landsturm regiments in the fortress.

The Russians launched a particularly strong attack against the Honvéd troops on February 20, which developed into a fierce battle. The combatants fought within 150 paces of each other, utilizing shrapnel, machine guns, infantry salvos, and other destructive means. Tsarist troops fell in rows by the hundreds, while at some perimeter positions not one soldier survived. One Honvéd regiment received orders to storm and seize a Russian strong point with a bayonet attack despite the extreme garrison troop exhaustion. Despite months of horrific conditions and shot nerves, they still had to continue to resist enemy assaults.

The last enemy storm attack also took its toll on the weary tsarist soldiers and, on February 23, they halted their attack and began to retreat. Habsburg bulwark artillery fire continued, while garrison civilians continued to hope for a rapid liberation of the bulwark. During the evening, the fortress city streets became filled with people on the first warm, spring-like day of the year. For four weeks the city had endured Russian bombings, with one commentator remarking, "As I write these lines, I can hear the explosions one after the other. During the afternoon, Russian Flyers again visited us."[64]

On February 19, a Honvéd officer recorded in his diary that Honvéd Infantry Regiment 6 (in the Pod Mazurami area) had sustained 50 percent casualties during the bloody battle. He claimed that corpses, pierced by bayonets, had piled up at the fortress defensive lines. Battle had lasted all night; thus, only in the morning did the garrison troops realize that they had repulsed the tsarist attack. A captured Russian officer revealed that he knew the Honvéd units would attack when they did. The diarist also mentioned that friendly artillery failed completely, a too common complaint. On February 21, still complaining about Honvéd casualties at Pod Mazurami, the officer emphasized that when the Russians retreated after the initial sortie attack, they knew that they would return shortly to their original positions, and again lamented that the enemy had received information about the Honvéd foray beforehand.[65] On February 27, he also recorded that the Russians placed fortress garrison prisoners of war in front of their attacking troops to prevent defensive fortress fire. He complained that the fortress Honvéd units did not have proficient noncommissioned officers and that the regular soldiers were ignorant and lacked common sense.

On the Carpathian Mountain front on February 18, overwhelming enemy counterfire halted any Habsburg troops' attempts to advance. The unfavorable weather conditions compounded the horrendous traffic problems. The usual fog shrouded the battlefield until noon. The remaining heavily laden supply wagons accelerated the further deterioration of roads and bridges, while several key road sections required constant major repair. The Russians launched attacks, resulting in hand-to-hand combat on February 19. The heavily wooded mountain terrain allowed them to assemble their forces undetected by Habsburg defenders. Then, on February 20, heavy enemy artillery fire stymied Habsburg troops as thick fog again enveloped the battlefields until early afternoon. Habsburg troops, however, successfully repelled two enemy attacks and maintained the terrain they had seized earlier.

Meanwhile, General Böhm-Ermolli, commander of the Habsburg Second Army, still deployed on the German front, received orders to return to the Habsburg front and launch a second Carpathian Mountain offensive in conjunction with Third Army units to be placed under his command. The objective for this second major offensive included the recapture of the Lupkov Pass to regain access to its narrow-gauge railroad to alleviate the very difficult Habsburg supply situation, recapture the key Mezölaborcz transportation and communications junction, and then ultimately liberate Fortress Przemyśl. Conrad insisted that he did not pressure the Second Army to capture Fortress Przemyśl on February 18, but nevertheless maintained that it should be liberated as quickly as possible. Attacking troops were advised not to wait for late-arriving divisions before launching the offensive operation. Six and one-half additional infantry divisions would reinforce the Second Army's intended frontal attack against well-fortified tsarist defensive positions, which blocked the most direct route to Fortress Przemyśl.

The new offensive operation would launch its main forces along both sides of the road system Cisna-Baligrod-Lisko. A considerable disadvantage was that only one major supply route provided for the attacking force's four army corps. This explains why a major priority for the offensive encompassed seizing the Lupkov to Cisna railroad connection. The Third Army main force received the mission to reconquer Mezölaborcz, thus a XIX Corps offensive on that army's flank would be launched before the main operation commenced. Although the chosen invasion route to Fortress Przemyśl was certainly the shortest, it also represented the most difficult—steep cliffs and narrow passageways gave the enemy a great advantage. New obstacles appeared at every terrain turn. The

Russians, of course, recognized the significance of this area for attempted offensive operations and had themselves utilized the region for their own purposes. They secured and blocked all of the possible invasion routes before the Habsburg offensive commenced. Heavy rainfall caused snow and ice to melt rapidly, compounding the supply traffic problems.

General Böhm-Ermolli faced an extraordinarily difficult situation before launching the second Carpathian Mountain offensive. All but one of the Third Army corps commanders that participated in the first offensive operation reported total troop exhaustion after the three-week campaign. Their efforts had been seriously retarded for many reasons, but the lack of sufficient numbers of mountain artillery batteries proved devastating partly because they did not have the appropriate equipment to transport the artillery into the mountains, so many batteries remained idle far behind the front. The priority for the deployment of mountain artillery batteries, however, was assigned to the Balkan-Serbian campaign. Thus, similar to the first offensive, the infantry suffered many casualties because they had to attack without the necessary artillery support, although the weather again proved an important factor in the battle's outcome.

Before the Second Army could launch its offensive, the casualties from the first operation had to be replaced because of the huge losses sustained during that campaign, while the Russians threatened to attack Habsburg forces before the Second Army could be organized to launch its offensive. To help refill the depleted ranks, Second Army command preferred to deploy replacement troops to its front before the six reinforcing infantry divisions would be transferred to participate in the offensive because of the present inadequate troop numbers at the front.

Although the offensive was set to commence on February 22, sudden melting conditions created extremely difficult communications problems. All supply and troop movement had to contend with terrain that had become quagmires of mud. Masses of snow melted and flooded passageways and trenches; the smallest brooks became tremendous obstacles, and the few roads that previous status reports termed "neck-breaking undertakings" had now been totally washed out. Such desperate conditions resulted in the Second Army offensive being delayed. Just prior to the scheduled operation, a report revealed that twelve kilometers of supply roads critical for the maintenance of the operation had been destroyed by overuse and the inclement weather conditions. The only recourse became to postpone the invasion.

On February 21, the offensive's launch day was rescheduled for February 26 because of the horrendous terrain conditions. Two hours after the order had been issued, two more messages reported similar catastrophes: "Ground totally destroyed, countless wagons broke down and stuck in the mud, horses stranded on the roadside." It became necessary to initially postpone the operation for twenty-four hours. General Boroević reported to Second Army command on February 25 that only a very slim chance existed of reconquering Mezölaborcz. Meanwhile, the unrelenting rain continued to wreak havoc on any efforts to maintain the supply traffic. The road conditions became so horrendous that all supply efforts had to be suspended for forty-eight hours to allow for repair work.

The XIX Corps finally launched its preliminary attack toward Mezölaborcz on February 27, followed by the main attack force on the next day. Unfortunately, the Habsburg effort ended quickly, again owing to inadequate artillery support. Infantry reinforcements and the few available mountain artillery batteries had extreme difficulty in reaching the front lines; most artillery pieces had to be left behind at the lower base camps, far behind the vulnerable assault troops. Fighting continued on March 1 as fog and heavy, driving snow set in, destroying all sense of direction. Entire regiments became lost in the mountains. The result was catastrophic.

Military and political pressure to liberate the fortress remained a constant and influential factor throughout the second Carpathian Mountain offensive, which lasted from February 27 until mid-March 1915. The fortress leadership submitted multiple exaggerated reports claiming that the citadel garrison's resistance power had rapidly declined, which certainly influenced Conrad's decision to initiate the Second Army offensive along the shortest route to the citadel to coincide with a neighboring Third Army advance.

Limited rail access to the front lines and incessant pressure relative to Fortress Przemyśl caused General Conrad to transfer troops to the Third Army right flank positions during the second half of February.

A simultaneous fortress breakout operation accompanied the Second Army offensive effort. Pressing time constraints relative to the fortress food situation resulted in the Second Army launching its offensive before all assigned troop units had been assembled on the delayed February 27 launch date. The undertaking, similar to the first Carpathian Mountain Winter War offensive, lacked sufficient materiel and manpower to accomplish its overly optimistic mission. Campaign planners also ignored severe weather warnings because recent Russian battlefield successes had to be neutralized. Renewed enemy assaults in the same area where the offensive would occur necessitated further Habsburg retrograde movements, raising serious concerns about any chance of success for the forthcoming endeavor to liberate Fortress Przemyśl.

Emperor Franz Joseph meanwhile admonished Habsburg Supreme Command to prevent the surrender of the fortress, only one example of the mounting pressure to liberate the citadel because of its deteriorating food situation and troop conditions. The emperor's pressure also caused General Conrad to increase pressure on General Böhm-Ermolli to launch the Second Army offensive as soon as possible. Meanwhile, on the field army battlefields, severe Habsburg casualties and the concomitant deterioration of the soldiers' psychological and physical condition continued unabated.

In the interim, the slaughter of additional horses in the fortress presented yet another attempt to extend food rations a few more days. Any additional decrease in the already starvation-level food portions would further diminish the troops' physical health and ability to adequately perform their military duties. The loss of additional horses also significantly lessened the fortress's rapidly diminishing maneuver capabilities. During early February, fortress troops suffered a sharp decline in combat effectiveness as illnesses became epidemic and a noticeable increase in mortality rates resulted from accelerating troop exhaustion. Calculations now had fortress food supplies lasting only until March 16, adding to the increasing pressure to launch a relieving offensive to liberate the citadel as quickly as possible.

The obsession with liberating Fortress Przemyśl resulted in the Second Army receiving the formidable mission of initiating a renewed offensive on the limited twelve-kilometer front compared to the far more extensive one-hundred-kilometer Third Army first offensive effort. When the second offensive finally commenced after the weather and supply delays, the Second Army would launch a frontal assault against strong enemy defensive positions established on dominating terrain with inadequate artillery support for its attacking forces. Meanwhile, sudden dense, pouring rain and windy conditions produced further snowmelt, causing additional serious road erosion. The bitter cold nights and wet conditions exacted a heavy toll on the troops' health. Every day thousands became ill, many suffering from frostbite or succumbing to exposure as the losses to illness doubled. But Fortress Przemyśl had to be liberated!

7

✠ ✠ ✠

The Third Carpathian Mountain Offensive

EARLY MARCH 1915

AT THE BEGINNING OF MARCH 1915, THE PROLONGED FOOD rationing in Fortress Przemyśl had taken an enormous toll on garrison troops. In increasing numbers, they simply collapsed and died, while sickness rates became much more prevalent. Between March 1 and 10, the fortress reported 12,140 sick and 6,900 lightly wounded troops.[1] General Kusmanek focused his attention on maintaining the fortress's battle-worthiness, but that suffered as his troops' health steadily declined and Russian military activity around the fortress accelerated.[2] March would be the fatal month for Fortress Przemyśl as General Conrad continued his second Carpathian Mountain military campaign to liberate the citadel. When that operation failed, he launched a third, smaller offensive effort; but after the fortress's surrender, that effort was doomed to failure before it even commenced. Several higher command officers suggested that the offensive not be launched until the severe snowstorms slackened and the extreme cold dissipated somewhat. They were justifiably concerned about the effects of frostbite; one unit reported that 200 of its 350 casualties resulted from frostbite rather than battle.[3] Exposed to the elements day and night, the soldiers were particularly vulnerable to frostbite. Conrad's critics argued that launching the renewed offensive under more favorable weather conditions would produce fewer casualties, but the Habsburg commander maintained that the military situation at Fortress Przemyśl was too critical to ignore and pushed ahead with his planned offensive regardless of the likely consequences.

In the fortress, the cost of tobacco skyrocketed, as smoking became almost as important as eating for the troops. When they ran out of cigarette paper, they used every imaginable substitute, even book pages. Meanwhile, horse meat had become inexpensive, and the fortress magazines even distributed it to the civilian population, each person receiving five kilograms per month. In addition, it became increasingly difficult to transport the swelling numbers of sick and overworked troops into the inner fortress from the outer walls. To accommodate the wounded, the city's Polish theater was converted into a hospital. The need for beds, blankets, and straw for sick and wounded troops continued to escalate as the bulwark's situation worsened daily. The working conditions for hospital personnel progressively worsened. One hospital's sick bay even came under fire from enemy forces, requiring its evacuation.

A civilian recorded in her diary on March 4 that "yesterday there was great alarm as the Russians stormed the southern fortress front. By evening, the first wounded began arriving in the fortress, in the meantime it appeared that the Russians had begun to retreat." The fortress enjoyed three days of improved weather before the snowfall intensified once again, this time bringing the heaviest snows of the entire winter. During the day, snowy and sunny conditions alternated as many as five or six times. The Russians received additional reinforcements while battle reports indicated that a major encounter was being fought south of the Dniester River.[4]

Incessant rumors continued to circulate throughout the fortress as the days passed, none of which received official confirmation or comment. Following the release of a secret report that delineated the Russian theater military activities, General Conrad began developing plans for the next Habsburg military operation to drive the enemy out of western and middle Galicia. The effort was of extreme significance, since its success would facilitate Fortress Przemyśl's liberation. Recognizing that the fortress's food supply would reportedly not last beyond mid-March, Conrad also formulated plans for a major breakout attempt in the event that the Galician field army operation failed.

Conrad ordered General Böhm-Ermolli to renew the Second Army offensive operation on March 6 in a further attempt to liberate the fortress and hurl enemy forces out of Galicia. To assure any hope for success of the reactivated offensive, the Second Army's right flank desperately needed the cooperation of the Fourth Army southern flank, but Fourth Army had yet to reinforce those positions and even initiate intensive artillery preparations for its operation. Eager to get the offensive under way, Conrad suggested that they move their positions rearward, which left unusually weak forces in the Fourth Army's forward ranks.

The Second Army then advanced toward Fortress Przemyśl, supported by Third Army right flank units. The Fourth Army assembled its strongest troop units at its right flank in preparation for the renewed operation, while its remaining forces moved into position to prevent an enemy advance over the Biala and Dunajec Rivers. Third Army left flank troops had to prevent enemy forces from intervening against the Fourth Army's southern flank attack. What successes the Habsburg forces achieved would soon be negated by a Russian counterattack against the XIX Corps, which produced enormous casualties on both sides. Battle lasted day and night as troops became increasingly combat-fatigued.

Even before the March 1915 offensives commenced, the troops' physical condition and morale declined enormously. Corps commanders reported increased casualties as frostbite and extreme weather conditions took their toll on the poorly equipped troops. Too weak to complete the required strenuous marches, soldiers vanished into the frozen abyss, their compasses all but worthless in the heavily wooded, snow-shrouded terrain. Many units lost their way and often found themselves marching in circles. Uniforms froze to the men's skin as nighttime temperatures sank to below −20°C. Crossing creeks and moving through the snow only exacerbated the already widespread cases of frostbite. The continued lack of reserve troops and reinforcements contributed to the pervasive apathy that rapidly spread through the army ranks throughout the winter campaigns. Reports of exhaustion in the face of such miserable conditions, particularly among troops that had to be in close contact with enemy positions, became a fixture in Habsburg military unit communications.

Recruit basic training times were reduced from eight to two weeks as Habsburg casualties mounted. None of their limited and inadequate training prepared the troops for the rigors of mountain battle or the unique extreme weather and terrain conditions. Rather than being placed in combat units to replace battle losses, replacement troops were simply hurled into combat, often without trained officers, after long marches to the front. Facing a numerically superior enemy, the troops quickly became cannon fodder because of the lack of reserve troops to fill the many gaps that opened in the front lines.

Furthermore, logistical support troops proved incapable of transporting food to the forces attempting to advance. Hunger further weakened the troops, leaving them with little energy to march through the deep snow and mud. The shortage of draft animals forced the starving troops to help transport machine guns, ammunition, and artillery pieces over the difficult terrain. Icy slopes had to be hacked and shoveled step by step under enemy fire.

General Kusmanek had to determine the garrison troop numbers necessary to either launch an offensive action or defend the citadel.[5] Conrad dispatched a revealing letter to the Emperor's Military Chancellery justifying his March 6 decision to renew the stalled Second Army offensive. He reiterated that the objective of the second Carpathian Mountain offensive operation remained to liberate Fortress Przemyśl and drive the Russians out of Galicia. To achieve this mission, the Second Army's operation received support from four Fourth Army southern flank divisions. The South Army's six infantry divisions and Army Group Pflanzer-Baltin's six (later seven) infantry divisions assisted the South Army's attempt to escape from its mountain entrapment. Conrad claimed that every available division had been deployed to the Carpathian Mountain hellhole to achieve success, a serious exaggeration of the truth. He emphasized that the Austro-Hungarian army's main objective remained the liberation of Fortress Przemyśl.[6]

The consistent Habsburg battlefield defeats in the Carpathian Mountain campaigns again raised the critical issue of neutral countries, especially Italy, entering the war if the fortress had to capitulate. Its food stores would be depleted by March 23, adding four days to the previous estimates. Conrad claimed that the time pressure to liberate Fortress Przemyśl had not yet become critical, but the Carpathian Mountain offensive operations continued nevertheless. In the meantime, Colonel Veith reported:

On March 1, fog and heavy snow falls, we have lost all sense of direction; entire regiments are getting lost, resulting in catastrophic losses. March 6 brings a complete change in the weather: clear skies, thaw during the day and −20 degrees at night; with the result that all slopes are iced over. On March 20, a snowstorm breaks over us with a ferocity found only in Arctic regions. All forward movement ceases; none of our wounded can be evacuated; entire lines of riflemen appear as if covered with a white cloth. The icy ground, sanded smooth by the storm, we are unable to move in front of the enemy defensive work; the artillery is several days march behind.[7]

Fortress inhabitants nevertheless harbored great hopes of being liberated. They had not thought it would be possible during the worst winter months, but in March, their high expectations were revived.[8] By March 6, fortress troop losses reached twenty-four thousand, the majority resulting from battle.[9] Complicating the situation, food supplies, boots, uniforms, and other bare necessities kept dwindling at an alarming rate. Increasing numbers of artillery pieces failed because their barrels had worn out, and the firing range of those that remained operable had decreased from eight to six and one-half kilometers. The supplies of 15-centimeter howitzer granite shells were expended, and already during December, artillery shell supplies had vanished at a rapid rate. Meanwhile, newly constructed fortress factories continued to produce the most sorely lacking primitive goods, creating whatever basic day-to-day commodities were possible under the circumstances, while army cooks continued to add unhealthy fillers, such as sawdust, to food to extend the provisions for the troops. In early March, the Second Army received its orders to renew the offensive along the same direct route to Fortress Przemyśl in a new attempt to liberate the garrison.[10] The Russians, fearing a disruption of their major transportation and communications links between Galicia and Poland, also accelerated their military activities.

Meanwhile, the March 6 Second Army offensive collapsed during its first day. By not launching cooperative attacks to bind opposing enemy units, adjacent Habsburg armies certainly contributed to the operation's failure. However, both the Second and South Armies' units conducted their efforts in two meters of snow, dense fog, and −25°C temperatures. The troops suffered terribly from the debilitating and frigid conditions, but again attacked with insufficient troop numbers on too narrow a front to obtain a decisive victory despite the soldiers' sacrificial efforts. The Second Army had orders to cooperate with a fortress troops' sortie for mutual benefit.[11] Second Army Command received numerous messages from Habsburg Supreme Command urging it, because of the extreme time pressure, to liberate Fortress Przemyśl.[12]

On the fatal day of the failed renewed attack effort, General Kusmanek informed Habsburg Supreme Command that he had to report the horrendous conditions within the fortress following the six months of uninterrupted close contact and battle with the enemy. Since September 1914, the majority of the garrison had continued to wear summer-issue uniforms, particularly the men serving in fortress forefield earthen positions or huts. The troops also endured more than three months of reduced food rations, thus the Landsturm and even the more physically fit Landwehr units exhibited progressively worsening troop conditions. Complete exhaustion became rampant and over sixty front-line troops died in February from exhaustion soon after their arrival at a fortress hospital. The number of soldiers reporting to sick call also continued to escalate.[13]

The fortress command now wrestled with the problem of establishing which combat units they would designate for either a major fortress breakout effort or a breakthrough operation to attempt to reach the Habsburg field armies fighting to liberate the citadel. Enemy action naturally became a major factor in determining which forces would participate in either effort. General Kusmanek reported in January that he could mobilize a maximum of twenty-four to twenty-six battalions consisting of about eight hundred troops each for a breakout effort toward Na Gorach. The main fortress units could advance along the road to Bircza, while security forces had to deploy at the northern and southern flank positions toward the important railroad connection at Nizankovice. General Kusmanek anticipated attacking an equal number of enemy forces, but the unfavorable fortress conditions in March rendered multiple citadel regiments incapable of battle.[14]

On March 3, tsarist artillery fire increased against the fortress, especially against the barracks at the airfield of Zuravica and Siedliska in Defensive District VI. During early March, Russian troops easily broke through Habsburg Second and Third Army lines with impunity, bleeding the troops white and creating a precarious Habsburg military situation that continued until the conclusion of the early April Easter battle. The Habsburg armies continued to sustain defeat after defeat under the most atrocious conditions. Meanwhile, also on March 3, General Ivanov informed Stavka that Austria-Hungary and Germany had reputedly launched a powerful offensive toward Sanok-Lisko with the ultimate objectives of liberating Fortress Przemyśl, unhinging the extreme left flank tsarist positions, and forcing the enemy's evacuation of Galicia. He further insisted that if he could halt the Habsburg offensive, it would be possible to destroy the Dual Monarchy's armies. Surprisingly, Stavka accepted Ivanov's arguments.

Meanwhile, the constant interruptions of heavy support supply traffic along the single Habsburg supply route to the Second Army again created significant delays. This allowed the Russians time to transfer reinforcements to any threatened portion of their front, enabling them to successfully counter all Habsburg offensive efforts. Defensive flanking artillery fire halted the Russian attack along portions of the front, but increasingly Habsburg units reported that their offensive capabilities had been destroyed as a result of the battles. During March, in near-continuous battle while fighting the elements, daily Habsburg casualty figures rose enormously.

By March 7, it already appeared evident that the fortress could not be liberated before it had to capitulate.[15] An airplane pilot was informed in the strictest confidence on March 6 that there was no possibility of the fortress being liberated and that a breakout attempt would be launched. All aircraft were prepared to depart from the fortress. This resulted in repair work becoming necessary because the aircraft were worn out and would have to fly in the same appalling weather conditions that had originally grounded the planes. When they finally departed, the aircraft carried official documents and files from the fortress command.

Meanwhile, the Fourth Army's reinforced southern flank forces continued their offensive efforts in the key Gorlice-Jaslo area, but transporting artillery forward through the deep snow retarded its movement. After a twenty-four-hour delay, four Fourth Army infantry divisions (the 8th, 10th, 12th, and 39th) launched an unsuccessful attack toward Gorlice. The excellent enemy defensive positions, as Fourth Army Command had anticipated and reported to Habsburg Supreme Command, proved much too formidable, and the failure to reposition artillery pieces in a timely fashion hindered the infantry attack, resulting in wasted effort and heavy casualties. Six weeks later, on May 2, the Central Powers achieved their greatest victory of the war during the Gorlice-Tarnov campaign when German forces launched an offensive in the exact same area. The German army provided the manpower that Conrad lacked, and the May operation ultimately rescued the Dual Monarchy from a potentially catastrophic defeat.

After anticipated replacement troops had arrived and been assimilated into their new units, the Third Army could recommence its right flank attack activity, but it had to maintain its western flank positions until those replacement troops arrived. The Austrian official history of the war emphasized that the unrelenting winter snowstorms forced rapid termination of all offensive efforts. Transport of sick and wounded soldiers from the front lines proved futile on the impassible snow- and ice-covered terrain. In the meantime, intelligence reports indicated that the enemy had constructed additional defensive lines twenty-five to thirty kilometers behind the present front, which precluded any timely liberation of Fortress Przemyśl. Tsarist forces utilized the inclement weather conditions to their advantage by launching counterassaults after Habsburg offensive efforts had been halted, which resulted in numerous retreat movements.

Possessing no reserve formations, the Habsburg forces could not initiate the customary counterattack to halt the Russian assaults. Man-high snow blanketed the fronts, while losses to battle and unfavorable conditions continued to mount. For example, the 41st Honvéd Infantry Division numbers had plummeted from 12,000 to 2,110 troops since February 20. Artillery support proved useless because of the wind-driven snow, while machine gun mechanisms continued to freeze and malfunction. Troops continued to starve while the repetitive High Command order to "unconditionally maintain positions" remained meaningless.[16]

The blizzard conditions also severely reduced the troops' resistance powers, while the continued arrival of tsarist reinforcements and escalating casualties made defending the front lines increasingly difficult. The physically and psychologically exhausted troops realized the futility of continuing to assault the well-fortified enemy positions even if Conrad did not. In early March alone, forty thousand frostbite cases were reported.[17] The various battles repeatedly witnessed failed attempts at coordination between attacking units, and fatal communication breakdowns remained a common occurrence. The time pressure to rescue Fortress Przemyśl prevented levelheaded minds from creating a more advantageous strategy. General Böhm-Ermolli meanwhile prodded his battered Second Army troops to continue their attempts to seize their key objective, Baligrod, while Conrad constantly harangued his field commanders about the deteriorating Fortress Przemyśl situation. However, the enemy successfully countered all Habsburg offensive efforts by rapidly transferring reinforcements to any threatened frontal areas and launching counteroffensives.

The commander of the 8th Honvéd Infantry Regiment, explained on March 7 that everyone spoke of the possibility of launching some type of action outside the fortress, but all believed that such an undertaking would be impossible to achieve, particularly since the troops could no longer walk ten kilometers (6.25 miles). He claimed that his regiment was thoroughly enfeebled from the continuous lack of adequate food and equipment. It could be anticipated that in a desperate foray, those troops that did not immediately retreat into the fortress would surrender. The commander complained bitterly that senior officers did not check the condition of field combat units and distrusted their field officers' reports.[18]

On March 9, fortress inhabitants witnessed the passage of heavy mobile guns (30.5- and 24-centimeter mortars) through the city streets toward the southern fortress perimeters. The Russians apparently concentrated their main troop numbers to await the anticipated Habsburg attack. "We know nothing about the details. Many rumors continued to circulate without confirmation," one fortress inhabitant lamented. It appeared that most inhabitants had lost all hope of the fortress being liberated; the lack of details in recent war reports only exacerbated the situation.[19]

Reports from Vienna, reputedly from a reliable source, claimed that the fortress would be liberated in five days. The expectations of the inhabitants of the bulwark rose again, but both troops and civilians remained apprehensive. Meanwhile, the troops stationed in the forefield positions continued to suffer from extreme nervousness and psychological pressure from being so close to the enemy, the perpetually inadequate food supply, inhuman conditions, and the stress of continuous battle. However, the expectation that the fortress would soon be liberated transformed these exhausted troops. Such renewed expectations released some of the fearful pressure on the troops and civilians. "God be with us" became the prayer.

Meanwhile, the number of citadel troops suffering from illness steadily increased. For example, during one night, eighty Honvéd troops entered the hospital, the majority suffering from complete exhaustion. Positive war reports from other fronts increased on March 4. "Strong Russian attacks had been repulsed in the Carpathian Mountains. Hundreds of dead soldiers lie before their positions." The Russians also reportedly suffered serious setbacks in southeast Galicia. A four-day-old report dated March 9 stated that the liberation army was now only seventy kilometers from the fortress. Such reports gave the unrealistic impression that the citadel would be liberated in a matter of days.

Strong tsarist counterattacks abruptly halted the Habsburg field army efforts to advance on March 11. An enemy assault broke through the XIX Corps front on March 13. This terminated any chance of liberating Fortress Przemyśl as the enemy proceeded forward through the Uzsok and Lupkov Passes.[20] On the same day, the Second Army's commander reported to Habsburg Supreme Command that he had not guaranteed that his army could obtain its objective of Lisko by March 18. Thus, General Conrad determined that the fortress should launch a breakthrough attempt in the general direction of the Second Army for the honor of Habsburg arms.[21] To most observers, however, such an effort was mere insanity.

Habsburg Supreme Command again drew the attention of the field armies to the deficiency in battle effectiveness of their artillery combat arm. A number of field commanders emphasized the need to conserve shells because of the monthlong trench battles and the unanticipated large number of rounds fired. Lengthy bombardments against reinforced enemy positions, especially those using shrapnel shells, had no effect and served merely to consume more artillery ammunition. Military planners noted that the most necessary and effective utilization of artillery occurred when the Russians attacked Habsburg positions. The important connection between infantry front lines and observation of enemy activity, as well as the necessity of changing artillery positions frequently for security purposes, had become obvious. Airplanes also added a new dimension to artillery reconnaissance and observation, including at Fortress Przemyśl.

On March 12, following ten days of continuous snow, icy wind, and frost conditions, sunlight appeared for the first time, thus ending the constant precipitation and −10°C temperatures that had endured for so long. When the snow finally melted, trenches filled with muddy slime and roads turned into running streams. Such conditions raised serious health risks for troops. A fortress civilian lamented: "This post-winter is a bad thing for us and for our armies because it delayed them for weeks, which was just one result of the inclement weather conditions. We cannot wait much longer."[22] Bulwark inhabitants also saw a major fire burning in the direction of Lemberg. Many believed that the Russians had evacuated Medyka and Dynov and set them on fire.

Within the fortress, military authorities seized large numbers of dairy cows and food supplies from the civilian population, extending fortress rations until March 24. On the mountain battlefields, the horrific terrain conditions and enormous snow masses delayed the initiation of the ill-fated third Carpathian Mountain offensive effort. A March 13 order to the citadel conveyed a much more serious message than previous communications had as General Conrad finally acknowledged that the fortress could not be liberated in a timely fashion. Extensive preparations had commenced in February for the last great fortress offensive action before it had to capitulate. These preparations included Landsturm and military laborers receiving infantry training to fill depleted garrison troop ranks.

The only possibility for a successful fortress breakthrough attempt would have required Third Army troops to simultaneously attack toward Bircza to establish contact with the fortress troops attempting to advance toward them. The minimal number of garrison troops remaining in the fortress during the breakthrough effort had to ward off any enemy assaults. According to Habsburg Supreme Command's March 14

orders, the fortress distributed rations to the participating troops before the mission to assure success.[23] Given the logistical circumstances,
the offensive action could not be initiated before the early hours of
March 19.

A fortress civilian working in the citadel hospital recorded that on the
previous day, March 13, enemy artillery fire increased enormously during
the day and recommenced between midnight and 2 a.m. Fortress morale
sank as the enemy bombardment intensified. During the morning of
March 14, the enemy barrages slackened somewhat and the frost conditions eased, although it continued to snow. The same civilian lamented
how horrible it must be for the troops stationed in the forward fortress
positions: "The [fortress] inhabitants are more dead than alive!"[24]

On March 13, tsarist forces sapped closer to the fortress, in particular
at Defensive District III and forefield positions at Pod Mazurami and
Helica. During the night, strong enemy forces approached the fortress,
attacked, and successfully overran the forefield positions at Na Gorach–
Batycze and the northern section of Fort Dunkowiczki. The surprised
and weakened defending troops of Landsturm Infantry Regiment 35
could not halt the Russian assaults and surrendered some of their positions. Lacking sufficient numbers, the fortress troops could not launch
a counterattack. Malnutrition and exhaustion forced the evacuation of
all remaining forward forefield positions.[25]

The main Russian thrust at Na Gorach proved a complete success.
Close to midnight, large enemy troop numbers overpowered the weakened Landwehr forces in hand-to-hand combat. A vast majority of defending troops became casualties, whereupon the few surviving troops
retreated into the fortress. At Batycze, the Russians defeated Honvéd
Infantry Regiment 5 troops when they approached their defensive positions; large numbers became prisoners of war. Defensive Districts IV
and II artillery opened fire against the lost positions, resulting in an
artillery duel.

The fortress's Zuravica airfield remained a safe haven for airplanes
only as long as fortress troops occupied the high terrain in the area of
Na Gorach at Defensive District VI (Siedliska). At the commencement
of the second fortress siege, two additional airfields were constructed,
the first at Buszkovice, north of the San River, and the second at Iwowski,

south of the river. Once the Na Gorach positions surrendered to the enemy, the Zuravica airfield came under heavy tsarist artillery barrages and suffered extensive damage. This forced aircraft to be flown out. Toward the end of February, the airfield located at Iwowski also had to be abandoned because of the excessively muddy conditions. Flight company Flik 11 remained for fortress service until the end of the siege.

For protection against enemy aerial attacks, the airfields received 9-centimeter field guns to be utilized as antiaircraft weapons. Originally deployed at Buszkowice, these artillery pieces never shot down any enemy airplanes but often succeeded in turning them away. Nevertheless, the airfield would be bombed on numerous occasions, resulting in extensive damage and casualties.

The Russians continued to take advantage of the stormy weather to attack the battered garrison troops. The field army defenders did not have the advantage of artillery support to halt the enemy advance. During the Carpathian Mountain offensives, tsarist troops continued to employ their usual tactics to avoid battle when they abandoned offensive operations, and then they would launch night assaults. The major improvements in the Fortress Przemyśl forefield positions, such as the construction of new defensive areas with connecting trenches, proved extremely beneficial. However, the primitive cover and barbed wire emplacements offered inadequate protection for the troops.[26] By the end of the second offensive to liberate the fortress, field army troop desertions had increased. The most frequently cited example in the historiography involved Czech Infantry Regiment 28, which will be discussed later. Tsarist propaganda promised Ruthenian soldiers that if they surrendered, they could safely return to their homes located behind the front lines.

The inclement weather conditions made it impossible for Habsburg artillery to locate and neutralize enemy guns. Tsarist artillery barrages fired against Defensive District III caused little damage but did destroy telephone wires, disrupting vital communications for a few days. The continuous enemy artillery fire further lowered garrison morale. The inability of fortress artillery to neutralize its tsarist counterpart left the bulwark inhabitants feeling helpless. Sustained high-intensity enemy artillery fire usually occurred between 11 a.m. and 3 p.m. and then tapered off.

As the days progressed and troop conditions worsened, the fortress could initiate only defensive actions. The projected breakout troops now consisted of only twelve to fifteen infantry battalions with an average seven-hundred-man battle stand, far smaller than the earlier estimates that twenty-four to twenty-eight battalions, each with eight hundred soldiers, could participate in such an operation. Garrison troops prepared to launch their fateful effort, aware that the bulwark's food supply would last only until March 24. Troops also had to defend the fortress while they destroyed all useful war materiel before the fortress capitulated. Because of the declining food supplies, the attempted breakthrough effort had to be initiated before the afternoon of March 20. The smaller "minimal" defensive group remaining in the citadel during the operation had to follow the offensive troops no later than the second day after the attempt commenced. The soldiers then possessed only four days of reserve food rations, the absolute minimum, assuming that they could reach Sambor and seize food supplies from enemy depots.

After temporarily defending the fortress, the "minimal" troop garrison also had to perform a rearguard action against the enemy to protect the attacking forces' rear echelon positions. A unified command structure was an absolute necessity to ensure operational success. General Kusmanek originally hoped to command both garrison groups but later determined that he could not. He requested that Habsburg Supreme Command accept his operational plans for the fortress breakthrough effort as he outlined them in a dispatch to General Conrad.[27] Habsburg headquarters received that fortress communication at 10:45 a.m. on March 15.

Between December 1914 and the fortress's capitulation on March 22, 1915, the number of troops reporting to sick call expanded enormously. The only detailed report of garrison troop casualties determined that this occurred mainly during the March 19 breakthrough attempt. Illnesses that earlier in the siege would not have been considered dangerous or life-threatening now became lethal for even lightly wounded soldiers because of their prolonged malnourishment. The first reports of a serious decline in fortress garrison troop numbers had appeared in January 1915. By February 1915, troops serving in forward perimeter positions displaying no symptoms of illness other than total exhaustion would die within half an hour of reaching a hospital. On December 1, 1914, 4,879 garrison troops had been listed as sick, while another 4,683 suffered from exhaustion. These numbers increased significantly by March 1915. On March 1, 10,581 citadel soldiers were reported ill and 6,441 listed as totally exhausted. Fortress hospitals had become so overcrowded that they could admit only the most serious cases. By March 10, the number of troops listed as ill had risen to 12,140, and those listed as exhausted to 6,920. Between March 8 and 10, many soldiers reported to hospitals suffering from complete exhaustion; twenty-seven died quickly. On March 13, of the 7,873 soldiers designated as ill, 2,493 consisted of exhaustion cases, of which 10 died immediately. Meanwhile, on the field army's battlefield, a Russian counteroffensive, launched during the fierce snowstorms, crippled the Second Army's offensive operation toward Baligrod. The troops retreated to new defensive positions. The Second Army's main attack force commander claimed that he required forty thousand additional soldiers merely to hold the new front because of the heavy losses his forces had sustained.[28]

On March 12, Captain Rudolph Holecka reported the first defection of a Habsburg pilot to the enemy. A fortress Flight Company 10 Czech pilot flew to Tarnov, in tsarist territory, where the Russians captured the mail and medicine destined for the fortress his plane was transporting. The Russians then dispatched airplanes over the citadel's Brzesko airfield and dropped a parcel with a letter thanking the personnel for the airplane they had just captured, but they did return the mail that had been on board. Meanwhile, flights to the fortress continued, delivering military and civilian correspondence. An individual described how on March 13, 1915, five k.u.k. airplanes took off from the Fortress Buszowiczki airfield in extremely inclement weather. All had to return, but engine failure forced one plane to land behind Russian lines. The Russians probably captured the operational plans for the March 19 fortress breakthrough attempt because of this unanticipated turn of events.[29]

Additional flights into the fortress during March included one airplane carrying mail from Brzesko on March 17, two with mail on March 21, and a flight out of the fortress toward Brzesko on March 22

carrying additional mail from the fortress. A large number of mail pack-
ets fell into Russian hands when airplanes and balloons were forced to
land behind enemy lines.[30]

Habsburg Supreme Command ordered General Kusmanek to
launch the citadel's major breakthrough effort in the general direction
of Lisko, Stary-Sambor, or Turka, declaring that the latter target selection
would probably surprise the enemy the most. The destruction of San
River area railroad connections, though, received General Conrad's
highest priority. The order further specified that the fortress commander
should assure, to the maximum degree possible, that the remaining fortress garrison defend the fortress and, if necessary, destroy all materiel
and equipment that could be utilized the enemy.

By March 17, it remained apparent that the fortress would capitulate,
but the garrison continued its "honorable activities." In addition to maintaining Habsburg military honor, a large mobile fortress offensive force
had to attempt to break through enemy siege lines toward the field
armies in a direction that provided the best chance for success and, in
addition, inflicted maximum damage on the enemy. In light of the fortress's critical food situation, General Kusmanek had to report the latest
day that he perceived the breakthrough effort could commence.

Kusmanek ultimately chose to launch the offensive in an eastern
direction, basing his decision on the fortress troops' terrible physical
condition, but he did not have much confidence in the mission's success.
Although General Conrad considered the Lemberg-Sambor and Lemberg-
Stryj railroad lines much more significant objectives, General Kusmanek
opposed attempting to advance toward the field armies because all previous fortress sorties had been launched in that direction and experienced
only fleeting success. In the interim, the Russians had constructed additional rear echelon fortified positions since earlier battles in February.
The difficult terrain conditions and forced marches required to reach the
field army positions raised the question of whether the garrison troops
would be physically capable of making such an effort. Two-thirds of the
fortress regiments had, after all, been designated as incapable of battle.[31]
Company commanders, understanding the terrible condition of their
troops, considered it preposterous to even suggest that the garrison
troops could reach the field armies.

General Kusmanek had determined that only the eastward advance direction remained feasible for the fortress mission, because of the reputed enemy weakness in that region (possibly only the 48th Reichswehr Infantry Brigade defended that entire region). Furthermore, if successful, the starving garrison formations could reach enemy food depots.[32]

By March 1915, all Second Army corps deployed in the Carpathian Mountains had reported that their troops had developed serious psychological problems. The units remained deployed in incredibly squalid conditions with no protection from the adverse elements and had sustained enormous casualties, most resulting from frostbite and disease.[33] As a result, depression and apathy had become rampant in the ranks. Then, on March 15, General Falkenhayn telegraphed Conrad that he could not transfer the desperately requested German reinforcements until March 24, which would be too late to affect the fate of the fortress.

Citing the increasing urgency to liberate the fortress, General Conrad ordered the launching of a renewed Second Army offensive on March 16, barely one week before the fortress would have to capitulate, although Second Army troop offensive and resistance powers had declined precipitously. The unrelenting, bone-chilling weather and impassable terrain conditions placed extreme physical and mental demands on the soldiers. The recent severe winter storms on March 6, 10, and 11 further demoralized the already apathetic troops. The consistent lack of artillery shells, continued Russian numerical superiority, and horrendous weather conditions more than justified the termination of the Second Army's offensive efforts on March 14. As during the first Carpathian Mountain efforts, the Habsburg Second Army had to surrender significant territory that it had previously captured with great human sacrifice. Although the Second Army offensive was unlikely to have made a difference in the fortress's fate, its cancelation assured that Fortress Przemyśl's surrender was inevitable.[34]

As Conrad's plans for a final offensive effort crumbled, the Russian 81st Reserve Infantry Division besieged Defensive District VIII and the southern and southeastern fortress areas. The elevated terrain opposite the fortress perimeter walls at those locations allowed enemy troops to easily outflank the defensive positions. The southeast and southern fortress positions also contained impassable areas, making them unsuitable as marching targets.

On March 15, General Conrad apprised General Kusmanek of the friendly and enemy military situations. Habsburg Second Army center and right flank units remained in battle, while the South Army and Army Group Pflanzer-Baltin remained deployed south of the fortress in extremely difficult mountain terrain. The fortress commander received additional information on March 16.[35] Habsburg intelligence sources placed the following tsarist units at the respective fortress fronts: northwestern: 82nd Reserve Infantry Division; northern: 21st Reichswehr Infantry Brigade; eastern: half of the 58th Reserve Infantry Division; southeastern: 68th Reserve Infantry Division; southwestern: a reserve division; western: 9th Cavalry Division reinforced by infantry units. Half of the 58th and the entire 60th and 69th Reserve Infantry Divisions redeployed to the Carpathian Mountain front, representing a significant weakening of the siege army.

On March 16, General Kusmanek informed Conrad that because of the desperate food situation and poor physical condition of the troops, the breakthrough attempt had to occur no later than March 19. The proposed operation sought to disturb and destroy local enemy railroad traffic in that vicinity and reach enemy food depots to alleviate the terrible physical condition of the garrison troops. The advance direction would be toward Mosciska and Lemberg, but Kusmanek still had little faith that the mission could succeed. The element of surprise would be critical, but with so many citadel infantry regiments incapable of sustained battle, the fortress commander believed that any attempt to advance toward the field armies would be disastrous.[36]

Despite the prevailing blizzard conditions, an airplane flew urgent orders and information relative to the Habsburg military situation to General Kusmanek. The orders demanded the launching of the breakthrough attempt to cooperate with Second Army eastern flank units within the next three days. On its attempted return flight, enemy fire caused the plane to burst into flames. The pilot managed to land in a field between fortress fortifications, and the crew returned safely to the fortress.

General Conrad had previously judged the fortress situation too optimistically when he ordered General Kusmanek to launch a sortie rather than attempt a major breakthrough operation to the field armies. Launching a sortie operation would have signified that the field armies had to liberate the fortress rather than the fortress garrison having to undertake a major military effort to reach the field armies. The breakthrough attempt, to the contrary, would prevent the enemy from deploying additional troops against Habsburg Third Army rear echelon positions. The new Habsburg Supreme Command attack order also ignored the fact that the exhausted and apathetic Second Army troops critically required rehabilitation.[37] When responding to a Conrad question regarding the fortress's choice of operational direction, General Kusmanek replied that the fortress would make the greatest possible effort to complete the newly assigned mission, but he also emphasized that his starving troops would be attacking, at a minimum, an equal number of enemy forces.[38] In addition to preparing a breakthrough attempt toward Sambor, the evacuation of the fortress and destruction of any war equipment or materiel had to be accomplished by March 21.[39]

A fortress inhabitant's diary entry for March 17 indicated that "yesterday dread and dismay" swiftly affected the hospital atmosphere where the writer worked as rumors quickly circulated that the Habsburg Third Army had been forced to retreat. Most of the local conversations that followed dwelled on the impending "death march" of the garrison troops. The starved fortress Honvéd troops were described as being at the end of their physical capacities, while the civilian inhabitants realized that the field armies could not save the fortress within the next few days.[40]

Thousands of Honvéd fortress troops had earlier been sacrificed in attempts to reach the intended liberation army, but it now appeared that all those efforts had been for naught and that the fortress would soon have to surrender nevertheless. Rumors circulated that wounded officers had been issued weapons for the defense of the fortress, while in fact Sanitation Department medical troops were armed, as large unit formations began to march through the fortress city on the evening of March 18. The soldiers' malnourished faces mirrored the seriousness of the situation and the weight of the looming circumstances. Although suffering from extreme overexertion, garrison troops had to endure yet another battle. During March 17, they began to prepare for the breakthrough operation, many units requiring seven hours to march through the snow on the next day from their fortress deployment areas to reach their offensive positions in a timely manner.

In the meantime, Second Army V Corps continued preparations for the doomed third Carpathian Mountain field army offensive attempt to relieve the fortress. It required three days just to transport additional artillery units to the mountain front positions to support the ridiculously small number of attacking troops. V Corps units engaged in a moderate evening firefight, while the 31st Infantry Division began preparing its troops to participate in the offensive effort.[41] The restricted attack front area and inadequate troop numbers (33,000) could not liberate the fortress in sufficient time to prevent its capitulation. Regrettably, no additional plans existed to reinforce the attack force or provide the necessary labor units to prepare and maintain the roads required for proper supply and troop movement for the impending relief operation.

The offensive mission of V Corps' primary attack force, Group Lieb, supported by seven additional artillery batteries, began to attack the objective, Loziov, and then secure the surrounding high mountain terrain by March 20. Neighboring Group Szurmay units supported Group Lieb's operation. An additional seven-infantry battalion group, Group Fox, would follow Group Lieb's attack. The artillery batteries designated to support the offensive, however, did not possess their full quotas of guns; therefore, the only effective artillery support for the attack emanated from neighboring Group Szurmay.

On March 18, General Kusmanek determined that the fortress's financial assets must be destroyed the next day. At the commencement of Fortress Przemyśl's second siege in early November 1914, Kusmanek and those authorized to destroy the monetary assets determined to burn all the money resources if and when it became necessary. On March 16, the fortress commander ordered that all paper money be burned on March 19 before the military breakthrough operation transpired. The only exception would be the troops' April payroll, to be distributed to them in advance because it could not be distributed during the actual operation. A commission to destroy the financial assets assembled on the morning of

March 19 and convened until 5:00 p.m. The members first counted the money (6.7 million kronen), then burned it and destroyed the ashes at 9:00 p.m., concluding the commission's work.[42]

On March 18, General Kusmanek telegraphed Habsburg Supreme Command that he had granted his troops a rest day and increased their food rations for the next day's military operation. He then appealed to his soldiers.[43] The garrison troops received their last rations at midnight when they also learned that they must fight their way through Russian territory to reach the field armies.

As the garrison troops made preparations to launch their ill-fated mission, citadel civilians had no idea what the future had in store for them. Reportedly, the last flour had been consumed and all horse meat eaten, and there only remained enough food to suffice for a few more days. Starving soldiers desired additional bread rations to supplement the quarter-loaf they had received daily for many weeks. This paltry sustenance did not halt their hunger pangs. Meanwhile, hurried preparations commenced at the fortress perimeters for the approaching operation, while the troops awaited the release of the attack order. Officers' faces revealed their innermost feelings, while the troops despaired on the eve of their "last fearful death struggle." The garrison troops could barely stand because of their extreme exhaustion. General Kusmanek's attack order, when released, contained no mention of the attack direction to prevent further panic spreading in the ranks. Emperor Franz Joseph opposed launching the endeavor, contrary to the opinion of Habsburg Supreme Command. Meanwhile, all airplane and balloon pilots prepared to leave the citadel in haste on March 19 as snowstorm conditions continued.[44]

The main garrison units, 23rd Honvéd Infantry and Combined Division Waitzendorfer, commenced preparations for the March 19 operation. During the night of March 18–19, garrison troops marched silently from their bivouac areas to their designated fortress perimeter jump-off points. At daybreak, they received orders to carry only forty rifle rounds for their personal defense. Only a relatively small garrison detachment would remain to defend the fortress perimeter positions against possible enemy attacks. Officers, recognizing their troops' terrible physical condition, marched them at a snail's pace to their attack assembly areas.

Nevertheless, multiple starving soldiers collapsed and even died during the pre-offensive preparation period, while all troops harbored strong forebodings concerning the approaching operation. Many hoped to merely be taken as prisoners of war. One officer claimed that his troops required fourteen days of nourishment just to be capable of attempting the mission.

In frigid weather conditions, which consisted mainly of light rain mixed with snow, the troops trudged through the fortress's ankle-deep, snow-covered mud. Defensive District artillery barrages commenced, intended to distract the enemy to believe that the breakthrough effort would emanate from a location other than the one designated. General Kusmanek rushed all available reserve artillery units to that defensive district to increase the firepower. Earlier, confidants and spies spread false rumors and reports to further confuse the enemy as to where they would launch the operation. The troops marched through the citadel area without talking, smoking, or using any light in an effort to camouflage their actions from the enemy. Apathy prevailed throughout the ranks, while the soldiers who collapsed and died prior to the actual operation were labeled *stille* Helden, or "silent heroes."[45]

On March 18 at 4:20 p.m., when the alarm sounded for the various infantry battalions to prepare to move out by 6:00 p.m., General Kusmanek transmitted his final operational concept to General Conrad. He also telegraphed Emperor Franz Joseph, declaring that after six months of uninterrupted battle with the enemy, hunger would finally force the fortress to surrender.[46] The emperor and nominal armed forces commander Archduke Friedrich also forwarded telegrams to the fortress, but they arrived after battle had already commenced outside the bulwark on March 19.

When General Waitzendorfer, Combined Division commander, heard grumbling about the operation orders from some of his officers, he replied, "If we are ordered to die, so must we die!"[47] The commander of Honvéd Infantry Regiment 2 cut the unit's battle flag into pieces and passed them out to his officers to preserve. The other Honvéd Infantry Regiment flags would likewise be distributed; a piece of one resides in the Budapest military museum today.

Of the participating units, only the 23th Honvéd Infantry Division and the 97th Landsturm Infantry Brigade arrived at their assembly area destinations on time, the Combined Division not until 2:35 a.m. This tardiness cost valuable time and delayed the commencement of the attack, which proved fateful for the overall action. Habsburg commanders neither reconnoitered the advance area nor oriented most troop units about the minefields that had been dug outside the Defensive District VI perimeter, which they now had to traverse. Only 97th Landsturm Infantry Brigade troops had been informed of the local field conditions and minefields.[48] This resulted in miscommunication and friction, but also atrocious troop casualties as enemy artillery fire wreaked havoc when the troops paused and bunched up at the minefields and barbed wire entanglements.

Although apathy permeated the ranks, some troops initially exhibited unwarranted optimism only because of their lack of knowledge about the rapidly approaching situation. General Kusmanek demanded a solemn pledge of secrecy from his field commanders concerning the timing and direction of the breakthrough attempt. Thus, to prevent any treasonous acts or panic in the ranks, the weary troops were given no indication of their ultimate destination. Garrison officers understood that the Russians would have attacked the fortress in force earlier if they had known how thinly manned the citadel walls actually were.

On the Carpathian Mountain front, the V Corps offensive preparations included accelerated roadway maintenance efforts in an attempt to overcome the unfavorable march conditions and to supply winter-issue uniforms for the troops assigned to the mission. The Second Army V Corps' third Carpathian Mountain offensive operation, however, commenced three days after the fortress's March 19 attempt had failed. According to documented orders, the two operations should have occurred simultaneously. Neither Second Army Command nor V Corps headquarters received information concerning the fortress's fateful and disastrous March 19 breakthrough attempt prior to the launching of their doomed offensive action. Thus, both the bloody fortress effort and the ill-fated third Carpathian Mountain offensive proved unnecessary, merely increasing Habsburg casualty lists.

Nevertheless, on March 18, persistent lower valley melting conditions and heavy mountain snowfall negatively affected the transport and deployment of the seven designated artillery batteries into their mountain positions to support the V Corps attack. Road conditions continued to deteriorate, and an insufficient number of labor units were made available to maintain the roads required for troop and supply movement. This delayed initiating the operation until the night of March 20–21 and allowed the Russians adequate time to prepare countermeasures to thwart the operation.[49]

As attack preparations continued, the flaws in the proposed V Corps operation became increasingly obvious. The thirty-three thousand designated mission troops were barely sufficient to seize the initial objective, Loziov, let alone take control of any further significant terrain or liberate the fortress in time to prevent its capitulation.[50] The reinforced V Corps 31st Infantry Division and Infantry Regiment 76 ultimately launched the ill-fated undertaking, supported by the 33rd and 37th Honvéd Infantry Divisions.

Those in the fortress witnessed "silent despair" because the troops recognized that the forthcoming action was a doomed effort. Pre-offensive activity included the burning of all army service books at the last minute.[51] Troops meanwhile prepared explosives to destroy any military objects that the enemy could utilize, while pilots hastily prepared fortress aircraft and balloons to depart the citadel. Meanwhile, snow fell for the seventeenth straight day.

By March 1915, little hope remained that the fortress could resist a major Russian assault. If the fortress could not be liberated immediately, capitulation was inevitable. As this realization became apparent, the rumor began to circulate that the fortress commander intended to launch a last great offensive undertaking, the aforementioned "death march," despite the fact that the main fortress offensive weapon, the 23rd Honvéd Infantry Division, had already sacrificed much of its battle worth. To garrison troops, a breakthrough effort seemed absolute nonsense, and most troops did not believe it would occur. There were no longer sufficient horses to transport the artillery around the fortress environs. Also, many troops proved physically incapable of marching even a few kilometers with full field packs. Small sleds were built for troops to pull machine guns, because of the lack of healthy horses. Also, ski patrols were organized. While earlier rumors concentrated on the fervent hope that the fortress would soon be liberated, especially when the sound of cannon fire could not be heard in the distance, that hope had by now disappeared.

8

✠✠✠

Breakthrough Attempt and Surrender of the Fortress

MARCH 1915

ALTHOUGH IT WAS RELATIVELY QUIET AT THE FORTRESS IN the days leading up to the March 19 breakthrough attempt, the tension became unbearable for the garrison troops. Once they realized that there would be a final offensive military action, the only unknown factor remained in which direction it would be launched. Weather conditions alternated between bright sunshine and fog, rain, snow, and storm conditions. The troops anxiously awaited a final decision for the operation, which was finally announced on March 18. When the order became public on that cloudy and rainy day, the fortress streets were still covered with deep mud. "Thus," noted one unfortunate participant, "we soldiers marched slowly, very slowly." Despite being specifically ordered not to do so, many soldiers immediately wolfed down their extra rations, leaving empty containers strewn everywhere. One frustrated observer saw no way to prevent the starving troops from consuming the extra food: "What were we supposed to do, shoot all the men who had eaten?" Several troops suffered heart attacks after gorging themselves, which served as a warning for their compatriots not to follow their example.

Most of the troops who consumed their extra rations likely did so in the hope that it would increase their strength. After months of grueling conditions and starvation rations, the garrison soldiers could barely carry their rifles and ammunition, let alone their usual field gear.[1] Troop morale sunk so low that even officers reported to sick call. As troops quietly marched to their assembly areas, they passed the corpses of soldiers who had collapsed in the streets and died from exhaustion. The men resembled walking skeletons, their bodies ravaged from months of malnutrition. Some attempted to commit suicide. Most waited for what they anticipated to be the moment of their death.

As the troop units marched toward their assembly areas through the wide, desolate city streets, they also saw the broken windows caused by constant tsarist aerial bombardment and artillery barrages. When the weary soldiers finally reached their assembly areas, they learned, to their surprise, that the attack would be launched in a southeasterly direction. The fortress perimeter walls had to be passed by midnight for the troops to reach the enemy lines within an hour using the protection of darkness. The troops could not believe the operation's direction, where the Russians had reputedly constructed some of their strongest defensive positions, protected by their best artillery units and possessing their most favorable communication networks constructed over many months.[2] However, for the soldiers, at least their dreadful situation would finally be resolved within twenty-four hours, even if it meant their own deaths.[3]

Artillery and supply train columns became intermingled with each other, which blocked streets or crossed troop marching routes, making command control over the troops increasingly difficult despite all attempts to facilitate forward movement. By midnight, several units had not reached the citadel walls, but the troops could not march any faster. Many simply lay down along the streets to be left behind.[4] One-third to one-half of the troops dropped out of the ranks before they reached the citadel perimeter. Futile attempts to retrieve those soldiers failed. Many others did not reach the fortress walls until 1 a.m.[5]

During the morning of March 18, General Kusmanek informed his generals that he would launch the breakthrough attempt the next day. If the operation failed, all fortress war materiel useful to the enemy had to be destroyed before the citadel capitulated. Fortress field grade officers realized that no historical example existed of a strong fortress garrison successfully escaping from a major enemy siege. However, the Austro-Hungarian army had a long, admirable, and proud military history and, despite its numerous nineteenth-century battlefield defeats, it had never suffered dishonor on the battlefield. Thus, General Conrad ordered the fortress garrison to launch the breakthrough operation to maintain the Royal and Imperial Army's reputation and honor.[6] The order willfully ignored the terrible physical condition of the participating troops: there was no possibility that the exhausted soldiers could battle their way across one hundred kilometers of treacherous mountain terrain in the extreme weather conditions against a reinforced enemy with plentiful Ersatz troops.

General Kusmanek's dramatically worded operation order demanded that the participating troops be in position at 12:30 a.m. on March 19 behind the eastern Defensive District VII perimeter. The attack force consisted of two infantry divisions and three separate infantry brigades. The Combined Division Waitzenhofer deployed at the northern flank, its objective to reach Lemberg; the Hungarian 97th Landsturm Infantry Brigade and 23rd Honvéd Infantry Division mobilized at the fortress's southern flank. At 1 a.m., the Combined Division Waitzendorfer received orders to advance from the fortress perimeter zone until it became roughly parallel to the 23rd Honvéd Infantry Division positions. It would then advance. Landsturm Infantry Regiment 35 gave its northern flank security, other units protected the 23rd Honvéd Infantry Division's flanks, while the 108th Landsturm Infantry Brigade deployed in the rear echelon area. If the offensive operation succeeded, the remaining fortress troops would initially destroy the citadel positions extending from Werks IV to X.[7] Because the inclement weather conditions and troop exhaustion delayed launching the operation, it did not commence until just before daylight, making the troops easy targets for enemy gunners. All attempts to reach and penetrate enemy trenches failed, leaving the hapless troops in direct Russian defensive fire for seven hours. The resulting senseless casualties raised the moral question of why the bloody endeavor had been deemed necessary.[8]

As the operation commenced, snowfall reduced visibility to less than one hundred meters and prevented observation of enemy positions, forcing a pause in the attack. When the snow finally lifted, the Russians immediately unleashed heavy artillery barrages and machine gun fire at and behind the hapless Habsburg troops and then launched several assaults against them. Eyewitnesses described the deafening battlefield noise as hellish. Landsturm Infantry Regiment 18 lost half its troop strength preparing to assemble for the operation; thus, it did not participate in the ensuing battle.[9] Pre-offensive unit reports revealed that only

25 to 30 percent of Landsturm Infantry Regiment 6 remained healthy, as did only 70 percent of Infantry Regiment 97 and only half of Landsturm Infantry Regiment 33—a good indication of the percentages of combat-ready troops for the other participating units.

Garrison troop units initially approached the rows of protective barbed wire entanglements outside the fortress perimeter and then zig-zagged to navigate the minefields located immediately before them. Increased enemy artillery barrages blasted tree branches into tiny pieces that tore soldiers' bodies apart until one could not differentiate between the dead and wounded. Enemy guns specifically targeted the barbed wire emplacements, accelerating their crossfire at the helpless troops. The Russians then immediately launched a counterattack with their 58th Infantry Division. Many dead and wounded were abandoned on the battlefield when retreat became necessary. Units quickly lost half of their troop numbers in the hapless situation; soldiers could not believe the tenacity of the enemy defensive fire or the strength of tsarist defensive positions.[10] The close proximity of enemy positions and advancing fortress troops prohibited friendly artillery support, and the troops could not find shelter on the open terrain. Tsarist artillery fire steadily increased in tempo and remained out of range of the fortress guns. Citadel troops found themselves in a hopeless situation when a Russian storm attack resulted in bitter hand-to-hand fighting.[11]

The operation was aimed toward Medyka-Mosciska-Lemberg on a four-kilometer front. The weather remained poor; it had even worsened into snow and sleet with the accompanying cold temperatures and low cloud cover. In detail, the Combined Division Waitzendorfer attack, ordered to commence at 2 a.m., did not begin until 3:15 a.m. because of the delays in assembling the troops. The division received orders to advance from the Fort I/1 perimeter zone, but only Colonel Szathmary's Honvéd Infantry Regiment 2 pressed forward, while supporting artillery fire from that Siedliska position attempted unsuccessfully to counter the fierce enemy barrages. A fortress radio message to Habsburg Supreme Command, received at 6:00 p.m. on March 19, reported that General Waitzendorfer's Combined Division advanced toward Lemberg and the 23rd Honvéd Infantry Division toward Nowosiolki, while the 97th Landsturm Infantry Brigade deployed between these two main attack units. Before the garrison troops were fully deployed, the Russians launched a powerful counteroffensive that halted the operation. Russian artillery shells already filled the air before the operation commenced. Combined Division troops rapidly retreated; its exhausted soldiers deployed on the open terrain sustained severe losses, while 23rd Honvéd Infantry Division troops reached their immediate objective, the high terrain at Nowosiolki, before being forced to retreat.

Initially, Habsburg patrols reached the forward Russian outposts located within five hundred paces of their troops and quickly overpowered these weak tsarist positions. In the meantime, a major portion of Honvéd Infantry Regiment 5 encountered difficulties traversing the fortress perimeter minefields because, similar to other units, they had not been properly oriented about them.[12] Thus, Regiment 5 initially remained inactive, while Honvéd Infantry Regiment 7 did not advance because its commander had not received orders to do so. Honvéd Infantry Regiment 2 continued its isolated attack, which immediately encountered enemy artillery fire from every direction.[13] Shortly thereafter, the various regiments lost contact with each other.

Honvéd Infantry Regiment 2 initially captured a few enemy listening posts but failed to report its success to command headquarters. The regiment launched a bayonet attack as it approached forward enemy positions and forced the opposing weak enemy troop numbers to flee, abandoning their wounded and numerous prisoners of war. This enabled the Honvéd troops to advance to within three or four hundred paces of the main Russian defensive positions, where harrowing, blistering enemy fire quickly halted them. Attacking troop units became intermixed while gaps formed between them. The failure of Honvéd Infantry Regiment 5 to advance exposed Honvéd Infantry Regiment 2's flank position, while severed telephone connections prevented any contact with brigade command. Honvéd Infantry Regiment 2 quickly found itself totally isolated, in desperate need of reinforcements, and having to reestablish liaison with neighboring units. Otherwise, it could not continue any forward movement and faced imminent disaster. Then, at 9:00 a.m., the Russians launched a powerful assault against that regiment's northern and unprotected southern flank positions. Hundreds of Honvéd troops surrendered after the enemy encircled them following a brief hand-to-hand struggle. Many dead and severely wounded officers and troops had to be abandoned on the battlefield.

After the massed Russian troops extended their attack, they annihilated Honvéd Infantry Regiment 2 and threatened to encircle adjacent Honvéd units. They steadily increased their pressure as the Honvéd troops continued to exhaust themselves with their futile efforts. Nevertheless, after a brief pause, the surviving garrison troops attempted to continue to advance, initially overcoming some light enemy resistance. However, heavy rifle and machine gun fire stymied the attacks, and the desperate units began to flee back toward the fortress. A four-hour pause ensued before the Russians attempted to isolate the various Honvéd units and then encircle their flank positions. Enemy firepower and the lack of sufficient troop numbers halted any further Habsburg forward progress. The endangered Honvéd flank positions required immediate reinforcements as the devastating enemy fire continued to inflict heavy casualties. Entire infantry companies simply vanished, while others were almost overrun. The desperate requests for reinforcements proved fruitless because of the interruption of telephone communication.

Following the annihilation of Honvéd Infantry Regiment 2, tsarist troops quickly advanced toward the fortress as their supporting artillery fire intensified. This forced the surviving Honvéd Infantry Regiments 5 and 7 troops to retreat. Meanwhile, the 23rd Honvéd Infantry Division commenced its delayed advance at 4:40 a.m., but encountered further time-consuming impediments while traversing the fortress minefields and blocking positions.[14] Thus, both the Combined Division Waitzendorfer and the 23rd Honvéd Infantry Division failed to initiate immediate action.[15] Using Honvéd Infantry Regiment 5 as an example, the unit prepared to attack from the Siedliska Defensive District VI positions. When the troops passed the fortress perimeter zone and through the narrow protective barbed wire emplacements to launch their attack, they bunched up, losing some individual troop and unit cohesion in the process. Hundreds died or were wounded as they cleared the barbed wire entanglements because enemy mortar, artillery, and machine gun crossfire commenced when they reached the fortress protective barbed wire. One could hear the screams of the dying and wounded over the battlefield noises, but the sick and those soldiers who simply collapsed from exhaustion could not be heard. Some unit commanders reported immediately that they could not advance because the enemy crossfire had inflicted too many casualties.

Honvéd soldiers following the center of the attacking battalions could not fire their rifles, fix their bayonets, or utilize machine guns for fear of killing their compatriots directly in front of them. When these troops ultimately retreated behind their barbed wire entanglements, the Russians continued to fire at them. Once the few surviving troops returned to the fortress environs, a deadly silence hung over them. Honvéd Infantry Regiment 2 supply trains became intermingled, creating chaos, as the regiment's artillery columns had advanced in the wrong direction. The valuable time it required to untangle the confusion produced an adverse effect on the 93rd Landsturm Infantry Brigade's situation. It commenced a retreat, and the entire division soon followed when the 85th Landwehr Infantry Brigade was nearly isolated. Honvéd Infantry Regiment 5 provided flanking fire to assist the 97th Landsturm Infantry Brigade advance when the latter had to cross a difficult and swampy area to reach the roadway leading to Medyka.[16] A 9:45 a.m. report revealed that a powerful enemy counterattack had also hurled the 97th Landsturm Infantry Brigade and the 23rd Honvéd Infantry Division rearward.[17] Both units retreated to the fortress, leaving the Combined Division Waitzendorfer troops exposed on open terrain and forcing them to also join the retreat movement.

As the garrison regiments initially advanced, tsarist forces utilized powerful searchlights to pinpoint the attackers. At 6:30 a.m., flanking cannon, machine gun, and rifle crossfire struck the hapless troops, halting any possible advance while killing or wounding many soldiers who had received little effective fortress artillery support.[18] A soldier's description of the post- operation period conveyed the dire situation:

> I knew we were in our old positions and had only suffered a few losses from the granite fire. Again, mud, filth, and the unbearable tiredness. Many troops remained in their positions and could not be moved by threat. We marched back into the city to our original positions, but there we found that everything had been plundered, windows broken, and doors knocked down. Nevertheless, we all collapsed in the dirt and fell asleep.
>
> After hardly any sleep the troops were suddenly awakened by an alarm, because the Russians had reputedly attacked the northern fortress front. It proved

to be a false alarm, but mass hysteria caused wild rifle fire everywhere, which spread to the other defensive districts. No one knew what the wild shooting was about. Spending the night in the trenches was true torture as the icy winds tore through us. We did not have sufficient protection from the cold. Conditions were such that many could no longer hold their weapons because their fingers were frozen.[19]

The Russians then fired shrapnel shells into the city beginning at 7 a.m. on March 19. According to a fortress civilian, the barrages were greater than those during the October 7, 1914, storm attacks during the first tsarist siege. Shells whistled through the air, and detonation followed detonation.[20] People become more fatalistic as the stormy weather bent trees over. While airplanes attempted to leave the fortress, balloon passengers had to wait for favorable winds before launching their craft. Unfortunately, a counterwind was the norm for several days. Thus, very little time remained for the pilots to depart before the fortress had to capitulate.

Those troops still in outlying forefield positions remained in their cold and damp posts, starving and mentally drained, waiting for their anticipated death. Then, during the afternoon, word spread rapidly through the citadel that the Galician regiments had been hurled back to the fortress. This left the fate of the citadel to the Honvéd troops still in the field, but there was little they could achieve. The attempted breakthrough operation faced the immediate problem of overcoming the enemy's front lines, which a lack of artillery preparation for the garrison's attacks did not help. Garrison troops had to overcome enemy fire and overrun entrenched defensive positions, an impossible task given the circumstances. To the participating troops, the best hope would be to die a hero's death or be captured.[21]

The morning after the disastrous March 19 folly, the apathetic troops marched through the fortress streets. During the late afternoon hours, they learned that the fortress would capitulate and that all the fortress military equipment and ammunition that could be of use to the enemy had to be destroyed. Meanwhile, tsarist artillery lobbed high-explosive and shrapnel shells into the city.[22]

Unbeknownst to Habsburg Supreme Command and the fortress commander at the time, the enemy had foreknowledge of the March 19 breakthrough operation details; therefore, they deployed their troops and artillery positions accordingly. During January 1915, Habsburg Supreme Command ordered the Third Army not to correspond with the fortress by radio. Three months later, a special Habsburg ciphered code reputedly allowed safe radio contact, but later evidence indicates that the Russians had broken it as early as January. Thus, fortress, Third Army, and Habsburg Supreme Command communications provided the enemy with vital information, such as the direction and time of the March 19 fortress breakthrough attempt, although not revealing the participating units or the number of reserve units stationed in the fortress.[23]

The Austro-Hungarian government portrayed the March 19 military fiasco to the public as a heroic and honorable deed after its disastrous conclusion. Fortress headquarters and the Emperor's Military Chancellery exchanged numerous self-serving, congratulatory telegrams in an attempt to glorify the senseless and unnecessary bloody action.[24]

Archduke Friedrich dispatched a telegram to the fortress garrison, stating that "after four and a half months of honorable battle . . . futile enemy attempts to storm the fortress resulted in enormous losses. Recently, especially March 20 and 21, the enemy launched day and night attempts to seize the fortress, but the brave fortress garrison, which on March 19 could not break through the powerful enemy siege lines, ultimately was forced by hunger to surrender. This occurred only after destroying all works, bridges, weapons, ammunition and other war materiel. Only rubble remained for the enemy."[25] The Archduke further expressed his appreciation to the troops for their commitment and emphasized that hunger, not the enemy, had forced them to surrender by presenting a "noble example of honorable duty to the utmost human capacity." His message concluded, "Fortress Przemyśl remains forever a shining example of glory for the army." Friedrich signed and forwarded the telegram to all Habsburg field armies.[26]

During the March 19 bloodbath, the 23rd Honvéd Infantry Division sacrificed 68 percent of its troops, and the Combined Division and the 97th Landsturm Infantry Brigade suffered comparable losses for the perceived honor and prestige of the Habsburg army.[27] There is, however, some disagreement concerning the total fortress losses during that fateful March 19 operation. Some sources claimed that 10,000 troops were killed or wounded.[28] On March 19, the Russians claimed to have captured 110 officers and 4,000 men during the fortress breakout fiasco. The 23rd Honvéd Infantry Division sustained 5,838 casualties, while Combined Division Waitzendorfer suffered 3,000. The 97th Landsturm Infantry Brigade sacrificed between 1,500 and 2,000 soldiers, and one Honvéd Infantry Regiment lost 254 officers and 2,600 troops.[29] Numerous deaths, as mentioned, resulted from utter exhaustion and starvation.

The fortress's unfavorable artillery situation further undermined the ill-fated breakout attempt. Certain caliber artillery shells had already disappeared well before March. The fortress obviously could not replace damaged artillery pieces, gun tubes, other necessary supplies, or faulty artillery telephone materiel. Some artillery barrels, particularly those for 12- and 15-centimeter cannons, were unserviceable by the end of December 1914. Thus, the deteriorating condition of garrison artillery raised a major concern because, in addition, M 80 15-centimeter howitzers and 9-centimeter M 75 cannons had run out of shells.

Skeleton Landsturm formations, military labor sections, and other miscellaneous formations manned fortress ring defensive positions during the failed attempt.[30] After the retreat of the defeated garrison force, fortress perimeter artillery fire prevented the enemy from approaching too close to the citadel. Because the tsarist Eleventh Army siege commander realized that the fortress had expended its last fighting power, he planned to launch a strong assault against it on March 20. He calculated that there would be another fortress breakout attempt, but the fierce fortress defensive artillery fire prevented him from determining a location from where it could be launched.

An interesting saga during Fortress Przemyśl's fateful events involved an armored train constructed specifically for the breakthrough attempt. Its armament consisted of two improvised M 75 15-centimeter field cannons and four machine guns. In addition to encountering enormous obstacles in its preparation, the train commander had not been informed which railroad line should be used or even a specific mission. When the enemy blew up the Wiar River bridges, the armored train's story ended.[31] The wasted effort emphasized the lack of coordination and detail in planning the March 19 operation.

Troop exhaustion prohibited any further offensive efforts after March 19, but General Kusmanek was determined to defend the fortress as long as possible, or at least until the garrison troops had destroyed all useful military objects. The soldiers protecting the fortress received orders to repulse any enemy attacks until they had disposed of the fortress equipment.

During the night of March 20, as a glacial snowstorm enveloped the Carpathian Mountain front, Russian artillery unleashed a massive barrage against the Third Army's right flank and all Second Army positions and commenced a major offensive operation to break through the Dukla Pass, once again utilizing the inclement weather conditions to their advantage. The renewed tsarist offensive eliminated any possibility of Habsburg forces either liberating Fortress Przemyśl before it had to capitulate or encircling the besieging Russian forces from the south. The Carpathian Mountain front remained in a state of constant flux between the major March 20 attack and mid-April 1915 as General Ivanov repeatedly launched assault operations attempting to smash through the Habsburg Carpathian Mountain positions onto the Hungarian plains, his ultimate goal, in an effort to end the war on that front. The unanticipated Russian operation resulted in rapid enemy seizure of critical terrain, which also prevented the Second Army and V Corps Group Lieb from successfully completing its offensive mission toward Fortress Przemyśl. The ill-fated and unnecessary Habsburg attempts to recapture those lost positions caused further casualties and additional delay in launching the limited third Carpathian Mountain offensive.

The main tsarist military objective remained to pierce the Habsburg Second and Third Army fronts that defended the important approaches to the Hungarian plains and then encircle the Habsburg forces at both flanks.[32] The offensive battered the Habsburg cornerstone inner flank positions along the dominating Beskid ridges. Colonel Veith described the operation: "On March 20, a snowstorm broke over us with a ferocity found only in glacial regions. All forward movement ceases; no wounded can be evacuated; entire lines of riflemen became covered as if by a white blanket. The icy ground, sanded smooth by the storm, was impossible to dig into; the infantry had no protective cover and could not move in front of the enemy's defensive works; the artillery is several days' march behind."[33]

General Böhm-Ermolli reported that his V Corps attack group could not attain its objective by March 22, the day Fortress Przemyśl surrendered. Meanwhile, V Corps launched its last futile effort to reach the fortress on March 21. Unfortunately, the effort occurred three days after the fortress attempt had failed. Astonishingly, Habsburg Supreme Command did not inform either Second Army Command or the fortress of that fact, making the last of the Second Army's bloody sacrifices to reach the citadel completely unnecessary. On March 20, only V Corps and some Group Szurmay troops at the Second Army's extreme eastern flank could continue the futile attempt to relieve the embattled fortress. Neighboring units received orders to launch simultaneous offensive actions, but Group Szurmay's left flank units could not participate in the effort because of unanticipated serious enemy attacks unleashed against them between March 17 and 19.

Back at Fortress Przemyśl, the order to destroy useful military equipment in the fortress resulted in General Kusmanek convening a meeting attended by the commander of the 23th Honvéd Infantry Division, General Waitzendorfer, commander of the northern fortress defensive districts and Combined Division, the artillery and engineering staff chiefs, and the Fortress chief of staff.[34] General Kusmanek informed these senior commanders that the garrison's physical condition and poor morale precluded any further major action outside the fortress. On March 20 and 21, despite the garrison troops' extreme exhaustion, lessened battle capabilities, and loss of morale resulting from the failed breakthrough attempt, they halted all enemy attacks against the northern, western, and northeastern fortress fronts. When the tsarist efforts failed on March 21, they terminated any further siege army active attempts against the fortress. Meanwhile, garrison troops could not halt another night attack and indeed could no longer perform any substantial military duty, which raised the serious question whether they could destroy fortress war materiel in time before the capitulation. All commanders reported that troop morale suffered badly from the failed military attempt; thus, they could not consider participation in any future major military action. Since the fortress food supply would reportedly last only until March 24, commanders had to unconditionally reserve rations for the garrison troops until the anticipated surrender to prevent them from dying of starvation when they had to march from the fortress to the next Russian food magazines. The destruction of railroads in the fortress area signified that the Russians could not rapidly replenish the fortress's food supplies when it capitulated. On March 21, the troops received four rations of biscuits and a two-day supply of canned meat. Enough food also had to be reserved for the fortress hospital to last until the end of March. The evening before the surrender, the troops attended a religious ceremony, while all remaining horses were slaughtered during March 20 and 21.[35]

Fortress airplane pilots received orders to leave the fortress even if the weather did not cooperate; in particular, counterwinds and poor visibility remained a problem for fourteen days. In addition, several aircraft engines were described as either defective or unreliable. Some planes even failed to take off, and one aircraft flew toward Russia, while another had to return to the fortress area because of engine trouble. Only one airplane successfully flew into the clouds and headed toward home. The Austrian record balloon captain, because of the counterwinds, fell into enemy hands after being wounded near Brest-Litovsk.[36]

During the evening of March 20, three telegrams arrived at the Brzesko aviation camp. The first one indicated that some pilots left the fortress on March 18 in four balloons, but no information arrived concerning their fate. The second telegram requested any information about the flights, while the third stressed that two airplanes had to fly to Przemyśl. That evening pilots received orders to prepare to depart for the fortress the next morning. Thus, on March 21, a day before the fortress capitulated, two aircrews left from the Brzesko airfield, on the last flight to the besieged fortress. Both airplanes carried five sacks of mail as well as two telegrams for General Kusmanek. One pilot carried about 140 kilograms of the last mail delivery to the fortress. The flight covered 200 kilometers, lasting only one hour and fifteen minutes because a strong tailwind pushed the airplane to a speed of 180 kilometers per hour.[37]

The second airplane departed shortly afterward but developed engine problems. After the pilot landed and repaired his apparatus, he flew to the fortress on only three cylinders. The first pilot, a Lieutenant

Stanger, landed at the Zuravica airfield amid fierce tsarist gunfire and immediately reported to General Kusmanek's headquarters, where he received a warm welcome. "I reported to General Kusmanek, who joyfully received me with the words 'so here you are again with us.' "[38] He continued:

> The general read two telegrams from the Emperor. I'll never forget the moment when this heroic commander with tears in his eyes told me, "You see . . . after five months of day and night combat, the enemy did not defeat us. Hunger forced us to surrender." I felt a lump in my throat. When he shook my hand in farewell, he told me, "You are probably the only human being who will get out of this fortress. Tell everyone what you have seen here and let people know that we suffered; make certain they are aware that we fought to the last moment and fulfilled our soldier's duty." General Kusmanek shook Lt. Stanger's hand and asked him to "Please take this card to my wife and daughter."[39]

Lieutenant Stanger also described artillery shells falling on Fortress Przemyśl buildings. For dinner, he and senior fortress officers dined on the last surviving carrier pigeons. The fortress's "Last Supper" revealed the depressing mood of the officers; some even stared at maps wondering where they would spend their prisoner of war days. Intermittent explosions interrupted conversation. Lieutenant Stanger recalled, "About 10 p.m. at my farewell, the officers gave me messages for their acquaintances and letters to their beloved families. I promised to deliver the parcels and letters." He witnessed the city police rousing inhabitants from their homes; the starving people solemnly trudged out onto the streets. The lieutenant meanwhile received orders to depart before 5 or 6 a.m., but stated, "I can't sleep because of the terrible explosions, which rattle the window panes."[40]

Around 4:00 a.m., Lieutenant Stanger heard an airplane take off despite the darkness, one of the last flights out of Fortress Przemyśl. According to one account, the plane was later shot down and burned by the Russians. Another version of the events, however, suggested that the Czech pilot deliberately flew his plane toward Russian positions. After March 22, 1915, that pilot would be listed in the Austro-Hungarian army registers as missing in action. On April 20, 1920, he enlisted in the Czechoslovakian air force as a major.[41]

When Lieutenant Stanger arrived at the airfield at 5:15 a.m. to oversee repairs to his airplane, shrapnel shells were landing all around him, so he decided to depart quickly. Once his plane took off and attained an altitude of one hundred meters, he witnessed the terrible sight of flames shooting high into the sky, and explosions buffeted the airplane from all directions. The aircraft became filled with the smell of fire and smoke as parts of buildings and fortifications blasted up into the air within enormous clouds of dust. Stanger altered his course of flight over the city, climbed to three hundred meters, and flew over a bridge just as it exploded. The city by then had been covered with vast flames, turning the morning clouds into a glowing red. The plane eventually crossed Russian lines at a height of six hundred meters, three and a half hours after leaving the fortress. Stanger would eventually land the plane safely at Brzesko.[42]

On March 19, after waiting several days for favorable weather that never arrived, and while the Russians unleashed artillery barrages against the Zuravica and Hurezco airfields, six airplanes exited the fortress's main airfield at Buszowiczki. Despite the constant enemy shelling, Flight Company 11 airplanes took off for Brzesko in a raging blizzard that lowered visibility to less than one hundred meters. Five planes returned to the fortress, where they would be destroyed, and their crews then attempted to depart in balloons. The sixth plane, which contained the plans for the breakthrough operation, went missing and probably ended up in enemy hands. Documents flown out by balloon on March 17 also landed in enemy territory. Immediately after takeoff the wind shifted, pushing the balloons toward the enemy front. Twelve aircraft were destroyed in the fortress, while seven pilots and observers became Russian prisoners of war.

Four overloaded balloons carrying documents, twelve men, and an unknown number of unmanned "Pareval" observation models eventually took off. Those carrying mail unfortunately encountered unfavorable wind currents and could not fly west over the Carpathian Mountains, but rather drifted northeast toward enemy positions. They finally landed thirty-two kilometers southeast of Brest-Litovsk. The "Przemyśl" balloon landed in Russian territory, the "Austria" and "Erz. Joseph Ferdinand" near Brest-Litovsk, while the "Schicht" landed near Sokal. The final balloon, the "Steiermarkt," was destroyed when it attempted to take off. None of the balloons reached friendly territory.[43]

Fearing that the Russians would storm and conquer the fortress on March 20, Conrad ordered that "as soon as the food situation makes it impossible to hold the fortress any longer, all war materiel must be destroyed" according to Dienstbuch E-9/70 regulations pertaining to fortresses.[44] A fortress commission determined to commence such action at 5 a.m. on March 22. This was due to the garrison troops' terrible physical condition, which drastically worsened following the bloody March 19 fiasco and the March 20 and 21 Russian attacks on the fortress. Fortress Commander Order Number 94 of March 21, 1915, declared that between 5 and 6 a.m. on March 22, all fortress artillery pieces must be destroyed after firing their remaining shells. During this time, the interval battery positions had to continue to protect the fortress and forefield troops to halt any enemy attack. Then came the destruction of optical instruments, telephones, and any other worthwhile equipment.[45]

Thus at 5 a.m. on March 22, garrison troops overloaded the last granite rounds into artillery barrels and fired them off. They spared the obsolete M 1861 artillery pieces, because the troops reputedly possessed neither the shells nor necessary black powder to destroy them.[46] A few minutes before 6 a.m., infantry troops abandoned their fortress positions. According to Fortress Operation Number 233, the remaining horses—with the exception of those belonging to commanders, artillery horses, and two horses for each lower unit—were shot and their saddles torn up; signal and telephone equipment, railroad rolling stock, tracks, and ancillary materials such as coal, gasoline, and oats were destroyed. The fortress radio station reported at 6:55 a.m. that the army had liquidated everything within the citadel.[47]

By 6 a.m., the major works themselves and other major objects and materiel had been destroyed. The process then commenced in the interval positions, which the troops evacuated. All buildings were burned to the ground. Afterward, the troops had to assemble and march through the connecting trenches; however, the central fortress areas still had to be maintained. Telephone installations were destroyed before the Werks themselves. Meanwhile, the troops destroyed their weapons: machine guns, rifles, bayonets, and swords.

Six soldiers in every infantry company who had earned medals for bravery in battle would keep their weapons to maintain discipline and order in the ranks. The only troops to remain completely armed were the civil police, the prisoner of war guards, and the fortress command staff. The troops could carry only their blankets and bread sack. All other material was destroyed. In the fortress girdle, observation positions and officer patrols had to ensure that the enemy realized that the fortress had capitulated, and then parliamentarians would be sent to Russian siege headquarters.[48]

A Fortress Przemyśl civilian diary entry of March 20 revealed some very disturbing facts: on March 19, attacking Honvéd troops were hurled back and fearfully decimated, with an unknown number of dead, wounded, missing, and prisoners of war. The author described the returning troops as trudging along, appearing to be ghosts on the verge of collapse. "The dread has no end," she wrote. They begged for bread, but there was none available. The hospitals had no empty beds, and a large number of private homes were commandeered for housing the wounded. Only half-healed troops were transferred to the houses, while "the fortress has become one enormous hospital."

Conditions in the fortress hospitals became increasingly horrendous, the putrid stench of human waste assaulting the senses as soon as one entered one of the facilities. Casualties before the bloody effort of March 19 had already overtaxed fortress medical services. When fifteen hundred wounded troops and a thousand cholera cases received treatment, the Medical Corps personnel tried to prevent the outbreak of cholera, typhus, and dysentery. Then the many wounded soldiers from the ill-fated breakthrough attempt required immediate medical attention, overwhelming medical personnel.

Patients often received tea brewed from foul water. Many succumbed the very next day and were transferred to the morgue. Gravediggers remained busy throughout the siege ordeals. Initially, during the first encirclement, ceremonial military burials would be held for the dead. Later, corpses would be buried with little fanfare and, eventually, disposed of without ceremony because the starving survivors were too weak to dig the graves. The number of wounded who succumbed increased, and toward the end of the siege, as many as three hundred men died each day of starvation. Petty crime, embezzlement, and robbery became more common as the military authorities, often complicit in the corruption, struggled to maintain order as the death toll mounted.

Then came descriptions of the destruction of equipment as enemy artillery bombardment of the fortress continued. One airplane took off and quickly disappeared into the clouds, "hopefully heading for the homeland." Further entries added:

> Since 7 a.m. Russian shrapnel shells could be heard all over the city. One heard the shells whistle through the air and explode one after another; thus, the entire fortress shook. The incessant booms caused windows to rattle and iron doors to shake. The blasts destroyed glass while the salvos of the last firing cannons and heavy mortars created incredible noise, was "all hell breaking loose?" Fatalism pervades, meanwhile it continues to snow as trees bend in the cemetery under its weight.
>
> Troops serving outside the fortress walls suffered from cold and dampness and wished death to end their misery. Rising flames and clouds of smoke could be seen at the fortress rings. The troops that returned from the March 19 travesty were nothing but skin and bones, tattered uniforms hang off them—the last horses have been slaughtered, tears welled in the soldiers' eyes. They had given their last efforts, the inhuman pain they suffered kills us. Soldiers think of only one thing—eat—eat—they can do no more. They cannot talk.[49]

At 9 a.m., General Kusmanek forwarded the following message to the tsarist siege commander: "Food is exhausted. The works destroyed. I surrender the open city and await your command with no conditions." The new fortress commander issued the command that Habsburg officers could keep their swords because of their bravery.[50]

A fortress inhabitant recorded the scene of destruction on March 22, 1915: "Get up! Get up! Everyone out of the house! Open all the windows! The works are being blown up! The bridges are being blown up!" There was no time for civilians to wash or to comb their hair. People threw on their clothes and entered into the endless mass of humanity being directed along the streets by military personnel. Faces were pale as death in the early morning light of dawn. A fortress civilian provided an interesting description of the troops:

> The men fall into formation. They are merely skin and bones—their too large uniforms are baggy. With pale faces, their stare is dead. They can hardly stand up on their legs. A cook passed by, carrying a raw horse drumstick on his shoulder. The people should be able to eat well one last time. Tears well in eyes as the cook walks past. Thousands waited in silence, but no one complained or spoke. In the

cold morning light, their hard white faces look like they had been made of stone. At 4 a.m., the first mines burst into flames. Then all around the fortress, thunderclap after thunderclap, explosion after explosion followed. The force of the air pressure shook the people like a high voltage electrical shock. Windows and doors flew off their hinges and crashed to the ground. Iron shutters bent outwards, in seconds, the streets were covered with splintered window and door frames, bricks from the rooftops and pieces of window sills and gutters. One fort after the other collapsed. Mines exploded. Toxic materials burned, producing black and white columns of smoke as the fortress became engulfed in fire, the flames reaching for the sky. The three San River bridges exploded. An enormous detonation forced the tree branches in the old cemetery to bend almost completely over. Within seconds, people became engulfed in a cloud of gunpowder smoke and covered head to foot in soot.

The fortress civilian continued to describe the happenings:

> Is the tragedy over, or is it just beginning? How dreadful this fateful night. At 9 p.m., they began to shoot off the ammunition. A volley around the entire fort like we have never heard before. The walls began to cave upon one another, all of the works raised their terrible voices simultaneously, all of the exterior and interior walls. A constant rolling wave formed in the air. Windows rattled, steel girders shook. Thunder led to more thunder, the roar of heavy mortars, the crackling of rapid fire cannons. All the sounds of hell rang out. You would think it was a volcano erupting. We understood. The time has come. Every thunderclap struck us deep in the heart. We clenched our fists. Every thunderclap a cry of the dead, the bleeding, the starving. Every thunderclap a cry of the hundred thousand martyred souls that gave up their blood for this fort. And so it went the entire night. From time to time a solitary car made a mad dash down the streets. An airplane clattered so close to our window that you would have thought it was in your room. The last airplane flew away. Now and then I dozed. Half asleep having a nightmare from which you want to wake up. Half sleep and full of unexplained, dreadful sounds, like a wicked laugh emanating from hell. At 4:30 in the morning, the police rushed through the streets going house to house.[51]

Before the fortress surrendered, the Russians fired 28-centimeter mortar rounds against the northern, northwestern, and northeastern fortress fronts; the southwest Pod Mazurami position was targeted as well. General Kusmanek feared that the enemy might attempt to seize individual fortress ring positions; thus, citadel troops had to unconditionally defend the fortress during the night.[52] Troop morale posed a serious problem, especially among the Ruthenians, whose commanders no longer trusted them to fulfill their military duties.

It would have been impossible for the weakened troops to march far as prisoners of war with just reserve rations, so they also received their March 24 allotment. This influenced the decision for the fortress to surrender on March 22, because the destruction of the railroads around the citadel area, as previously mentioned, would prevent the transport of food to the fortress before March 24.

On the day of Fortress Przemyśl's surrender, civilians stormed and plundered food magazines, creating chaos. Typical of Austrian historiography, it has been claimed that not one morsel of food could be found in the citadel on the day of its surrender. Contrary to those assertions, civilians discovered thirty-six thousand tins of canned meat and large amounts of coffee and biscuits at the Bakonczyce food magazine. The army also left thousands of cans of preserved food and numerous other food items at the Zasani magazine. At the Slovakigasse, hysterical, starving civilians carried away huge amounts of smoked meat, sugar, rice, and biscuits. At Spitalgasse magazine, civilians discovered beef, coffee, canned meat, and other items. The Russian army distributed some supplies to the people, and they burned or hurled the remainder into the San River.[53] Civilians seized everything they could carry, many returning multiple times to plunder any remaining supplies. At some locations, tsarist soldiers intervened to control the frenzied inhabitants but nevertheless allowed them to confiscate the food. They also plundered the food magazines after the fortress surrender. It reputedly required four days to remove the remaining food supplies. They also discovered a farm with ample hay and twenty milk cows that provided the hospitals with their milk supply.

The surrender of the fortress represented a major military event during this period. Stavka had a great celebration, while the popularity of the Russian commander in chief, Crown Prince Nicolai Nicholovic, soared. In one blow, it appeared that the eastern front situation had been transformed, releasing the siege troops for battle in the mountain campaigns. Naturally, the Russian press proclaimed that the capture of the fortress was a major victory, while Habsburg newspapers attempted to downplay its capitulation. Until March 22, the Dual Monarchy press announced daily that Fortress Przemyśl remained in their possession.

In an effort to minimize the loss of prestige resulting from the surrender, official reports asserted that the capitulation "had no influence on the general situation." Entente newspapers carried stories claiming that the capture of Fortress Przemyśl was the greatest victory of the war. Emperor Franz Joseph reputedly wept upon hearing the news of the fortress's capitulation. Thus, a significant chapter in the history of Fortress Przemyśl ended. The fortress disappeared from the headlines until its recapture on June 3 during the victorious allied Austro-Hungarian-German Gorlice-Tarnov offensive, but its legacy would endure long after the war. Some European historians have even compared the Carpathian Winter War and the fortress surrender to the apocalyptic battle of Stalingrad in 1943 during World War II.[54]

For General Conrad, the surrender of Fortress Przemyśl was a major tragedy, but he was more concerned with the political implications of the defeat than with the military consequences. He feared that internal and external enemies would portray the event as a catastrophe. The perception that the loss had inflicted such a fearful blow to the Habsburg war effort could further undermine troop morale and perhaps even convince Italy to enter the war soon. Given these circumstances, Conrad foresaw a sad Easter.

In the meantime, the Russian Eleventh Army commander had planned to launch a major attack to conquer the fortress, but with its surrender he simply occupied it.[55] At noon on March 23, Russian troops entered the fortress environs in complete order, initially with only a few infantry battalions and Cossack formations. According to some sources, city inhabitants remained in their homes; others claimed that the Russians received a warm greeting. Tsarist soldiers attempted to retrieve rifles and other equipment hurled into the shallow waters of the San River. Observers also reported that Habsburg officers ate well, stealing food from their own troops, who starved during the siege. Thus, at the capitulation, many officers were fat, while the troops were skin and bones. A British observer called it "simply a burlesque."[56]

With the fortress's capitulation, the Russians captured nine generals, ninety-three staff officers, about 2,500 lower-rank officers and military officials, 117,000 soldiers (9,000 sick or wounded), and 16,000 military and 4,000 civilian workers. Approximately 2,000 Russian prisoners of war also received their freedom.[57] On March 24, General Artamonov issued the first Russian command for Fortress Przemyśl personnel, strongly demanding the maintenance of full order and quiet in the entire fortress area. Everyone had to remain in their quarters and provide the same service as they had before, including doctors and medical officers. Each officer and his server would be allowed fifty kilograms of prepacked luggage for transport to prisoner of war camps. Everyone appeared extremely tired as they wrestled with the idea of being captured. Many troops collapsed, totally exhausted. The remainder of General Artamonov's order asked for "absolute fulfillment of my commands and demands of all my representatives":

> War action has been halted, but if my commands are not followed, or if there is any anti-Russian action taken siege artillery will open fire against Przemyśl city and destroy it. Food supplies will also be terminated. In addition, I demand the prevention of epidemics and sickness. Thus, sanitary methods must be adhered to in the city and fortress. Further plunderers would be shot, the selling of alcohol would be punished, Russian troops would be quartered (housed) and all fortress officers could carry their saber, but no other weapons.[58]

Following the capitulation, entire regiments marched to Radymno, two miles away, where they received a meal that night. Then the new prisoners of war found themselves herded into secluded buildings surrounded by guards. The next day they were marched into town, where many Ruthenians were finally reunited with the families, whom they had not seen throughout the entire winter. When questioned about their personal circumstances, family members answered with frightened expressions on their faces. The soldiers noted that the town had been destroyed, with filth, crosses, and graves everywhere: "The Russians then fed us bread, one loaf for every three soldiers. Following the meal they moved us back to the fortress once again where they now provided us nothing to eat, and then they marched us to Zarawica, because the destroyed railroad tracks around the fortress had not been repaired. Thus no food could be delivered to the fortress environs."[59]

The new prisoners of war ate vegetable soup as well as very good smoked fish conserves for dinner. Then, for the first time, they were fed meat as the provision depots opened and food was divided between the military and civilian population. Ten Honvéd soldiers died because they ate too much food too quickly.[60] When the wounded were transferred from hospitals, those buildings would be evacuated. The seriously wounded troops were transferred into two or three hospitals. On April 4, the Russian commander called for the rapid evacuation of medical personnel by the end of May.

The fortress garrison learned that the first transport of prisoners of war would commence on March 26; in the meantime, the situation at the hospitals remained stationary. The Russians seemed to treat their troops well and proved very tactful in their dealings with fortress officers. Streets remained quiet, and all doors had to be locked by 7 p.m. Civilians and Habsburg officers had to be home or in their quarters by the curfew time of 10 p.m. Daily, one witnessed fires and clouds of smoke as objects that had been blown up on March 22 continued to burn. Many Russian trains began to transport supplies to the fortress daily.[61]

The Carpathian Mountain front military situation increasingly favored the Russians after Fortress Przemyśl's capitulation. The tsarist Eleventh Army immediately was redeployed into the brutal Carpathian Mountain front lines, promptly enhancing Russian numerical advantage there as their Third and Eighth Armies received an additional army corps with which to continue to attack the Habsburg Third Army. The troops attempted to seize the Dukla Pass through the Carpathian Mountains during the Easter battle. A successful tsarist Carpathian Mountain campaign still had the potential advantage of bringing Romania into the war to assist in the destruction of the Austro-Hungarian army.

General Ivanov could now finally attempt to fulfill his goal of crushing Habsburg military resistance and invade Hungary. With the addition of former siege troops, he launched the aforementioned deadly attack against Habsburg Second and Third Army flank and rear positions on March 20. Only the lack of suitable roads and the unfavorable weather and terrain conditions prevented a rapid tsarist success. Following the Fortress Przemyśl capitulation, the Third Army could not halt the enemy offensive as the hard-pressed Second Army Command desired to relieve the pressure against it. Russian troops broke through the Second and Third Army fronts with impunity, creating further chaos in their ranks. The Third Army required reinforcements merely to maintain its right flank positions, which forced the Fourth Army to relinquish additional troops to it.

On the mountain front during the last week of March, relentless enemy pressure forced reeling Habsburg defenders back though the hilly terrain toward the Hungarian plains, preventing the normal Habsburg procedure of redeploying exhausted troops from a nonendangered front area to a newly threatened one. When the Third Army continued to retreat, the Russians extended their offensive to the Fourth Army front.

The April 1915 Easter battle provided General Ivanov's last major effort to defeat the Austro-Hungarian army and bring Italy and Romania into the war on the Entente side. Meanwhile, the Habsburg Second Army front also crumbled, leaving it unable to push encroaching enemy troops back across the San River. The beleaguered Habsburg field army troops would have to recapture recently surrendered territory before they could even contemplate recapturing Fortress Przemyśl.

Weather and climate also influenced the "Easter battle," but this time the Russians suffered as the attackers. Snowstorms alternating with warming trends caused flooding and icy glaciers. The end of March and the beginning of April brought a repeated series of events as attacking forces sank so deep into the softened ground that the dead remained standing in an upright position. The steady warming trend brought the threat of epidemics, which the severe winter weather had suppressed.

During late fall 1914, cholera claimed many lives before retreating to a subordinate role in the winter months as the climate, frostbite, and cold-related illnesses became the principal causes of troop suffering. In the spring, cholera returned because of the terrible shelter conditions, the poor supply situation, and the unbelievable indolence of the populace. Civil authorities, in many instances, hindered much-needed precautionary sanitation measures. Some immunization met with passive resistance among the troops. Personal hygiene meant little to the troops at the front. They wore the same uniforms for weeks and months at a time and rarely washed themselves, which facilitated the spread of cholera and other infectious diseases such as typhus, which had broken out earlier in the Serbian theater. Fortunately, it proved rare during this campaign.

Troops also became infested with lice. At one upper Hungarian base camp's sanitary camp, fifteen liters of lice were collected from hundreds of wounded soldiers. Everyone, officers and regular troops alike, accepted the lice problem with resignation as one of the many obvious "hardships of war." Unfortunately, no one understood the connection between lice and typhus. Under the circumstances, it is remarkable that the pestilence did not become more widespread.

In the meantime, 15,819 Habsburg soldiers in the fortress reported to sick call or had nonthreatening infectious illnesses on March 25, and between March 17 and 23, forty-nine officers and 6,258 troops were hospitalized. Fortress medical personnel, including civilian employees, numbered about 115 doctors, 40 medical students, 300 sister nurses, and 2,400 medical troops.[62] The new tsarist fortress commander ordered a rapid evacuation of the sick and wounded on April 4, as well as imprisoned medical personnel. By the end of May, only some of the patients had been transported from the fortress.

The first Russian newspapers arrived from Kiev, which provided descriptions of the military events on the Galician front. The transport of Red Cross sisters out of the fortress occurred approximately three weeks after the prisoners of war and wounded were evacuated. The sisters would be shipped to Finland and Sweden; the trip and food for fourteen days would be free.[63]

By March 26, the former fortress commander, General Kusmanek, his personal adjutants, and three servers arrived in Kiev as prisoners of war. They and five hundred other officers became the first to evacuate the fortress. Later, another two hundred officers and three thousand troops departed by train. By early April, the generals and almost all officers had been evacuated, as well as some Carpathian Mountain front prisoners of war.[64]

The largest number of prisoners of war, 1,725 officers and 66,700 troops, departed the fortress by train between March 31 and April 6; another large group left between the second and third weeks of April. Then, between April 28 and May 5, an additional 41 officers and 5,600 men departed the fortress. The Russians claimed that by May 1915, 4,200 officers and 126,000 men (8,400 sick) departed the fortress. No additional reports have been found between April 21 and 27. Thus, by mid-May, the greatest number of fortress prisoners of war had been evacuated. Tsarist sources further claimed that by the second evacuation effort most officers and troops had been moved to their prisoner of war locations in Russia. This ignored an ordered multiple-day Russian quarantine period. However, some sick and wounded soldiers remained in the fortress until May. Tsar Nicholas II visited the conquered citadel between April 23 and 25.

The Russians used two railroad routes to evacuate Habsburg prisoners of war. Previously, these routes were used to transport supplies to the Carpathian Mountain front and fortress siege troops. To the north, the evacuation route direction extended from Fortress Przemyśl to Lemberg and then to Kiev and beyond. Approximately one hundred thousand to three hundred thousand soldiers were evacuated within ten days. At the turn of the month, the Russian war minister ordered that the prisoners of war be prepared to perform work details. On April 9, the railroad line between Lemberg and Brody and Tarnopol reputedly had been overtaxed, indicating the enormous movement of prisoners of war to Kiev.[65]

In an interesting sidelight to the Fortress Przemyśl saga, Austrian Dr. Robert Bárány received the Nobel Prize in Physiology in 1914. His main medical contribution involved the clinical application of experimental data to human beings. This ultimately resulted in the doctor investigating the human equilibrium system. He became professor extraordinar just before the war erupted but volunteered for military service despite suffering from physical problems. Dr. Bárány, deployed to Fortress Przemyśl as a medical officer, did not accept the customary methods of treating infected cranial wounds. He realized that when bullets penetrated the brain, they carried infected skin and clothing particles with them, causing infection and eventually death. He introduced the system of carefully cleaning the brain cavity, and then closing the wound to prevent infection from entering. He sought to have his new method of head wound treatment become common practice.

He became a prisoner of war when the fortress surrendered and found himself transported by cattle car to Central Asia. As a result of the unsanitary conditions he endured, the doctor contracted malaria. Outside public intervention brought his eventual release from a Russian prisoner of war camp in 1916, but in the interim, Dr. Bárány had no means to conduct experimentation or read medical literature during his time as a prisoner.

With the "spring battle" of Gorlice, the Austro-Hungarian winter campaign in the Carpathians ended. One of the most difficult episodes of the war, a time of unspeakably bitter suffering, had reached its conclusion. The Habsburg military crisis, however, was far from over. After Fortress Przemyśl surrendered, the Russians threatened to break through the remaining Carpathian Mountain ridges to invade Hungary. The Habsburg army found itself on the brink of collapse. Would April determine its ultimate fate? Would the Russians invade Hungary and force Austria-Hungary out of the war? Would Italy and/or Romania enter the war to perform the coup de grâce to the hapless Austro-Hungarian army? Or would Germany again rescue its floundering Habsburg ally as after the disastrous retreat following the two battles of Lemberg? Would Fortress Przemyśl be reconquered by the Central Powers? These questions will be answered in the next chapter.

9

Gorlice-Tarnov and After

THE BATTLE OF GORLICE-TARNOV, WHICH COMMENCED ON May 2, 1915, proved the greatest Central Powers victory of the war and represented the apex of Austro-Hungarian and German coalition warfare. Germany's successful tactics of short but massive artillery preparations followed by frontal infantry attacks became the norm for General Falkenhayn's operations for the next two years. The offensive not only rescued the floundering Habsburg ally in the Carpathian Mountains but also prevented Romania from renouncing its neutrality and declaring war on Austria-Hungary.[1]

The Central Powers' military situation on the eastern front in early April 1915 appeared very unfavorable. On the western front, the French and the English had launched offensives with a numerical superiority of six hundred battalions. The outcome of these western front battles remained uncertain, but the Germans anticipated that the Entente armies would achieve only local victories because of previous defensive successes. On the eastern front, the Austro-Hungarian armies continued to retreat from incessant Russian attacks throughout winter and spring 1915, particularly during the Easter battle. The tsarist Eighth Army and part of its Third Army had successfully battled their way across the key ridgelines to the western side of the Carpathian Mountains. General Conrad repeatedly demanded German reinforcements to buttress that faltering front, where the Russians continued their assaults unabated. He callously pressured his battered troops, including X Corps, which had been bled white, to halt the enemy's progress. By early spring, Austro-Hungarian forces had come perilously close to collapse. As the Habsburgs continued their successive retreats, the threat increased that Italy would soon enter the war against Austria-Hungary to gain its irredenta territory within the Dual Monarchy. Conrad needed a major offensive success against Russia to prevent this.[2] Constant Russian advances toward the Hungarian plains also encouraged Romania to enter the war to gain Transylvania and the Bukovina. Although Fortress Przemyśl capitulated in late March, the Russians themselves suffered enormous losses as Dual Monarchy troop numbers also rapidly decreased. The Habsburgs also desperately needed a victory to hold the k.u.k. army together. Increasing war weariness was taking a toll on the troops, and it appeared that the army had begun to disintegrate.[3] A noticeable decline in troop effectiveness also became evident within certain Austro-Hungarian army units, especially those with Czech, Romanian, Italian, and South Slav soldiers. In a number of cases, predominantly Slavic units allegedly surrendered en masse to the enemy.

Although tsarist forces continued to succeed militarily during April 1915, they lacked the necessary troop strength to fully exploit their victories by mid-April. After sustaining such enormous losses throughout the war, Russia had been forced to deploy inadequately trained and armed troops, which effectively transformed its forces into a peasant army. In addition, the Russians increasingly suffered from a shortage of weapons and ammunition, particularly artillery shells, which quickly became an acute weakness.

Compounding Austria-Hungary's difficult eastern front situation was that the outcome of the French and British Gallipoli campaign in the Dardanelles remained unclear. The Entente hoped to open the straits to Russia and the Black Sea and possibly knock the Ottoman Empire out of the war. General Falkenhayn desired, as a priority, to relieve Entente pressure in the Dardanelles, but had to await the victorious allied October 1915 campaign against Serbia to finally achieve his Balkan plans. The successful campaign became possible as a result of the Gorlice-Tarnov operation. Throughout the Carpathian Winter War campaigns, he suggested to Conrad that the allies launch a campaign against the Serbs, but the Habsburgs had no extra troops at their disposal. However, the real military emergency existed on the Habsburg eastern front, as the Russians, by early April 1915, threatened to invade Hungary and defeat

Austria-Hungary. The German High Command realized that it had to assist its reeling ally, but since the entire Carpathian Mountain region had proved so unfavorable for successful battle, General Falkenhayn sought a more appropriate location to initiate a major military operation. However, the German Beskid Corps was scraped together and transferred to the threatened Habsburg front to prevent its immediate collapse. The insertion of the German troops halted further tsarist successes against the battered X Corps, bringing some relief to their ally.

On April 4, as battle raged in the Carpathian Mountains, Generals Conrad and Falkenhayn conferred in Berlin and agreed to remain on the defensive on the Habsburg Balkan front. They also determined to maintain a defensive position on the Italian front should Italy enter the war. However, General Falkenhayn failed to be completely honest with his counterpart during their meeting. A few days earlier, he had begun to consider launching an offensive in the area west of Fortress Kraków to relieve pressure on the Habsburg mountain front. Thus, when Conrad returned to his headquarters after their meeting, he learned that the German liaison officer, General August Cramon, had met with Habsburg Railroad Bureau personnel to investigate the possibility of major German troop transports to the region south of Fortress Kraków. Cramon had replied to a Falkenhayn telegram that such a deployment would require eight days. The initial objective of the operation was the Wisloka River toward the Dukla Pass and Fortress Przemyśl. General Falkenhayn therefore had to terminate his plans for a western front offensive effort in order to rescue his hapless Habsburg ally.

Conrad responded to Falkenhayn immediately on April 6, requesting that seven German divisions be deployed to the Italian frontier and three to the Romanian frontier as a defensive measure to free Habsburg troops for deployment to support the threatened Carpathian Mountain front. By April 10, the Russian Eighth Army and a portion of its Third Army had reached the far side of the Carpathian Mountains. Three tsarist divisions had been transferred to the Bukovina and three deployed into the Carpathian Mountains, weakening the tsarist Third Army. If the Russians came within striking distance of the Hungarian plains, Romania would also certainly attack Austria-Hungary. General Falkenhayn did not inform Conrad of his intentions until three weeks before the allied offensive occurred.[4] Then, on April 13, at their next meeting in Berlin, General Falkenhayn announced, without revealing specific details, that he intended to create a new German Eleventh Army, to be deployed to the Gorlice-Tarnov area where the Habsburg Fourth Army had battled in early March. At that battle, the Fourth Army's VI Corps failed to conquer its objective because of inadequate troop numbers, the unfavorable winter weather conditions, and particularly strong enemy defensive positions on that front.

Gorlice served as a crucial transportation center for the Russian southwest front with its good railroad connections. Conrad originally anticipated that General Falkenhayn would deploy four German divisions to the Russian front for the approaching offensive operation, but now learned that he intended to deploy four army corps instead. On April 14, the two generals reconvened and finalized the planning details, in full agreement about the campaign.[5] The plan called for the newly formed German Eleventh Army to launch an offensive toward Zmigrod, Sanok, and the Dukla Pass, and then liberate Fortress Przemyśl. Then, with the Habsburg Third and Fourth Armies protecting its flanks, it would attack tsarist Eighth Army positions at the Lupkov Pass. The Germans, however, demanded some command control over the two Habsburg armies during the operation. Although irritated by the request, General Conrad appreciated that General Falkenhayn finally intended to intervene on the Carpathian Mountain front, where Habsburg troops fought on the last mountain ridges before they would have to retreat onto the Hungarian plains.[6]

On April 20, General Conrad learned the offensive goals of the mission. The German Eleventh and the Habsburg Fourth Army would break through tsarist positions west of the Lupkov Pass saddle from the west. The southern flank troops would move in the general direction of Zmigrod-Dukla-Sanok to pierce tsarist defensive lines along the Becken (basin) line Gorlice-Jaslo. On April 21, the first German soldiers began their railroad transport to the Galician front.

A controversy arose that continued long after the war concerning whether Conrad or Falkenhayn had conceived the original idea for what became the most successful Central Powers victory of the war. Was it General Conrad, who had earlier recognized the critical military significance of the Gorlice area, or General Falkenhayn, who also recognized the strategic importance of this area, but could provide the troop strength necessary to achieve the victory? The debate raged long after the war ended. It should be noted that General Falkenhayn, aware of the Habsburg army's debilitating defeats in August and September 1914 and then during the 1915 Carpathian Mountain Winter, held little regard for the Dual Monarchy's military capabilities.

Meanwhile, when Fortress Przemyśl capitulated in March, the Russians occupied it and began reconstructing some destroyed citadel positions to improve defensive capabilities should it be attacked. As mentioned earlier, Tsar Nicholas II visited the compound between April 23 and 25, after which serious improvement work on the fortress commenced. Heavy tsarist artillery pieces and numerous troop units converged on the desolate fortress.

By the end of April 1915, the Central Powers' military situation remained very unfavorable. On all fronts, they stood on the military and political defensive and had lost the military initiative. The threat of Italy entering the war against Austria-Hungary escalated, which could also bring neutral Bulgaria and Romania into the conflagration. Indications abounded of major allied offensive plans for the western front, and by April 25 the second phase of the Gallipoli campaign against the Dardanelles had commenced. This raised the question of the fate of Turkey and, to General Falkenhayn, the necessity of launching an offensive against Serbia to open the Danube River and enable Austria-Hungary and Germany to supply the Ottoman ally with the materials necessary to continue the war and simultaneously relieve allied pressure in the Balkan Peninsula. The Central Powers' military and diplomatic leadership also desired to shift the Balkan Peninsula balance of power back in their favor, but this required leaving multiple German units in the Balkan theater after a successful campaign against Serbia. Between February and March, allied offensives failed at Champagne and Artois on the western front. Now that the Central Powers felt free to strike in the east, Falkenhayn targeted the northern portion of Russia's southwest front for the Gorlice-Tarnov operation.

By late April 1915, one-third of a million Central Powers troops had assembled to launch a surprise offensive against the unsuspecting

Russian Third Army formations. Superior troop numbers would assault the defending tsarist forces. The German artillery complement included approximately five hundred heavy and light artillery pieces, ninety-six trench mortars, and six hundred machine guns, the greatest concentration of artillery to date on the eastern front. The operation was even more successful than expected because the Russians proved so ill-prepared to counter the offensive. The Russian Third Army possessed 675 light artillery pieces, 4 defective heavy artillery guns, 600 machine guns, and no trench mortars. The army's frontline trenches were only three feet deep, this portion of the front having been quiescent for weeks. Although some sources claim that the Russians had previous notification of the military operation, tsarist commanders appeared not to have noticed that the peasants, who had been tilling the fields between the opposing lines, had disappeared for several days.

Before the Gorlice-Tarnov offensive was launched on May 2, General Falkenhayn pressured General Conrad relative to negotiations with Italy. He demanded that Vienna meet Rome's territorial demands. He also urged Vienna to commence negotiations with Bulgaria concerning an alliance against Serbia. General Conrad replied that he encouraged the Habsburg foreign minister to seek an agreement with Sofia.[7] He also declared that even if the Galician campaign proved to be a decisive victory and Italy remained neutral, a military campaign against Serbia was out of the question before the end of May. He refused Falkenhayn's request to divert forces from his Fifth Army, which was deployed on the Serbian front, because he feared a surprise enemy attack into Bosnia.[8] General Falkenhayn replied that the Serbians could not launch an offensive into Habsburg territory because of the swollen rivers. Therefore, if the Serbians could not attack, General Conrad could shift troops from his Fifth Army.[9] General Conrad then recontacted his German counterpart, inquiring about the required strength of the participating forces and the time factor involved, as well as when he could anticipate German military units being deployed to assist his forces against Italy if it came to war against the perfidious ally. General Conrad also pressured his foreign minister to keep Italy out of the war and informed General Falkenhayn of his action.[10]

As the Gorlice-Tarnov offensive approached, Russian artillery had proved ineffective in combat due to the serious lack of artillery shells. Following the opening German artillery barrages against the opposing tsarist Third Army trenches, at 9 a.m. on May 2 mortars commenced an hour of devastating fire against the shallow enemy trenches. The artillery shifted its fire forward to usher in the first German infantry attack wave. This first assault operation advanced rapidly, a desperate necessity given the lingering threat of neutral European states entering the war. The German hurricane artillery bombardment, the greatest in the war so far, quickly pulverized the Russian Third Army trenches and destroyed all communications links between the defending units. The result produced an enormous, yet unanticipated, early success as large Russian troop numbers surrendered when German soldiers easily overran the inadequately prepared tsarist trench lines. According to one of the corps commanders, the troops quickly vanished into dust and smoke. Soon thousands of Russian soldiers became visible marching down a slope, but they were not attacking German positions; they had become prisoners of war. The first breach in the enemy positions had occurred.[11] Significant numbers of tsarist troops were killed or wounded in the initial artillery barrages, and because there was no second tsarist defensive line, although the army commander had been ordered to establish one on April 16, many Russian soldiers died as they fled rearward over the open terrain. Of the 250,000-man Russian Third Army not involved in the Carpathian Mountain battle, 210,000 became casualties in just one week, including 140,000 prisoners of war. Two tsarist corps (X and XXIV) had been destroyed. A pilot of Flight Company 10 witnessed the destruction during the battle because of well-directed artillery fire resulting from excellent ground and air observation.[12]

The newly created German Eleventh Army and Habsburg VI Corps had launched their offensive at a very weak portion of the Russian front, the tsarist Third Army northern front position, which served as the connecting point between the Romanov, German, and Austro-Hungarian theaters (north and southwest fronts). After intense consideration of the potential locations to launch a successful offensive operation, German military planners selected the thirty-mile area in western Galicia between the villages of Gorlice and Tarnov. The opposing tsarist Third Army had deployed many of its troops as reinforcements for the Carpathian Mountain front offensive. Thus, when attacked, there was insufficient time for the Russians to transfer reinforcements from the mountain front to the suddenly threatened army.

The subsequent multimonth troop movements and battles created enormous devastation, the worst occurring during the six weeks before the great Russian retreat that eventually extended three hundred miles into the defeated enemy's interior. Artillery barrages, plundering troops, or the burning of villages completely or partially destroyed the remaining village homes east of Fortress Przemyśl. Fleeing civilians filled local roads, delaying the forward movement of Central Powers troops and hindering tsarist retreat efforts.

When Italy declared war on Austria-Hungary on May 23, 1915, Generals Conrad and Falkenhayn quickly agreed to maintain a defensive stance against the former ally and to continue the successful Gorlice offensive operation. Fortunately for the Dual Monarchy, the Italians waited a month to launch the first of eleven Isonzo assaults at the end of June 1915 with overwhelming troop numbers. The attempted invasion of Austria-Hungary failed, however, because the inexperienced Italian troops attacked uphill, without machine guns and artillery support, against a numerically inferior but well dug-in Habsburg defensive force. In addition, the small, ragtag number of defenders had gained enough time to rush reinforcements to hold the line because of the Italian hesitancy in launching the offensive.[13]

General Conrad desired to crush his former Italian ally immediately, but lacked the necessary troop numbers to accomplish this because of the Gorlice-Tarnov offensive on the Russian front. He therefore had to pin his hopes on the defensive capabilities of his few local troops defending their mountain terrain. The sheer size of the eastern front ensured that it would be extremely difficult to obtain a decisive victory in that theater against the tsarist foe. Four Russian armies soon became entrapped in the Carpathian Mountain terrain in a desperate situation. The more deeply Russian troops penetrated into the mountains, the more problematic their circumstances became. As the Gorlice-Tarnov offensive progressed further east, it outflanked the tsarist troops, now entrapped in the Carpathian Mountains.

In order to provide new formations for the Gorlice-Tarnov operation, a reorganization of the German army occurred. German divisions reduced the number of their regiments from four to three, which added eight hundred soldiers or more and machine guns to each one. This created eight new infantry divisions that General Falkenhayn originally intended to utilize on the western front and to launch an offensive against Serbia. However, the extremely precarious situation on the Habsburg front forced the German general to alter his plans.[14]

The German Eleventh Army consisted of combat-hardened veterans from the western front. These troops had training superior to that of the Russians and much higher morale. Before commencing the offensive operations, well-supported military feints and demonstrations were launched along the eastern front at Courland and Bukovina to conceal the assembly of soldiers and heavy artillery deploying for the Gorlice operation. General Falkenhayn also launched an offensive on the Flanders Ypres front to camouflage the transfer of eight German divisions to the eastern front to participate in the offensive on the rolling hilly terrain, a much more favorable terrain than the inhospitable Carpathian Mountain theater.

However, already on April 27, a telegram from Grand Duke Nicholas to General Ivanov ordered the southwest front commander to prepare to launch an offensive to finally invade the Hungarian plains. The communication also reported a German raid far into the Baltic area lines, termed a diversionary assault. The next day the grand duke informed the tsar of a large concentration of Central Powers troops in the Gorlice region, repeating the message on April 28. As one Russian historian has written, Nicholas did not appear to realize the magnitude of the potential threat, so he did not order any major military measures.

Earlier attempts to create a unified Central Powers command on the eastern front had not succeeded. This difficulty continued to plague the allies when bitter problems arose in directing and controlling the joint theater operations. The Russian army remained in semi-good order, able to fight very effective rearguard actions. The Habsburg Third and Fourth

Armies protected the German Eleventh Army flanks during the campaign, which represented the first Austro-Hungarian–German troops fighting under unified command. General Falkenhayn demanded that a German command the Gorlice-Tarnov campaign. He chose General August von Mackensen, who would be subject to orders from the German High Command and the formal commander. Conrad ultimately had to accept General Mackensen, which forced him into the background during the successful campaign. Since the numerically superior German army led the offensive against Russia to rescue the Austro-Hungarian army, Conrad had to accept his field commanders receiving German Supreme Command orders. To ease Conrad's mind, General Falkenhayn claimed that he did not desire to bypass him and that he would personally inform him and seek his acceptance of all major orders to German units.[15]

General Falkenhayn's minimal campaign goal encompassed crippling Russian military potential to the extent that time and his resources allowed and seizing and maintaining the strategic initiative on the eastern front. Falkenhayn remained wary of the inherent dangers as well as problems with large-scale operations against tsarist Russia. His immediate objective was to relieve the Habsburg Carpathian Mountain front, which was very close to collapse, and to defeat the opposing Russian forces. The initial operational successes provided that opportunity, while the immediately discernible Russian battlefield weaknesses enabled the Central Powers forces to obtain further victories. During the initial Gorlice attack, the Russians could neither rapidly nor effectively reinforce their Third Army, which proved disastrous. Within forty hours that army had been shattered, and within three days its defensive positions had been completely overrun. Under heavy German artillery fire, thousands of Russian soldiers fled rapidly from their shallow trenches into open country to be massacred by German artillery shrapnel shells and low-trajectory rounds. This rapid defeat resulted partially from the insufficient and fragmented tsarist High Command (Stavka).

By the end of the first day of battle, allied attacking troops had advanced one and a half to three and a half miles. Part of the explanation for the rapid tsarist defeat was that their Third Army lacked strength in depth. The majority of troops deployed in forward defensive lines were decimated by the pre-offensive artillery bombardment. General Ivanov now had to depend on the III Caucasus Corps for reinforcements, as it served as the major southwest front reserve force. Already Stavka failed to initiate an effective response.

On May 3, the German Eleventh Army had accomplished a fifteen- to twenty-kilometer-wide breakthrough. The Habsburg Fourth and Third Armies' advance on the German army's two flanks worsened the enemy's already perilous situation and caused them to retreat further, to the San River. Although the Russians had already suffered enormous battle losses and lost many prisoners of war as well as huge quantities of weapons and equipment in their sudden defeat, they attempted to launch a counterattack with their III Caucasus Corps at the Carpathian Moun- tains Dukla Pass. One division received orders to be transferred from the tsarist northwest front to the southwest front.

Generals Falkenhayn and Mackensen realized that the opposing tsarist forces were fighting and retreating on their own terrain with a still-intact railroad network and unlimited opportunities to continue withdrawing. They also recognized the geographical obstacles to be overcome and the necessity to extend their supply efforts as their troops advanced, but the critical Habsburg military situation had left General Falkenhayn with no alternative but to launch the May offensive cam- paign. Falkenhayn's main concern, however, remained the western front situation. Therefore, one of his major objectives involved continuing the eastern front offensive in the hopes of inflicting unacceptable casualties, crippling the Russian army, and forcing them to sign a separate peace treaty.[16] To that end, he launched small, limited, but effective offensive actions to paralyze Russia's offensive power and stabilize the eastern front situation for the Central Powers before turning his major attention back to the trenches on the western front.

Falkenhayn concentrated on obtaining limited offensive successes, cautiously planning each operation. He did not seek enormous territorial acquisitions, which could prove illusory and create major problems, but rather to always protect his limited gains. He remained cognizant of the pitfalls and dangers inherent in conducting large-scale operations in Russia. Thus, in early May his initial operational goal was to seize the road junction at Zmigrod, which would effectively sever the tsarist army's lateral communication in the Carpathian Mountains. He then intended to outflank them. Zmigrod fell on May 9. On May 4, the third day of the Gorlice offensive, as the tsarist Third Army continued its retreat, Stavka (headed by Grand Duke Nicholas) assumed he could halt the Central Powers advance without major difficulty. One week after the offensive commenced, the Eleventh Army had achieved all its objectives ordered on April 24.[17]

As the offensive progressed, General Falkenhayn had agreed that the Habsburg Third Army could have the honor of reconquering Fortress Przemyśl when the victorious troops approached the citadel. Thus, the Third Army marched toward the fortress with the intent to seize it by storm attack.[18] However, that army's progress lagged because of enemy resistance, so Eleventh Army units ultimately captured the fortress. The poor roads leading to Fortress Przemyśl slowed supply movement and created difficult problems for the allies. General Falkenhayn determined that because of the lack of Habsburg Third Army progress, his Eleventh Army had to alter its attack direction and plans for seizing the citadel, as it advanced more rapidly than the Habsburg Third and Fourth Armies.

The rapid and overwhelming success of the Gorlice-Tarnov offensive kept Romania from entering the war, while the tsarist military weakness provided the opportunity to achieve the great Central Powers military victory, which included the recapture of Fortress Przemyśl. The tsarist front meanwhile rapidly collapsed in the area of Tarnov as the German Eleventh and the Habsburg Fourth Armies quickly advanced, while the Russian Eighth Army, entrapped in the Carpathian Mountains, retreated to the Lupkov Pass because of the threat of being encircled. Effective German artillery played a major role throughout the campaign. Its heavy guns proved indispensable in laying the groundwork for the multiple short infantry attacks against the defending Russian troops. As during much of the war, Habsburg artillery during this campaign was described as ineffective and inadequate.

The Russians, for example, claimed not to have had to move their battery positions during the entire Carpathian Mountain Winter campaign because of the total lack of effectual Habsburg counterfire.[19] German artillery forward observers proved extremely effective, particularly when their efforts were combined with air reconnaissance missions, both of which precisely charted Russian artillery positions down to the individual gun, often enabling German gunners to neutralize enemy defensive firepower. Airplane reconnaissance pilots witnessed the destruction caused by the well-directed artillery fire and tsarist reinforcements rushing to the endangered battlefront.[20]

The Russian army suffered from numerous disadvantages during the campaign, although it remained in semi-good order and conducted its customary effective rearguard retreat actions. Difficulties included an increasing shortage of weapons, particularly rifles, ammunition, and artillery shells, while the faulty early May Third Army troop dispositions had made it impossible to halt the determined German advance. Tsarist field commanders at the operational level often dispersed their reinforcements ineffectively as well as piecemeal into the front lines, thus consuming them too rapidly when launching counterattacks into German artillery barrages. Meanwhile, the Russians continued their previous Ninth Army offensive operation in the Habsburg province of the Bukovina, which had also consumed multiple Russian Third Army units throughout the month of May. This operation threatened Habsburg forces deployed at the Romanian frontier and increased the danger of that country entering the war against Austria-Hungary.

The III Caucasus Corps had been deployed in two groups far to the rear of the Gorlice battlefront; therefore it could not arrive on the battlefield until May 4 as the major southwest front reserve force. Their intervention slowed the allied advance for the next two days, but on May 4, the German Eleventh Army accomplished its tactical success when its right flank forces pierced the Russian Third Army front. On May 4 the Russian Supreme Command did not believe their military situation to be too serious, thus they launched a counterattack with the III Caucasus Corps. Meanwhile, the tsarist Third Army had retreated behind the Wisloka and Wislok Rivers. The Russian command hoped for local military successes that would have changed the military situation in their favor.[21]

The Russian Carpathian Mountain front also began to crumble, as the allies determined to continue their advance toward the San River, which trapped the four tsarist armies ensconced in the mountains. The Germans had begun to advance ten miles a day, forcing tsarist armies in the mountains to retreat to the San River to avoid annihilation. Thousands of tsarist troops either perished from machine gun fire or drowned attempting to cross the river. During the next two weeks, Central Powers troops reached the San River line; however, the advancing troops soon encountered serious supply, logistical, and transport problems because the Eleventh Army's main railroad supply depot was situated more than fifty miles to the rear of the troops.

During the night of May 4, Habsburg Fourth Army troops crossed the Dunajec River and then advanced. The army's middle forces attained mountain positions south of Tarnov where the Russians established serious resistance, while continuing to protect the Eleventh Army's left flank. It achieved success on both its flanks on that day, and the Austro-Hungarian Third Army approached Fortress Przemyśl from the west and south to attempt to capture it.[22] Once Jaroslau became the major allied objective, the German Eleventh Army had to shift its main forces across the San River to the right bank. Allied corps then received the mission to seize that objective.

The tsarist X Corps received the brunt of the enemy offensive and had to retreat, creating an enormous gap in the Russian line. In the meantime, tsarist X Corps numbers had dropped to fifteen hundred troops.[23] The overall Central Powers success forced a tsarist retreat to the Wisloka River area, a short distance to the east of their present positions. General Ivanov, however, wanted to retreat to the San River line. Stavka negated this idea; the retrograde movement must halt at the Wisloka River.

Between May 5 and 8, the advancing Central Powers armies completed a series of planned short advances; the mountain roads and the necessity of resupply, particularly of artillery shells, still delayed the main effort, which enabled Russian troops to escape to the northeast. With Eleventh Army corps in pursuit, the Russians failed to destroy the pontoon bridges constructed by the advancing Central Powers divisions. Meanwhile, at the Eleventh Army flanks, the Habsburg Third and Fourth Armies commenced additional offensive efforts, Third Army forcing the Russians out of the Dukla Pass. Habsburg troops advanced through the series of basins at Jaslo-Krosno-Sanok, which made the tsarist Lupkov Pass position untenable. After constructing bridgeheads that offered the opportunity to expand the operation eastward, the German army crossed the river. The width of the river required that the troops initially capture the most favorable crossing points. The selected Jaroslau and Radymno areas, where the major north-south railroad line traversed, partially isolated Fortress Przemyśl.

On May 5, the III Caucasus Corps, instead of launching a tsarist counterattack against the German offensive formations, became drawn into battle and was badly mauled. By late May 5, the corps contained only 4,000 to 5,000 troops of its original 34,000. The Russian Third Army's X Corps, which received the brunt of the German attack, was annihilated. By May 6, Central Powers troops had forced open a large gap into the Russian Third Army front, while tsarist forces were in total disarray.

The May 5 seizure of the Lupkov Pass, the immediate geographic target objective to exploit the Gorlice breakthrough, resulted in the victorious allied troops continuing their advance to the San River as the Russian Carpathian Mountain front began to crumble. German advances forced the tsarist armies in the Carpathian Mountains to retreat as quickly as possible to the San River to avoid annihilation.

On May 6, General Falkenhayn notified General Conrad that the German ambassador and the military attaché in Rome had recommended that the Dual Monarchy submit its maximum concessions to Rome within twenty-four hours. General Falkenhayn emphasized that "we stand at a crossroads."[24] The general agreed that they could not launch an allied offensive against Serbia before the end of May and that it was necessary to obtain Bulgaria as an ally.[25] He then strongly suggested to General Conrad that the Habsburg diplomats avoid war with Italy "under any circumstances."[26] On May 4, he pressured Foreign Minister Istvan Burian to keep Italy neutral and notified General Falkenhayn of this action. Conrad continued to press the Habsburg Foreign Office relative to the ongoing Italian negotiations on May 5. By April 28, Conrad had also appealed to Emperor Franz Joseph to drop his opposition to initiating military defensive measures along the Italian frontier.[27]

Meanwhile, the tsarist supply lines extended fifty miles west of the San River, while Russian units increasingly became threatened by Habsburg troops advancing in the Carpathian Mountains. At the same time, the Russian Third Army inserted its few reserves (two infantry regiments) between Fortress Przemyśl and Jaroslau. The Russian Carpathian

Mountain front also began to crumble, as the allies determined to continue their advance toward the San River, which trapped the tsarist
armies in the mountains.

The Russians established a defensive line on the Wisloka River that
extended almost one hundred kilometers in a north-south direction
eighty kilometers west of the San River. Habsburg troops advancing
from the Carpathian Mountain front could have outflanked the new
tsarist position. Initially, General Ivanov requested that he be able to
retreat to the San River, but Stavka ordered him to defend that line
because they anticipated that Italy would enter the war soon. In addition,
they expected that tsarist Ninth Army success in the Bukovina theater
would bring Romania into the war on the Entente side.

On May 7, III Caucasus Corps launched its counterattack just as
German reinforcements initiated their own assault across the Wislok
River; on May 7 and 8, the Central Powers continued their advance
toward the San River. This trapped the tsarist armies ensconced in the
Carpathian Mountains. Again, General Ivanov sought to retreat to the San
River to save what remained of the Third Army, but Grand Duke Nicholas
had announced that no retreat could be initiated without his permission.
This condemned the Russian Third Army. Two divisions from the tsarist
northwest front received orders to reinforce the buckling southwest
front. Without large numbers of reserve troops, units would be drawn
helter-skelter.

Stavka originally ordered the Third Army to hold its positions, but
the intervening events made the order superfluous. The tsarist armies in
the Carpathian Mountains proceeded to retreat to the San River to avoid
annihilation. The Germans utilized every means available to rebuild the
local railroad lines and repair destroyed bridges as rapidly as possible.
They constructed bridgeheads from which to launch further advances,
which proved of great assistance as they pushed further east, and expanded
their maneuver room so that the Eleventh Army could shift its attack
direction, which soon became necessary.

When General Mackensen discussed the next operational allied objectives with General Conrad, he proposed that the offensive continue
to hurl the retreating Russians behind the San River line. The successful
Central Powers tactical battle had become a strategic triumph. Then, on

May 10, General Ivanov received orders to defend the San-Dniester River line when his forces remained deployed well forward of that line.

Russian command issued multiple confused orders, countered and reissued, to defend the San-Dniester River line. Three other corps (Habsburg VI, German XLI Reserve, and ad hoc Corps Kneussl) mobilized to the south and southwest to isolate the fortress from the north and east. The strong Russian defensive positions west of Jaroslau hindered Habsburg Third Army forward progress, so it could not rapidly capture Fortress Przemyśl; therefore, the German Eleventh Army had to halt its movement to accomplish that mission.

In addition, Conrad requested further German troops for deployment on General Planzer-Baltin's front in the southern Carpathian Mountains because the Russians launched a major attack in the Bukovina. General Falkenhayn replied by emphasizing that he could not spare additional German troops from the western front because the long-awaited Anglo-French offensive had just commenced, which bound all available German reserves on that front.[28] Falkenhayn also stated that the "spearhead" of the offensive should not be weakened for a secondary front.

Claiming that the two requested German divisions were necessary to support the Bukovina front, General Conrad also raised the question of neutral Romania and Italy, stressing that a major Habsburg defeat in the Bukovina could entice Bucharest to enter the war against Austria-Hungary. Conrad and Falkenhayn agreed on the necessity of continuing the Gorlice-Tarnov offensive but momentarily failed to determine a specific objective. Thus, their personal long-distance exchanges proved inconclusive, and they required private meetings to decide such matters as the disposal of captured materials, weapons, ammunition, and equipment. The allied generals exchanged a flurry of memoranda between May 9 and 12, when they met personally. Consensus quickly followed, and on May 12 they continued the offensive to the San River. The broad attack objectives included attaining the river to the north and east of Fortress Przemyśl, which the disarray of Russian military forces made easier.

On May 9, General Falkenhayn wired General Conrad that his Eleventh Army had to complete its original mission, then requested his counterpart's input relative to future allied strategy. The German chief of the General Staff also stated that the success of the present offensive would most likely make it easier to transfer troop reinforcements against Italy. General Conrad replied that the successful operation should include the "relentless pursuit of the defeated enemy with all our forces." The Russians had to be prevented from constructing a strong defensive line so that Central Powers troops could cross the San River in pursuit of the enemy. General Conrad also reported that the Russians had mounted a massive offensive against the Habsburg Seventh Army in the Bukovina, forcing him to dispatch two divisions to halt the tsarist advance.[29] Meanwhile, the Germans established new eastern front headquarters, indicating that for the time being the main German war theater remained in the east.

On the same day, the Russians attempted to establish defensive positions on the San River, but these had not been prepared in time, and they did not establish any such lines north of Fortress Przemyśl. They began to suffer from low troop numbers while being attacked on the San River during the original offensive. General Ivanov's forces had few reserves; for example, only two infantry regiments defended against Central Powers forces between Fortress Przemyśl and Jaroslau. Grand Duke Nicolas personally telegraphed General Ivanov, reemphasizing that he could not initiate a retreat movement without specific orders from Stavka.

General Conrad's May 9 telegram to General Falkenhayn also emphasized that the main goal of Habsburg diplomacy remained preventing a war with Italy.[30] On that same day, he reported to the Emperor's Military Chancellery about the May 7 conference at German headquarters, where a consensus was reached that Italy would most likely intervene against Austria-Hungary in the war. Germany promised solidarity with Austria-Hungary; its contribution of military forces, however, would be dependent upon the momentary situation. Falkenhayn also accepted that absolutely no chance of any agreement existed with Italy, thus he turned to studying various defensive measures to initiate on the southwest front. Yet, he continued to pressure Habsburg diplomats to avoid war with Italy "under any circumstances" and argued that the present offensive would most likely make it easier to transfer troops to the threatened Italian front.[31]

General Falkenhayn again indicated to Conrad that the newly launched Anglo-French offensive made it impossible to divert any forces from the western to the eastern front, while the divisions promised by Hindenburg and Ludendorff had not yet been freed.

Then, on May 10, the tsarist Third Army center buckled; the severely weakened army had lost much of its fighting capability. This forced Stavka to reverse its earlier decision and order a retreat to the San River. The Grand Duke (Nicolas) stipulated that tsarist forces defend the San-Vistula River lines and prepare to launch an offensive. Stavka's main concern had become that tsarist troops must not surrender Galicia. However, the Third Army had to retreat behind the San River, which forced the entire theater's forces to retreat.

By May 10, the tsarist Third Army had lost nearly 200 artillery pieces and 140,000 prisoners of war. From the original 200,000 Russian troops and 50,000 replacement troops hurled into the battered front lines, only 40,000 unwounded soldiers now defended the threatened San River line. The Russian losses proved so severe that the X and XXIV Corps barely existed; the IX Corps had lost 80 percent of its manpower, and III Corps 75 percent; and its XXI Corps now consisted of only 2,000 troops.[32] Tsarist commanders possessed few reserve formations—only the two infantry regiments mentioned between Fortress Przemyśl and Jaroslau.

As Franz Joseph approved initiating military activity on the southwest front, the Germans launched a diplomatic offensive in a last-ditch effort to prevent the Italians from entering the war. Naturally, Habsburg concerns about a possible third front also increased. The allied generals, Conrad and Mackensen, exchanged a series of memoranda before they met personally. Consensus quickly followed and, on May 12, they had determined to continue the offensive to the San River. The broad attack objectives became attaining the river to the north and east of Fortress Przemyśl, which the chaotic Russian retreat facilitated. Tsarist forces had to be prevented from constructing a strong defensive line so that Central Powers troops could rapidly defeat them, cross the San River, and pursue the retreating soldiers.

The Russian Third and Eighth Army forces had almost been annihilated, while the Central Powers recovered 130 kilometers of Galician terrain extending to the San River. During the next two weeks, carefully controlled assault efforts would be launched over the San River. German air reconnaissance reports provided accurate and invaluable information on the movement of tsarist forces and their artillery emplacements.[33] The May 12 events ended the first phase of the Gorlice-Tarnov campaign. During that period, western Galicia had been recaptured and the tsarist front hurled back to the Nida River and Carpathian Mountain forelands. The depleted Habsburg morale that resulted from the disastrous Carpathian Mountain winter campaign disappeared in their frontline formations and civilians in the hinterland.

Renewed self-confidence and elation replaced the gloom and doom of the Carpathian Mountain campaign, and again hopes for victory emerged. However, while the bulk of the allied troops deployed forward, General Falkenhayn noticed a continuous disintegration of Habsburg units, particularly those of the Fourth Army, as tsarist reinforcements began to arrive on the battlefield. Meanwhile, General Conrad admitted that the Gorlice military success resulted from the German efforts.[34]

The Germans found themselves delayed more by logistical problems than by any serious Russian resistance. Russian forces were in complete disarray by this time. Over the next two weeks, the Germans initiated their series of carefully controlled advances toward the San River. A major objective became to build bridgeheads to extend the allied advance over the river to the east and also provide maneuver space if necessary for the Eleventh Army to change its offensive's direction. The most feverish activity, however, occurred on the railroads, because the nearest major railhead was sixty miles from the advancing armies. Changing the direction of the attack would be vital for the offensive, targeted toward the southeast.

Meanwhile, the Habsburg Third Army accomplished only slow forward progress against the Russian Eighth Army at the San River, which defended the southern and western approaches to Fortress Przemyśl. The terrible condition of the supply roads slowed all efforts east of the Carpathian Mountains. The German X Corps and the Prussian Garde Corps advanced east of the San River to establish blocking positions to protect the Eleventh Army's right flank position. The remaining three corps, the VI, the German XLI reserve, and the ad hoc Corps Kneussl, would swing to the south and southeast to isolate the fortress from the north and east.[35]

When the Russian Ninth Army launched the mentioned major offensive into the Bukovina, General Falkenhayn did not want to weaken the main offensive operation against the Russians by diverting divisions to the Habsburg Seventh Army defending that province. He refused to weaken the Third, Eleventh, and Fourth Armies for the sake of what he termed a secondary theater and a highly questionable action. To him it was of little significance if the Habsburg Seventh Army had to retreat multiple kilometers. General Conrad, however, replied that if the Seventh Army suffered a decisive defeat, it would reverse the favorable situation of the Gorlice offensive and make a major negative impression on neutral European states. Thus, he intended to transfer his III Corps to that theater. A meeting at German headquarters did not produce any change.[36]

In the meantime, the Russian Ninth Army won a considerable but basically irrelevant success in that province; thus, by mid-May the Habsburgs had lost much of the Bukovina (120,000 tsarist troops had attacked 80,000 Habsburg Seventh Army soldiers).[37] On May 13 an interesting exchange occurred between the Central Powers generals relative to the deployment of German Alpine Corps with Habsburg troops at the Italian frontier. The Germans requested that General Conrad instruct his forces to avoid any incident that might unfavorably influence an Italian response. Conrad immediately instructed his commander on the Italian front to avoid any provocation.[38] Then General Falkenhayn stated that it was absolutely essential that the Habsburg deployment not disturb the diplomatic efforts in Rome at this critical moment.[39]

When Conrad and Falkenhayn met in Pless, they discussed the situation in Galicia and the Balkan front, deciding that the Bulgarians should be informed that now was the time to "immediately" prepare for a campaign against Serbia, but the uncertain situation relative to Italy caused Bulgaria to shy away.[40]

The German Eleventh Army and Habsburg VI Corps commenced another short advance on May 13 along the northern San riverbank as General Mackensen prepared to launch an attack on Fortress Przemyśl. Air reconnaissance efforts extended into the area north of the fortress.

The bridgehead at Jaroslau provided a position for the German XLI Corps to push through Russian positions at Radymno from which to attack the fortress. This action also covered the flank of German Corps Kneussl approaching from the west. That corps, consisting of the 11th and 119th Infantry Divisions, attacked the fortress from the northwest after coordinating its advance with the Habsburg ally.[41] The troops then advanced from Sanok toward Bircza and the fortress. However, those forces encountered serious Russian resistance, which slowed them down.

The slackened combat activity that commenced on that day provided a welcome respite for Eleventh Army troops who had just endured nine straight days of battle, partly in pursuit of the retreating Russians. Conrad dispatched a memorandum to Falkenhayn and Burian suggesting that the allied offensive be halted at the San-Dniester River line and that a defensive posture commence. This, he calculated, would free twenty infantry divisions to counter an Italian attack.

Air reconnaissance reports provided continual accurate and invaluable information to higher field commanders on the tsarist forces and artillery locations.[42] The next major concern dealt with potential Russian intentions. German aerial reconnaissance revealed that tsarist troops had initiated a retreat movement, but a question remained: Did they intend to defend Fortress Przemyśl? Throughout early May, the Russians actually could not determine whether to defend or surrender the fortress. Meanwhile, wagons rapidly prepared to transport troops and weapons out of the citadel, as commanders had actually taken the initial steps toward evacuating it during mid-May. Then, during the latter part of the month, they reversed the decision and determined to defend the fortress as a May 12 Russian radio transmission indicated. Then, on May 21 they determined to abandon it, as heard on the radio traffic. The German assumption that the Russians would attempt to avoid decisive battle on the San River, however, proved erroneous.

On May 14, a Habsburg and German corps (VI and Garde) attacked and seized the key tsarist defensive positions west and south of Jaroslau. The Russians hoped to halt enemy progress with arriving reinforcements to protect Fortress Przemyśl and the lower San River defensive line. A tsarist counterattack followed. The important San-Dniester

River line had not yet been crossed, although the Habsburg Second and Third Armies had attacked enemy positions at the southern Fortress Przemyśl front.[43]

Meanwhile, on May 11, Emperor Franz Joseph finally approved the activation of the forts on the Italian frontier.[44] Habsburg leaders anticipated Rome's intervention in the war in the immediate future. The following day, Foreign Minister Burian agreed, as did both Central Powers emperors, to the secession of nearly all Habsburg territory inhabited by Italians. The territory, however, could not be surrendered until the end of the year, but the effort proved fruitless. General Conrad informed General Falkenhayn relative to the stable condition on the Galician front and the fact that Serbia could not presently launch an offensive. Therefore, the Bulgarians needed to be informed that the time for a military campaign against Serbia had arrived. The tumultuous situation relative to Italy, however, caused the Bulgarians to decline a treaty with the Central Powers to launch an offensive against Serbia.[45]

Allied discussions commenced relative to appropriate military measures to be initiated on the Italian front when that country declared war. Habsburg military leadership anticipated Italy entering the war by July 4. On May 14 orders approved by Emperor Franz Joseph were disseminated to initiate defensive measures against an Italian attack at the Italian frontier.[46] Meanwhile, General Falkenhayn raised the question of the probability, with the assistance of German and Bulgarian troops, of simultaneously knocking Serbia out of the conflict.[47] The next day, Conrad suggested that if Italy could be kept neutral in the near future, a joint allied operation with Bulgarian and Turkish troops could be launched against Serbia.[48]

The next day the Eleventh Army offensive continued during rainy conditions. That army's right flank positions became protected against the launching of a possible tsarist sortie from Fortress Przemyśl when the German X and Garde Corps successfully advanced east of the San River and established blocking positions to protect its flank.[49] The arrival of a critical resupply of artillery shells allowed renewal of the assault, which finally drove some Russian troops across the San River. Air reconnaissance, however, confirmed that significant enemy forces remained ensconced west of the river.

To the south Russian forces retreated into Galicia from the Carpathian Mountains. General Ivanov received orders to maintain their present positions, while the Ninth Army continued its attack in the Bukovina. The tsarist shortage of artillery shells began to be a major factor for the Russians' tactical decision making.

Then, on May 16, German Corps Kneussl crossed the river and advanced, as it appeared that the Russians had prepared to resist behind the San River, forcing enemy units protecting Jaroslau to capitulate. (Jaroslau was one of the earlier bridgeheads defending the approaches to Fortress Przemyśl from tsarist attack during September 1914). The rapid collapse of tsarist Jaroslau positions negated any tsarist plan to launch a counterattack. In the meantime, as the allied advance continued, air reconnaissance units would be deployed forward to enable long-range missions and provide reconnaissance reports and pictures of tsarist units and artillery.[50]

The Eleventh Army's southern flank units arrived at the bridgehead at Radymno on May 16, but because of a heavy tsarist counterattack and supply difficulties, those troops' offensive would also be halted. Meanwhile, X Corps attacked the fortress positions at Fort Pralkowce, but could not seize them owing to insufficient pre-attack artillery support. Tsarist resistance increased against the Fourth, Third, and Eleventh armies even as they retreated across the San-Dniester River line. Seven divisions stood ready to pursue the defeated enemy if the Armee Ober Kommando (AOK) approved.

During mid-May, the Third and Fourth Habsburg Armies advanced toward the south, southwest, and western Fortress Przemyśl fronts, while the German Eleventh Army approached the citadel from the southern San River after capturing the important Radymno bridgehead. However, because of the mentioned tsarist counterattack and continuing supply difficulties, the Austro-Hungarian and German troops were forced on the defensive.

Also on May 16, General Falkenhayn replied to Conrad's earlier telegram, declaring that once the allied troops attained the San-Dniester River line, the allied front extending from the Vistula River to the Bukovina could be held with thirty Habsburg divisions. That would free troops for deployment against both Italy and Serbia. Conrad had explained that if Italy could be kept neutral during the near future, a joint front could be maintained by only seven divisions, freeing seventeen to eighteen Austro-Hungarian and seven German divisions excluding the Eleventh Army. Twenty-four or twenty-five divisions could then be utilized to attack Italy and Serbia if the Russian forces continued to retreat. A combined German, Austro-Hungarian, Bulgarian, and Turkish offensive could be launched again Serbia.[51]

Falkenhayn also claimed that the Vistula River to Bukovina front could be maintained by three Habsburg divisions. On May 17, Conrad expressed his regrets that General Falkenhayn now contemplated removing his Eleventh Army after it attained the San-Dniester River line. Furthermore, he considered that no more than twenty divisions could be made available against Italy when it declared war on Austria-Hungary (the Eleventh Army's nine divisions, Beskid Corps [one division], and ten Habsburg divisions) under Habsburg command.[52]

The Central Powers' assault continued toward the San River, where forced crossings proved successful. In the meantime, Stavka commanded General Ivanov to defend particularly the left bank to prevent the loss of Fortress Przemyśl. Everything must be done to prevent having to abandon the citadel.[53] On the next day the Grand Duke informed General Brusilov that the fortress must be kept and the general situation maintained.

The following six days were spent making those preparations necessary for launching the next phase of the operation, again requiring the stockpiling of artillery shells and awaiting the arrival of Ersatz troops to replace recent severe casualties. Between May 20 and 23, the Eleventh Army received orders to sever the eastern Fortress Przemyśl communications while the Habsburg Third and Second Armies captured the citadel. Stavka now became concerned about their northwest front against Germany, as it had to protect its positions along the Vistula and Narev Rivers. That front could initiate a retreat only as a last resort. Grand Duke Nicholas, although consistently ordering his troops not to retreat, reluctantly rescinded his resistance because of the continuing battlefield setbacks.

On May 18, Generals Conrad and Falkenhayn agreed to continue the attack toward Fortress Przemyśl. On May 20, General Falkenhayn determined to maintain the overall offensive operation to eliminate the Russian military danger, and by May 22, the Central Powers forces had advanced fifty-five miles in just three weeks.[54] Meanwhile, the poor mountain roads hampered Habsburg Third Army efforts to approach and attack Fortress Przemyśl positions because heavy artillery shells could not be transported to that area. The continued slow progress against the tsarist Eighth Army forces defending the western and southern fortress approaches also delayed the Third Army's commencement of assaults against the fortress. The German Eleventh Army therefore shifted its advance direction after a short battle pause to attack the fortress from the north. Meanwhile, another battle pause became necessary on May 19 to restock artillery shells to support further offensive action at the San River.

The operation also had to be halted until supply trains could reach the advance formations because of the destroyed roadways, bridges, and railroad lines that delayed the delivery of much-needed equipment and food. The German Eleventh Army had meanwhile advanced sixty-two miles from its nearest supply railhead depots, the insufficient road networks and inclement weather conditions seriously compounding its supply problems.[55] Feverish repairs continued on the damaged railroads. The unrelenting logistical problems could be resolved only by moving railroads closer to the front and restocking artillery shells as rapidly as possible. Fortunately, the Russians proved incapable of launching counterattacks, although they managed to increase resistance against the Central Powers forces, particularly the Habsburg Fourth Army.[56] Generals Conrad and Falkenhayn had to reassess the strategic situation, particularly because of the Italian threat to enter the war against the allies.

But even as Habsburg and German forces prepared to liberate the fortress, the question of when Italy would declare war also dominated military planning. General Falkenhayn particularly became concerned about the protection of Bavaria and southern Germany. Because of the time pressure, Habsburg troop transports started moving to the Italian frontier and preparations commenced on preparing fortified defensive lines. The situation also raised questions about Romania's intentions. Conrad wanted twenty divisions from the eastern front to launch a powerful offensive against Italy but reported that two-thirds of Habsburg forces on the Serbian front were not capable of launching an effective offensive.[57] The German High Command, however, wondered what effect such a troop movement would have on the Russian theater. In the meantime, Stavka ordered the transfer of a corps from its German northwest front to the Habsburg southwest front. The question of whether to defend Fortress Przemyśl became increasingly significant. The argument became whether it would be expedient to defend the citadel from a military point of view or whether it should be abandoned if defending it did not assist the field armies and their travail. Grand Duke Nicholas believed that defending Fortress Przemyśl made no military sense, but it had to be held for political reasons.[58]

General Falkenhayn also suggested launching an offensive against Serbia to draw Bulgaria to the Central Powers' side, but for the time being Conrad rejected the proposal. Such an offensive called for the deployment of fourteen German and three Habsburg divisions under Habsburg Supreme Command control. Conrad also argued that if the Habsburg forces had to go on the defensive against Russia, the Romanians might attack them from the rear.

The next major strategic question concerned troop numbers necessary to obtain military success against Serbia, particularly units that Bulgaria would deploy, and whether Turkey would provide up to six infantry divisions for the operation. When comparing numbers, estimates had Germany deploying 140,000 troops and the Bulgarians 120,000. These troop numbers should be sufficient to overpower the Serbs, who could muster 200,000 troops. Falkenhayn wanted to attack Serbia first before launching a surprise attack against Italy, because he did not judge Italian troops to be particularly good.[59]

Conrad calculated that in the Tyrol, a division would be strong enough to defend the frontier, and the Germans promised to transport and deploy their Alpine Corps made up of twelve Bavarian battalions. On May 19, Conrad contacted Foreign Minister Burian, emphasizing that ruthless measures against Italy had become necessary and that any delay would prove disastrous. Because of insufficient troop numbers on the Italian front, the Habsburg military initially had to use guerrilla warfare tactics against an Italian invasion. Meanwhile, Bulgaria announced that it would remain neutral if the Central Powers invaded Serbia so as not to give the impression that a secret treaty existed between Germany and Bulgaria.[60]

The Habsburg Fifth Army would be transferred from the Balkan front as a first echelon force to the Italian frontier. Crown Prince Eugene would command new southwest front forces. Naturally, the strongest possible number of troops had to be deployed against Italy, but the numbers would be pathetically low. General Falkenhayn telegrammed Conrad to remind him that a decision needed to be made to maintain the Russian front before any units could be deployed against Italy.

On May 21, Falkenhayn declared that no indication existed of a possible Serbian offensive being launched against the Dual Monarchy, and he doubted that the Italians would initiate an offensive immediately if war broke out.[61] He did, however, promise some German units to be deployed on the Italian front, so long as they did not emanate from the eastern front. Conrad replied that he anticipated an Italian invasion of the Dual Monarchy almost immediately. His defensive forces would be too weak to launch a counteraction or a counteroffensive, leaving the Italians free to march almost unopposed into Habsburg territory.

The German commander, however, adamantly opposed fielding large numbers of troops against Italy, especially from the Galician front. Falkenhayn eventually convinced Conrad at a meeting at Teschen that the offensive against Russia had to be continued and that any forces intended for Italy should be fielded at the frontier.[62] It remained unclear, however, whether the potential ten divisions (five from the Balkans, two German, and three Austrian) could halt an Italian offensive.

Conrad ordered his few *Landesschutzen* troops to hold the Italians at the frontier if possible, because the five divisions that would eventually be deployed would be too weak to launch an offensive. He also accepted Falkenhayn's advice to delay launching an attack under all circumstances until a major military decision could be obtained against Russia. General Falkenhayn calculated that the Italians could only advance slowly and that they would not attain combat operational readiness until later in June.[63]

While Falkenhayn's attention remained focused on the western front, he recognized the necessity of exploiting his military successes on the eastern one, at least for the near future. Conrad also accepted the necessity of defending the Habsburg frontier against Italy with the weak available forces. In return for this, his German counterpart promised to deploy token German troops at the Italian frontier to bolster Habsburg morale. His consistent pressure to launch an offensive against Serbia had to be momentarily dropped because of the Bulgarians' refusal to join the Central Powers at that time. However, General Falkenhayn refused to relinquish his ideas on this matter because of Turkish requirements for weapons and ammunition to remain in the war.

Preparations commenced for the May 24–June 6 battle to conquer Fortress Przemyśl, including stockpiling artillery shells and awaiting the arrival of troops to replace the recent casualties. Multiple problems arose before the continuation of the operation. The foremost difficulty involved a critical shortage of large-caliber artillery shells and the persisting negative effect of delayed logistical efforts, partially because the closest railhead head lay between sixty and ninety kilometers behind the present front. In addition, besides a lack of motor vehicles, a shortage of fodder limited horse productivity during this rapidly moving battle. The military could utilize few roads because of the terrible terrain conditions, thus the presently attained positions represented the furthest possible operational distance until railroads could be constructed and extended farther east.[64] Such logistical problems impeded the German offensive more than enemy resistance.

On May 24, two hours of preparatory artillery barrages initiated an artillery duel with the enemy and the launching of a major attack against Fortress Przemyśl, particularly against heavy tsarist gun positions, until Forts XI and XII capitulated. Central Powers troops launched a major offensive during the next three days once enemy positions at Radymno collapsed and the German XLI Reserve Corps had reached striking distance of that village, where the last eastward road from the fortress came within German artillery range. The Habsburg Third and Second Armies' advances continued slowly to the northeast toward Mosciska. Increased pressure would be applied on the fortress from the south. Aerial reconnaissance reports, however, indicated that tsarist preparations to abandon the fortress had commenced.

As the allied forces approached Fortress Przemyśl, Falkenhayn became increasingly concerned with the slow advance of Habsburg troops at the Eleventh Army's southern flank. He telegraphed General August

Cramon, ranking liaison officer at Conrad's headquarters, to request that he order his Second and Third Armies to attack with all means possible, because the Eleventh Army's success could only be attained through such cooperation. General Cramon replied that such an order had already been issued from Habsburg headquarters.[65] The Eleventh Army, advancing north through Radymno to the northwest fortress front, and Third Army, advancing from the southwest, would seize the fortress.

With the offensive to recapture Fortress Przemyśl under way, Conrad turned his attention to the pressing matter of Italy. There was some confusion regarding the May 23 Italian declaration of war. On May 25, the commander of the Habsburg Railroad Bureau stated that no one could guarantee when railroad transports would be ready to commence, while Conrad decided that the first arriving troops could not be thrown into battle at the frontier.[66] That same day, allied troops crossed the San River and regrouped while receiving reinforcements for the attack on Fortress Przemyśl. Meanwhile, the Third Russian Army had been forced to retreat rapidly, forcing the Fourth, Eighth, and Eleventh Armies to similarly withdraw from their Carpathian Mountain positions to avoid being encircled.

Conrad remained concerned about Romania's intentions. If it intervened on the Habsburg side, he postulated that then the Central Powers could win the war. Victory remained possible even if the Romanians simply remained neutral. But Conrad had become convinced that if Romania joined the war against the Central Powers, defeat was inevitable. He recommended incorporating Romania into the Dual Monarchy as the Germans had done with Bavaria. The suggestion raised questions about Bulgaria, which sought to seize Macedonia to the Enos-Midia line. Conrad believed that if Bulgaria could not be gained as an ally, Romania would certainly join the Entente to ensure military defeat for the Central Powers. The diplomatic and political machinations of Bulgaria and Romania thus remained pivotal factors in the Central Powers' calculations.[67]

Allied forces meanwhile continued to push toward Fortress Przemyśl, and the Eleventh Army's heavy artillery barrages forced six tsarist divisions to retreat. On May 26, as the Central Powers advanced to the fortress, fighting continued along the San River, causing a shortage of supplies for several days. Then, beginning May 27, tsarist forces launched a powerful counterattack from the northern and northeastern fortress fronts against the German Eleventh and Habsburg Fourth Armies. Grand Duke Nicholas reported to the tsar on May 28 that the situation remained most serious, but by May 30 he felt somewhat more confident.[68]

On May 29, Stavka altered its strategy; now determined to defend the fortress, it deployed reinforcements to the citadel.[69] It chose, however, not to defend the bulwark with the demoralized Third Army but rather with VIII Corps troops.[70] On May 30 at 11:00 a.m., heavy German artillery began bombarding the citadel. An assault was planned for the next day despite the numerous supply and troop delays caused by multiple destroyed bridges and damaged roads. Toward evening, two Habsburg infantry regiments stormed Fort Prakovce but failed to seize it because of insufficient artillery support. This convinced the tsarist command that the enemy would launch their major attack at this location. Therefore, they considered the fighting occurring at the northern citadel front merely to be a feint. Thus, the mass of tsarist reserve artillery pieces was transferred to the southwest fortress front.

On May 31, at 11 a.m., heavy artillery fire, assisted by precise aerial guidance, turned several of the Fortress Przemyśl forts into rubble. A Bavarian division stormed several ruined fortress walls and seized the three northernmost positions. The German High Command then had to postpone plans for any further assaults until June 1, again because of a lack of heavy artillery pieces and shells. Available gun batteries, however, continued blasting the fortress on May 31. Night artillery barrages, including devastating 42-centimeter heavy mortar fire, targeted fortress Forts X, Xa, XI, and XIa, transforming several into rubble. Central Powers troops then stormed two fortress fronts, and X Corps attacked the southwestern portion. The Germans now determined to initiate a more direct approach to attacking the fortress.

The 11th Bavarian Infantry Division, part of a larger force, stormed several fortress work ruins and seized the three northernmost ones. Also, a Habsburg regiment finally pierced the western fortification area near Fortress Work VII, while artillery fire battered the ramparts at Fort Work XI's locations. A lucky German howitzer shell destroyed key Russian trenches on the west flank of the bulwark, and several other citadel positions received the brunt of powerful artillery barrages. Precise aerial artillery observation continued to improve German firing accuracy significantly. On June 1, German offensive units finally directly attacked the citadel, whereupon a Bavarian infantry unit seized Forts X and XI and another battalion seized Fort XII. By evening, German troops had successfully penetrated the fortress defenses; although Russian reinforcements had arrived, they were too late to affect the outcome of the battle.

During the early morning hours of June 2, the Russians launched a heavy counterattack at the Fortress Defensive District XI, but effective allied rifle, machine gun, and artillery barrages halted the effort. Russian defensive positions then quickly collapsed, and the soldiers who could escape the battle retreated to the east. Remaining tsarist troops burned the remaining fortress supplies and destroyed the last bridge across the San River. They then attempted to establish a defensive position north of Zuravica, but this also collapsed. A plan to launch a major assault against the fortress city on June 3 proved unnecessary, since it capitulated during the afternoon hours. At this point, German Eleventh Army troops occupied the bulwark, capturing eight thousand prisoners of war.[71] Estimates of Russian losses during the battle for the fortress vary. The Central Powers' spoils, however, proved disappointingly small.

When the Russians abandoned the citadel during the night of June 2, they established defensive positions to the east of the fortress along a line extending between Medyka and Siedliska. Central Powers troops advanced toward the critical Siedliska fortresses and captured them.[72] At 3:00 a.m., the Bavarian 11th Infantry Division had entered the citadel from the north, and a Habsburg cavalry division from the northwest. Habsburg X Corps followed them several hours later. Allied forces then rapidly drove tsarist units from the Siedliska fortress area and continued their advance. Once tsarist forces retreated, the Central Powers military situation became very complicated when Italy declared war on Austria-Hungary (but not Germany) on May 23, 1915. Habsburg Supreme Command had to immediately strengthen its very thinly manned defensive lines along the Italian frontier while the two allied commanders adjusted to the new military situation.

In the interim, the Austro-Hungarian–German forces advanced eastward to Mosciska and then Lemberg; therefore, Fortress Przemyśl would have no further influence on the overall Habsburg strategy and military situation. No one considered rebuilding the entire damaged fortress, but because the citadel presently remained so close to the immediate front, some repair work had to be performed on the northern and eastern bulwark perimeter areas. Infantry strong points were established, although the earlier artillery damage proved too extensive at Forts I/1, XI, XII, and XIII for any improvement. However, many of the remaining fortress works could be partially utilized, despite the Russians having destroyed them once again before their retreat.

Although Generals Conrad and Falkenhayn had originally agreed that Habsburg forces should recapture the fortress for prestige reasons, German forces actually achieved the capture. General Falkenhayn, in a tactless gesture, offered the fortress at the feet of Emperor Franz Joseph, while General Conrad had to accept German units liberating the fortress.[73] The citadel capitulated just 4 days after being attacked, compared to the 137 days the Russians had to starve the garrison during their second siege before its surrender in March 1915. The tsarist retreat from Fortress Przemyśl signified that the Russian army had relinquished its most powerful defensive pivot point on the San River front. The Habsburg Second Army then continued its advance toward Lemberg, the capital of Galicia.

Following the two-month Russian occupation, the fortress's civilian population welcomed the arrival of the conquering Central Powers troops. The successful campaign also provided a diplomatic success, because an original objective—to prevent Italy and Romania from entering the war—was partially accomplished. The major Russian military collapse convinced the Romanian leadership to maintain their neutrality. The Gorlice-Tarnov campaign continued after the capture of Fortress Przemyśl as the German Eleventh and the Habsburg Third Armies now had to assist the embattled Austro-Hungarian Fourth Army, which had suffered from some battlefield defeats and compelled General Falkenhayn to adjust his offensive plans. A Russian counterattack against the Fourth Army's southern flank positions had forced it to retreat behind

the San River, which interrupted the Habsburg Third and South Armies'
forward progress. The overall Gorlice-Tarnov campaign proved disastrous for the Russian southwest front. Tsarist armies sacrificed at least
412,000 troops and, by May 17, surrendered 170,000 prisoners of war and
huge quantities of war materiel.

Once tsarist military leaders had determined not to defend the San
River line, their defensive positions at Jaroslau and Radymno had to
surrender and their occupation of Fortress Przemyśl was doomed. The
Russian High Command should have accepted that situation and reacted accordingly; however, General Ivanov brought in reinforcements
but deployed them too slowly.[74] The Central Powers' campaign to recapture Fortress Przemyśl neutralized the four tsarist armies embroiled in
the Carpathian Mountain battle by threatening to encircle them and
finally ended the Russian threat to invade Hungary. This greatly improved morale on the Habsburg home front. By the end of June 1915, the
Central Powers had regained most of the territory the Habsburg troops
had surrendered during the Carpathian Mountain Winter War campaign.[75] The Gorlice-Tarnov campaign continued throughout the
summer of 1915 and into the fall season. Russia lost at least one million
prisoners of war during the campaign and another million to combat
casualties. The German offensive methods utilized during the entire
operation characterized their later tactics—rapid, deep breakthrough
movements with excellent artillery support that produced a string of
unbroken Central Powers victories on the eastern front.

On June 6, a large parade was staged in the reconquered citadel.
Habsburg Supreme Command then dispatched an officer to the northern fortress front to investigate the possibility of rebuilding the fortress
works in that area. At the same time, the Habsburg liaison officer to the
German Eleventh Army reported that the destruction of the fortress
positions before the March 22 capitulation was not as effective as had
been reported or assumed. For example, many of the old 1861 vintage
cannons remaining in the fortress interval positions between the works
remained in good condition with plentiful shells. Tsarist troops had prepared hundreds of these antique artillery pieces to be transported into
Russia as war spoils, but the rapid recapture of the citadel prevented it.
Even the German High Command claimed that, with a few exceptions,

the destruction of fortress material in late March had been largely insufficient.[76]

In hindsight, the recapture of Fortress Przemyśl on June 3 did not provide as significant a victory as is usually proclaimed in Austrian historiography. The attacking Central Powers troops failed to encircle and capture the tsarist forces deployed in the fortress, which enabled them to evacuate the bulwark in a timely fashion. The Russians, however, committed a major blunder when they deployed all their reserve artillery pieces to the southern citadel front to counter what they anticipated would be the main Austro-Hungarian–German assault. This reduced the northern front's defensive capabilities just as Central Powers troops attacked there. Even Austrian newspapers reporting the battle that drove the Russians out of Fortress Przemyśl did not claim it to be a major victory.

The bloody failure of the French-British offensives on the western front resulted in the transfer of three German divisions from that front and two from the Hindenburg-Ludendorff forces to the north to reinforce the Eleventh Army. General Mackensen maintained command of the Habsburg Second and Fourth Armies, while Third Army was disbanded and multiple units transferred to the Italian front. The offensive continued through the summer months until fall 1915.

By June 21, 1915, garrison troops had performed all the required restoration work within the fortress with the construction of multiple infantry defensive positions. No extra artillery batteries were provided to support these troops. Given the potential cost of reconstruction and the fact that the fortress had lost much of its previous military significance, it was not rebuilt. Habsburg Landsturm units and ten thousand Russian prisoners of war reconstructed the few selected infantry positions, while life returned to normal within the fortress city. Twenty Russian, five Polish, and two Italian prisoner of war labor companies relocated to the citadel to complete the few reconstruction projects.[77]

Court hearings were scheduled to punish citadel collaborators during the Russian occupation, but few were convicted. However, after the war's end, on December 19, 1918, serious charges were leveled at both General Kusmanek and the Habsburg Supreme Command General Staff. One of the more serious allegations involved the failure of the military to construct a railroad line during peacetime extending from the rear of Fortress Przemyśl toward the hinterland to expedite traffic to it. Three rail lines existed, from the northwest, east, and south of the citadel, but not one led to the west of the San Valley toward the interior of Hungary. Two officers were charged with criminal negligence.[78] Although the Habsburg General Staff had requested that such a railroad line be constructed since 1902, no government money had been allocated for it. The investigation commission completed its sessions by April 1921, reporting that the serious and fatal problems encountered at the fortress had resulted from a deficiency in government financing for prewar military preparations. Thus, neither General Conrad nor General Kusmanek would be found guilty of committing treasonous acts during the war, and the World War I saga of Fortress Przemyśl finally ended. The documents utilized for the commission's hearing can be found in AOK, faszikel 523, in the Vienna War Archives.

In another story that circulated for years after the war, Lieutenant Colonel Molnar, commander of Honvéd Infantry Regiment 8, had reputedly hidden his diary and documents in his living quarters although the fortress commander had ordered that all such material be destroyed before the surrender of the bulwarks. Immediately after the war, several searches for these materials proved fruitless. Decades later, when that building was being renovated, the cache was finally discovered under some floorboards; it included maps, military orders, and fortress newspapers.

After the recapture of the fortress on June 3, 1915, it remained in Habsburg possession for the duration of the war. Its garrison was skeletal, as the major battle raged much further east. At the dissolution of the Dual Monarchy, a struggle exploded between Poles and the Western Ukrainian People's Republic for possession of the fortress environs, and Polish Legion forces quickly occupied the fortress. Habsburg officers had not understood the extent of the hostility and turmoil between the two ethnic factions, but they also wanted to avoid becoming involved in the region's nationality machinations.[79]

On June 3, 1915, plans were finalized to continue the offensive after a meeting at Pless. The objective of the new operation would be Lemberg. General Mackensen received operational command of the Habsburg

Second and Fourth Armies, while the Third Army would be removed from the Russian front and deployed on the Italian war theater. A ten-day pause in operations allowed the Eleventh Army to receive badly needed replacement and reinforcement troops, rebuild its stockpile of artillery shells, and conduct a thorough aerial reconnaissance of the Russian defensive positions located between the San River and Lemberg. The renewed attack objective became the railroad line located between Lemberg and Rava Russka.

The Eleventh and Fourth Armies received the mission to secure the crossings at the San River, then all three armies continued the offensive. Following Italy's declaration of war on Austria-Hungary, the touchy problem arose of how to utilize the German Alpine Corps, which produced a bitter conflict between Generals Conrad and Falkenhayn. Falkenhayn notified Conrad that he had learned that the Alpine Corps had been ordered to be deployed to the Habsburg front lines, which placed them partially in Italian territory. The German general insisted that they not invade Italy because that country had not declared war on Germany.[80]

General Conrad quickly informed General Falkenhayn that he would take corrective action, but in the meantime Falkenhayn had already dispatched orders to the Alpine Corps over Conrad's head. If a clash occurred between German and Italian troops on Tyrolean territory, the Italians had to appear to be the aggressors.[81] An infuriated General Conrad quickly informed his counterpart that the Tyrolean defense command had corrected the orders to the German troops. Conrad's direct orders to German commands (to be under Habsburg Supreme Command) should be sent to them as well, as would occur if Habsburg commanders were fighting within German armies.[82] General Falkenhayn extended his apologies the next day to his counterpart.[83]

Meanwhile, the Russians broke through the Habsburg Seventh Army's right flank positions between Delatyn and Kolomea, but Conrad was discreetly informed that he should avoid deploying reinforcements to this front area, because it would be advantageous if the Russians would be occupied in that direction.[84]

By June 13 the allied troops were prepared to resume the offensive, which resulted in the collapse of Russian defensive positions within two days. Following a subsequent four-day advance, the Eleventh Army attained the area along the chain of lakes and forests west of Lemberg. After another brief pause to receive reinforcements and supplies, renewal of the attack resulted in piercing the Russian defensive positions.

The allied forces severed the railroad line between Lemberg and Rava Russka on June 20. The demoralized Russian troops, fearing they would be encircled, quickly retreated from Lemberg.

The Habsburg Second Army conquered the capital of Galicia on June 23. This substantially raised Dual Monarchy morale.[85] The southwest tsarist front lost an army; only the tsarist Eighth, Ninth, and Eleventh Armies remained. The badly mauled Third Army retreated north from Lemberg to the Russian northwest front. Now consideration of two different courses of action followed the conquest of Lemberg. The logical move appeared to be to advance to the north into Russian Poland. The major objective became Brest-Litovsk, the hub of the Russian Polish railroad network. Its capture would be a serious blow to the Russian army.

After being briefed, Generals Conrad and Falkenhayn agreed on June 24 that a successful campaign in Russian Poland could possibly force Russia to conclude a separate peace. Then the German Eleventh Army crossed the frontier into Russian Poland during June 28 and 29, encountering very little enemy resistance except for some weak rearguard actions. On the Eleventh Army's left flank, the Habsburg Fourth Army crossed the Tanev River and advanced into the region east of the Vistula River, then made liaison with the Eleventh Army's right flank X Corps.

South Army forces fought their way across the Dniester River southeast of Lemberg on June 30, then halted briefly to replace their losses and equipment before advancing to their next objective, the Gnila-Lipa River line. The Habsburg Second Army lagged behind the South Army as they advanced.

During the last week of June, combat eased; strenuous marches occupied the allied troops as they approached the northern edge of the Carpathian Mountains. In the meantime, the weather remained favorable. Much of the terrain to be traversed was flat, but there were also some swampy areas. The sandy roads turned into bottomless pits of mud with heavy rainfall.

On July 1, the advancing Eleventh Army encountered a new Russian defensive position on both sides of the Wiar River. Meanwhile, during the last week of June, the Russian retreat movement created a much shorter and straighter front line along the southern portion of the Russian Polish salient.

Once assaulting infantry penetrated the Russian lines, they widened the shoulders of the newly created salient while other units drove as far as possible into the Russian positions. At times the strategy was costly in terms of the number of casualties, but proved most successful in destroying frontline Russian units and defeating local reserve formations deployed behind the front lines. These efforts were greatly aided by Russian defensive tactics, which included the launching of immediate counterattacks in attempts to regain any lost terrain.[86] The resultant penetrations of enemy lines achieved sufficient width and depth that such assaults normally resulted in the collapse of entire enemy frontline positions. Examples of this included the opening battle of Gorlice-Tarnov and the crossing of the San River.

Logistics proved to be a major factor on the eastern front battle, so the Germans' slow, methodical approach worked very well. Once General Mackensen's victorious forces advanced about sixty miles from the nearest railroad depot location, they were forced to pause to resupply, which usually took about a week. During this activity rearward lines were extended forward, ammunition stocks—especially artillery shells—were replaced, reinforcements were placed in their units, and heavy artillery batteries moved forward.

German aerial reconnaissance quickly proved of extreme significance during the entire campaign, aided by the Central Powers' aerial superiority, which ensured that they encountered very little opposition. In-depth photographic images of Russian defensive positions helped identify crucial targets for allied artillery, which proved extremely helpful, because for the Central Powers every artillery shell counted. Another major factor explaining the success of the offensive operations was that the Russians' primitive trench systems could not withstand heavy German artillery barrages, which usually lasted between ninety minutes and two hours, unlike the major western front artillery preparations, which could last for days and weeks.

10

✠✠✠

Conclusion

THE PRZEMYŚL ENVIRONS HAD BEEN USED AS A FORTIFIED area dating back to the seventh century. This strategic region witnessed battle for hundreds of years. Fortress Przemyśl was significant because of its important geographic location along the San River at the foothills of the Carpathian Mountains. Along with Fortress Kraków, two hundred kilometers to the northeast, it served as the only impediment to a Russian invasion of eastern Galicia.

Russian troops had only to advance into the province of Galicia to be in a position to encircle Habsburg defensive forces because of the lack of geographic hindrances and the bow shape of the province. The fortress was the location to halt or at least impede tsarist egress into the Carpathian Mountains to invade Hungary, one of Russian's major strategic goals during late 1914 and early 1915.

Since the French revolutionary period and the rise of Russia as a great power, the problem of where to establish a fortress to defend the province of Galicia from a potential Russian threat had grown in significance. In the final third of the nineteenth century, Fortress Przemyśl evolved into a major bulwark. Yet, with all the improvements and construction that took place there throughout the century, the citadel proved obsolete in 1914. This resulted from a miserly allotment of funding over multiple decades for fortress construction and improvement. Once Conrad von Hötzendorf became chief of the General Staff of the Austro-Hungarian army in 1906, his bias against the construction of fortresses became obvious. The sparse funds that became available for building and improving fortresses during his tenure would be utilized mainly for constructing new bulwark positions along the Italian frontier. Conrad, however, considered that fortified positions would serve mainly as depot sites during and after a mobilization, because of their construction and garrison costs and his fear of disaster if one had to capitulate to the enemy.

With the Austro-Hungarian mobilization in July 1914, the fortress became significant because of the Rückverlegung and the Fourth Army and X Corps commander deployed there. General Conrad's botched 1914 offensive plan resulted in defeat after the two disastrous battles of Lemberg in August and early September 1914. The resulting hastily ordered Habsburg retreat on September 11, which had not been anticipated or prepared for, brought Fortress Przemyśl to the forefront of eastern front warfare until its surrender on March 22, 1915, and again briefly with its recapture in June 1915.

During that chaotic 150-kilometer retreat, Third Army troops passed through the bulwark, leaving many sick and wounded soldiers behind. The fortress fulfilled its missions well during its first siege between October 9 and November 8, 1914. It tied down nine tsarist infantry divisions and two cavalry divisions and remained a major impediment for the Russian troops who attempted to cross the Carpathian Mountains into Hungary. Such an enormous number of troops in their rear echelon area provided a constant threat to tsarist military endeavors.

Following the futile but bloody Russian storm attacks to conquer the fortress between October 6 and 8, 1914, and the liberation of the citadel on October 9, Habsburg Third and Second Army forces plundered its food, ammunition, and artillery supplies as troops traversed through the bulwark. This ultimately had a disastrous effect on the fortress's destiny, as the foraged materials could not be replaced because of the ensuing tsarist military actions. The Russians quickly launched another major offensive, which resulted in the fortress being besieged again before its resupply could be completed.

The unfortunate German–Austro-Hungarian October campaign at the Ivangorod crossing of the Vistula River resulted in the retreat of the allied front. The Habsburg armies had to retreat because of the newly created threat that its northern flank positions could easily be enveloped once German forces withdrew. The second siege of the fortress lasted for 137 days, until its capitulation on March 22, 1915. During the second siege, however, the major military activity on the eastern front had shifted to the northern German theater. This compelled the Russian High Command to refrain from launching storm attacks against the citadel as they had during the first siege. Instead, the Russians chose to starve out the fortification garrison. They besieged the fortress with far fewer troops—only three reserve divisions and ancillary units as time progressed—but these few troops proved more than successful in maintaining the siege of the bulwark.

The unanticipated allied military setback occurred so rapidly that the frantic attempts to resupply the fortress with the required food, ammunition, and other necessities could be attempted only between October 27 and November 4, 1914. A major impediment to this effort resulted from the Russian troops' destruction of railroads as they retreated after the early October Austro-Hungarian offensive. Thus, before any provisions could be transported back into the fortress, multiple railroad bridges had to be reconstructed, which required much time and concentrated work. At best, the fortress was able to restock only half of its basic requirements, particularly food, by the time the second siege began.

The multiple sorties launched from the fortress were intended to tie down enemy forces and to determine the composition of the opposing Russian forces. These attacks resulted in more than twenty-four thousand garrison casualties. These heavy troop casualty numbers were partially due to repeated and predictable military efforts, which were not only launched in the same direction but also utilized the same units. Advancing fortress troops quickly found themselves outgunned and outnumbered by Russian defensive positions. Instead of raising garrison morale, as the commanders anticipated, these attacks ended with a demoralizing retreat into the fortress. Several fortress efforts attempted to reach the Habsburg Third Army right flank positions fifty to sixty kilometers distant, which launched several offensives to liberate the bulwark. Inevitably, the Third Army offensives collapsed; thus, fortress sortie efforts to reach the approaching troops proved futile.

During December 1914, when serious rationing commenced within the fortress, the troops' physical and mental condition began to suffer greatly. Garrison soldiers increasingly proved unable to perform their duties, and soon thousands of horses had to be slaughtered to extend the garrison's food supplies. However, the resulting shortage of horses increasingly crippled the maneuverability of the garrison forces in moving artillery and shells to the perimeter walls when necessary. December witnessed the greatest number of casualties. It also signaled the rapid approach of a time when the troops proved incapable of launching an effective major effort outside the fortress.

In late December, General Conrad determined that he must take immediate action to prevent the surrender of the fortress and thus prevent tsarist forces from invading Hungary. Disturbing diplomatic reports arriving from Italy and Romania suggested that the neutral European powers harboring territorial aspirations against the Habsburg monarchy could enter the war very shortly if the Habsburg army sustained further major battlefield defeats. This information, coupled with pressure from Emperor Franz Joseph, convinced Conrad that he had to launch an offensive during January 1915 in an attempt to liberate the fortress and roll up the enemy's extreme left flank positions. From October 1914 through the surrender of the fortress on March 22, 1915, the liberation of the bulwark remained the main corollary of Conrad's military planning.

After careful consideration, Conrad determined to launch a winter offensive through the Carpathian Mountains to liberate the fortress. However, what evolved into three separate Carpathian Mountain offensives occurred during horrendous winter weather and mountain terrain conditions, leading to battle conditions never before witnessed except perhaps during the 1812 Napoleonic invasion of Russia. The Habsburg Third Army launched the first offensive on January 23, 1915; however, even though it faced only weak enemy troop contingents, it lacked sufficient mass and troops, as well as adequate artillery support, to succeed. The few initial battlefield victories could not be sustained because of the lack of reserve forces and reinforcements. The troops also suffered horribly from disease, frostbite, and hypothermia, because neither the fortress garrison nor the field army troops had winter uniforms or appropriate equipment to battle the elements.

The failure of the Third Army offensive, which resulted in 80 percent casualties for the attacking forces, led General Conrad to appoint his Second Army commander, General Böhm-Ermolli, to launch the second

offensive operation, but on a much narrower front—only twelve kilometers and against extremely strong Russian defensive positions. On the
eve of the new offensive, melting snow and ice made the roadways necessary to supply the attacking army formations impassable, delaying the
offensive for several days. Several Habsburg commanders suggested that
the offensive should not be launched until weather conditions were more
favorable and the troops had had time to recover from their debilitating
first effort. Conrad refused all such suggestions, demanding that the
offensive operation be launched to liberate the fortress before the garrison
troops had to surrender from starvation. This second offensive effort
terminated on March 14 after unsuccessful battles and the endurance of
some of the worst weather in the history of the Carpathian Mountains
region. Second Army units were decimated, losing forty thousand of
their complement of ninety-five thousand soldiers. Astonishingly, it was
claimed that only six thousand casualties occurred on the battlefield, the
vast majority resulting from illness, frostbite, and hypothermia. Powerful blizzards struck several times during the operation, halting Habsburg
military action and causing untold misery for the troops on both sides
of the front.

    With Habsburg field army troops still almost one hundred kilo-
meters from the fortress area and in horrendous physical condition, Conrad ordered that yet a third offensive be launched to liberate Fortress
Przemyśl. This effort consisted of only a single reinforced corps, which
was intended to attack simultaneously with a fortress breakout attempt.
The catastrophic breakthrough effort on March 19, 1915, occurred several
days before the launching of the third field army offensive. Neither Second Army Command nor the commander of the attacking troops was
informed of the failure of the fortress breakout attempts, during which
the attacking units needlessly suffered 75 percent casualties.

    The fortress ultimately surrendered on March 22, 1915, and the military
situation of the Austro-Hungarian army after the Easter battles in the
Carpathian Mountains forced the Germans to launch their famous
Gorlice-Tarnov offensive, which produced the greatest Central Powers
victory of the war. In the process of this campaign, Fortress Przemyśl
would be reconquered on June 3, but by then the saga of the last fortress
had officially ended. The citadel garrison outperformed its mission dur-

ing the first siege (September–October 1914). Its long second siege produced the conditions for its surrender at the end of March 1915.

For the remainder of the war the bulwark would be garrisoned by very few troops and would not be restored to its prewar condition. Multiple books have been written in Polish on all aspects of the history of the fortress during World War I. But today it remains merely a relic to visit in Poland, and its history is basically unknown. Fortress Przemyśl, a relatively unknown entity until the outbreak of World War I, provided the main focus of battle on the Austro-Hungarian front from the Habsburg mobilization until its surrender and recapture in 1915, by which time it had become the Verdun of the east.

Notes

ABBREVIATIONS

AC	Archiv Conrad
AOK	Armee Ober Kommando
BWA	Budapest War Archives
fasz.	*faszikel*
KA	Kriegsarchiv
Kdo.	Kommando
k.k.	kaiserlich- königliche (Hungarian referent for army)
k.u.k	kaiserlich und königlich (Imperial and Royal Army)
LU	Luftfahrte Archiv
MKSM	Militärkanzlei Seiner Majestät
Ms., Mss.	Manuscript, Manuscripts
MTM	*Militärwissenschaftliche und -technische Mitteilungen*
NFA	Neue Feld Akten
NL	Nachlässe
nr., nrn.	number, numbers
Op. Nr.	Operation Number
ÖULK	*Österreich-Ungarns letzter Krieg 1914–1918*
RAWK	*Der Weltkriege 1914 bis 1918: Die militärischen Operationen zu Lande*

1. INTRODUCTION

1. Österreichisches Bundesministerium für Heereswesen-Kriegsarchiv Wien, *Österreich-Ungarns letzter Krieg 1914–1918* (hereafter ÖULK), vols. 1–7 (Vienna: Verlag Militärwissenschaftlicher Mitteilungen, 1930–1938), 1:1.

2. The original sources for this book include (1) Kriegsarchiv (KA, War Archive, Vienna); (2) Armee Ober Kommando (hereafter AOK), Operations Abteilung, fasz. 523,

Festung Przemyśl, a small Operations Bureau *faszikel* with documents resulting from a postwar investigation relative to the fortress and General Kusmanek's actions during the siege; (3) KA Nachlässe (NL) B/1137, Kusmanek Nr. 2, Hermann von Burgstädten Kusmanek, "Festung Przemyśl," a manuscript written by General Kusmanek justifying his actions as commander of the fortress during its travail (hereafter cited as KA NL, B/1137, Kusmanek, "Festung Przemyśl"); (4) KA NL, B/1041, Bornemann, Kriegsgeschichte-Vortragsentwürfe Weltkrieg 1914–1918—Przemyśl (hereafter cited as KA NL, B/1041, Bornemann, Przemyśl), containing diverse papers on various battles; and (5) KA Seiner Majestät (hereafter MKSM), Separate fasz. 100, particularly Reserve Nr. 1956, a report from Habsburg Supreme Command to Emperor Franz Joseph concerning the provisioning of food to the fortress before the second siege. Published and unpublished works by Franz Stuckheil include the following: (1) a massive manuscript, KA, Manuscripte 1. Weltkrieg, Russland, 1914 (hereafter KA Ms. 1 Wkg, Russland, 1914), Nr. 19, Stuckheil, "Festung Przemyśl"; and (2) his condensed eleven-article series about the fortress's travails published in the periodical *Militär-wissenschaftliche und -technische Mitteilungen* (hereafter MTM): "Die strategische Rolle Przemyśls auf dem östlichen Kriegsschauplatz," MTM 54 (1923): 60–78, 132–146; "Die Festung Przemyśl in der Ausrüstungszeit: Provisorische Darstellung," MTM 55 (1924): 201–230 (hereafter cited as Stuckheil, "Ausrüstungszeit"); "Die zweite Einschliessung der Festung Przemyśl III," Abschnitt das Ende, MTM (1924): 289–309, 395–417; MTM 56 (1925): 110–133, 222–236, 346–367; MTM 57 (1926): 162–173, 286–296, 405–410, 530–535. Monographs include Franz Forstner's excellent *Przemyśl: Österreich-Ungarns bedeutendste Festung* (Vienna: Österreichische Bundesverlag, 1987) and Hermann Heiden's *Bollwerk am San: Schicksal der Festung Przemyśl* (Oldenburg: Gerhard Stalting, 1940. See also Hans G. M. Schwalb, "Die Verteidigung von Przemyśl, 1914–1915," *Mitteilungen über Gegenstücke des Artillerie und Geniewesens* 149 (1918): 1373–1392, a short article. Valuable information can also be found in the KA AOK, Operations Abteilung (Operations Bureau) and various NL files. Short summaries can be found in Manfried Rauchensteiner's significant book, *Der Tod des Doppeladlers: Österreich-Ungarn und der Erste Weltkrieg* (Graz: Styria, 1993); in Bruno Wolfgang, *Przemyśl 1914–1915* (Vienna: Payer, 1935); and in Franz Conrad von Hötzendorf, *Aus meiner Dienstzeit, 1906–1918*, 5 vols. (Vienna: Rikola Verlag, 1921–1925).

3. The k.u.k. army sacrificed an estimated eight hundred thousand troops to liberate the fortress, which nevertheless had to surrender.

4. KA AOK, Übersetzung Nordost, Nr. 14, "Sturm Octobre 1914," Tscherkassow, 122–123 (hereafter cited as KA, Übersetzung Nordost, Nr. 14, "Sturm," Tscherkassow).

5. KA MKSM, Separate fasz. 100, Reserve Nr. 1956, MKSM Nr. 1375 (69-6/13).

6. KA Manuscripte 1. Weltkrieg, Russland, 1915 (hereafter KA Ms. 1 Wkg, Russland, 1915), Nr. 6, Joly, "Der Winterfeldzug in Polen und Galizien," 11.

7. KA NL, B/1137, Nr. 2, Kusmanek, "Festung Przemyśl"; KA MKSM, Separate fasz. 100, Reserve Nr. 1956; KA Ms. 1 Wkg, Russland, 1914, Nr. 19, Stuckheil, "Festung Przemyśl," and the various articles by Stuckheil cited in note 2; Eduard Ritter von Steinitz and Theodor von Arenau Brosch, *Die Reichsbefestigung Österreich-Ungarn zur Zeit Conrads von Hötzendorf: Ergänzungsheft 1 zum Werke Österreich-Ungarns letzter Krieg* (Wien: Verlag der Militärwissenschaftlichen Mitteilungen, 1930). See also Heiden, *Bollwerk am Sam,* 23; and especially Forstner, *Przemyśl.*

8. KA Ms. 1 Wkg, Russland, 1914, Nr. 19, Stuckheil, "Festung Przemyśl"; KA MKSM, Separate fasz. 100, Reserve Nr. 1956, MKSM Nr. 1375 (69-6/13); Forstner, *Przemyśl*.

9. KA Ms. 1 Wkg, Russland, 1915, Nr. 6, Joly, "Der Winterfeldzung in Polen und Galizien"; KA Ms. 1 Wkg, Russland, 1914, Nr. 19, Stuckheil, "Festung Przemyśl"; KA NL, B/1137, Nr. 2, Kusmanek, "Festung Przemyśl."

10. KA NL, B/1137, Nr. 2, Kusmanek, "Festung Przemyśl"; KA Ms. 1 Wkg, Russland, 1914, Nr. 19, Stuckheil, "Festung Przemyśl."

11. ÖULK, vol. 1; KA Ms. 1 Wkg, Russland, 1914, Nr. 19, Stuckheil, "Festung Przemyśl."

12. KA NL, B/1137, Nr. 2, Kusmanek, "Festung Przemyśl"; KA Ms. 1 Wkg, Russland, 1914, Nr. 19, Stuckheil, "Festung Przemyśl," and articles cited in note 2; see Heiden, *Bollwerk am Sam*, 23; Wolfgang, *Przemyśl 1914–1915*; Forstner, *Przemyśl*.

13. Conrad, *Dienstzeit*, vol. 5; ÖULK, vol. 1. See also note 12 for this chapter.

2. THE OPENING BATTLES, AUGUST–SEPTEMBER 1914

1. See Graydon Tunstall, *Planning for War against Russia and Serbia: Austro-Hungarian and German Military Strategies, 1871–1914* (New York: Columbia University Press, 1993), for details on the field army battles.

2. Minimal "B" (Balkan) deployment refers to the twelve designated divisions to be fielded against Serbia if Russia intervened in the war.

3. KA NL, B/726, Nr. 8, Robert Nowak, "Die Klammer des Reiches: Das Verhalten der elf Nationalitäten Österreich-Ungarn in der k.u.k. Wehrmacht 1914–1918"; Stuckheil, "Ausrüstungszeit," 205, 208, 215; Forstner, *Przemyśl*.

4. Budapest War Archives (hereafter BWA), TGY 99, Pamperl, Chronicle; Stuckheil, "Ausrüstungszeit," 208; see also Rudolph Hecht, "Fragen des Heeresergänzungen der Gestalten Bewaffneten Macht Österreich-Ungarns während des ersten Weltkrieges" (PhD thesis, University of Vienna, 1969.

5. Conrad, *Dienstzeit*, 5:650.

6. BWA, TGY 99, Pamperl, Chronicle.

7. BWA, TGY 99, Pamperl, Chronicle.

8. KA Ms. 1 Wkg, Russland, 1914, Nr. 19, Stuckheil, "Festung Przemyśl"; KA NL, B/1137, Nr. 2, Kusmanek, "Festung Przemyśl," 14; Rauchensteiner, *Der Tod des Doppeladlers*, 124; Forstner, *Przemyśl*, 152.

9. KA NL, B/1137, Nr. 2, Kusmanek, "Festung Przemyśl," 14; KA Ms. 1 Wkg, Russland, 1914, Nr. 19, Stuckheil, "Festung Przemyśl."

10. Jan Lenar, *Pamietnik z walk o Twierdze Przemyśl* (Przemyśl: Wydawnictwo Fort, 2005).

11. Heiden, *Bollwerk am San*, 93.

12. KA NL, B/1137, Nr. 2, Kusmanek, "Festung Przemyśl," 14; KA Ms. 1 Wkg, Russland, 1914, Nr. 19, Stuckheil, "Festung Przemyśl"; Forstner, *Przemyśl*.

13. Conrad, *Dienstzeit*, 4:62.

14. KA MKSM, Separate fasz. 100, Reserve Nr. 1956, 69-6/13; KA NL, B/1137, Nr. 2, Kusmanek, "Festung Przemyśl"; KA Ms. 1 Wkg, Russland, 1914, Nr. 19, Stuckheil, "Festung Przemyśl"; see Conrad, *Dienstzeit*, vol. 5; Forstner, *Przemyśl*.

15. Conrad, *Dienstzeit*, 4:692, 693.

16. Conrad, *Dienstzeit*, 4:690, 692, 693, 712.

17. Conrad, *Dienstzeit*, 4:734–735; KA NL, B/1137, Nr. 2, Kusmanek, "Festung Przemyśl"; KA Ms. 1 Wkg, Russland, 1914, Nr. 19, Stuckheil, "Festung Przemyśl"; Forstner, *Przemyśl*.

18. Conrad, *Dienstzeit*, 4:727.

19. ÖULK, 1:312, 342.

20. Conrad, *Dienstzeit*, 4:731; ÖULK, 1:342–343; *Reichsarchiv: Weltkriege 1914 bis 1918: Die militärischen Operationen zu Lande* (Berlin: E. S. Mittler & Sohn, 1929) (hereafter cited as RAWK) 5:403.

21. Conrad, *Dienstzeit*, 4:699, 701, 726; ÖULK, vol. 1.

22. Conrad, *Dienstzeit*, 4:727.

23. Norman Stone, *The Eastern Front, 1914–1917* (New York: Charles Scribner's Sons, 1975), 95; see also Holger Herwig, *The First World War: Germany and Austria-Hungary* (New York: Arnold, 1997), 107.

24. Conrad, *Dienstzeit*, 4:699, 700, 702, 724–725, 730, 732, see especially Operations Order Nr. 154, Conrad to Moltke.

25. KA Ms. 1 Wkg, Russland, 1915, Nr. 6, Joly, "Der Winterfeldzug in Polen und Galizien"; Rauchensteiner, *Der Tod des Doppeladlers*.

26. Heiden, *Bollwerk am San*; Conrad, *Dienstzeit*, vol. 5; ÖULK, vol. 1.

27. Heiden, *Bollwerk am San*, 89.

28. Conrad, *Dienstzeit*, 4:710.

29. See ÖULK, vol. 1, and Graydon Tunstall, *Blood on the Snow: The Carpathian Winter War, 1915* (Lawrence: University Press of Kansas, 2010), for further details.

30. Conrad, *Dienstzeit*, 4:752; Tunstall, *Blood on the Snow*.

31. BWA, TGY 99, Pamperl, Chronicle.

32. Conrad, *Dienstzeit*, 4:755.

33. ÖULK, 1:341.

34. ÖULK, 1:343; RAWK, 5:402ff.; Paul von Hindenburg, *Aus meinem Leben* (Leipzig: Herzel, 1920), 101; Graf von Joseph Stürgkh, *Im deutschen grossen hauptquartier* (Leipzig: Paul List Verlag, 1921), 414.

35. Erich von Ludendorff, *Meine Kriegserinnerungen 1914–1918* (Berlin: E. S. Mittler & Sohn, 1921), 55.

36. ÖULK, 1:343; RAWK, 5:408; Conrad, *Dienstzeit*, vol. 4.

37. Conrad, *Dienstzeit*, 4:735, 738, 742, 752, 755, 756; ÖULK, vol. 1.

38. KA AOK, fasz. 4, AOK Op. Nr. 7442.

39. Conrad, *Dienstzeit*, 4:752, 754.

40. Conrad, *Dienstzeit*, 4:708.

41. Conrad, *Dienstzeit*, 4:724, 767, 786, 797.

42. Conrad, *Dienstzeit*, 4:779, 786; KA AOK, fasz. 512, Conrad-Falkenhayn Korrespondenz, Russland; ÖULK, vol. 1; RAWK, vol. 5.

43. ÖULK, 1:379.

44. KA Ms. 1 Wkg, Russland, 1914, Nr. 19, Stuckheil, "Festung Przemyśl."

45. Conrad, *Dienstzeit*, 4:754–756, 767, 791.

46. ÖULK, 1:343.

47. ÖULK, 1:345; Conrad, *Dienstzeit*, 4:796ff.; RAWK, 5:412ff.; Stone, *Eastern Front*, 90.

48. ÖULK, 1:347; RAWK, 5:413.

49. ÖULK, 1:345–347; Max Schwarte, *Der grosse Krieg 1914–1918*, vol. 5, *Der österreichisch-ungarische Krieg* (Leipzig: Barth in Ausg1., 1922), 39.

50. Conrad, *Dienstzeit*, 4:791, 800, 813.

51. Heiden, *Bollwerk am San*, 102.

52. Conrad, *Dienstzeit*, 4:103.

53. Conrad, *Dienstzeit*, 4:816, 820.

54. KA Ms. 1 Wkg, Russland, 1914, Nr. 19, Stuckheil, "Festung Przemyśl."

55. KA Ms. 1 Wkg, Russland, 1914, Nr. 19, Stuckheil, "Festung Przemyśl."

56. KA, Übersetzung Nordost, Nr. 14, "Sturm," Tscherkassow; ÖULK, 1:344.

57. Conrad, *Dienstzeit*, 4:789; ÖULK, vol. 1.

58. Conrad, *Dienstzeit*, 5:816.

59. KA NL, B/1137, Nr. 2, Kusmanek, "Festung Przemyśl"; AOK, Op. Nr. 2096; KA AOK, fasz. 523, Festung Przemyśl; KA MKSM, Separate fasz. 100, Reserve Nr. 1956; Conrad, *Dienstzeit*, vol. 5; Forstner, *Przemyśl*.

60. Conrad, *Dienstzeit*, 5:704–705, 727.

61. ÖULK, 1:378; KA MKSM, Separate fasz. 100, Reserve Nr. 1956; KA NL, B/1137, Nr. 2, Kusmanek, "Festung Przemyśl"; KA Ms. 1 Wkg, Russland, 1914, Nr. 19, Stuckheil, "Festung Przemyśl."

62. Conrad, *Dienstzeit*, 5:755, 778–779, 791.

63. Conrad, *Dienstzeit*, 5:789; KA NL, B/1137, Nr. 2, Kusmanek, "Festung Przemyśl"; KA Ms. 1 Wkg, Russland, 1914, Nr. 19, "Stuckheil, Przemyśl."

64. Conrad, *Dienstzeit*, 5:727.

65. BWA, "Auszug aus dem Berichte über die Aktion im III Verteidigung Bezirk: Während der Einschliessung," General der Infantry (GDI) Karl Waitzendorfer (hereafter cited as Waitzendorfer, "III Verteidigung Bezirk Während der Einschliessung"), 107; Conrad, *Dienstzeit*, 5:727, 789.

66. Heiden, *Bollwerk am San*, 214; ÖULK, vol. 1.

67. Waitzendorfer, "III Verteidigung Bezirk Während der Einschliessung," Nordost 10.

68. KA Ms. 1 Wkg, Russland, 1914, Nr. 19, Stuckheil, "Festung Przemyśl"; KA, Übersetzung Nordost, Nr. 14, "Sturm," Tscherkassow, 35; ÖULK, 1:379.

69. ÖULK, 1:342.

70. ÖULK, 1:342, 344.

71. Conrad, *Dienstzeit*, 5:705, 800–803, 816, 820, AOK Op. Nr. 2230 daily log, AOK, Op. Nr. 2278 daily log, September 19 Tagebücher.

72. Conrad, *Dienstzeit*, 5:807; ÖULK, 1:344.

73. Conrad, *Dienstzeit*, 5:816.

74. ÖULK, 1:346, 379.

75. ÖULK, 1:379–380.

76. KA, Übersetzung Nordost, Nr. 14, "Sturm," Tscherkassow.

77. Landsturm Infantry Regiment 54 from Defensive District IV assisted in the effort.

78. Waitzendorfer, "III Verteidigung Bezirk Während der Einschliessung."

79. Conrad, *Dienstzeit*, 5:832.

80. J. V. Michaelsburg, *Im belagerten Przemyśl: Tagebuchblätter aus grosser Zeit* (Leipzig: C. F. Amelangs Verlag, 1915), 15–16, 23–24, 25.

81. Michaelsburg, *Im belagerten Przemyśl*, 14.

82. Michaelsburg, *Im belagerten Przemyśl*.

83. Michaelsburg, *Im belagerten Przemyśl*; KA Ms. 1 Wkg, Russland, 1915, Nr. 6, Joly, "Der Winterfeldzug in Polen und Galizien."

84. Chudenitz, Franz Czernin von. *Das Chudenitz in der ÖU. Festung Przemyśl Während der Beiden Belagerungen, 1914–1915*. Viena: Selbstverlag, 1985, 16.

85. Chudenitz, 2–4.

86. Michaelsburg, *Im belagerten Przemyśl*, 26; Chudenitz, 8.

87. Michaelsburg, *Im belagerten Przemyśl*, 27.

88. Conrad, *Dienstzeit*, 5:838–840, 842; see also ÖULK, vol. 1.

89. Conrad, *Dienstzeit*, 5:843, 858; ÖULK, vol. 1.

90. KA, Übersetzung Nordost, Nr. 14, "Sturm," Tscherkassow.

91. Stone, *Eastern Front*, 96; ÖULK, 1:347.

92. Michaelsburg, *Im belagerten Przemyśl*.

93. Conrad, *Dienstzeit*, 5:871.

94. Conrad, *Dienstzeit*, 5:866, 902.

95. Conrad, *Dienstzeit*, 5:873.

3. SIEGE AND LIBERATION, OCTOBER 1914

1. General A. A. Brusilov, *A Soldier's Notebook, 1914–1918* (Westport, CT: Greenwood Press, 1930), 80; KA NL B/1040, Bornemann, Przemyśl; KA Ms. 1 Wkg, Russland, 1914, Nr. 19, Stuckheil, "Festung Przemyśl"; Forstner, *Przemyśl*.

2. ÖULK, 1:373, 381.

3. General Max Hoffmann, *War Diaries and Other Papers*, trans. Eric Sutton (London: M. Secker, 1929), 49; see ÖULK, vol. 1; RAWK, vol. 5.

4. KA NL, B/1137, Nr. 2, Kusmanek, "Festung Przemyśl"; KA MKSM, Separate fasz. 100, Reserve Nr. 1956; KA Ms. 1 Wkg, Russland, 1914, Nr. 19, Stuckheil, "Festung Przemyśl."

5. KA NL, B/1137, Nr. 2, Kusmanek, "Festung Przemyśl"; KA MKSM, Separate fasz. 100, Reserve Nr. 1956; KA Ms. 1 Wkg, Russland, 1914, Nr. 19, Stuckheil, "Festung Przemyśl."

6. BWA, TGY 99, Pamperl, Chronicle.

7. Heiden, *Bollwerk am San*, 121–123.

8. Conrad, *Dienstzeit*, 5:26, 64.

9. KA Ms. 1 Wkg, Russland, 1914, Nr. 9, "Die Geschichte der Festung Przemyśl," ÖULK, vol. 1; Heiden, *Bollwerk am San*, 119–120.

10. ÖULK, 1:380.

11. ÖULK, 1:380.

12. ÖULK, 1:380–381.

13. Conrad, *Dienstzeit*, 5:40, 43, AOK Op. Nr. 2870.

14. Conrad, *Dienstzeit*, 5:39–41, AOK Op. Nr. 2821.

15. KA NL, B/1137, Nr. 2, Kusmanek, "Festung Przemyśl"; KA Ms. 1 Wkg, Russland, 1914, Nr. 19, Stuckheil, "Festung Przemyśl."

16. ÖULK, 1:373; KA, Übersetzung Nordost, Nr. 14, "Sturm," Tscherkassow; KA Ms. 1 Wkg, Russland, 1914, Nr. 19, Stuckheil, "Festung Przemyśl."

17. Conrad, *Dienstzeit*, 5:39–40, 43, AOK Op. Nrn. 2913 and 2821.

18. KA, Übersetzung Nordost, Nr. 14, "Sturm," Tscherkassow.

19. XII Corps (12th and 19th Infantry Divisions). The 65th Reserve Infantry Division served as a reserve force. The siege force consisted of the 3rd Schützen

Brigade and the 58th, 60th, 69th, 78th, and 82nd Reserve Infantry Divisions; ÖULK, 1:381.

20. Only one-twelfth of the tsarist artillery consisted of field howitzer and heavy artillery pieces. ÖULK, 1:381.

21. KA Ms. 1 Wkg, Russland, 1914, Nr. 19, Stuckheil, "Festung Przemyśl"; KA NL, B/1137, Nr. 2, Kusmanek, "Festung Przemyśl"; KA NL, B/1040 and 1041, Bornemann, Przemyśl; Forstner, Przemyśl; KA Ms. 1 Wkg, Russland, 1915, Nr. 6, Joly, "Der Winterfeldzug in Polen und Galizien."

22. ÖULK, vol. 1.

23. Conrad, Dienstzeit, 5:50, 183.

24. Conrad, Dienstzeit, 5:231.

25. KA AOK, Op. Nr. 2726.

26. Heiden, Bollwerk am San, 134.

27. KA, Übersetzung Nordost, Nr. 10, G. Korolkow, "Strategische Studie über den Weltkrieg, 1914–1918 (14 Sept. bis 20 Nov. 1914)."

28. KA NL, B/1137, Nr. 2, Kusmanek, "Festung Przemyśl"; KA Ms. 1 Wkg, Russland, 1914, Nr. 19, Stuckheil, "Festung Przemyśl."

29. Wolfgang, Przemyśl, 1914–1915.

30. KA Ms. 1 Wkg, Russland, 1914, Nr. 19, Stuckheil, "Festung Przemyśl"; Forstner, Przemyśl, 171.

31. KA Ms. 1 Wkg, Russland, 1914, Nr. 19, Stuckheil, "Festung Przemyśl"; Forstner, Przemyśl, 171.

32. KA MKSM, Separate fasz. 100, Reserve Nr. 1956, 69-6/3; KA NL, B/1137, Nr. 2, Kusmanek, "Festung Przemyśl"; KA Ms. 1 Wkg, Russland, 1914, Nr. 19, Stuckheil, "Festung Przemyśl"; see also Conrad, Dienstzeit, 5:56, 61; ÖULK, vol. 1; Forstner, Przemyśl, 197–198; KA, Übersetzung Nordost, Nr. 28, "Von Lodz bis Gorlice Jänner–März 1915," A. M. Zajonstschowsky, 29.

33. Conrad, Dienstzeit, 5:51, 55.

34. Conrad, Dienstzeit, 5:51, 55.; see KA, Übersetzung Nordost, Nr. 28, "Von Lodz bis Gorlice Jänner–März 1915," A. M. Zajonstschowsky; ÖULK, 1:382. The Russians launched a powerful attack against Werk I/4 on the southeast front and about a division against Werk I/5+6. Conrad, Dienstzeit, 5:56.

35. Conrad, Dienstzeit, 5:56.

36. Heiden, Bollwerk am San, 139, 142–145.

37. ÖULK, 1:383.

38. KA, Übersetzung Nordost, Nr. 14, "Sturm," Tscherkassow.

39. KA, Übersetzung Nordost, Nr. 14, "Sturm," Tscherkassow.

40. Rudolf Reiser, "Der Kampf um das Werk I/I der Gruppe Siedliska am 7. Octobre 1914," Österreichische Wehrzeitung, Folge 29, 1925.

41. KA, Übersetzung Nordost, Nr. 14, "Sturm," Tscherkassow, 124.

42. Heiden, Bollwerk am San, 157; Forstner, Przemyśl, 172.

43. Conrad, Dienstzeit, 5:92.

44. Laslo Szabo, A nady temető Przemyśl ostrema 1914–1915 (Budapest: Kossuth, 1982).

45. Conrad, Dienstzeit, 5:52.

46. Conrad, Dienstzeit, vol. 5, Tagebericht, Op. Nr. 3007, Oct. 7, 52; ÖULK, 1:383, 384; KA, Übersetzung Nordost, Nr. 14, "Sturm," Tscherkassow; Herwig, First World War, 108.

47. ÖULK, 1:384.

48. KA NL, B/1041, Bornemann, "Przemyśl."

49. KA, Übersetzung Nordost, Nr. 14, "Sturm," Tscherkassow.

50. ÖULK, 1:383–384.

51. Conrad, Dienstzeit, 5:67; ÖULK, 1:393.

52. ÖULK, 1:386, 391, 387–388.

53. ÖULK, 1:384, 390–391.

54. ÖULK, 1:386.

55. Conrad, Dienstzeit, 5:89.

56. Conrad, Dienstzeit, 5:67ff., 384, 387, 398; ÖULK, 1:387–391; KA NL, B/1041, Bornemann, "Przemyśl."

57. Conrad, Dienstzeit, 5:72, 90, 92, Op. Nr. 3076; ÖULK, vol. 1.

58. Conrad, Dienstzeit, 5:67; ÖULK, 1:384, 385.

59. Conrad, Dienstzeit, 5:102; ÖULK, 1:399.

60. RAWK, 5:458ff.; ÖULK, 1:385.

61. ÖULK, 1:419.

62. Forstner, Przemyśl, 198.

63. Conrad, Dienstzeit, 5:65ff.

64. Conrad, Dienstzeit, 5:100.

65. ÖULK, 1:425–427.

66. ÖULK, 1:406.

67. Conrad, Dienstzeit, 5:86, 100; ÖULK, 1:400, 407.

68. Conrad, Dienstzeit, 5:98–100, 107; ÖULK, 1:408.

69. ÖULK, 1:420; KA MKSM, Separate fasz. 100, Op. Nr. 1375, 4/3, 1915, 69/6-13; Conrad, Dienstzeit, 5: 90, AOK Op. Nr. 3092.

70. Heiden, Bollwerk am San, 153.

71. AOK Op. Nr. 2992.

72. KA NL, B/1137, Nr. 2, Kusmanek, "Festung Przemyśl"; KA Ms. 1 Wkg, Russland, 1914, Nr. 19, Stuckheil, "Festung Przemyśl."

73. KA Ms. 1 Wkg, Russland, 1914, Nr. 19, Stuckheil, "Festung Przemyśl," chap. 6.

74. KA Ms. 1 Wkg, Russland, 1914, Nr. 19, Stuckheil, "Festung Przemyśl," chap. 6; KA Ms. 1 Wkg, Russland, 1915, Nr. 6, Joly, "Der Winterfeldzug in Polen und Galizien."

75. KA Ms. 1 Wkg, Russland, 1914, Nr. 19, Stuckheil, "Festung Przemyśl;" see KA AOK, fasz. 523, Festung Przemyśl, AOK Op. Nr. 3852 for slightly different numbers.

76. KA MKSM, Separate fasz. 100, Op. Nr. 1375; MKSM 69-6/3, k.u.k. AOK Auszug aus dem Memoir über die Versorgung Festung Przemyśl.

77. KA MKSM, Separate fasz. 100, Op. Nr. 1375, MKSM 69-6/3, k.u.k. AOK Auszug aus dem Memoir über die Versorgung Festung Przemyśl.

78. KA NL, B/1137, Nr. 2, Kusmanek, "Festung Przemyśl"; Forstner, Przemyśl, 199.

79. Anton Pitreich, Der österreich-ungarisch Bundesgenose in Sperrfeuer (Klagenfurt: Arthur Killitsch, 1930), 141.

80. Pitreich, Der österreich-ungarisch Bundesgenose in Sperrfeuer; KA AOK, fasz. 523, Festung Przemyśl, AOK Op. Nr. 3852.

81. KA NL, B/1137, Nr. 2, Kusmanek, "Festung Przemyśl"; KA Ms. 1 Wkg, Russland, 1914, Nr. 19, Stuckheil, "Festung Przemyśl," and articles cited in chapter 1, note 2. See also Conrad, Dienstzeit, vol. 5.

82. Conrad, Dienstzeit, 5:97, 98–99, 100, Op. Nr. 3205.

83. *ÖULK*, 1:417.

84. KA NL, B/1137, Nr. 2, Kusmanek, "Festung Przemyśl"; KA Ms. 1 Wkg, Russland, 1914, Nr. 19, Stuckheil, "Festung Przemyśl," Ms. Przemyśl and articles by Stuckheil cited in chapter 1, note 2.

85. Conrad, *Dienstzeit*, 5:131, 199, Tagebuch, Op. Nr. 3247; k.u.k. Armee Ober Kommando, Nachtrichtenabteilung K/r Nr. 1198.

86. Conrad, *Dienstzeit*, 5:98.

87. It had been blown up on September 19.

88. *ÖULK*, 1:443.

89. Conrad, *Dienstzeit*, 5:170, 180, 185; *ÖULK*, 1:425–427, 430, 443; Forstner, *Przemyśl*, 190.

90. Conrad, *Dienstzeit*, 5:215; Rudolph Hecht, "Fragen zur Heeresergänzung der Gestalten Bewaffneten Macht Österreich-Ungarns während des ersten Weltkriegs" (dissertation, University of Vienna, 1969); Stone, *Eastern Front*; Manfried Rauchensteiner, *Der Erste Weltkrieg und das Ende der Habsburgermonarchie 1914–1918* (Vienna: Böhlau Verlag, 2013).

91. *ÖULK*, 1:443, 450.

92. Conrad, *Dienstzeit*, 5:176, Op. Nr. 3365, 180.

93. Also on that date, the first article appeared in the Vienna *Neue Freie Presse* from the reporter Roda Roda, entitled "Die Erste Belagerung Przemśyl."

94. *RAWK*, 7:35, 489.

95. *RAWK*, 7:431, 485.

96. Conrad, *Dienstzeit*, 5:460, 463.

97. *ÖULK*, 1:191–192.

98. Conrad, *Dienstzeit*, 5:244, 249ff., 490; *RAWK*, 7:489, 490.

99. Conrad, *Dienstzeit*, 5:457–460, 452–454.

100. Conrad, *Dienstzeit*, 5:254, 191.

101. *ÖULK*, 1:470, 490–491.

102. *ÖULK*, 1:481.

103. *ÖULK*, 1:192.

104. *ÖULK*, 1:192–193; *RAWK*, 1:316.

105. *ÖULK*, 1:491.

106. Conrad, *Dienstzeit*, 5:341.

4. THE SECOND SIEGE, NOVEMBER 1914

1. Rauchensteiner, *Der Tod des Doppeladlers*, 188.

2. Conrad, *Dienstzeit*, 5:498–499.

3. KA AOK, Op. Nr. 3834; see Conrad, *Dienstzeit*, 5:357.

4. *ÖULK*, 1:482.

5. Conrad, *Dienstzeit*, 5:352, 367, 370, 381; Herwig, *First World War*.

6. KA AOK, fasz. 523, Fortress Przemyśl (4 November), Op. Nr. 153/1.

7. *ÖULK*, 1:502.

8. KA AOK, Op. Nr. 3696; Conrad, *Dienstzeit*, 5:362, 501.

9. KA AOK, Kdo. Op. Nr. 3854.

10. *ÖULK*, 1:483.

11. *ÖULK*, vol. 1.

12. Conrad, *Dienstzeit*, 5:379; KA NL, B/800, Rudolf Kiszling, "Die k.u.k. 2. Armee von 10 November 1914 bis zum Jahresschluss" (hereafter cited as KA NL, B/800, Kiszling, "Die k.u.k. 2. Armee").

13. Conrad, *Dienstzeit*, 5:379, AOK Op. Nr. 3903.

14. *Chudenitz*, 18–19, 21–22, 32, 35–36, 38, 42; see Herwig, *First World War*.

15. Conrad, *Dienstzeit*, 5:364–365.

16. KA, Übersetzung Nordost, Nr. 14, "Sturm," Tscherkassow; ÖULK, 1:514; Herwig, *First World War*, 193.

17. KA NL, B/1137/14, Kusmanek, "Festung Przemyśl"; Heiden, *Bollwerk am San*, 145; Rudolf Völker, *Przemyśl: Sieg und Untergang der Festung am San* (Vienna: Tyrolia 1927), 126; Herwig, *First World War*, 201–202.

18. KA MKSM, Separate fasz. 100, Reserve Nr. 1956; KA Ms. 1 Wkg, Russland, 1914, Nr. 19, Stuckheil, "Festung Przemyśl"; Stuckheil, "Die zweite Einschliessung der Festung Przemyśl III," MTM 57 (1926): 170–172.

19. KA NL, B/1137, Nr. 2, Kusmanek, "Festung Przemyśl"; KA Ms. 1 Wkg, Russland, 1914, Nr. 19, Stuckheil, "Festung Przemyśl"; Stuckheil, "Die zweite Einschliessung der Festung Przemyśl III," 171.

20. Conrad, *Dienstzeit*, 5:363.

21. The 23rd Honvéd Infantry Division contained 11,200 of the combat troops. Conrad, *Dienstzeit*, 5:385.

22. Conrad, *Dienstzeit*, 5:359, 382, 392ff., 503; RAWK, 7:38; ÖULK, vol. 1.

23. Herwig, *First World War*, 108.

24. Conrad, *Dienstzeit*, 5:362, 371, KA AOK, Op. Nr. 3696.

25. Conrad, *Dienstzeit*, 5:385, 392.

26. KA NL, B/1137, Nr. 2, Kusmanek, "Festung Przemyśl"; KA MKSM, fasz. 100, AOK Op. Nr. 1956; KA Ms. 1 Wkg, Russland, 1914, Nr. 19, Stuckheil, "Festung Przemyśl."

27. Conrad, *Dienstzeit*, vol. 5, AOK Op. Nr. 3950.

28. KA NL, B/1137, Nr. 2, Kusmanek, "Festung Przemyśl"; KA Ms. 1 Wkg, Russland, 1914, Nr. 19, Stuckheil, "Festung Przemyśl."

29. KA, Übersetzung Nordost, No. 14, "Sturm," Tscherkassow; ÖULK, 1:514; Herwig, *First World War*, 193.

30. KA, Luftfahrte Archiv, Ms. 72, "Als Flieger in Przemyśl," Oberst Feldpilot Nikolaus Wagner Edler von Florhein (hereafter cited as KA LU, Ms. 72, "Als Flieger in Przemyśl").

31. KA LU, Ms. 72, "Als Flieger in Przemyśl."

32. KA LU, Ms. 72, "Als Flieger in Przemyśl."

33. Conrad, *Dienstzeit*, 5:404, 415, 565.

34. ÖULK, vol. 1; KA Ms. 1 Wkg, Russland, 1914, Nr. 19, Stuckheil, "Festung Przemyśl"; KA NL, B/800, Kiszling, "Die k.u.k. 2 Armee."

35. The Second Army units still to be utilized in the Carpathian Mountains included VII Corps (17th and 34th Infantry Divisions), the 20th and 38th Honvéd Infantry Divisions, the 103rd Landsturm Infantry Brigade and the 1st, 2nd, and 17th Landsturm Territorial Brigades, as well as the 1st, 5th, and 8th Cavalry Divisions.

36. A. Pitreich, *Der österreich-ungarische Bundesgenosse im Speerfeuer*, 5; Conrad, *Dienstzeit*, vol. 5.

37. Conrad, *Dienstzeit*, 5:352. Brigade troop numbers were less than a fully manned regiment.

38. Conrad, *Dienstzeit*, 5:536, 564; KA Ms. 1 Wkg, Russland, 1914, Stuckheil, "Festung Przemyśl"; Rauchensteiner, *Der Tod des Doppeladler*, 199.

39. Conrad, *Dienstzeit*, 5:506.

40. ÖULK, 1:565.

41. Conrad, *Dienstzeit*, 5:413, 414, 416, 418.

42. Conrad, *Dienstzeit*, 5:407; KA NL, B/800, Kiszling, Die k.u.k. 2 Armee.

43. Conrad, *Dienstzeit*, 5:411, 418.

44. KA AOK, Eigene Evidenz russichen Meldungen and Nachrichten, 11/9, Op. Nr. 4082/2; AOK, fasz. 523, Festung Przemyśl, Op. Nr. 100/12; Forstner, *Przemyśl*.

45. Conrad, *Dienstzeit*, 5:418; AOK Op. Nr. 4045.

46. Conrad, *Dienstzeit*, 5:536, 564.

47. KA LU, Ms. 72, "Als Flieger in Przemyśl," 138.

48. Conrad, *Dienstzeit*, 5:443, daily report of November 9, AOK Op. Nrn. 4104, Heiden, *Bollwerk am San*, 153, 197.

49. Conrad, *Dienstzeit*, 5:566.

50. Conrad, *Dienstzeit*, 5:564; Forstner, *Przemyśl*, 205–207.

51. KA NL, B/1137, Nr. 2, Kusmanek, "Festung Przemyśl"; KA Ms. 1 Wkg, Russland, 1914, Nr. 19, Stuckheil, "Festung Przemyśl"; ÖULK, vol. 2; Forstner, *Przemyśl*; see KA AOK, fasz. 523, Festung Przemyśl, AOK Op. Nr. 7960, December 3.

52. Michaelsburg, *Im belagerten Przemyśl*, 59–61.

53. Conrad, 5:511; ÖULK, vol. 1.

54. Conrad, *Dienstzeit*, 5:442.

55. Conrad, *Dienstzeit*, 5:566, 567; ÖULK, vol. 1.

56. Conrad, *Dienstzeit*, vol. 5, AOK Op. Nr. 4097, 448; KA NL, B/800, Kiszling, "Die k.u.k. 2 Armee".

57. Conrad, *Dienstzeit*, 5:452; RAWK, 6:232.

58. ÖULK, 1:508–519.

59. ÖULK, 1:509–510, 512.

60. KA Ms. 1 Wkg, Russland, 1914, Nr. 19, Stuckeil, "Festung Przemyśl," 208; Heiden, *Bollwerk am San*, 158; Conrad, *Dienstzeit*, 5:449, 477.

61. Conrad, *Dienstzeit*, 5:451, 458–460, 477; ÖULK, vol. 1.

62. Conrad, *Dienstzeit*, 5:449, 477, 3. Armee, Op. Nr. 1705, AOK Op. Nr. 4209.

63. KA AOK, Eigene Evidenz R und Nachrichten, November 12, AOK Op. Nr. 4160; Conrad, *Dienstzeit*, 5:517, 567.

64. ÖULK, 1:513.

65. Conrad, *Dienstzeit*, 5:442, 470, 471, 498; KA Ms. 1 Wkg, Russland, 1914, Nr. 19, Stuckheil, "Festung Przemyśl."

66. KA Ms. 1 Wkg, Russland, 1914, Nr. 19, Stuckheil, "Festung Przemyśl"; Stuckheil, "Ausrüstungszeit," 206–209; KA NL, B/1137, Nr. 2, Kusmanek, "Festung Przemyśl"; Conrad, *Dienstzeit*, 5:497, 503; KA AOK, fasz. 523, Festung Przemyśl, Op. Nr. 103.

67. Michaelsburg, *Im belagerten Przemyśl*, 64–65.

68. KA Ms. 1 Wkg, Russland, 1914, Nr. 19, Stuckheil, "Festung Przemyśl."

69. See RAWK, vol. 7; Conrad, *Dienstzeit*, 5:517, 567.

70. Conrad, *Dienstzeit*, 5:478, 484; ÖULK, 1:519–520, 2:40.

71. Conrad, *Dienstzeit*, 5:506, AOK Op. Nr. 4353.

72. Conrad, *Dienstzeit*, 5:569; ÖULK, vol. 2.

73. Stone, *Eastern Front*; see RAWK.

74. Conrad, *Dienstzeit*, 5:506, 514–516, 518–519, 520, 524, see p. 534, AOK Op. Nrn. 4353, 4385, 4632; ÖULK, vol. 2.

75. Conrad, *Dienstzeit*, 5:543.

76. KA AOK, Op. Nrn. 4438, 4536, 4539.

77. Conrad, *Dienstzeit*, vol. 5, AOK Op. Nr. 4472, 551–553; see ÖULK, vols. 1, 2.

78. Heiden, *Bollwerk am San,* 209; see KA Ms. 1 Wkg, Russland, 1914, Nr. 19, Stuckheil, "Festung Przemyśl."

79. Heiden, *Bollwerk am San,* 201.

80. Michaelsburg, *Im belagerten Przemyśl;* KA Ms. 1 Wkg, Russland, 1914, Nr. 19, Stuckheil, "Festung Przemyśl."

81. Conrad, *Dienstzeit,* 5:57ff.

82. KA Ms. 1 Wkg, Russland, 1914, Nr. 19, Stuckheil, "Festung Przemyśl," 395–396; Conrad, *Dienstzeit,* 5:574.

83. Conrad, *Dienstzeit,* 5:580.

84. Conrad, *Dienstzeit,* 5:580–581. The 20th Honvéd, the 17th, most of the 28th, and a portion of the 22nd Infantry Division, as well as the 105th Landsturm Infantry Brigade.

85. Conrad, *Dienstzeit,* 5:520; see ÖULK, vol. 2.

86. Conrad, *Dienstzeit,* 5:511, 589, 597–598, AOK Op. Nr. 4662: see KA AOK, fasz. 512, Conrad-Falkenhayn Korrespondenz, Russland.

87. Conrad, *Dienstzeit,* 5:600, 602–603; see ÖULK, 1:585.

88. Conrad, *Dienstzeit,* 5:616, 617.

89. KA AOK, Op. Büro, fasz. 14, k.u.k. Infantrie Regiment 74, III Corps, Nr. 10, Reserve, AOK Op. Nr. 5761.

90. Conrad, *Dienstzeit,* 5:586.

91. Conrad, *Dienstzeit,* 5:587–588; ÖULK, vol. 1.

92. Conrad, *Dienstzeit,* 5:638–639; AOK Op. Nr. 4040; KA Ms. 1 Wkg, Russland, 1914, Nr. 19, Stuckheil, "Festung Przemyśl." Honvéd Infantry Regiment 8 also participated in the sortie.

93. ÖULK, vol. 1.

5. LIMANOVA-LAPANOV AND DEFEAT, DECEMBER 1914

1. It proved to be a catastrophe that almost all M 80 15-centimeter howitzer and field cannon M 75/96 9-centimeter guns had to stop firing during December. Field cannon M 05 8-centimeter shells had to be reserved for enemy attacks. During the first siege large numbers of short-range shells were utilized against the tsarist storm attacks, then long-range shells and field artillery for the numerous garrison sorties.

2. KA Ms 1. Wkg, Russland, 1914, Nr. 19, Stuckheil, "Festung Przemyśl"; Forstner, *Przemyśl,* 246.

3. KA NL, B/54, Pitreich.

4. AOK, Evidenz der eigenen Situation 1915 "R" 1914, *Nachrichten, Kriegsnachrichten, k.u.k. Festungskommdo.* 1914 and 1915; KA AOK, Op. Nr. 4840/8.

5. Their exchanges can be found in KA AOK, fasz. 512, Conrad-Falkenhayn Korrespondenz, Russland.

6. ÖULK, 1:814–815; Conrad, *Dienstzeit,* 5:682.

7. ÖULK, 1:814–818.

8. KA, Übersetzung Nordost, Nr. 3.

9. RAWK, 6:302.

10. Conrad, Dienstzeit, 5:697; ÖULK, 1:786.

11. KA NL, B/509, Schneller, Nr. 2: Kriegstagebuch; Conrad, Dienstzeit, 5:786.

12. Conrad, Dienstzeit, 5:789; ÖULK, vol. 2.

13. ÖULK, 1:803; 2:41.

14. Conrad, Dienstzeit, 5: 791; ÖULK, 1:791, 805; KA NL, B/509, Schneller, Tagebücher.

15. Conrad, Dienstzeit, 5:746–782, AOK Op. Nrn. 5299, 5338.

16. Conrad, Dienstzeit, 5:792; KA NL, B/509, Schneller, Tagebücher.

17. ÖULK, 2:33.

18. Emil Ratzenhofer, "Die Aufmarsch hinter den Karpaten im Winter 1915," Militärgeschichtliche Mitteilungen, 61 (1930), 498.

19. Rauchensteiner, Der Tod des Doppeladlers, 182–183.

20. ÖULK, 2:34.

21. Conrad, Dienstzeit, 5:722, 754ff.; RAWK, 6:406.

22. Conrad, Dienstzeit, 5:754ff., 722.

23. RAWK, 6:406ff.

24. KA Ms 1. Wkg, Russland, 1914, Nr. 19, Stuckheil, "Festung Przemyśl," 197.

25. KA AOK, Op. Nr. 5303.

26. KA Ms 1. Wkg, Russland, 1914, Stuckheil, "Festung Przemyśl," 116, 121; Forstner, Przemyśl, 213; KA AOK, fasz. 523, "Festung Przemyśl."

27. KA MKSM, Separate fasz. 100, AOK Op. Nr. 1856; KA AOK, fasz. 523, "Festung Przemyśl," Op. Nr. 139/9; ÖULK, vol. 2; KA Ms 1. Wkg, Russland, 1914, Nr. 19, Stuckheil, "Festung Przemyśl"; KA NL, B/1137, Nr. 2, Kusmanek, "Festung Przemyśl"; Forstner, Przemyśl, 216.

28. RAWK, 6:310; Conrad, Dienstzeit, 5:809, 817, 819.

29. Herwig, First World War, 119–120, 145.

30. Conrad, Dienstzeit, 5:861; Heiden, Bollwerk am San, 195; Forstner, Przemyśl, 216–217; Rauchensteiner, Der Tod des Doppeladlers, 200.

31. KA Ms 1. Wkg, Russland, 1914, Nr. 19, Stuckheil, "Festung Przemyśl," 288; ÖULK, VOL. 2; Rauchensteiner, Der Tod des Doppeladlers, 183; Forstner, Przemyśl, 216.

32. ÖULK, 2:58; KA NL, B/509, Schneller, Tagebücher; KA Ms 1. Wkg, Russland, 1914, Nr. 19, Stuckheil, "Festung Przemyśl," 225; Forstner, Przemyśl, 211; Rauchensteiner, Der Tod des Doppeladlers, 183.

33. ÖULK, vol. 2; KA NL, B/509, Schneller, Tagebücher. That number represented two-thirds of a full division complement.

34. Wolfgang, Przemyśl 1914–1915.

35. Michaelsburg, Im belagerten Przemyśl, 95.

36. KA Ms 1. Wkg, Russland, 1914, Nr. 19, Stuckheil, "Festung Przemyśl"; Stuckheil, "Die zweite Einschliessung der Festung Przemyśl III," 227; Forstner, Przemyśl; Wolfgang, Przemyśl 1914–1915, 114; Forstner, Przemyśl, 214, 217.

37. KA NL, B/1137, Nr. 2, Kusmanek, "Festung Przemyśl"; KA Ms 1. Wkg, Russland, 1914, Nr. 19, Stuckheil, "Festung Przemyśl," 227; Forstner, Przemyśl.

38. Michaelsburg, Im belagerten Przemyśl, 99.

39. KA NL, B/509, Schneller, Tagebücher; Conrad, Dienstzeit, 5:927; KA AOK, fasz. 615, Tagesberichte/Kaiserberichte Anfang Jänner bis Ende Juni.

40. KA Ms 1. Wkg, Russland, 1914, Nr. 19; Stuckheil, "Festung Przemyśl," 357; Forstner, *Przemyśl*, 214–215; ÖULK, 2: 68.

41. KA Ms 1. Wkg, Russland, 1914, Nr. 19, Stuckheil, "Festung Przemyśl," 356.

42. Second Army units had been redeployed from the Carpathian Mountain theater to the German front to fill a 180-kilometer gap in the lines and to defend industrial Silesia during November.

43. AOK, Op. Nr. 5771.

44. KA Neue Feld Akten (hereafter NFA), fasz. 42, 3. Op. Armee Kdo., Tagebücher.

6. THE FIRST TWO CARPATHIAN MOUNTAIN OFFENSIVES, JANUARY TO MID-MARCH 1915

1. KA, Übersetzung Nordost, Nr. 14, "Sturm," Tscherkassow.

2. KA AOK, fasz. 512, Conrad-Falkenhayn Korrespondenz, Russland.

3. Keith Tranmer, *Austro-Hungarian A.P.O.'s, 1914–1918*, rev. ed. (Hornchurch: Keith Tranmer, 1973), 9.

4. Michaelsburg, *Im belagerten Przemyśl*, 99–101.

5. Michaelsburg, *Im belagerten Przemyśl*, 103–104.

6. Forstner, *Przemyśl*.

7. Franz Czernin von Chudenitz, *Das Postwesen in der ÖU. Festung Przemyśl Während der Beiden Belagerungen, 1914–1915*, (Viena: Selbstverlag, 1985).

8. Tranmer, *Austro-Hungarian A.P.O.'s*.

9. KA AOK, fasz. 512, Conrad-Falkenhyn Korrespondenz, Russland, Op. Nr. 4840; Op. Nr. 6127 Auf Nr. 4801.

10. KA AOK, fasz. 512, Conrad-Falkenhayn Korrespondenz, Russland, various; Hermann Wendt, *Der italienische Kriegschauplatz in europäischen Konflikten: Seine Bedeutung für die Kriegführung an Frankreichs Nordostgrenze* (Berlin: Junker und Dunnhaupt Verlag, 1936).

11. See figures on the percentage of Ruthenian troops in the introduction and notes.

12. Michaelsburg, *Im belagerten Przemyśl*, 104–106.

13. KA AC, B/13, Kundmann Tagebücher.

14. ÖULK, vol. 2; Rauchensteiner, *Der Tod des Doppeladlers*; see Tunstall, *Blood on the Snow*, for the details of the three Carpathian Mountain offensives.

15. Michaelsburg, *Im belagerten Przemyśl*, 108.

16. Michaelsburg, *Im belagerten Przemyśl*, 111–112.

17. KA Ms 1. Wkg, Russland, 1914, Nr. 19, Stuckheil, "Festung Przemyśl," 74.

18. See Tunstall, *Blood on the Snow*, for details.

19. KA AOK, Op. Nrn. 2543, 2537, 2531/25, 2560, 2560/4.

20. Michaelsburg, *Im belagerten Przemyśl*, 112–115.

21. See Tunstall, *Blood on the Snow*.

22. KA AOK, Op. Nr. 2560/4, 7; KA NFA, fasz. K 1812, X Corps, Op. Nr. 347/1.

23. KA AOK, fasz. 615, Ober Kommando Tagebücher.

24. Tranmer, *Austro-Hungarian A.P.O.'s*, 56.

25. KA AOK, Op. Nr. 2575; KA NFA, 3. Armee, fasz. 42, Tagebücher, Op. Nrn. 2575, 3082; KA NL, B/240, Nr. 3, Fiedler.

26. KA NFA, 3. Armee, Op. Nr. 3019 op.; KA NL, B/240, Nr. 1, 42; KA NL, B/509, Schneller, Tagebücher.

27. KA AOK, Op. Nr. 6804.

28. AOK, Etappen Oberkommando, Op. Nr. 21773; Tranmer, *Austro-Hungarian A.P.O.'s*.

29. Istvan Lagzi, ed., *Wegrzy w Twierdzy Przemyskiej w latoch 1914–1915* (Przemyśl: Wegierski Instytut Kuttury-Muzeum Narodowe Ziemi Przemyślu, 1985), 144.

30. Forstner, *Przemyśl*, 233, footnotes 64, 65.

31. Michaelsburg, *Im belagerten Przemyśl*, 115.

32. ÖULK, vol. 2; KA NFA, VII Korps, Op. Nr. 516/6, 30.

33. KA, NFA, 3. Armee, fasz. 42, Tagebücher, 3. Armee Auf Op. Nr. 3106, AOK, Op. Nr. 6850; ÖULK, 2:138.

34. ÖULK, vol. 2; KA NFA, 3. Armee, fasz. 42, Tagebücher, 3. Armee Op. Nrn. 3096, 3107.

35. KA NFA, 3. Armee, Op. Nr. 3242; VII Korps, 784/32 (Standabgänge), Infantrieregiment 81 and 88.

36. KA NFA, 20, Infantrie Division, Op. Nr. 44/18.

37. KA AOK, fasz. 615, Ober Kommando Tagebücher; KA NFA, 3. Armee, fasz. 42, Tagebücher; 4. Armee, fasz. 70, Tagebücher.

38. KA NFA, 3. Armee, fasz. 42, Tagebücher, Zu Op. Nr. 309, 2600/7; see ÖULK, vol. 2.

39. KA NFA, 3. Armee, fasz. 42, Tagebücher, Op. Nr. 3088, AOK, Op. Nr. 6804; KA NFA, 3 Armee, fasz. 13, Op. Nr. 3151; KA AOK, Op. Nr. 6804, 3. Armee Op. Nrn. 2500/2, 2501/1.

40. KA NFA, 3. Armee, Op. Nr. 2597, 2597/II; ÖULK, vol. 2.

41. KA AOK, fasz. 501, AOK, Op. Nrn. 6904, 6898.

42. KA AOK, fasz. 501; AOK, Op. Nrn. 6898, 6904; KA NFA, 3. Armee, fasz. 42, Tagebücher; Lagzi, *Wegrzy w Twierdzy Przemyskiej*, 145–146.

43. KA NFA, VII Korps, Op. Nr. 781/33; 3. Armee Op. Nrn. 3171, 3173; AOK, Op. Nr. 6946.

44. KA NFA, 3. Armee, Op. Nrn. 2597, 3128, 3082.

45. KA NFA, 4. Armee, Op. Nr. 2597; AOK, fasz. 615, Armee Ober Kommando Tagebücher; AOK, Op. Nrn. 6915, 6946.

46. KA Ms. 1 Wkg, Russland, 1914, Nr. 19, Stuckheil, "Festung Przemyśl," 75; Lagzi, *Wegrzy w Twierdzy Przemyskiej*, 146.

47. Michaelsburg, *Im belagerten Przemyśl*, 116.

48. Michaelsburg, *Im belagerten Przemyśl*, 116–117.

49. Michaelsburg, *Im belagerten Przemyśl*, 118.

50. Michaelsburg, *Im belagerten Przemyśl*, 118, 119–120.

51. KA AOK, Op. Nrn. 6946, 6986; 3. Armee Op. Nrn. 3,173, 3,190; KA NFA, 20. Infantrie Division, Op. Nr. 44/18; Forstner, *Przemyśl*, 234.

52. KA AOK, Op. Nr. 7095; Heiden, *Bollwerk am San*, 234–235.

53. Lagzi, *Wegrzy w Twierdzy Przemyskiej*, 147.

54. KA NFA, VII Korps, 17. Infantrie Division, Tagebücher.

55. KA MKSM, Separate fasz. 100, Reserve Nr. 1956.

56. KA Ms. 1 Wkg, Russland, 1914, Nr. 19, Stuckheil, "Festung Przemyśl," 62.

57. Michaelsburg, *Im belagerten Przemyśl*, 120–121.

58. Lagzi, *Wegrzy w Twierdzy Przemyskiej*, 150.

59. KA Ms. 1 Wkg, Russland, 1914, Nr. 19, Stuckheil, "Festung Przemyśl," 77–78.

60. Michaelsburg, *Im belagerten Przemyśl*, 121.

61. Michaelsburg, *Im belagerten Przemyśl*, 121–122; Forstner, *Przemyśl*, 234.

62. KA AOK, Evidenzbüro, Eigene Op. Nr. 7840; KA AOK, Op. Nrn. 7250/2, 17, and 7310/2, 7340/15.

63. KA Ms. 1 Wkg, Russland, 1914, Nr. 19, Stuckheil, "Festung Przemyśl," 72–73.

64. Michaelsburg, *Im belagerten Przemyśl*, 125.

65. Lagzi, *Wegrzy w Twierdzy Przemyskiej*, 151.

7. THE THIRD CARPATHIAN MOUNTAIN OFFENSIVE, EARLY MARCH 1915

1. KA NL, B/1137, Nr. 2, Kusmanek, "Festung Przemyśl."

2. *ÖULK*, 2:203.

3. KA, Op. Nr. 2917.

4. Michaelsburg, *Im belagerten Przemyśl*, 129–132.

5. KA AOK, fasz. 523, Festung Przemyśl, AOK Op. Nr. 7810.

6. Tunstall, *Blood on the Snow*.

7. Allgemeine, A4, Veith, "Werdigang und Untergang"; Forstner, *Przemyśl*, 243; Michaelsburg, *Im belagerten Przemyśl*, 244.

8. Michaelsburg, *Im belagerten Przemyśl*, 129.

9. KA AOK, fasz. 523, Festung Przemyśl, AOK Op. Nrn. 7800, 7008/1, 7690.

10. Tunstall, *Blood on the Snow*.

11. KA AOK, fasz. 523, Festung Przemyśl, AOK Op. Nr. 7810.

12. KA NFA, 2. Armee, fasz. 95, Tagebücher.

13. KA AOK, fasz. 523, Festung Przemyśl, AOK Op. Nr. 7810.

14. KA AOK, fasz. 523, Festung Przemyśl, AOK Op. Nr. 7810, Festung Op. Nr. 230/5.

15. Forstner, *Przemyśl*, 242.

16. Tunstall, *Blood on the Snow*, 159–160, 192.

17. Stone, *Eastern Front*.

18. Lagzi, *Wegrzy w Twierdzy Przemskiej*, 159–160.

19. Michaelsburg, *Im belagerten Przemyśl*, 132.

20. Brusilov, *A Soldier's Notebook*, 96.

21. KA AOK, fasz. 523, Festung Przemyśl, AOK Op. Nrn. 7810, 8008, 2. Armee Op. Nr. 226/10.

22. Michaelsburg, *Im belagerten Przemyśl*, 133.

23. KA AOK, fasz. 523, Festung Przemyśl, Op. Nr. 226/10, AOK Op. Nr. 8008.

24. Michaelsburg, *Im belagerten Przemyśl*, 135.

25. KA Ms. 1 Wkg, Russland, 1914, Nr. 1, "Die k.u.k. 2. Armee in der Karpatenschlacht 1914/15," Karl Mayern (hereinafter cited as Mayern, "Armee in der Karpatenschlacht 1914/15); Forstner, *Przemyśl*, 224–246.

26. KA Ms. 1 Wkg, Russland, 1914, Nr. 19, Stuckheil, "Festung Przemyśl."

27. KA AOK, fasz. 523, Festung Przemyśl, Op. Nr. 226/10, AOK Op. Nr. 8008.

28. KA Ms. 1 Wkg, Russland, 1914, Nr. 19, Stuckheil, "Festung Przemyśl"; KA Ms. 1 Wkg, Russland, 1914, Nr. 1, Mayern, "Armee in der Karpatenschlacht 1914/15," 338, 358, 360; see, *ÖULK*, vol. 2; Op. Nr. 2051.

29. Michaelsburg, *Im belagerten Przemyśl*; KA Ms. 1 Wkg, Russland, 1914, Nr. 19, Stuckheil, "Festung Przemyśl"; KA NL, B/1137, Nr. 2, Kusmanek, "Festung Przemyśl"; Forstner, *Przemyśl*.

30. Tranmer, *Austro-Hungarian A.P.O.'s*, 51.

31. KA AOK, fasz. 523, Festung Przemyśl, Op. Nr. 230/5.

32. KA AOK, fasz. 523, Festung Przemyśl, Op. Nr. 229/11; KA Ms. 1 Wkg, Russland, 1914, Nr. 19, Stuckheil, "Festung Przemyśl"; Tunstall, *Blood on the Snow.*

33. KA AC, B/13, Kundmann Tagebuch; Tunstall, *Blood on the Snow,* for a detailed description.

34. KA Ms. 1 Wkg, Russland, 1914, Nr. 1, Mayern, "Armee in der Karpatenschlacht 1914/15"; KA NFA, 2. Armee, fasz. 95, Tagebücher; KA Ms. 1 Wkg, Russland, 1914, Nr. 19, Stuckheil, "Festung Przemyśl."

35. KA, AOK, Op. Nr. 8057 (R1678); KA AOK, fasz. 523, Festung Przemyśl, AOK Op. Nr. 8080; Tunstall, *Blood on the Snow.*

36. KA AOK, fasz. 523, "Festung Przemyśl," Op. Nr. 230/5; KA Ms. 1 Wkg, Russland, 1914, Nr. 19, Stuckheil, "Festung Przemyśl"; Forstner, *Przemyśl.*

37. KA AOK, Op. Nr. 8679; KA NFA, 2. Armee fasz. 42, 95, 2 *Armee* Op. Nrn. 2066, 2067; KA Ms. 1 Wkg, Russland, 1914, Nr. 1, Mayern, "Armee in der Karpatenschlacht 1914/15," 360.

38. KA AOK, fasz. 523, "Festung Przemyśl," AOK Op. Nr. 8080.

39. AOK Op. Nr. 8080 (R 1685); KA Ms. 1 Wkg, Russland, 1914, Nr. 1, Mayern, "Armee in der Karpatenschlacht 1914/15," 360.

40. Michaelsburg, *Im belagerten Przemyśl,* 135-136.

41. KA Ms. 1 Wkg, Russland, 1914, Nr. 1, Mayern, "Armee in der Karpatenschlacht 1914/15"; Tunstall, *Blood on the Snow.*

42. KA Ms. 1 Wkg, Russland, 1914, Nr. 19, Stuckheil, "Festung Przemyśl," 409; Forstner, *Przemyśl.*

43. Michaelsburg, *Im belagerten Przemyśl,* 141-142.

44. Wolfgang, *Przemyśl 1914-1915,* 152, 159; Michaelsburg, *Im belagerten Przemyśl,* 137.

45. Heiden, *Bollwerk am San.*

46. KA AOK, fasz. 523, "Festung Przemyśl," Op. Nr. 230/5 (AOK Op. Nr. 8165); KA Ms. 1 Wkg, Russland, 1914, Nr. 19, Stuckheil, "Festung Przemyśl"; Forstner, *Przemyśl.*

47. KA NL, B/1137, Nr. 2, Kusmanek, "Festung Przemyśl."

48. KA AOK, fasz. 523, "Festung Przemyśl," Op. Nr. 231/13; see ÖULK, vol. 2.

49. See Tunstall, *Blood on the Snow.*

50. KA Ms. 1 Wkg, Russland, 1914, Nr. 19, Stuckheil, "Festung Przemyśl"; Forstner, *Przemyśl.*

51. Michaelsburg, *Im belagerten Przemyśl,* 133, 136.

8. BREAKTHROUGH ATTEMPT AND SURRENDER OF THE FORTRESS, MARCH 1915

1. Bruno Proschaska, *Przemyśl 1914/15* (Vienna: Kommanditgesellschaft Payer & Co, 1935); Heiden, *Bollwerk am San,* 246-247; Wolfgang, *Przemyśl 1914-1915.*

2. Proschaska, *Przemyśl,* 70; Wolfgang, *Przemyśl 1914-1915.*

3. KA Ms. 1 Wkg, Russland, 1914, Nr. 19, Stuckheil, "Festung Przemyśl"; Proschaska, *Przemyśl;* Wolfgang, *Przemyśl 1914-1915.*

4. Proschaska, *Przemyśl,* 70; Wolfgang, *Przemyśl 1914-1915.*

5. KA Ms. 1 Wkg, Russland, 1914, Nr. 19, Stuckheil, "Festung Przemyśl."

6. Heiden, *Bollwerk am San,* 244.

7. KA Ms. 1 Wkg, Russland, 1914, Stuckheil, "Festung Przemyśl," 15–18; Wolfgang, *Przemyśl 1914–1915*, 152, 159; Heiden, *Bollwerk am San*, 226.

8. KA AOK, fasz. 523, Festung Przemyśl, AOK Op. Nr. 8205; see KA NL, B/1137, Nr. 2, Kusmanek, "Festung Przemyśl."

9. KA Ms. 1 Wkg, Russland, 1914, Stuckheil, "Festung Przemyśl"; KA NL, B/1137, Nr. 2, Kusmanek, "Festung Przemyśl."

10. Heiden, *Bollwerk am San*, 249.

11. KA AOK, fasz. 523, Festung Przemyśl, Op. Nr. 231/15, 17, 24; KA Ms. 1 Wkg, Russland, 1914, Nr. 19, Stuckheil, "Festung Przemyśl."

12. KA AOK, fasz. 523, Festung Przemyśl, Op. Nr. 231/13.

13. KA AOK, fasz. 523, Festung Przemyśl, Op. Nr. 231/14, 20; KA NL, B/1137, Nr. 2, Kusmanek, "Festung Przemyśl."

14. KA Ms. 1 Wkg, Russland, 1914, Nr. 19, Stuckheil, "Festung Przemyśl," 11.

15. KA AOK, fasz. 523, Festung Przemyśl, Op. Nr. 231/7.

16. KA Ms. 1 Wkg, Russland, 1914, Nr. 19, Stuckheil, "Festung Przemyśl," 42; KA AOK, fasz. 523, Festung Przemyśl, Op. Nr. 231/18.

17. KA AOK, fasz. 523, Festung Przemyśl, Op. Nr. 231/18, 24.

18. Laslo Szabo, *A nagy temető Przemyśl ostrema 1914–1915* (Budapest: Kossuth, 1982).

19. Proschaska, *Festung Przemyśl*, 71; Wolfgang, *Przemyśl 1914–1915*.

20. Michaelsburg, *Im belagerten Przemyśl*, 137.

21. Forstner, *Przemyśl*, 225.

22. Michaelsburg, *Im belagerten Przemyśl*, 139.

23. KA AOK, fasz. 523, Festung Przemyśl, Op. Nr. 231/32; KA Ms. 1 Wkg, Russland, 1914, Nr. 19, Stuckheil, "Festung Przemyśl."

24. Kusmanek to his soldiers, Forstner, *Przemyśl*, 245–246; Franz Joseph 19 March, 248–249; AOK reply to radio telegram, "your report understood," Forstner, *Przemyśl*, 252.

25. KA AOK, fasz. 523, Festung Przemyśl; KA Ms. 1 Wkg, Russland, 1914, Stuckheil, "Festung Przemyśl"; Heiden, *Bollwerk am San*.

26. KA AOK, fasz. 523, Festung Przemyśl, AOK, Op. Nr. 8282.

27. KA AOK, fasz. 523, Festung Przemyśl, AOK, Op. Nr. 8205.

28. Forstner, *Przemyśl*, 234; Heiden, *Bollwerk am San*, 228; KA Ms 1. Russland, 1914, Nr. 19, Stuckheil, "Festung Przemyśl," 688; Wolfgang, *Przemyśl 1914–1915*, 174, claimed that ten thousand died. One unit log claimed that one-third of the attackers died and one-third became prisoners of war, while the other third returned to the fortress (p. 227).

29. KA AOK, fasz. 523, Fortress Przemyśl, AOK Op. Nr. 8205; KA Ms. 1 Wkg, Russland, 1914, Nr. 19, Stuckheil, "Festung Przemyśl"; Forstner, *Przemyśl*.

30. KA AOK, Op. Nr. 7690.

31. KA AOK, fasz. 523, Festung Przemyśl, Op. Nr. 231/32.

32. General Jury N. Danilov, *Russland in Weltkriege 1914–1915* (Jena: Verlag Fromman, 1925), 458.

33. KA Ms. 1 Wkg, Russland, 1914, Nr. 19, Stuckheil, "Festung Przemyśl"; *Allgemeine*, A4, Veith, "Werdigang und Untergang."

34. KA Ms. 1 Wkg, Russland, 1914, Nr. 19, Stuckheil, "Festung Przemyśl"; Forstner, *Przemyśl*, 228.

35. KA AOK, fasz. 523, Festung Przemyśl, Op. Nr. 223/2; KA Ms. 1 Wkg, Russland, 1914, Nr. 19, Stuckheil, "Festung Przemyśl," 409–410.

36. Michaelsburg, *Im belagerten Przemyśl*, 138, 142–143.

37. Jerzy W. Kupiec-Weglinski, "The Siege of Przemyśl, 1914–15," *American Philatelist* 126, no. 6 (June 2012).

38. Kupiec-Weglinski, "The Siege of Przemyśl, 1914–15."

39. See Forstner, *Przemyśl*, 262–263.

40. Kupiec-Weglinski, "The Siege of Przemyśl, 1914–15."

41. Kupiec-Weglinski, "The Siege of Przemyśl, 1914–15."

42. Kupiec-Weglinski, "The Siege of Przemyśl, 1914–15."

43. Forstner, *Przemyśl*, 233–234.

44. KA AOK, fasz. 523, Fortress Przemyśl; Forstner, *Przemyśl*, 227–228.

45. Forstner, *Przemyśl*, 229, KA AOK, fasz. 523, Festung Przemyśl, Op. Nr. 233/1.

46. After the recapture of the fortress on June 3, multiple intact guns were found with shells. It was learned that March 22 attempts to destroy the artillery and fortress works positions, particularly Werks I, IV, V, VII, VII1/2, and XII, had been only partially successful, while works VI, VIII, IX, X, and XIII had basically been destroyed.

47. KA AOK, fasz. 523, Festung Przemyśl, Op. Nr. 233/2; Forstner, *Przemyśl*, 231, 234; KA Ms. 1 Wkg, Russland, 1914, Nr. 19, Stuckheil, "Festung Przemyśl."

48. KA Ms. 1 Wkg, Russland, 1914, Nr. 19, Stuckheil, "Festung Przemyśl," 407; Wolfgang, *Przemyśl 1914–1915*.

49. Michaelsburg, *Im belagerten Przemyśl*, 138, 142–143.

50. Michaelsburg, *Im beleaguered Przemyśl*, 147, 157.

51. Michaelsburg, *Im belagerten Przemyśl*, 143.

52. KA Ms. 1 Wkg, Russland, 1914, Nr. 19, Stuckheil, "Festung Przemyśl"; KA AOK, Op. Nr. 8250/19.

53. See KA NL, B/1137, Nr. 2, Kusmanek, "Festung Przemyśl"; KA Ms. 1 Wkg, Russland, 1914, Nr. 19, Stuckheil, "Festung Przemyśl."

54. Rauchensteiner, *Der Tod des Doppeladler*, 61, 64.

55. KA Ms. 1 Wkg, Russland, 1914, Nr. 19, Stuckheil, "Festung Przemyśl"; Stuckheil, "Die zweite Enschliessung der Festung Przemyśl III," 232–233.

56. Michaelsburg, *Im belagerten Przemyśl*; Alfred Knox, *With the Russian Army, 1914–1917*, 2 vols. (London: Hutchinson, 1921).

57. Forstner, *Przemyśl*, 233ff.

58. Proschaska, *Festung Przemyśl*, 75; see Michaelsburg, *Im belagerten Przemyśl*, 154; Wolfgang, *Przemyśl 1914–1915*.

59. Jan Lenar, *Twierdza Przemyśl w Galicji* (Przemyśl: Regionalny Ośrodek Kultury, Edukacji i Nauki w Przemyślu, 2003).

60. Michaelsburg, *Im belagerten Przemyśl*, 154.

61. Michaelsburg, *Im belagerten Przemyśl*, 152.

62. Reinhard Nachtigal, *Russland und seine österreich-ungarichen Kriegsgefangenen (1914–1918)* (Remshalden:Verlag Berrhard Albert Greiner, 2003), 33, 34.

63. Michaelsburg, *Im beleaguered Przemyśl*, 153–154.

64. Forstner, *Przemyśl*, 259; Nachtigal, *Kriegsgefangenen*, 34.

65. Nachtigal, *Kriegsgefangenen*, 34; Forstner, *Przemyśl*.

9. GORLICE-TARNOV AND AFTER

1. For the battle of Gorlice-Tarnov, see ÖULK, vol. 2; RAWK, vol. 7; and Richard DiNardo, *Breakthrough: The Gorlice-Tarnow Campaign, 1915* (Santa Barbara, CA: Praeger, 2010).

2. *ÖULK*, 2:297–300.

3. KA AC, B/13, Kundmann Tagebuch.

4. Rauchensteiner, *Der Tod des Doppeladlers*, 211.

5. *ÖULK*, 2:306; DiNardo, *Breakthrough*.

6. Rauchensteiner, *Der Tod des Doppeladlers*, 211–212.

7. KA AOK, fasz. 512, Conrad-Falkenhayn Korrespondenz, Russland, Persönlich Op. Nr. 7720; KA AOK, fasz. 551, document unnumbered.

8. KA AOK, fasz. 512, Conrad-Falkenhayn Korrespondenz, Russland, Op. Nr. 9700.

9. Wendt, *Der italienische Kriegschauplatz*; Nr. 46, 432–433, Op. Nr. 769 1b; KA AOK, fasz. 512, Conrad-Falkenhayn Korrespondenz, Russland.

10. KA AOK, fasz. 512, Conrad-Falkenhayn Korrespondenz, Russland, Op. Nr. 9763.

11. Artur Arz, *Zur Geschichte des Grossen Krieges, 1914–1918* (Vienna: Rikola Verlag, 1924), 60.

12. KA LU Ms. 13, "Die FLIK 10-vor und nach der grossen Durchbruch offensive bei Gorlice-Jaslo," Erich Kahlin.

13. The first-line Italian troops numbered 800,000, another 500,000 served as reserves.

14. Austrians intercepted Russian radio messages and deciphered them; Cramon, *Unser Österreich-Ungarn Bundesgenosse: Erinnerungen aus meiner vierjährigen Tätigkeit als bevollmächtigter deutscher General beim k.u.k. Armeeoberkommando* (Berlin: E. S. Mittler & Sohn, 1922).

15. Rauchensteiner, *Der Tod des Doppeladlers*, 213.

16. *ÖULK*, 6:409: Holger Afflerbach, *Falkenhayn: Politischens Denken und Handeln im Kaiserreich* (Munich: R. Oldenbourg, 1994), 176–177, 249; Stone, *Eastern Front*, 176.

17. KA AOK, fasz. 512, Conrad-Falkenhayn Korrespondenz, Russland, Falkenhayn to Conrad.

18. *ÖULK*, 2:372.

19. Knox, *With the Russian Army*, 1:282.

20. KA LU Ms. 13, Kahlin, "Die FLIK 10-vor und nach der grossen Durchbruch offensive bei Gorlice-Jaslo."

21. *ÖULK*, 2:353–356.

22. *RAWK*, 7:426.

23. Stone, *Eastern Front*, 137.

24. KA AOK, fasz. 512, Conrad-Falkenhayn Korrespondenz, Russland, Op. Nr. 9763.

25. KA AOK, fasz. 512, Conrad-Falkenhayn Korrespondenz, Russland, Op. Nr. 777 Ib.

26. KA AOK, fasz. 607, Cramon to Falkenhayn 1/6; Stone, *Eastern Front*, 138.

27. KA AOK, fasz. 512, Conrad-Falkenhayn Korrespondenz, Russland, Op. Nr. 780 Ib.

28. KA AOK, fasz. 512, Conrad-Falkenhayn Korrespondenz, Russland.

29. KA AOK, fasz. 512, Conrad-Falkenhayn Korrespondenz, Russland, Op. Nrn. 1054r, 9991.

30. KA AOK, fasz. 512, Conrad-Falkenhayn Korrespondenz, Russland, Op. Nr. 9970.

31. KA AOK, fasz. 607, Cramon, " "Abschriften Berichten beim k.u.k. AOK. Cramon an die DOHL 1915/1916," Cramon to Falkenhayn (6 May).

32. Stone, *Eastern Front*, 139, 140.

33. KA LU Ms. 13, Kahlin, "Die FLIK 10-vor und nach der grossen Durchbruch offensive bei Gorlice-Jaslo."

34. Gina (Virgina) Conrad von Hözendorf, *Mein Leben mit Conrad von Hözendorf: Sein geistiges Vermächtnis* (Leipzig: Grethlein & Co. Nachf.), 1935, 138.

35. See DiNardo, *Breakthrough*.

36. KA AOK, fasz. 512, Russland, Conrad-Falkenhayn Korrespondenz, Op. Nrn. 1017, 1072, 9991, 10017.

37. Stone, *Eastern Front*, 139.

38. KA AOK, fasz. 561, Conrad-Falkenhayn Korrespondenz, Italien, enclosed in AOK Op. Nrn. 10323, 1138r.

39. KA AOK, fasz. 560, Conrad-Falkenhayn Korrespondenz, Italien, enclosed in AOK Op. Nr. 10138.

40. *RAWK*, 8:5.

41. *ÖULK*, 2:375.

42. KA LU Ms. 13, Kahlin, "Die FLIK 10-vor und nach der grossen Durchbruch offensive bei Gorlice-Jaslo."

43. KA AOK, fasz. 512, Conrad-Falkenhayn Korrespondenz, Russland, Op. Nr. 10200.

44. MKSM, 1915, Documents 69-10/17-1.2; KA AOK, fasz. 560, Conrad-Falkenhayn Korrespondenz, Italien, Op. Nr. 10170.

45. *RAWK*, 8:5.

46. KA AOK, fasz. 560, Conrad-Falkenhayn Korrespondenz, Italien, Op. Nr. 10170.

47. KA AOK, fasz. 560, Conrad-Falkenhayn Korrespondenz, Italien, Op. Nrn. 10170, 10176.

48. KA AOK, fasz. 512, Conrad-Falkenhayn Korrespondenz, Russland, Op. Nr. 10200.

49. *RAWK*, 8:14.

50. KA LU Ms. 13, Kahlin, "Die FLIK 10-vor und nach der grossen Durchbruch offensive bei Gorlice-Jaslo."

51. KA AOK, fasz. 512, Conrad-Falkenhayn Korrespondenz, Russland, Op. Nr. 10200.

52. KA AOK, fasz. 512, Conrad-Falkenhayn Korrespondenz, Russland, Op. Nrn. 572, 10285.

53. Paul Robinson, *Grand Duke Nicolas Nikolavich, Supreme Commander of the Russian Army* (Dekalb, IL: NIU Press, 2014), 418–419.

54. KA AOK, fasz. 551, Conrad-Falkenhayn Korrespondenz, Balkan.

55. *RAWK*, 8:148.

56. KA AC B/13, Kundmann Tagebuch.

57. KA AOK, fasz. 512, Conrad-Falkenhayn Korrespondenz, Russland, Op. Nr. 10350.

58. Robinson, *Grand Duke Nicolas*, 420–421.

59. KA AC, B/13, Kundmann Tagebuch.

60. KA AC, B/13, Kundmann Tagebuch.

61. KA AOK, fasz. 560, Conrad-Falkenhayn Korrespondenz, Italien, AOK Op. Nr. 1392r.

62. *RAWK*, 8:109–110.

63. KA AOK, fasz. 607, Op. Nr. 1553r.

64. *RAWK*, 7:428.

65. KA AOK, fasz. 607, Nr. 1553r.

66. KA AC, B/13, Kundmann Tagebuch.

67. KA AC, B/13, Kundmann Tagebüch.

68. Robinson, *Grand Duke Nicolas"*, 426.

69. KA Ms. 1 Wkg, Russland, 1914, Nr. 19, Stuckheil, "Festung Przemyśl."

70. *RAWK*, 8:149.

71. *RAWK*, 8:181–182.

72. *RAWK*, 8:107.

73. ÖULK, 2:440; Forstner, *Przemyśl*, 273.

74. Erich von Falkenhayn, *General Headquarters and its Critical Decisions* (London: Hutchison & Co., 1919), 101; see ÖULK; RAWK.

75. Rauchensteiner, *Der Tod des Doppeladler,* 282. See DiNardo, *Breakthrough,* for details.

76. Forstner, *Przemyśl*, 274; Paul Kneussl, *Aus der Kriegsgeschichte der 11. bayr. Infanterie-Division. [1], Przemysl : Mai - Juni 1915* (Munich: Selbstverl, 1925), 99.

77. Forstner, *Przemyśl*, 283.

78. Forstner, *Przemyśl*, 260, 277, 290.

79. Forstner, *Przemyśl*, 282.

80. KA AOK, fasz. 561, Conrad-Falkenhayn Korrespondenz, Italy, Op. Nr.11168/I.

81. KA AOK, fasz. 560, Conrad-Falkenhayn Korrespondenz, Italien, Op. Nr. 2076.

82. KA AOK, fasz. 560, Conrad-Falkenhayn Korrespondenz, Italien, Op. Nr. 11170.

83. KA AOK, fasz. 560, Conrad-Falkenhayn Korrespondenz, Italien, Op. Nr. 2076r.

84. KA AOK, fasz. 607, Cramon, Falkenhayn to Cramon.

85. KA AC, B/13, Kundmann Tagebücher.

86. Stone, *Eastern Front,* 136–137.

Bibliography

UNPUBLISHED DOCUMENTS

Kriegsarchiv (War Archives: Vienna)
Armee Ober Kommando (AOK) Operations Abteilung
Conrad-Falkenhayn

fasz. 512	Conrad-Falkenhayn Korrespondenz, Russland
fasz. 551	Conrad-Falkenhayn Korrespondenz, Balkan
fasz. 560, 561	Conrad-Falkenhayn Korrespondenz, Italien

Armee Ober Kommando (AOK)

fasz. 10–15	Aus Op. Nrs. 4801–6300

AOK Operations Abteilung (Operations Bueau)

fasz. 22–29	Aus Op. Nrs. 7,301–10,800

k.u.k. Operations Abteilung "R" Gruppe: 1915

fasz. 497	Oktober Aus Op. Nrs. 2684–3833
fasz. 498	November Aus Op. Nrs. 3740–4837
fasz. 499	Dezember Aus Op. Nrs. 4442/I–5873
fasz. 500	Jänner Aus Op. Nrs. 5878–6756
fasz. 501	Februar Aus Op. Nrs. 6651–7620
fasz. 502	März Aus Op. Nrs. 6651–7620
fasz. 503	Avril Aus Op. Nrs. 8624–9657
fasz. 523	Festung Przemyśl

Armee Ober Kommando (AOK)

fasz. 607	Abschriften Berichten beim k.u.k. AOK. Cramon an die DOHL 1915/1916
fasz. 614	Tagesberichte/Kaiserberichte 1914
fasz. 615	Tagesberichte/Kaiserberichte Anfang Jänner bis Ende Juni

AOK Tagerbücher

fasz. 679–680   1914–15 7/23–4/14
fasz. Tagebücher   I. vom 8/27 1914–2/19 1915
  der R-Gruppe   II. vom 2/20 1915–7/13 1916

Evidenz der eigenen Situation 1915

fasz. 796   12/16–12/31, 1914
fasz. 797   Februar 1915
fasz. 799   März 1915

Evidenz der feindlichen Situation

fasz. 873–875   Jänner–März 1915

Archiv Conrad (AC)

A-6   Varia
A-7   Varia
B-7   Januar 1915 bis Avril 1915
B-12   Kundmann Tagebuch 23 Juli–31 Dezember 1914
B/13   Kundmann Tagebuch vom 1/1 1915–4/XI 1916

Neue Feld Akten (NFA):
2. Op. Armee Kdo.

fasz. 15–18   2. Op. Armee Kdo. Op. Akten 2107–2931 vom 10/2–31/3, 1915
fasz. 46–49   Evidenz 1/1–3/31 1915
fasz. 95   2. Op. Armee Kdo. Tagebücher

3. Op. Armee Kdo.

fasz. 10   10 1/1–1/27 1915
fasz. 11   1/27–2/8 1915 Karpatenkrieg
fasz. 12–15   3. Op. Armee Kdo. Op. Akten Aus Op. Nrn. 3184–3298 vom
                     8/2–22/4, 1915
fasz. 27–31   Evidenz 1/1–3/31 1915
fasz. 42   3. Op. Armee Kdo. Tagebücher 1–6 1915

4. Armee

fasz. 14   Operative Akten 4/17–5/7 1915
fasz. 70   Tagebücher 8/1 '14–4/18 '15
fasz. 73   Evidenz russichen Situation
fasz. 78   Januar 1915
fasz. 79   Februar 1915
fasz. 80   Avril 1915

7. Armee 1915 (Group Pflanzer-Baltin)

fasz. 4   Januar 1915
fasz. 9   Avril

fasz. 10   Mai
fasz. 21   Tagebücher

Luftfahrte Archiv (LU)

Ms. 13	"Die FLIK 10-vor und nach der grossen Durchbruch offensive bei Gorlice-Jaslo." Erich Kalin
Ms. 40	"Improvisationen zur Bekämpfung von Luftfahr zeugung in der Festung Przemyśl 1914/1915." Generalmajor Hans Schwab
Ms. 61	"Meine Luftpost Reise Wien-Kiew." Major Tanner
Ms. 72	"Als Flieger in Przemyśl." Oberst Feldpilot Nikolaus Wagner Edler von Florheim
Ms. 77	"Letzter Flug aus Przemyśl" Roman Grutschnig

Militärkanzlei Seiner Majestät (MKSM)

Separate fasz. 78/77	Korrespondenz Conrad-Bolfras 1914, 1915
Separate fasz. 79/42	Korrespondenz Conrad-Bolfras
Separate fasz. 79/53	
Separate fasz. 84	
Separate fasz. 100	

Militärkanzlei Franz Ferdinand

14-24/ex 1913
Nachlässe (NL)

B/4	Boroević
B/23	Karl Mayern–2. "Armee in Karpathenschlacht 1915"
B/45	Veith, Werdegang und Untergang
B/54	Pitreich
B/75	Arthur Freiherr Bolfras von Ahnenberg
B/240	Fielder, Nr. 3
B/509	Karl Schneller, Nr. 2: Kriegstagebuch
B/544	Gottlieb Kralowetz von Hohenrecht, Karpatenkrieg–X. Korps–Manuskript
B/589	Pitreich
B/700	Hans Mailath-Pokorny
B/726	Robert Nowak, Nr. 8, "Die Klammer des Reiches: Das Verhalten der elf Nationalitäten Österreich-Ungarn in der k.u.k. Wehrmacht 1914–1918"
B/800	Rudolf Kiszling, Die k.u.k. 2. "Armee von 10 November 1914 bis zum Jahresschluss"
B/1040	Bornemann, Przemyśl Weltkrieg 1914: Russland
B/1041	Bornemann, Kriegsgeschichte-Vortragsentwürfe Weltkrieg 1914–1918—"Przemyśl"
B/1063	Nr. 6, "Auskünfte über Eisenbahn technische Fragen"
B/1137	Nr. 2, Hermann Kusmanek von Burgstädten, "Festung Przemyśl" (Kommandant Fortress Przemyśl)

Übersetzung Nordost

Nr. 2   Strategische Skizzen des Krieges der Jahre 1914–1918. Periode vom 12. (25.)
         Nov. 1914–15. (28) Feb. 1915. A. Nesmanow
Nr. 3   Unser Verlust von Galizien im Jahre 1915. M. Bontsch—Brujewitsch
Nr. 8   Das militärische Ubereinkommen Russlands
Nr. 10   Strategische Studie über den Weltkrieg, 1914–1918 (14 Sept. bis 20 Nov.
         1914). G. Korolkow
Nr. 14   "Sturm Octobre 1914." Tscherkassow
Nr. 28   Von Lodz bis Gorlice, Jänner–März 1915. A. M. Zajonstschowsky

MANUSCRIPTS

Allgemeine (General)
A4   "Werdigang und Untergang." George Veith

Manuskripte 1. Weltkrieg, Russland, 1914

Nr. 6   "Der Winterfeldzug in Polen und Galizien." 18/12. 1914–Anfang Jänner
         1915. Joly
Nr. 19   "Festung Przemyśl." Stuckheil

Manuskripte 1. Weltkrieg, Russland, 1915

Nr. 1   "Die k.u.k. 2. Armee in der Karpatenschlacht 1914/15." Karl Mayern
Nr. 2   Die Karpaten-Schlacht Mitte Jänner bis Ende Avril 1915 Karl Mayern
Nr. 5   Die westliche Flügelgruppe der 7. Armee in Karpaten. Paic
Nr. 9   Die Geschichte der Festung Przemyśl
Nr. 32   Die Winterschlacht in den Karpaten 1915. Schwarz
Nr. 36   Die deutsche Südarmee von Anfang Januar bis Juli 1915, Deutsch Reichsarchiv

Budapest War Archives (BWA)
"Auszug aus dem Berichte über die Aktion im III Verteidigung Bezirk: Während der Ein-
schliessung." General der Infantry (GDI) Karl Waitzendorfer.
Stuckheil Manuskript—"Festung Przemyśl"
TGY 99, Pamperl, Chronicle
TGY 2819 II 143, Armee Gruppe Szurmay

PERIODICALS (FOR SPECIFIC ARTICLES)

Galicja, Rok 2 Kultur A Tradycja Wspolczesność
Fortyfikacja Europejskim Dziedzictwem Kultry (Fortifications as a European Heritage).
   Vol. 10 of *Fortyfikacja Austriaka Twierdza Przemyśl*. Conference papers on Fortress
   Przemyśl, 30 September–3 October 1999. Articles:

   1) Jan Banbor and Jozef Dobrowolski, "Przemyśl I Verdun-Decydujace Twierdze I
      Wojny Swiatowej (Proba Analizy Porównawczej)," 23–56.
   2) Krzysztof Idzikowski, "Fortyfikacje Polowe Twierdzy Przemyśl . . . ," 111–150.

NEWSPAPERS

Kriegsnachrichten, k.u.k. Festungskommdo. 1914 and 1915 (fortress newsletter during siege). In German, Hungarian, and Polish.

PUBLISHED DOCUMENTS AND OFFICIAL COLLECTIONS

Official Military Histories
Austria
Österreich-Ungarns letzter Krieg 1914–1928. Vol. 1 of *Das Kriegsjahr 1914. Vom Kriegsausbruch bis zum Ausgang der Schlacht bei Limanowa-Lapanów.* Bundesministerium für Heereswesen und vom Kriegsarchiv. Vienna: Verlag Militärwissenschaftlicher Mitteilungen, 1930.
Österreich-Ungarns letzter Krieg 1914–1928. Vol. 2 of *Das Kriegsjahr 1915.* Bundesministerium für Heereswesen und vom Kriegsarchiv. Vienna: Verlag Militärwissenschaftlicher Mitteilungen, 1931.

Germany Reichsarchiv (RAWK)
Reichsarchiv Weltkrieg 1914 bis 1918. Vols. 1–8. *Die militärischen Operationen zu Lande.* Berlin: E. S. Mittler & Sohn, 1925–1932.

Monographs
Afflerbach, Holger. *Falkenhayn: Politischens Denken und Handeln im Kaiserreich.* Munich: R. Oldenbourg, 1994.
Albertini, Luigi. *The Origins of the War of 1914.* Vol. 1. London: Oxford University Press, 1952.
Arz, Artur. *Zur geschichte des grossen krieges, 1914–1918.* Vienna: Rikola Verlag, 1924.
Auffenberg-Komarów, Moritz Ritter von. *Aus Österreich-Ungarns Teilnahme am Weltkriege.* Berlin: 1920.
Aull, Otto. *Das K.K. Landsturm-Regiment St. Pölten, Nr. 21.* Wiener Neustadt, 1935.
Bardolff, Carl Freiherr von. *Soldat im alten Österreich: Erinnerungen aus meinem Leben.* Jena: E. Diederichs Verlag, 1943.
Beloy, A. *Galitsüskaya bitva.* Moscow: Gusudarstucennoye Izdatekstvo, 1929.
Bobusia, Bogusław, Marek Gosztyla, and Monik Zub. *Plany Twierdzy Przemyśl.* Przemyśl: n.p., 2004.
Brusilov, General A. A. *A Soldier's Notebook, 1914–1918.* Westport, CT: Greenwood Press, 1930.
Chrzanowski, Lukaz. *Artyleria Austro-Wegierska W. Zatach 1860–1890.* N.p.: Tomaz Idzikowski, 2008.
———. *Wielka Wojna in Galicji.* Przemyśl: Tomaz Idzikowski, 2008.
Chudenitz, Franz Czernin von. *Das Postwesen in der ÖU. Festung Przemyśl Während der Beiden Belagerungen, 1914–1915.* Vienna: Selbstverlag, 1985.
Churchill, Winston. *The Unknown War: The Eastern Front.* New York: Charles Scribner's Sons, 1931.
Conrad von Hötzendorf, Franz. *Aus meiner Dienstzeit, 1906–1918.* 5 vols. Vienna: Rikola Verlag, 1921–1925.
———. *Private Aufzeichnungen: Erste Veröffentilchung aus Paperiern des k.u.k. Generalstabs-Chefs.* Edited by Kurt Peball. Vienna: Amalthea, 1977.

Conrad von Hözendorf, Gina (Virgina). *Mein Leben mit Conrad von Hözendorf: Sein geistiges Vermächtnis.* Leipzig: Grethlein & Co. Nachf., 1935.

Cramon, August. *Unser österrich-ungarischen Bundesgenosse im Weltkriege: Erinnerungen aus meiner vierjährigen Tätigkeit als bevollmächtigter deutscher General beim k.u.k. Armeeoberkommando.* Berlin: E. S. Mittler & Sohn, 1922.

Cramon, August, and Paul von Fleck. *Deutschlands Schicksalsbund mit Österreich-Ungarn: Von Conrad von Hötzendorf zu Kaiser Karl.* Berlin: Verlag für Kulturpolitik, 1932.

Czermak, Wilhelm. *In deinem Lager war Österreich: Die österreichisch-ungarische Armee.* Berslau: Korn Verlag, 1938.

Danilov, General Jury N. *Russland in Weltkriege 1914–1915.* Jena: Verlag Fromman, 1925.

Dinardo, Richard. *Breakthrough: The Gorlice-Tarnov Campaign, 1915.* Santa Barbara, CA: Praeger, 2010.

Dobiasch, Sepp. *Kaiserjäger im Osten. Karpaten-Tarnow-Gorlice 1915.* Graz: Leykam-Verlag, 1934.

Ehrenstein, Leopold. *Der Fall der Festung Przemyśl.* Bratislava: Vilmek, 1935.

Falkenhayn, Erich von. *General Headquarters 1914–1916 and Its Critical Decisions.* London: Hutchinson, 1919.

———. *The German General Staff and Its Decisions, 1914–1916.* New York: Dodd, Mead, 1920.

———. *Die Oberste Heeresleitung 1914–1916 in ihren wichtigsten Entschliessungen.* Berlin: E. S. Mittler & Sohn, 1920.

Floericke, Kurt. *Das Ringen um Galizien: Lemberg, Limanova, Przemyśl.* Stuttgart: Frankh'sche Verlagshandlung, 1916.

Forstner, Franz. *Przemyśl: Österreich-Ungarns bedeutendste Festung.* Vienna: Österreichische Bundesverlag, 1987.

François, Hermann. *Gorlice, 1915: Der Karpthen durchbruch und die Befreiung von Galizien.* Leipzig: K.F. Koehler, 1922.

Gellert, Georg. *Der Kampf in Feindesland: Erzählung aus dem Völkerkriege 1914/15.*Berlin: Verlag Jugendhort, 1915.

Glaise-Horstenau, Edmund von. *Ein General im Zwielicht: Die Erinnerungen Edmund Glaises von Horstenau.* Edited by Peter Broucek. Vol. 1. Wein: Bohlau, 1980.

Golovin, Nicholas N. *The Russian Army in the World War.* New Haven, CT: Yale University Press, 1931.

Gomoll, Wilhelm Conrad. *Im Kampf gegen Russland und Serbien.* Leipzig: A. Brockhaus, 1916.

Heiden, Hermann. *Bollwerk am San: Schicksal der Festung Przemyśl.* Oldenburg: Gerhard Stalling, 1940.

Herwig, Holger H. *The First World War: Germany and Austria-Hungary, 1914–1918.* New York: Arnold, 1997.

Hindenburg, Paul von. *Aus meinem Leben.* Leipzig: Hirzel, 1920.

Hoffmann, General Max. *Der Krieg der versäumten Gelegenheiten.* Munich: Verlag für Kulturpolitik, 1924.

———. *War Diaries and Other Papers.* 2 vols. Translated by Eric Sutton. London: M. Secker, 1929.

Hornykiewicz, Theophiul, ed. *Ereignisse in der Ukraine 1914–1922.* Vol. 4. Philadelphia, PA: W.K. Lypynsky East European Research Institute, 1966.

Horst, Taitl. *Die Österreichisch-Ungarischen Kriegsefangenen in feindlichen Lagern 1914–1921.* Vol. 1. Dornbirn: Im Selbstverlag Dornbirn, 1992.

Idzikowski, Tomasz. *Fort I "Sali-Soglio."* Przemyśl : Tomasz Idzikowski - Fort VIII "Łętownia," 2004.

———. *Fort VIII "Łętownia,"* Przemyśl : Tomasz Idzikowski Fort VIII "Łętownia," 2004.

———. *Fort XV "Borek."* Przemyśl : Tomasz Idzikowski Fort VIII "Łętownia," 2004.

———. *Pierwszy obwod obronny.* Przemyśl : ROKEiN, 2002.

———. *Przemyśl w marcu 1915-im März.* Przemyśl : Tomasz Idzikowski Fort VIII "Łętownia," 2005.

Johnson, Douglas Wilson. *Topography and Strategy in the War.* New York: Henry Holt, 1917.

Josef, Feldmarschall Erzherzog. *A Világháború amilyennek én láttam.* 3 Vols. Budapest: Ungarische Akademie der Wissenschaften, 1926–1931.

Kaebisch, Generalleutnant Ernst. *Streitfragen des Weltkrieges, 1914–1918.* Stuttgart: Bergers Literarisches Bureau, 1924.

Kiszling, Rudolf. *Die Hohe Führung der Heere Habsburg im Ersten Weltkrieg.* Vienna: Bundesministerium für Landesverteidigung, Büro für Wehrpolitik, 1984.

———. *Österreich-Ungarns Anteil am ersten Weltkrieg.* Graz: Stiasny Verlag, 1958.

Kneussel, Paul. *Aus der Kriegsgeschichte der 11. bayr. Infanterie-Division. [1], Przemysl :* Mai - Juni 1915. Munich: Selbstverl, 1925.

Knox, Alfred. *With the Russian Army, 1914–1917.* 2 Vols. London: Hutchinson, 1923.

Kurek, Julian W., and Marcus Kurek. *Artyleria Twierdzy Przemyśl.* Przemyśl: Drukarnia San Set, 2002.

Lenar, Jan. *Pamietnik z walk o Twierdze Przemyśl.* Przemyśl: Wydawnictwo Fort, 2005.

———. *Twierdza Przemyśl w Galicji.* Przemyśl: Regionalny Ośrodek Kultury, Edukacji i Nauki w Przemyślu, 2003.

Lincoln, W. Bruce. *Passage through Armageddon: The Russian in War and Revolution, 1914–1918.* New York: Simon and Schuster, 1986.

Lucas, James S. *Austro-Hungarian Infantry, 1914–1918.* London: Almark, 1973.

Ludendorff, General Erich von. *Meine Kriegserinnerungen 1914–1918.* Berlin: E. S. Mittler & Sohn, 1921.

Ludwig, Max. *Neuzeitliche Festungen: Von der Ringfestung zur befestigten Zone.* Berlin: Mittler, 1938.

Matthes, Kurt. *Die 9. Armee im Weichselfeldzug, 1914.* Berlin: Junker & Dunnhaupt, 1936.

Merwin, Bertold. *Legiony w. Karpatach.* Vienna: Naczelny Komitet Narodowy, Skład główny w księgsrni, 1914.

Michaelsburg, J. V. *Im belagerten Przemyśl: Tagebuchblätter aus grosser Zeit.* Leipzig: C. F. Amelangs Verlag, 1915.

Partsch, J. *Die Kriegschauplätze.* Vol. 3 of *Der östliche Kriegsschauplatz.* Leipzig: Verlag von B. G. Teubner, 1916.

Pastor, Peter, ed. *Revolutions and Interventions in Hungary and Its Neighbor States, 1918–1919.* New York: Columbia University Press, 1988.

Peball, Kurt. *Conrad von Hötzendorf: Private Aufzeichnungen, Erste Veröffentlichungen aus den Papieren des k.u.k. Generalstabchefs.* Vienna: Amalthea Verlag, 1977.

Petho, Albert. *Agenten für den Doppeladler: Österreich-Ungarns Geheimer Dienst im Wettkrieg.* Graz: Stocker, 1998.

Pitreich, Anton. *Der österreich-ungarische Bundesgenosse im Sperrfeuer.* Klagenfurt: Arthur Killitsch, 1930.

Pitreich, Max von. *Lemberg, 1914*. Vienna: Verlag von Adolf Holzhausens Nachfolger Universitätsbuchdrucker, 1929.

———. *1914: Die Militärischen Probleme unseres Kriegsbeginnes; Ideen, Gründe und Zusammenhänge*. Vienna: Selbstverlag, 1934.

Popel', Nikolaï Kirillovich. *Panzer greifen an*. Berlin: Deutscher Militärverlag, 1968.

Proschaska, Bruno. *Przemyśl 1914/15*. Vienna: Kommanditgesellschaft Payer & Co, 1935.

Rauchensteiner, Manfried. *Der Erste Weltkrieg und das Ende der Habsburgermonarchie 1914–1918*. Vienna: Böhlau Verlag, 2013.

———. *Der Tod des Doppeladlers: Österreich-Ungarn und der Erste Weltkrieg*. Graz: Styria, 1993.

Rebolt, Genieoberst Jules. *Die Festungskämpfe im Weltkriege*. Zurich: Herausgeber: Gesellschaft für militärische Bautechnik, 1938.

Regele, Oskar. *Feldmarschall Conrad: Auftrag und Erfüllung, 1906–1918*. Vienna: Verlag Herold, 1955.

Robinson, Paul. *Grand Duke Nicolas Nikolavich, Supreme Commander of the Russian Army*. Dekalb, IL: NIU Press, 2014.

Ronge, Max. *Kriegs- und Industriespionage: Zwölf Jahre Kundschaftsdienst*. Zurich: 1930.

Rothenberg, Gunther. *The Army of Francis Joseph*. West Lafayette, IN: Purdue University Press, 1976.

Rozanski, Jan. *Przemyśl w I Wojnie Siviatowej*. Przemyśl: Muzeum Ziemi Przemyskieg, 1969.

———. *Twierdza Przemyskiej*. Rzeszów: Krajowa Agencja Wydawnicza, 1983.

Rutherford, Ward. *The Russian Army in World War I*. London: Gordon Cremonesi, 1975.

Schenk, Gerhard. *Przemyśl 1914–1915: Monographia über eine historischen Ereignis*. Vienna: Verlag Polbschanosky, 2003.

Schwarte, Max. *Der grosse Krieg 1914–1918*. Vol. 5 of *Der österreichisch-ungarische Krieg*. Leipzig: Barth in Ausgl., 1922.

Schwartz, Engelbrecht. *Frauen in Przemyśl Festung, 1914–1915*. Leipzig: Darnstadt, 1936.

Shanafelt, Gary W. *The Secret Enemy: Austria-Hungary and the German Alliance, 1914–1918*. New York: Columbia University Press, 1985.

Silberstein, Gerald E. *The Troubled Alliance: German-Austrian Relations, 1914 to 1917*. Lexington: University Press of Kentucky, 1970.

Singer, Roland. *Karpatenschlachten: Der Erste und Zweite Weltkrieg am oberen Karpatenbogen*. Berlin: Pro Buseness, GmbH, 2012.

Sondhaus, Lawrence. *Franz Conrad von Hötzendorf: Architect of the Apocalypse*. Boston: Humanities Press, 2000.

Steinitz, Eduard Ritter von, and Theodor von Arenau Brosch. *Die Reichsbefestigung Österrich-Ungarns zur Zeit Conrads von Hötzendorf: Ergänzungsheft 1 Österreich-Ungarns letzter Krieg*. Vienna: Verlag der Militärwissenschaftlichen Mitteilungen, 1937.

Stone, Norman. *The Eastern Front, 1914–1917*. New York: Charles Scribner's Sons, 1975.

Straube, [Bruno] Wolfgang Berhard. *Przemyśl 1914–15*. Vienna: Payer, 1936.

Stuckheil, Franz. *Drugie oblezenie Twierdzy Przemyśl*. Przemyśl: Wydawnictwo Fort,

———. *Okres dzialan ofensywnych*. Vol. 1 of *Drugie oblezenie Twierdzy Przemyśl*. Przemyśl: Wydawnictwo Fort, 2006.

Sturgkh, Graf Joseph. *Im deutschen grossen hauptquartier*. Leipzig: Paul List Verlag, 1921.

Szabo, Laslo. *A nagy temető Przemyśl ostrema 1914–1915*. Budapest: Kossuth, 1982.

Taitl, Horst. *Kriegsgefangen— Österreicher und Ungarns als Gefangene der Entente 1914–1921.* Vol. 1. Dornbinn: published by author, 1992.

Tisza, Stephen, Count. *Briefe, 1914–1918*. 2 vols. Edited by Oskar Werthheimer. Berlin: Reimer Hobing, 1928.

Tranmer, Keith. *Austro-Hungarian A.P.O.'s 1914–1918*. Rev. ed. Hornchurch: Keith Tranmer, 1973.

———. *Przemyśl 1914–1915*. Vienna: Arbeitsgemeinschaft Militaria Austriaca Philatelia im Heeres-Briefmarken-Sammler-Verein, 2003.

Tunstall, Graydon A., *Blood on the Snow: The Carpathian Winter War of 1915*. Lawrence: University Press of Kansas, 2010.

———. *Planning for War against Russia and Serbia: Austro-Hungarian and German Military Strategies, 1871–1914*. New York: Columbia University Press, 1993.

Urbanski von Ostrymiecz, August. *Conrad von Hötzendorf: Soldat und Mensch; dargestellt von seinem mitarbeiter feldmarschalleutnant August Urbanski von Ostrymiecz*. Vienna: Ulrich Mosers Verlag, 1938.

Vít, Jan. *Wspomnienia z mojego pobytu w Przemyślu podczas rosyjskiego oblezenia, 1914–1915.* (Memoir during Siege of Przemyśl) Translated from Polish by Ladislav Hofbauer and Jerzy Husar. Przemyśl: Poludniowo-Wschodni Instytut Naukowy, 1995.

Völker, Rudolf. *Przemyśl: Sieg und Untergang der Festung am San*. Vienna: Tyrolia, 1927.

Vormann, Nikolaus. *Der Feldzug 1939 in Polen: Die Operationen des Heeres*. Weissenburg: Prinz-Eugen-Verl, 1958.

Wendt, Hermann. *Der italienische Kriegsschauplatz in europäischen Konflikten: Seine Bedeutung für die Kriegführung an Frankreichs Nordostgrenze*. Berlin: Junker und Dunnhaupt Verlag, 1936.

Wieslaw, Baczkowski. *Samoloty bombowe I wajny sivatowej*. Warsaw: Wydawnictwa Komunikacji I Lacznosci, 1986.

Williamson, S. R., and P. Pastor, eds. *Essays on World War I: Origins and Prisoners of War*. New York: Columbia University Press, 1983.

Wisshaupt, Ernst. *Die Tiroler Kaiserjäger im Weltkriege 1914–1918*. Vienna: Verlagsanstalt Amon Fran Göth, 1935.

Wolfgang, Bruno. *Przemyśl 1914–1915*. Vienna: Payer, 1935.

Selected Articles

Baanbor, Jan, and Józef Dobrowolski. "Przemyśl und Verdun-entscheidende Festungen im ersten Weltkrieg." *Fortyfikacja Europejskim Dziedzictwem Kultury*. Vol. 10. Warsaw: Towarzystwo Przyjaciol Fortyfiksciji, 1999.

Barang, Robert. "Primäre Wundnaht bei Schussverletzungen speziell des Gehirnes." *Wiener Klinische Wochenschrift* 20 (1915): 524–529.

Bihl, Wolf-Dieter. "Die Ruthenen." In *Die Habsburgermonarchie 1848–1918: Die Völker des Reiches*, vol. 3, edited by Adam Wandruszka and Peter Urbanitsch, 555–584. Vienna: Verlag der Österreichischen Akademie der Wissenschaften, 1980.

Broucek, Peter. "Taktische Erkenntnisse aus dem russisch-japaischen Krieg und deren Beachtung in Österreich-Ungarn." *Mitteilungen des österreichischen Staatsarchivs* 30 (1977): Suppl., 191–220.

Collenberg, Ludwig von Rüdt. "Die Heersleitung und der Oberfelshaber Ost in Sommerfeldzug 1915." *Wissen und Wehr* 13 (1932): 291–296.

Demmer, Fritz. "Erfahrungen einer Chirurgengruppe in österreichisch-russichen Feldzuge 1915." *Wiener Medizinische Wochenschrifte* 12 (1915): 515–562; 14 (1915): 591–598; 15 (1915): 626–638.

Fellner, Fritz. "Zwischen Kriegsbegeisterung und Resignation-ein Memorandum des Sektionschefs Graf Forgách vom Jänner 1915." In *Beiträge zur allgemeinen Geschichte: Alexander Novotny zur Vollendung seines 70: Lebensjahres gewidmet*, ed. Von Hermann Wiesflecker and Othmar Pickl. Graz: Akademische Druck- u. Verlagsanstalt, 1975.

Fleischer, Obst. Rudolf. "Der Rückzug nach Przemyśl im Herbst 1914: Erinnerungen eines Truppenoffiziers." *Militärwissenschaftliche Miteilungen* 55 (1924): 18–26, 120–129.

Franek, Fritz. "Die Entwicklung der öst.-ung.: Wehrmacht in den ersten zwei Kriegsjahren." *Militärwissenschaftliche Miteilungen* 64 (1933): 15–31 and 98–111.

———. "Probleme der Organisation im ersten Kriegsjahre." *Militärwissenschaftliche Miteilungen* 61:11/12 (1930), 977–990.

Gilewicz, Alesky. "Twierda Przemyśl w XIX I XX w (Boudowa, oblezenie, rola e I wojnie swiatowej)." In *Rocznik Przemyśl: Towarzystwo przjaciól nauk w Przemyślu* 12 (1968): 149–192.

Golovin, Nicholas. "The Great Battle of Galicia (1914): A Study in Strategy." *Slavonic Review* 5 (1926–1927): 25–47.

Hölbelt, Lothar. "Schlieffen, Beck, Potiorek und das Ende der gemeinsamen deutschösterreichischen-ungarischen Aufmarchpläne im Osten." *Militärgeschichtliche Mitteilungen* 36 (1984): 7–30.

Kerchnahwe, Hugo. "Der Karpatenfeldzüge 1914/15." MTM 19 (1948): 594–604.

Kiszling, Rudolf. "Feldmarschall Conrad von Hötzendorf." *Österreich in Geschichte und Literatur* 4, no. 8 (1964): 157–167.

———. "Generaloberst Freiherr von Kusmanek." *Militärwissenschaftliche Mitteilungen* 65 (1934): 617ff.

———. "Das Nationalitätproblem in Habsburg Wehrmacht, 1848–1918." *Der Donauraum* 4 (1959): 82–92.

Kronenbitter, Günther. "Nur los lassen. Österreich-Ungarns und der Wille zum Krieg." In *Lange und kurze Wege in den Ersten Weltkrieg*, edited by Johannes Burkhart. Munich: Ernst Vögel, 1996.

Kupiec-Weglinski, Jerry W. "The Siege of Przemyśl, 1914–1915." *American Philatelist*, June 2001, 544–555.

Lagzi, Istvan, ed. *Wegrzy w Tiwierdzy Przemyskiej w latach 1914–1915*. Przemyśl: Wegierski Instytut Kuttury-Muzeum Narodowe Ziemi Przemyślu, 1985, 12–25.

Lipschutz, B. "Über sogenannte Blasenschwäche bei Soldaten (nach Beobachtungen in der Festung Przemyśl)." *Wiener Klinische Wochenschrift 1915*, July 1915, 948–951.

Luvaas, Jay. "A Unique Army: The Common Experience." In *The Habsburg Empire in World War I*, edited by Robert A. Kann, Béla K. Kiraly, and Paula S. Fichter. Boulder, CO: East European Quarterly Press, 1976, 87–103.

Mayern, Obstlt. d. R. "Die Karpathenschlacht: Mitte Jänner bis Ende Avril 1915." MTM 54 (1923): 354–364.

Olejko, Andrzej. "Zapomniane lotnicze epizody z c.k. Przemyśla 1914–1915." *Roczik Przemyśki* 40 (2004): 31–44.

Pamperl, Robert. "Chirurgische Tatigkeit in der belagerten Festung Przemyśl." *Medizische Klinik* 41 (October 10, 1915): 1126–1130.

Potpeschnigg, Karl. "Vom galizischen Kriegschauplatz." *Feldärtzliche Beilage zur Munch med Wochenschrift*, Nr. 14 (January 26, 1915): 136–139.

Ratzenhofer, Emil. "Die Aufmarsch hinter den Karpathen im Winter 1915." *Militärgeschichtliche Mitteilungen* 61 (1930): 499–513.

———. "Truppentransport zum Kriegsbeginn." *Militärwissenschftliche Mitteilungen* 10 (1929): 231–244.

———. "Verlust Kakül für den Karpatenwinter 1915." *Österreich-Ungarns letzter Krieg*, Suppl. 1, 1930.

Rauchensteiner, Manfried. "Zum 'operativen Denken' in Österreich 1814–1914." *Österreichische Militärische Zeitschrift* 12 (1974): 121–127, 207–211, 285–291, 379–384, 473–478; 13 (1975): 46–53.

Reiser, Rudolf. "Der Kampf um das Werk I/1 der Gruppe Siedliska am 7: Oktobre 1914." *Österreichische Wehrzeitung. Zeitschrift für Wehrfragen*, no. 29 (July 17, 1925): 3ff.

Rozanski, Jan. "Przemyśl w. I. Wojnie Swiatowy." Przemyśl: Muzeum ziemi Przemyskiej w Przemyslu, 1969.

———. "Tajemnice Twierdzy Przemyskiej." 2nd ed. Wydawnictwo "SAN-SET," Przemyśl, 2000, 62–132.

Schwalb, Hans G. M. "Die Verteidigung vom Przemyśl 1914–15." *Mitteilungen über Gegenstücke des Artillerie und Geniewesens* 149 (1918): 1373–1392.

Stuckheil, Franz. "Die Festung Przemyśl in der Ausrüstungszeit: Provisorische Darstellung." *MTM* 55 (1924): 200–230.

———. "Die strategische Rolle Przemyśl auf dem östlichen Kriegschauplatz." *MTM* 54 (1923): 60–78, 132–146.

———. "Die zweite Einschliessung der Festung Przemyśl II." Abschnitt Zeiten der Niederganges. *MTM* 55 (1924): 231–250.

———. "Die zweite Einschliessung der Festung Przemyśl III." Abschnitt das Ende. *MTM* 55 (1924): 289–309, 395–417; 56 (1925): 110–133, 222–236, 346–367; 57 (1926): 162–173, 286–296, 405–410, 530–535.

Tunstall, Graydon A. "The Carpathian Winter War, 1915." In *Essays on World War I*, edited by Peter Pastor and Graydon A. Tunstall. New York: Columbia University Press, 2012, 1–24.

———. "Die Karpatenschlachten 1915." Two-part series. *Truppendienst* 2 and 3 (1990), 132–137 and 226–231.

Wagner, Walter. "Die k.(u.)k. Armee—Gliederung und Aufgabenstellung." In *Die Habsburgermonarchie 1848–1918*, edited by Adam Wandruszka and Peter Urbanitsch. Vol. 5 of *Die bewaffnete Macht*. Vienna: Verlag der österreichischen Akademie der Wissenschaften, 1987, 142–633.

Wank, Solomon. "Foreign Policy and the Nationality Problem in Austria-Hungary, 1867–1914." *Austrian History Yearbook* 3, no. 3 (1967), 37–56.

———. "Some Reflections on Conrad von Hötzendorf and His Memoirs Based on Old and New Sources." *Austrian History Yearbook* 1 (1965): 74–88.

Zahálka, Jan. "Posledni let Psemyslu." *Historie a plastikové modelářství* 1, no. 3 (2001): 25–29.

Dissertations

Hecht, Rudolph. "Fragen zur Heeresergänzung der Gestalten Bewaffneten Macht Österreich-Ungarns während des ersten Weltkrieges." PhD thesis, University of Vienna, 1969.

Jerábeck, Rudolf. *Die Brussilowoffensive: 1916: Ein Wendepunkt der Koalitionskriegfuhrung der Mittelmächte*. Vienna: PHD, 1982.

Lein, Richard. "Das militärische Verhalten der Tschechen im Ersten Weltkrieg." Dissertation, University of Vienna, 2009.

Mörz, Kurt. "Der österreichisch-ungarische Befestigungsbau 1866–1914." Dissertation, University of Vienna, 1980.

Reinhard Nachtigal, *Russland und seine österreich-ungarichen Kriegsgefangenen (1914–1918)* (Remshalden:Verlag Berrhard Albert Greiner, 2003).

Seyfert, Günter. "Die militärischen Beziehungen und Vereinbarungen zwischen dem deutschen und dem österreichischen Generalstab vor und bei Beginn des Weltkrieges." Dissertation, University of Leipzig, 1934.

Index

For references to divisions of the armed forces, please see the Index of Military Units.

Index of Military Units

GRAYDON A. TUNSTALL is Senior Research Lecturer in the Department of History at the University of South Florida and author of *Blood in the Snow: The Carpathian Winter War of 1915*.

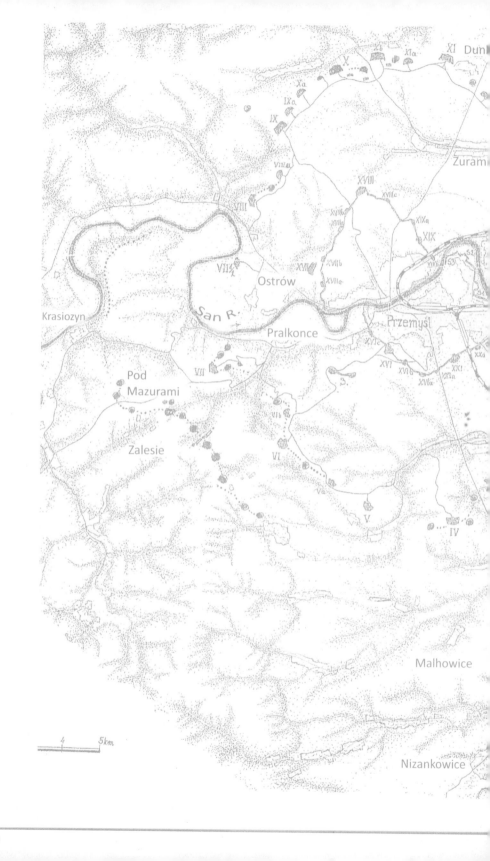